THE POLITICS OF PLACE

THE POLITICS OF PLACE

Montesquieu, Particularism,
and the Pursuit of Liberty

Joshua Bandoch

UNIVERSITY OF ROCHESTER PRESS

Copyright © 2017 by Joshua Bandoch

All rights reserved. Except as permitted under current legislation, no part of this work may be photocopied, stored in a retrieval system, published, performed in public, adapted, broadcast, transmitted, recorded, or reproduced in any form or by any means, without the prior permission of the copyright owner.

First published 2017
Reprinted in paperback 2022

University of Rochester Press
668 Mt. Hope Avenue, Rochester, NY 14620, USA
www.urpress.com
and Boydell & Brewer Limited
PO Box 9, Woodbridge, Suffolk IP12 3DF, UK
www.boydellandbrewer.com

ISBN-13: 978-1-58046-902-9 (hardcover)
ISBN-13: 978-1-64825-052-1 (paperback)

Library of Congress Cataloging-in-Publication Data

Names: Bandoch, Joshua, author.
Title: The politics of place : Montesquieu, particularism, and the pursuit of liberty / Joshua Bandoch.
Description: Rochester, N.Y. : University of Rochester Press, 2017. | Includes bibliographical references and index.
Identifiers: LCCN 2017030869 | ISBN 9781580469029 (hardcover) Subjects:
LCSH: Montesquieu, Charles de Secondat, baron de, 1689–1755. De l'esprit des lois. | Political science—Philosophy—History—18th century. | Liberty—Philosophy—History—18th century. | Particularism (Theology) | United States—Politics and government—Philosophy.
Classification: LCC JC179.M753 B36 2017 | DDC 320.01/1—dc23 LC record available at https://lccn.loc.gov/2017030869

To Maria

Contents

	Acknowledgments	ix
	Introduction	1
1	Montesquieu's Political Science	10
2	Security, Liberty, and Prosperity as Particularistic Political Goals	44
3	The Political Variables	79
4	The Subpolitical Variables	120
5	The American Founding as a Particularistic Achievement	157
	Conclusion	183
	Notes	189
	Bibliography	233
	Index	247

Acknowledgments

The seeds for this project were planted in a graduate seminar during my senior year at the University of Maryland, College Park, taught by Charles Butterworth. The class, on "Constitutionalism, the French Antecedents: Pascal, Montesquieu, Rousseau, and Constant," introduced me to Montesquieu. More than anything, I was struck by the complexity of Montesquieu's thought. My debt to Charles, my model teacher-scholar, is enormous. He has remained an invaluable mentor and has assisted with this volume in various ways, including helping me work through some complicated issues, and with some translations. (All remaining infelicities certainly are my own.)

My graduate studies at Notre Dame afforded me the opportunity to study Montesquieu extensively. Catherine Zuckert was an excellent advisor, always pushing me to improve, while providing direction and help to do so. Fortunately, I continue to benefit from her advice. I also profited greatly from working with Michael Zuckert, Fred Dallmayr, and Jim McAdams. Their insights strengthened my research on many fronts, and they were always ready, willing, and able to provide good feedback. The Nanovic Institute for European Studies was especially generous with its support throughout my time at Notre Dame. Nanovic facilitated much of my research, including stints in Munich, Paris, and Bordeaux. The staff at Nanovic was always a pleasure to work with.

I started research on this book at the Political Theory Project at Brown University, where I was a postdoctoral research associate for two years. John Tomasi provided an excellent environment in which to work and think. What's more, John helped me sharpen my project, my writing, and my thinking more generally, in critical ways. I'm grateful for all of his guidance. While at Brown I benefited from conversations with Gordon Wood, Sharon Krause, Bonnie Honig, and Annie Stilz. Dina Egge and Mary Massed helped facilitate many of my endeavors. My research assistants Alexia Ramirez and Marta Nicita provided valuable help on many fronts.

I completed this project at the University of Wisconsin–Madison while a postdoctoral fellow in the American Democracy Forum, housed in the

Department of Political Science. John Zumbrunnen provided another good work environment. I am especially grateful for the opportunity to have had a book workshop, where John, Vickie Sullivan, and Aurelian Craiutu provided me exceptional feedback that has helped me improve the manuscript. My research assistants Rebekah Cullum and Michael Promisel helped a great deal as I completed this project. Rebekah's diligence merits particular praise.

My debts extend well beyond these people and institutions. Special thanks to Céline Spector, who was a gracious host while I worked at Université Michel de Montaigne Bordeaux 3. She has shared many insights on Montesquieu over the years and sharpened my thinking about the Baron. Sophie Maloubier and Pascal Pierozzi made everything about my time in Bordeaux easier and more pleasant. Heinrich Meier was kind enough to permit me to sit in on one of his seminars, on Rousseau, in summer 2007 at Ludwigs-Maximilians-Universität in Munich. His attention to detail in the text is beyond meticulous, and our discussions were rewarding. I have benefited from conversations and insights from Catherine Volpilhac-Auger, Diana Schaub, Paul Rahe, Jason Brennan, Matthew Mendham, and Geneviève Rousseliere. The Institute for Humane Studies has been an intellectual home away from home. In particular, I'd like to thank Nigel Ashford and Bill Glod for their support. I owe much gratitude to the donors who have supported me over the years, especially donors to the Political Theory Project, American Democracy Forum, Nanovic Institute, and Institute for Humane Studies. Their generosity has made much of my work, and the work of countless others, possible. Thank you.

The University of Rochester Press has been a pleasure to work with. Sandy Thatcher reviewed the manuscript carefully, posed good questions, and found two top scholars to review my work. Dennis Rasmussen and Michael Mosher (both of whom kindly revealed their identities) provided remarkable feedback that helped me hone my argument further, clarify when necessary, and improve in many ways. Sonia Kane and Ryan Peterson have been insightful editors too, helpfully navigating the manuscript to completion. Robert Fullilove's careful copyediting improved the manuscript.

An earlier version of parts of chapter 1 first appeared as "The Politics of *esprit* in *De l'esprit des lois*," in *Diciottesimo Secolo* 2 (2017): 229–47; and an earlier version of parts of chapter 4 appeared as "Montesquieu's Selective Religious Intolerance in *Of the Spirit of the Laws*," in *Political Studies* 64, no. 2 (2016): 351–67. I wish to thank the publishers for their kind permission to reprint.

My friends and family have provided unending support as I worked on this project. My mother, Cheryl Bandoch, deserves more thanks than I can provide. In particular, her dedication to my education has opened innumerable doors for me. My late grandmother, Mary Forrest, taught me more about hard work than I could express. My father, John, sister, Christina, and Aunt Karen have been important sources of support. Pascal always makes me smile. Patrick Alban and Marcel Betsch have been valued friends for many years. Marcel has been an intellectual companion and a model for being so *fleißig*. To my wife, Maria, who is a Montesquieu expert by now after reading (and rereading) every chapter, I am grateful for her unending love, care, and patience. I dedicate this book to her.

Introduction

Is it possible to develop a universalistic account of the right political order?[1] Many Enlightenment-era philosophers thought so. Consider the cases of John Locke and Jeremy Bentham.[2] Locke, in his *Second Treatise*, develops a universal theory of political legitimacy. He asserts that men have natural rights, principally the right to life, liberty, and property. A government is legitimate, Locke claims, only insofar as it protects these natural rights. If a government does not protect these rights sufficiently, then the inhabitants of the country have a right, perhaps a duty, to dissolve the government. Sometimes, this dissolution must occur through force, as in a violent revolution. Locke's standards do not change over time and place—they are universal. Bentham's principle of utility is grounded in a universal imperative: to maximize the greatest good for the greatest number of people. This principle must guide all of our actions. Not following the principle is immoral and produces harmful consequences.[3] Consider also G. W. F. Hegel, who follows in the Enlightenment tradition in important ways. Hegel, in his *Lectures on the Philosophy of World History*, identifies an endpoint toward which History, guided by reason and *Geist*, points. Hegel found this endpoint in the Prussia of his day. Many states will not reach this endpoint, and those that do will take particular paths to get there; nonetheless, it remains the universally best political order. We take these thinkers as emblematic of the universalistic thinking present in crucial parts of the Enlightenment including, on some readings, the American founding.

The framers of the US Constitution widely are believed to have worked within this Enlightenment-era ideal, too. The Declaration of Independence proclaims that it is a "self-evident" truth that "all men"—not just Americans—are "created equal." Everyone is endowed "with certain unalienable Rights," principally "Life, Liberty, and the pursuit of Happiness." Men institute governments to protect these rights. Whenever a government fails to do so, it becomes illegitimate and the people have the right "to alter or to abolish it." In order to solidify these universal principles, the story goes, the founders crafted the US Constitution. Indeed, the writing and ratification of the US Constitution have been described as a "great rehearsal" toward what later thinkers would hail as the "end of history."[4]

There is a problem with this story, though. The thinker the founders relied on more than any other is Charles-Louis de Secondat, Baron de Montesquieu. Indeed, Baron de Montesquieu often is championed as the intellectual giant on whose shoulders America's Founding Fathers stood when it came time to write the US Constitution in the 1780s. *No author was cited more in America in the 1780s than Montesquieu.* Montesquieu leads by a wide margin of two to one over the next closest, Blackstone. Montesquieu retains first place when the data extend from 1760 to 1805—that is, the years leading up to the Revolution, the founding era, and the postfounding period.[5] Only the Bible was cited more than Montesquieu's *De l'Esprit des lois* (*Of the Spirit of the Laws*). James Madison succinctly captures Montesquieu's importance to the founders when he refers to Montesquieu, in *Federalist* No. 47, as the "oracle who is always consulted and cited on" the subject of the separation of powers, and by extension on Constitution writing more generally.[6]

Numerous scholars have attempted to fit Montesquieu into the tradition of identifying a universalistic account of the right political order. Some argue that he prefers the English regime, which in turn gave birth to the American system.[7] Others insist he prefers monarchy,[8] aristocratic liberalism,[9] ancient republicanism,[10] or even the feudal regime.[11] On these readings, Montesquieu prefers or favors one form of government.

But Montesquieu did not share the Enlightenment ambition I have described here. He did not think it was possible to develop a universalistic account of the right political order. Whereas Locke, Bentham, and Hegel offer clear answers to the question about the universally best political order, Montesquieu does not. It is the thesis of this book that Montesquieu is the great innovator of what I shall call the "politics of place."[12] He believed that the politics, economics, and morals of a society must fit a particular place and its people.[13] As long as states commit to pursuing security, liberty, and prosperity, states can—indeed, *should*—define and advance these universal goals in their own particular ways. These goals are universal insofar as all states should pursue them within set parameters; they remain particular, though, in how states implement them. As one of the first modern comparative political scientists, Montesquieu saw that we should look at the circumstances of a place—its religion, commerce, laws, institutions, physical environment, and *mœurs* (mores)—to determine the best political order for that place. When we understand Montesquieu in this way, we will understand the founding in a new way as well. Instead of having discerned the "right" political order, the founders instituted a good political order, of which there are numerous versions.

Rather than being a universalist, Montesquieu is a particularist:[14] each political order must fit its specific context. Many scholars have noted antiuniversalistic elements in Montesquieu's work. The French tradition of reading Montesquieu, going back to Alexis de Tocqueville, Émile Durkheim, and Raymond Aron, has noticed these elements.[15] More recently, French scholars like Céline Spector, Catherine Larrère, Bertrand Binoche, and Bernard Manin have observed that Montesquieu is a pluralist who identifies a worst regime (despotism), but not a best regime.[16] Others have made similar points.[17] Isaiah Berlin, for example, argues that Montesquieu "plainly did not believe in universal solutions, indeed in no simple or final solutions at all."[18] The accounts of what we might call the new Paris school, along with aligned English language literature, provide a valuable understanding of Montesquieu's project.[19] Building on these essential accounts, I treat Montesquieu's particularism as foundational to his thought. This study aims to offer the first extended account of Montesquieu's politics of place.[20]

Montesquieu's particularistic analysis has three components. Each component is central to understanding a state better, with the goal being to make the state more secure, free, and prosperous. First, legislators must understand how variables such as religion, commerce, and institutions operate in a particular society.[21] Montesquieu makes certain generalizations about how variables tend to function in societies. But even a specific religion (e.g., Christianity) does not have the same impact in all times and places. One might theorize that Christianity causes certain effects generally speaking. But it might not cause those effects in a particular place. It is necessary, therefore, to discern how commerce, religion, or any other variable actually functions in a particular place. Second, legislators must discern how the variables relate. The variables do not operate in a vacuum, separate from one another and society. To the contrary, they interact with each other, thus impacting how each functions in a given society. For example, Montesquieu argues that commerce softens *mœurs* and leads to peace. Commerce (re)shapes the political, moral, and social spheres, not just the economic. Third, legislators must determine how the variables interact in a particular society to form the *esprit* (spirit), ethos, or character of a society. Montesquieu does not provide a simple formula for understanding or identifying the *esprit*. Instead, he gives legislators the tools they need to understand, discern, evaluate, and if necessary change an *esprit*. In this work I treat Montesquieu's concept of *esprit* in depth, and show it to be central to his political philosophy.[22] Montesquieu's intricate analysis, particular to each society, shows the need to be careful about the extent to which political actors generalize principles and policies across societies.

Montesquieu's approach encourages variation. Even writers of constitutions need flexibility to operate effectively in different contexts. Many scholars interpret Montesquieu as having definitive opinions about the variables listed above, such as religion or form of government. To the contrary, I suggest that Montesquieu did not consider any single solution to be ideal or even appropriate for all societies. He allowed for different results in the form of government, principle, laws, institutions, *mœurs*, religion, commerce, and *esprit*. This is not to say that Montesquieu thought that all political orders were equally good. Despotic orders, for example, are always terrible. So Montesquieu is not a relativist: the politics of place, we might say, is not the politics of any-old-place.

How best to characterize Montesquieu? He is a liberal[23] who thinks that all societies should pursue security, liberty, and prosperity as aims. But he is a particularist: he realizes that diverse societies must understand and implement these ideas differently across time and place. Therefore, his liberalism is flexible.[24] Legislators establish security, liberty, and prosperity in a specific context. Contexts vary based on a host of factors. Montesquieu thus insists on flexibility in order to achieve security, liberty, and prosperity in different places.

Montesquieu certainly is not the only political theorist to pay attention to place; such a tradition dates back at least to Aristotle's study of constitutions. Other theorists who have discussed the importance of place include Vico, Rousseau, Burke, Hegel, and Tocqueville. Why, then, does Montesquieu stand out as the great innovator of the "politics of place"? There are two key reasons: the power and influence of his thought, and its superiority to alternatives.

Montesquieu's account of a politics of place is valuable and illuminating. The flexibility of his framework continually renews its effectiveness. More than simply identifying and philosophizing about three universally desirable goals in security, liberty, and prosperity, Montesquieu develops a framework for achieving them across time and place. His approach significantly increases the chances that legislators can advance these goods in their specific society. He does so by insisting on paying attention to how a wide range of factors shape societies, as well as how their interaction forms an *esprit*. *Esprit* (or something similar to it, like national character) receives insufficient consideration in the work of most political theorists.

The politics of place provides an insightful roadmap for changing societies. Montesquieu rejects the notion that some states are consigned to remain insecure, unfree, or impoverished. He seeks to provide all legislators with the tools to establish and maintain security, liberty, and prosperity. But when legislators seek to institute changes, they must proceed gradually, with caution. Change should occur incrementally, or via indirect methods. Legislators should not pursue dramatic, radical changes. Radical change not only will be ineffective; it likely will be dangerous. Moderation dictates that legislators not impose what they take to be the good regime, or a better regime, because that would result in a tyranny. Legal reform, for example, usually will be incremental. Change via commerce will be indirect. Rather than being an archconservative text, *De l'Esprit des lois* is meant to be a manual for cautious, lasting change. In this specific sense Montesquieu is conservative. And his approach is superior to those that seek quick, sweeping change.

Montesquieu's iteration of a politics of place also deserves attention because it influenced later thinkers to proceed in similar fashion. The cases of Edmund Burke and Alexis de Tocqueville are illustrative. In his *Reflections on the Revolution in France* Burke proclaims:

> But I cannot stand forward, and give praise or blame to anything which relates to human actions, and human concerns, on a simple view of the object, as it stands stripped of every relation, in all the nakedness and solitude of metaphysical abstraction. Circumstances (which with some gentlemen pass for nothing) give in reality to every political principle its distinguishing colour, and discriminating effect. The circumstances are what render every civil and political scheme beneficial or noxious to mankind.[25]

Montesquieu's insights into the role of circumstance help ground Burke's conservatism.[26] This caution fuels Montesquieu's as well as Burke's focus on moderation, a theme we will consider in chapter 2. Tocqueville, who receives attention in chapter 5 of this volume, identified Montesquieu as one of three men (along with Pascal and Rousseau) with whom he lived a little "every day."[27] *Democracy in America* is, in many ways, a Montesquieuian analysis of the United States. This is apparent when Tocqueville identifies three "causes" principally responsible for maintaining America's democratic republic: physical circumstance, the laws, and *mœurs*.[28] Throughout, Tocqueville analyzes America through a revised Montesquieuian framework. Burke, Tocqueville, and others build core parts of their political theories on Montesquieuian foundations.

Montesquieu's approach to *esprit* and circumstance is superior to alternative approaches. Consider briefly Hegel, the most relevant case. Hegel is perhaps the most famous philosopher of *Geist* (*esprit*). He argued that *Geist*, guided by reason, points History in a particular direction, that of the Prussian state of his time. There are particular instantiations of a *Geist* that manifest themselves in a people—a *Volksgeist*. Ultimately, though, Hegel suggests we judge societies based on the extent to which they approximate this Prussian endpoint of History. We know, though, that the premise of Hegel's philosophy of *Geist* is wrong—history is not directional. And Montesquieu shows that one endpoint is neither feasible nor desirable.[29] What's more, the consequences of Hegel's *Geist* have been negative. It inspired nineteenth-century nationalist movements, promoting a notion of "us" pitted against "them." Montesquieu's notion of *esprit*, by contrast, does not push things in a problematic direction.

To verify his claims, Montesquieu studied many different historical cases, ancient and modern, Western and Eastern. The tremendous amount of comparative analysis Montesquieu includes throughout his work makes him one of the first great modern comparative political scientists.[30] Cases like ancient Greece, Rome, and Persia captured his attention. He wrote an entire book on the rise and, especially, fall of Rome. Our focus will be on a number of prominent cases that represent different forms of government: England (mixed regime), France (monarchy), and Holland (federal republic).[31] Examining his discussions of these cases lets us see better how he analyzed aspects of particular societies as well as societies as a whole. I show that he judged England, France, and Holland to have the potential to be secure, free, and prosperous societies.

This study centers on *De l'Esprit des lois* (hereafter *EL*) because it is there that Montesquieu elaborates on his politics of place. *EL* is his most mature work on politics, morals, and economics. It is his final major statement on these matters. If we seek to understand his framework for analyzing societies, then our focus must be on his magnum opus. *EL* also is comprehensive. By contrast, his other major works, *Lettres Persanes* (*Persian Letters*) and *Considérations sur les causes de la grandeur des Romains et de leur décadence* (*Considerations on the Causes of the Greatness of the Romans and Their Decline*), do not provide comprehensive accounts of his political theory.

The purpose of this inquiry is not simply to establish that Montesquieu was a proponent of the "politics of place." This exegetical component of the study clearly is crucial to establishing Montesquieu as a particularist. But I seek to push Montesquieu's framework further. Students of politics generally should be more concerned with *universal* themes (normative and descriptive) and *particularity* in the way of setting, appraisal, and application. Montesquieu's framework remains valuable for analyzing both historical situations and contemporary societies and issues. The politics of place sheds light on contemporary debates over what sorts of political, economic, and moral orders states should adopt. It is a useful resource for societies seeking to become (more) secure, free, and prosperous. The politics of place should give pause to those seeking to define and implement universalistic solutions. More than that, in a world as diverse as ours, the politics of place provides legislators with the flexibility they need to improve their specific societies. This approach offers a more viable path to achieve security, liberty, and prosperity than the universalistic approaches of the Enlightenment and of today.

Montesquieu also presents his framework as superior to the alternatives, especially those of Enlightenment thinkers like Locke and Hobbes. Montesquieu is not a "social contract" thinker.[32] Nor is he a "state of nature" theorist.[33] He deemphasizes the language of rights. He thus diverges sharply from Thomas Hobbes and John Locke on these counts (and others). As Dennis Rasmussen's study of the "pragmatic Enlightenment" shows, this alternative approach adopted by Montesquieu (and, in Rasmussen's account, Adam Smith, David Hume, and Voltaire) offers us important resources unavailable in other strains of the Enlightenment. We live in an increasingly diverse, multicultural, cosmopolitan world. This diversity often spurs misunderstanding and conflict. Montesquieu offers us a more sensitive and subtle way to approach the varied political orders that we see around us, whether we are evaluating contemporary Singapore, Sicily, or Sweden.

The first four substantive chapters of this book focus on Montesquieu's political thought. Chapter 1 establishes Montesquieu as a proponent of the "politics of place" and identifies his notion of *esprit* (spirit) as central to this framework. The analysis centers on the most important chapter of *EL* for understanding Montesquieu's project: book I, chapter 3. His particularism comes out in two passages. He writes, "It is better to say that the government most in conformity to nature is the one whose particular arrangement best relates to the disposition of the people for whom it is established." He explains further that the laws "should be so appropriate to the people for whom they are made, that it is very unlikely that those of one nation can suit another." Montesquieu's analysis has three components: discerning how each variable functions separately, how it functions in relation to the other variables in a given state, and how the variables interact to form what Montesquieu calls the *esprit des lois* or the *esprit général*. Readers of *EL* have had much trouble discerning the organization of the work. My analysis sheds light on the logical structure of *EL*. The order of *EL* is dictated by its purpose, which is to help legislators understand what makes a state secure, free, and prosperous.

Chapter 2 shows that Montesquieu's recommendation of particularistic political solutions comes with the caveat that all states must pursue three goals (which are themselves universalistic in a sense): security, liberty, and prosperity. However, the realization of these aims is particularistic—states reasonably can define *and* achieve them in different ways. Still, some options like despotism are incompatible with a secure, free, prosperous society. Montesquieu insists that the achievement and definition of these universal goals must be particularistic.

Chapter 3 considers what I call the "political variables." Montesquieu examines these variables in parts I and II of *EL*, because they define the context in which legislators operate. The variables include form of government, the principle of each form of government, laws (especially criminal), liberty, institutions, and lawmaking. Montesquieu finds a spectrum of outcomes acceptable with each of these variables. He does not think that only regimes that resemble that of England could be secure, free, and prosperous. Rather, he shows that aristocratic republics, federal republics, and monarchies also can produce moderate political orders. He does not state a preference for any one of these forms of government. He also identifies numerous institutions that could successfully make power stop power.

Chapter 4 examines the "subpolitical variables"—environment, commerce, and religion. Montesquieu contends that the physical environment changes people biologically and affects their lifestyles substantially. Setting aside the biological analysis, his thoughts on how legislators must factor the physical environment into their calculations warrant consideration. Commerce is an agent of radical (positive) change for Montesquieu. He speaks little about the economic gains from trade, which he seems to take for granted. Commerce for Montesquieu is about the interaction of peoples, ideas, and cultures around the world. These interactions make peoples more peaceful and secure and their *mœurs* gentler, less pure, and thus better. Still, Montesquieu does not recommend that all peoples engage in the same amount and kind of commerce. The amount of commerce must be appropriate to a society. In matters of religion, Montesquieu is a proponent of what I call selective religious intolerance. He does not come down simply in favor of tolerating a religion—or not. He judges each religion individually based solely on the political effects it has in the context of a particular state. As such, there are times when he views religion generally, or a specific religion like Christianity, positively (or, at a minimum, as necessary), whereas in other situations he views the same religion negatively. He supports a religion if it has good effects in a state. This interpretation of Montesquieu's views on religion has implications for understanding his liberalism. He comes across as interested primarily, or solely, in the political effects of actions and issues, and unconcerned with the "truth" of such matters.

Chapter 5 offers an alternative interpretation of the American founding through the lens of the politics of place. Many have seen the Founding Fathers as discerning Montesquieu's "true" principles regarding the proper means for having a free state, primarily the distribution (or separation) of three governmental powers. They see the founders as making Montesquieu's recommendations more republican. Supporters of this interpretation often think the founders discovered the "right" or "best" way to structure political institutions. However, this narrow reading of Montesquieu, and of the founding, causes us to misinterpret what the founders really accomplished. The founders discerned one good way to apply (and adapt) Montesquieu's "politics of place." For this we can applaud them. But they did not discover the one "right" approach to politics. Indeed, there exist numerous political, economic, and moral paths states can take to achieve goodness. Those who see the American founding as the apex of "American exceptionalism" and who want to hold up the US political system as a model for all peoples are misguided. They skew the founders' accomplishments. What's more, such notions of American exceptionalism actually hinder many peoples from establishing a political, economic, and moral system that will make that particular people more secure, free, and prosperous. The guidance the founders provide for how to achieve this across time and place is what really makes their accomplishments exceptional.

CHAPTER ONE

Montesquieu's Political Science

Montesquieu's political science is founded on the idea that each state needs a political, economic, and moral order best suited to that particular society.[1] The keys to unlocking his political science are in the preface and book I of *De l'Esprit des lois*. Book I, chapter 3 is especially important, because here Montesquieu defines his enterprise and explains the order of *EL*. Montesquieu's goal is to explain how each state can overcome three "problems of politics": conflict between states, between persons, and between state and person(s). States and citizens must be secure from internal and external threats to freedom and prosperity. To achieve this goal, Montesquieu introduces the framework that I call the "politics of place." He insists that each state must discern which particular political order will address these problems most effectively. There can be no universal solutions to these matters. Rather, Montesquieu's recommendations are flexible and case sensitive. They take the particularities of a people into account when seeking to establish a good political order. Still, for "politics" to occur for Montesquieu, various conditions must be met; we consider them in chapters 1 and 2.

The key to addressing the problems of politics is Montesquieu's core concept of *esprit*. The *esprit* of a society is formed by a great many factors or variables. Montesquieu insists legislators must consider them carefully if they wish to understand and act prudently in a particular society. *Esprit* is so central because it defines—and is defined by—the society in which the politics of a particular place happen.

This reading of the "Introduction" to *EL* reveals the purpose and order of Baron de Montesquieu's magnum opus, something that has puzzled scholars since the work's publication. While some are tempted to skip ahead to Montesquieu's famous discussion of the forms of government in book II, the "Author's Foreword" (*Avertissement de l'auteur*), preface, and book I shed essential light on the order of a seemingly disorganized work. Montesquieu presents his project in surprisingly clear terms.

Lawmaking and the Politics of Place

The Introductory sections of *EL* culminate in Montesquieu's politics of place. Key passages in the beginning of *EL* point to this conclusion. We must read these and other passages in light of Montesquieu's declaration in the first paragraph of *EL*: Montesquieu says that he has had "new ideas" and that it has "been necessary to find new words, or give to old ones new meanings. . . . I have given a new day to all these things in this edition here."[2] This bold claim colors what follows, and comes in the context of one of his many controversial claims. He explains that when he uses the word virtue, he is speaking of "political" virtue (love of country and of equality), not Christian or moral virtue. The context—Catholic France and Christian Europe (*EL* was put on the Index Librorum Prohibitorum shortly after its publication)—makes this statement remarkable. Montesquieu's claim here reveals the nature of his enterprise. His focus is primarily, perhaps solely, on a political interpretation of ideas and events. There are a number of other cases where he puts forward a political understanding of things. The conceptions of liberty in which he is actually interested are political.[3] His evaluation of religion also is purely political.[4] His purpose is to shift attention to affairs related to politics, and away from religious or moral considerations. Indeed, he makes this kind of move a number of times in the Introduction.[5]

Montesquieu's rich preface warrants investigation on many fronts.[6] Over the course of less than three pages he makes a number of remarkable claims. He notes, for example, that *EL* is the work of twenty years, and readers thus should condemn or approve of the work as a whole, and not merely several passages. He insists that he thanks heaven for being born in the state he was (Preface.229). Here, we are most interested in his discussion of prejudices and principles.

In the preface Montesquieu reveals that his "principles" (*principes*) are central to his enterprise in *EL*. Accordingly, he discusses them more times (four) than anything else in the preface. He started and stopped his work many times, tossing away the pages he had written. Every day, he "sensed" that the "paternal hands" were falling. He struggled mightily to understand the design of his study, and found the truth only to lose it. "But, when I discovered my principles, everything for which I searched came to me; and, in the course of twenty years, I saw my work begin, grow, advance itself, and finish" (Preface.231). We therefore must consider what Montesquieu means by "principles," and what those principles are, since the discovery of his principles gave him the requisite knowledge to "penetrate in a stroke of genius the entire constitution of a State" (Preface.230). Being able to penetrate a constitution in this way, with the help of Montesquieu's principles, will help legislators improve their societies.

How, then, did Montesquieu develop his principles? Each of the other three mentions of them provides clues. In the first mention, he reveals that his principles are the product of a combination of philosophical analysis and historical observations: "I have set down principles, and I have seen particular cases yield to them as if by themselves; the histories of all nations being only the results; and each particular law being tied to another law, or depending on another more general" (Preface.229). Montesquieu deemed it insufficient to develop abstract principles based only on philosophical notions of, say, justice. Instead, he consciously worked to be sure that his principles were in conformity with history, lest historical events threaten the validity of his observations. He does claim, though, something more significant. Montesquieu suggests not only that his principles conform to history, but that history conforms to his principles. That is, he has gleaned certain insights into the historical process itself. Nations, he claims, are the results of the principles he identifies. Specifically, nations conform to the principles of *esprit*, to which we turn shortly.

Montesquieu's second and third mentions of his principles juxtapose the truths found in those principles against prejudices.[7] Montesquieu insists that he has taken his principles not from his "prejudices, but from the nature of things" (Preface.229).[8] We gain knowledge of the "nature of things," Montesquieu thinks, by studying societies in the way he outlines in *EL*. He works to understand the nature of a particular society. Legislators must undertake this task in order to promote security, liberty, and prosperity. Montesquieu continues, in the next paragraph, by connecting his principles to truth: "Many of the truths will make themselves felt here only after one will have seen the chain connecting them with the others. The more one will reflect on the details, the more one will feel the certainty of the principles" (Preface.229). Here, Montesquieu makes the weighty claim that *EL* contains "truths" (*vérités*). But we can discern these truths only by seeing the "chain" connecting them to others. We turn to the chain of *EL* in the final section of this chapter. Montesquieu provides a glimpse of the answer when he notes that the details are essential to these truths. These details are what distinguish societies from each other, giving each its *esprit*. Montesquieu continues his claims to having knowledge, even truth, a few sentences later when he proclaims: "It is not indifferent that the people be enlightened." Enlightenment Montesquieu can bring his readers, so long as they overcome their prejudices.

Montesquieu proclaims that one of the three things that would make him "the happiest of mortals" is if he could make it the case that "men can cure themselves of their prejudices." He continues by clarifying how he defines prejudices: "I call here prejudices, not what makes one ignorant of certain things, but what makes one ignorant of himself" (Preface.230). Someone without self-knowledge is, according to Montesquieu, ignorant. Ignorance, especially in the form of prejudices, is dangerous. Montesquieu asserts that prejudice is widespread, and it infiltrates society, growing and becoming more pernicious, spreading all the way to the top. "The prejudices of the magistrates were first the prejudices of the nation" (Preface.230). The consequence is that legislators become increasingly incapable of doing good things and preventing bad ones. Enlightenment, knowledge, and improvement cede to ignorance and decline. Rather than attempting to give men the content of their self-knowledge, Montesquieu deems it imperative to help men cure their own prejudices. The most famous mechanism he offers for doing so is commerce, which "cures destructive prejudices" (XX.1.585). Legislators then must listen to the artist who, with Corregio, has created something new and, in Montesquieu's mind, better: "'And I too am a painter,' have I said with Corregio." Montesquieu signaled as much with the critically important epigraph he attached to his magnum opus, from Ovid's *Metamorphosis*: *Prolem sine matre creatam*.[9] The creation begins in book I, which Montesquieu finishes by returning us to his principles.

Many readers overlook book I. To the extent that they examine it, they focus on three passages. The first is Montesquieu's famous definition of laws: "Laws, in the most extended signification, are the necessary relations which derive from the nature of things" (I.1.232).[10] This important definition ties directly into Montesquieu's political science. We return to it later in the context of Montesquieu's politics of place. The second is his analysis of five kinds of "beings" (*êtres*): the Divinity, the material world, intelligences superior to man (later called particular intelligent beings), beasts, and man (*homme*) (I.1.232).[11] Third, his chapter on the state of nature captures readers' attention, particularly because it is a response to Hobbes;[12] it also contains the seeds of Rousseau's state of nature.[13] While these passages are undoubtedly important, focusing too much attention on them obscures the movement of book I.

Montesquieu's discussion of five kinds of beings in I, 1[14] has the potential to distract the reader or divert his attention away from Montesquieu's primary concern, which is man. Montesquieu's discussion of the first four kinds of beings (the Divinity, the material world, intelligences superior to man, and beasts), especially his discussion of God, is by no means unimportant.[15] But make no mistake—he is most interested in the laws that govern men; as such, after discussing the first four,[16] he shifts his attention to man. Montesquieu examines how men are (best) governed. Three things potentially govern men: religion, philosophy, and laws. Montesquieu sees only laws as having a real chance at successfully governing men. Religion is insufficient. God has "called" men back to him by the laws of religion, but man "violates without ceasing the laws that God has established." Philosophers have "informed" man of "the laws of morality." But Montesquieu deems neither religion nor philosophy sufficient; they merely have "called" men back or "informed" them. Montesquieu reserves his strongest statement for legislators: "Made for living in society, they could have forgotten others; legislators have returned them to their duties by political and civil laws" (I.1.234). Legislation thus is the only means he identifies as having the potential to govern society effectively. Religion and philosophy only can play supplementary roles. The movement of I, 1 thus points to the centrality of man and his laws.

The movement of I, 2 again directs the reader to man's place *in society*, picking up on the notion from I, 1 that man is "made for living in society." Montesquieu discusses the idea of a state of nature and identifies five laws of nature.[17] Three such laws center on satisfying basic needs, and one deals with religion. The final law of nature is the most important: "Apart from the sentiment that men have to start with, they again get to have acquaintances; thus they have a second link that the other animals do not have. They therefore have a new motive for unifying; and the desire to live in society is a fourth natural law" (I.2.236).[18] Man, then, is naturally social for Montesquieu.[19] And so the trajectory of the chapter leads us to man's natural state, which is in society.

Montesquieu's initial portrait of society is bleak—a state of war: "as soon as men are in society, they lose the feeling of their weakness; the equality, which was between them, ceases, and the state of war commences" (I.3.236). As Thomas Pangle explains, "It turns out that nothing is so dangerous for man by nature as the association with his fellowman."[20] Both nations and individuals begin to sense their "force." They seek to "turn in their favor the principal advantages" of their position. These states of war lead to what I call Montesquieu's three "problems of politics": conflict between nations, conflict between nation and individual, and conflict between individuals. These problems threaten the existence of the nation.[21] A nation cannot be secure, free, and prosperous if it does not address each of these problems effectively. These "problems of politics" represent the puzzle Montesquieu seeks to solve. States must foster environments in which they are protected from internal and external threats, so far as possible. The question then becomes how each individual nation can address these issues successfully.

Montesquieu does not provide a universalistic solution for addressing these problems effectively in diverse societies across time and place. Rather, he proposes a particularistic approach I call the politics of place. He offers two formulations of his politics of place in I, 3. First, he writes, "it is better to say that the government most in conformity to nature is the one whose particular arrangement best relates to the disposition of the people for whom it is established" (I.3.237).[22] He explains further that the laws "should be so appropriate to the people for whom they are made that it is very unlikely that those of one nation can suit another". These passages from I, 3 have a great deal of interpretive and normative importance. As they are the clearest expressions of Montesquieu's politics of place, they offer core insights into understanding his political science. Circumstance requires that each state deal with these problems differently. Spector explains, "this diversity of peoples immediately requires the diversity of laws."[23] It is only possible to address the three problems of politics across time and place with a particularistic approach. Reason, Montesquieu explains, demands nothing else but such particularity.[24] Before explaining how Montesquieu thinks that political actors should go about applying this reason to particular cases, let us examine this notion of the politics of place more extensively.

By the politics of place I mean the idea that political, economic, social, and moral factors need to fit a particular people and advance security, liberty, and prosperity, broadly understood. Empirically, states vary substantially in their laws, institutions, *mœurs*, manners, religion(s), environments, modes of commerce, and in other ways. One core claim of the politics of place is that states *should* vary on these issues, too, for practical, political, philosophical, social, and moral reasons, with the caveat that this variation takes place within a certain spectrum of acceptability. We will examine what options are acceptable throughout this study. The politics of place is an appealing approach precisely because Montesquieu demonstrates beyond a reasonable doubt that the disposition of peoples varies greatly over time and place. What's more, he shows *how* and *why* their dispositions differ so markedly, and offers guidance on how to govern societies based on these differences.

Variation is necessary and desirable because Montesquieu's politics of place holds that the political good is indeterminate. As Aurelian Craiutu rightly notes, for Montesquieu "the political good can never be defined in an unambiguous and universal manner, independent of the particular social and political condition of each country."[25] One reason for this, Craiutu continues, is that Montesquieu "believed that the line between vice and virtue changes over time in such a way that what was previously considered a vice may later be seen as a virtue (or vice versa)." The political good also is indeterminate for Montesquieu because there is not one single political good, but multiple political goods.[26] Security, liberty, and prosperity, while universal goods, remain indeterminate.

The politics of place offers political actors the flexibility they need to achieve security, liberty, and prosperity in different situations. Dennis Rasmussen, in his study of the "pragmatic Enlightenment," has helpfully explored the flexibility of Montesquieu's thought. Montesquieu "adopted a practical, pragmatic outlook that supports the reform of existing institutions but opposes efforts to form a wholly new 'rational' order from scratch." While he "wanted to push" his "society in a broadly liberal direction," he "did not insist that these reforms be made all at once, or that the political and legal slates must be wiped clean in order to make room for a more liberal order."[27] Montesquieu's flexibility means that he "did not insist on (or even allow for) a single set of institutions or a comprehensive view of the good life that would be applicable in all times and places."[28] Rasmussen rightfully finds this approach appealing because it is "more realistic, moderate, flexible, and contextually sensitive than many other branches of this tradition."[29]

The politics of place also rejects any inclination to make societies uniform. In what originally was to be the penultimate chapter of *EL*, entitled "On Ideas of Uniformity," Montesquieu writes:

> There are some ideas of uniformity that sometimes seize great *esprits* (for they touched Charlemagne), but they infallibly strike small ones. They find there a genre of perfection that they recognize, because it is impossible not to discover it: the same weights in administering, the same measures in commerce, the same laws in the state, the same religion for all the sects. But is that always proper without exception? Is the evil of changing always less than that of suffering? Does not the grandeur of genius consist in better knowing in which case uniformity is necessary, and in which case differences are necessary? . . . When the citizens follow the laws, what does it matter whether they follow the same ones? (XXIX.18.882)

Still, legislators—both great and regular—are inclined toward universalism, Montesquieu contends. They are so inclined not only because it is easier but, more importantly, because they think that they are able to discern the "right" law that will be effective across societies. Montesquieu urges legislators to resist this temptation to try to figure out the right, true laws and then implement them wherever they can. Instead, he recommends the more careful approach that Solon, one of the great statesmen he considers a legislator, embraced: "One asked Solon whether the laws he had given to the Athenians were the best. 'I gave them,' he responded, 'the best that they could stand [*souffrir*].' Beautiful speech, which must be heard by all legislators" (XIX.21.571). To be successful, legislators should follow Solon and give a society the best, specific laws that it can handle, and reject the urge to universalize lawmaking.

On the point of uniformity, Montesquieu stands in contrast to other French Enlightenment thinkers, especially Condorcet. In his critique of book XXIX of *EL*, Condorcet takes particular aim at chapter 18. Arguing for uniformity, Condorcet proclaims that a "good law should be good for all men. A true proposition is true everywhere."[30] Lawmaking, then, appears as a sort of political and social mathematics. Once we deduce a solution to the problem, we need simply to implement that solution. And this process should be straightforward. "Uniformity in law may be established without trouble, and without producing any evil effects by the change."[31] Condorcet finds "commercial regulations" to be the only area where uniformity is not necessary; otherwise, differences are "founded on prejudices and habits, which should be extinguished."[32] But as Craiutu shows, Montesquieu eschews this kind of thinking. Montesquieu "rejected the idea of uniform legislation" and "refused to admit that political questions could ever be reduced to a few general and simple propositions or universally applicable recommendations."[33] Legislators must adapt laws and institutions to the diversity of institutions, peoples, and characters.[34]

The politics of place harbors deep reservations about both universalism and relativism. We begin with the former. Universalistic approaches seek to identify a "best" option or approach. Prominent universalists include John Locke and Jeremy Bentham. Universalists deem their standards to be true or correct across time and place. Subsequently, universalistic approaches tend to be "top-down": political actors should adopt these standards or principles, and then shape society to conform to them. Political actors are charged with enacting change in society to make it conform more closely to the ideas (and perhaps the practices) attached to the standards. Political actors thus understand themselves to be in control of the variables, as well as the events, practices, and policies that shape them. Some universalists recognize the impracticality, or the undesirability, of making all states conform to the universal standards these thinkers assert. Rather than forcing states to conform to them, these universalists accept that some states cannot live up to these standards. Such states must resign themselves to having a less than optimal, or even an undesirable, political order.

Such universalistic approaches are mistaken at best, and dangerous at worst. The politics of place rejects the notion that there is a "best" or ideal order; it does not exist. Rather, the politics of place affirms that "one size does not fit all"—that is, the same regime (however good) is neither possible nor desirable in all times and places for all peoples. It might be possible to identify an approach as best for a particular society while recognizing that it is not appropriate for diverse peoples across time and place. It is simply impossible for all states to adopt the same standards, to say nothing of the same institutions and practices. Reason being, they differ so markedly on matters of religion, commerce, law, institutions, geographical—and geopolitical—location, history, *mœurs*, and manners. Why, for example, should a deeply religious society embrace France's strong secular culture? Universalistic approaches are too divorced from fact and reality to work within the context of particular societies. Some rely on certain conceptions of human nature; by contrast, the politics of place holds that human nature is flexible.

It is more than just misguided to try to impose universal standards top-down; it is potentially—probably—perilous. Often, societies do not respond well to external or internal attempts to dramatically reorder society. Consider how a deeply religious society would respond to attempts to secularize it.

Although the politics of place is a particularistic approach to societies, I do not intend to imply that no generalizations can be made. Montesquieu certainly generalizes, and we should too. Rather, the point is that the interplay of multiple factors produces—and *should* produce—multiple results. Every case does not need to be treated sui generis. We can group nations into types as well as distinguish among them. The result of the kind of analysis I am advocating is that we must begin by treating each nation particularly, and only generalize when applicable.

The politics of place is not equivalent to relativism, because it does not view all options as morally equivalent.[35] All states should pursue security, liberty, and prosperity (Montesquieu's three general goals, which we will explore at greater length in chapter 2). The very parameters of these concepts restrict the number of potentially acceptable political orders. There is therefore a limit to the extent to which states should vary on political, economic, social, and moral issues. Within the range of acceptable options, some are superior to others because they do a better job of advancing these goods. Not all situations are equally good, and some, like despotism, are categorically bad. The politics of place encourages variation. While all states should pursue some kind of commerce, for example, the extent and nature of this commerce ought to vary. States can understand these general goals differently, and these differences can be perfectly justifiable. As such, I put Montesquieu's politics of place near the middle of a spectrum that has political universalism at one end and relativism at the other.[36] Montesquieu's moderate approach helps us to explain *why* societies differ, why they *should* differ, and *how* the legislator can understand and work in the context of these different situations. Montesquieu recognizes core values and standards, while affirming the necessity of having flexibility in understanding and implementing them. The politics of place is not the politics of any-old-place.

Montesquieu's politics of place is not a "rights"-based framework. To understand why, it helps first to consider the most prominent rights-based approach to which Montesquieu might have turned, that of John Locke. Locke argues in his *Second Treatise* that rights are "natural." We are born with these rights, and no one can take them from us. Rights are universal. We only can forfeit them by choosing to do so, or by violating someone else's rights; otherwise our rights are inalienable. We enter into society, Locke claims, to protect these rights. Men are willing to leave the state of nature "which, however free, is full of fears and continual dangers: and it is not without reason, that he seeks out, and is willing to join in society with others, who are already united, or have a mind to unite, for the mutual preservation of their lives, liberties, and estates, which I call by the general name, property."[37] Thus our three core rights, according to Locke, are life, liberty, and property. The citizens and the government form a social contract, an agreement that extends legitimacy to the government, in order to protect these rights. If the government ceases to protect these rights, it loses legitimacy altogether, and the citizens have the right, perhaps duty, to revolt and form a new political society.

Some scholars argue that Montesquieu follows Locke specifically on these matters.[38] Paul Rahe traces this line of natural rights thinking from Locke through Montesquieu to Jefferson.[39] Michael Zuckert argues that "Montesquieu, like Locke, finds the bedrock ground of political morality not in natural law but in right understood as self-ownership."[40] To make this claim, Zuckert turns to a passage in book X where Montesquieu claims that people have the right to kill in self-defense. "Montesquieu here clearly speaks of right [*droit*] in the sense of subjective rights, and the right he affirms derives from nature. That is, he recognizes a natural right of self-preservation. Not only natural law (i.e., the effectual natural forces in men) but also natural right prescribes preservation."[41] Even within Zuckert's essays we see some of the problems with this interpretation. Zuckert explains that Montesquieu "differs somewhat from Locke in that he emphasizes liberty rather than the securing of rights, and because he speaks of liberty in terms of security or the opinion of security. On the whole, Montesquieu subjectivizes the criteria of political right. For him, the good order is not so much a certain kind of order per se, but the order that produces a certain subjective state in citizens."[42] This difference is more significant than Zuckert acknowledges. The standard Montesquieu adopts of a good government is one that protects security, liberty, and prosperity. His standard is not of a government that protects rights per se, in sharp contrast to Locke. The case of Locke is more curious still because we know that Montesquieu read Locke's work and shared Locke's goals of distributing powers and protecting liberty. And yet, Locke is conspicuously absent in *EL*. Not once does Montesquieu cite Locke. Whereas Montesquieu specifically criticizes Hobbes in book I of *EL*, Locke never appears, despite the similarities of their political theories. Montesquieu's divergence from Locke on the central matter of rights is one reason for Locke's absence.

Despite having the language of rights as his disposal, Montesquieu downplays and minimizes the idea of rights. Fundamentally, he is not a rights thinker. Jean-Jacques Rousseau saw this. In *Émile or On Education*, Rousseau writes that Montesquieu "was careful not to discuss the principles of political right. He was content to discuss the positive right of established governments, and nothing in the world is more different than these two studies."[43] As David Lowenthal rightly notes, Montesquieu disagrees with Locke (and Hobbes) "by refusing to take the natural rights of man and the social contract as the new basis of orientation."[44] Montesquieu speaks of the "*droit des gens*" (right of peoples), of "*droit politique*" (political right), and of "*droit civil*" (civil right) in book I. But these terms refer to relations between states, between state and person(s), and between persons. They do not refer to things to which these entities have moral claims. A reader of *EL* would, when she considers Montesquieu's usage of *droit* in this chapter, be thinking of other prominent usages of the term based on Montesquieu's discussion in I, 2. Here, he criticizes state of nature constructs, specifically that of Thomas Hobbes.[45] Still, the reader would be thinking about the "rights" man is said to have in the state of nature. Montesquieu does not affirm the existence of rights, as Hobbes and Locke do. Montesquieu does not say that man enters society to protect these rights. Rather, Montesquieu argues that men naturally desire to enter society, and that once in society they want the state to address the three kinds of conflict related to the three kinds of *droit* indicated above.

Book XXVI provides further evidence that Montesquieu is not a rights thinker. There he does not offer a meaningful distinction between "right" (*droit*) and "law" (*loi*). He speaks, for example, of natural law and natural right interchangeably. In chapter 1 of book XXVI, entitled "Idea of This Book," Montesquieu identifies many kinds of "right" that govern men:

> Men are governed by diverse sorts of law: by natural right; by divine right, which is that of religion; by ecclesiastic right, otherwise called canonical, which is that of administering religion; by the right of peoples, that one can consider as the civil right of the universe, in the sense that each people is a citizen of it; by general political right, which has as its goal this human wisdom that has founded all societies; by particular political right, which is the focus of each society; by the right of conquest, founded on the fact that a people wanted, could, or needed to do violence to another; by the civil right of each society, by which a citizen can defend his goods and his life, against every other citizen; finally, by domestic right, which comes from a society being divided into diverse families who need a particular government.
>
> Therefore there are different orders of laws; and the sublimity of human reason consists in fully knowing to which of these orders are primarily related the things to be stipulated and in not introducing confusion into the principles that must govern men. (XXVI. 1.750–51)

Montesquieu identifies nine diverse sorts of law, which he refers to as kinds of "right." Throughout the rest of book XXVI, he explains the proper boundaries between these kinds of law, and grants precedence to natural, political, and civil right over all other kinds of law.

Montesquieu makes an important philosophical move here. He notes that "men are governed by diverse sorts of *laws*" (*lois*) and that "there are different orders of *laws*." He then speaks of kinds of "right" (*droit*). In doing so, he is saying that, words or terms notwithstanding, there is no difference between right and law. He takes it a step further: there is no such thing as divine law, no matter what people have said in the past. So while the *droit-loi* distinction goes back to the Latin *jus-lex* and then to the Greek *dike-nomos* distinction, Montesquieu is trying to show legislators that there is no difference between *loi* and *droit*. Montesquieu's denial of the distinction between "law" and "right" lends further support to my contention that he is not a "rights" thinker.

Regarding the passage from book X cited by Zuckert, the usage of "right" here comes in the midst of Montesquieu's consideration of offensive force. Montesquieu speaks of a "*droit de la défense naturelle*" (right of natural defense). This right derives from the fact that my life is my own, and so I have the "right" to kill in self-defense. Montesquieu quickly moves to discussing when a state has the "right" to attack and kill. His quick, basic mention of people having the "right" to kill in self-defense does not represent a significant usage of "rights."

Montesquieu's conceptions of liberty also do not rely on a notion of "rights." When he says that "liberty is the *droit* to do what the laws permit," he means *droit* in the sense of legally allowed or permitted. Montesquieu's usage of *droit* is in line with the lack of a distinction in French between *droit* as a "right" and *droit* as a system of laws. He does not use right in the sense of having a moral claim to, say, freedom of speech. Rather than defining political liberty as the right to do certain things, Montesquieu understands political liberty in relation to the constitution in the context of institutions and practices. He defines political liberty in relation to the citizen as feeling and being secure, which we examine in greater depth in the next chapter. As Craiutu explains, "Montesquieu refused to embrace the language of rights, preferring instead 'to put cruelty first.'"[46] Throughout his discussion of liberty in books XI and XII, Montesquieu does not appeal to the language of rights. Summarizing Montesquieu's position, Rasmussen writes: "Montesquieu certainly disapproves of infringements on people's basic desires, above all the desire to preserve the self and family. But he does not use these desires to formulate inalienable natural rights that individuals can assert against their government, or to judge all nonliberal regimes to be illegitimate."[47]

There are simple, compelling explanations for why the politics of place does not rely on the language of "rights." The language of "rights" can serve as a kind of barrier to the achievement of security, liberty, and prosperity in many places. Natural or human "rights" claims tend to be universalistic in nature.[48] If a "right" is a "human right" then everyone, across time and place, has a moral claim to it. Natural rights, if not positive rights, are fixed. The universalistic nature of these rights can come into conflict with the particularistic understanding of security, liberty, and prosperity that the politics of place provides. Montesquieu thinks that the best way to advance these goods is to focus on protecting the individual rather than asserting the existence of rights. It is for this reason above all that he focuses on the policies and practices that improve the lives of individuals. By contrast, there are many cases when a constitution or other legal document guarantees someone rights, but those rights are worth less than the paper on which they are written. Besides, we can say that someone ought to be free to do something without insisting that the action in question be enshrined as a "right." In this sense, the language of rights is, strictly speaking, unnecessary. The politics of place does not rule out rights as a legitimate or useful way of establishing and maintaining a good political order. But it does deny the necessity of "rights" to achieve this end.

Along similar lines, the politics of place does not understand the formation of a "social contract" to be necessary to the establishment of a good political order. A social contract might well serve these ends in certain situations. The United States again is a good example. But societies certainly can be good without such an agreement. Accordingly, Montesquieu is not a social contract thinker,[49] and the politics of place does not rely on social contract theorizing. Instead, the focus is on understanding the different aspects of a society and how they interact.

In order to identify effective particularistic solutions to the three problems of politics in a given context, legislators must discern the *esprit* of a society. In an extended passage Montesquieu explains his project:

> They [the laws] ought to be relative to the *physical make-up* [*physique*] of the country; to the icy, hot, or temperate climate; to the quality of the terrain, to the situation, to its size [*grandeur*]; to the lifestyle of the peoples, laborers, hunters, or shepherds; they must relate to the degree of liberty that the constitution can withstand [*souffrir*]; to the religion of the inhabitants, to their inclinations, to their wealth, to their numbers, to their commerce, to their *mœurs*, to their manners. Finally they have links among themselves; with their origins, with the goal of the legislator, with the order of things on which they are established. It is with respect to all these perspectives [*vues*] that they must be considered.
>
> It is that which I undertake to do in this work. I will examine all of these relations: they form all together that which is called the SPIRIT OF THE LAWS [*l'ESPRIT DES LOIS*]. (I.3.238; capitals in original)

This passage is extremely important for understanding Montesquieu's enterprise. Here we will focus on the nature of that enterprise; later we will examine it in relation to his notion of *esprit*.

For legislators to identify the best way to approach a particular people, they must do three things. First, political actors must examine intimately the host of variables Montesquieu identifies in the passage above. These include political, economic, moral, social, and environmental factors. The variables will differ from society to society. Montesquieu thinks it is necessary to account for these differences because they fundamentally impact the makeup of each society. Moreover, each variable is not static over time; therefore, to know how to continue to act appropriately and effectively within a society requires knowledge of the changes in this society. Such changes can occur gradually or rapidly. Especially in the case of rapid changes, not accounting properly for such changes can lead to harmful miscalculations.

The second step entails investigating, and understanding, how the variables interact with one another. Politics, morals, economics, and the environment all impact each other, as well as other aspects of society. As Markovits explains, "the variables do not define themselves independently from the others."[50] For example, Montesquieu demonstrates that the effects of commerce go well beyond the economic realm. He thinks commerce impacts morals by giving people softer, gentler *mœurs*. He thinks it gives people a sense of exact justice. Commerce makes states more peaceful. Commerce alleviates the need to acquire through force, because people can acquire through trade. Commerce has the potential to undermine religion. These few examples show some of the ways commerce can affect other aspects of a state in fundamental ways. It is insufficient to consider only the economic effects of commerce, for example. The variables do not function in a vacuum; rather, they influence each other in a great many ways. Still, Montesquieu insists that another step is required to truly understand societies.

Legislators must see how the variables interact to form what Montesquieu calls the *esprit des lois* or the *esprit général*. These two formulations of *esprit* are critical to understanding the nature of Montesquieu's entire project. Indeed, he writes that he will "undertake" to "examine all of these relations" in his work, as they form what he calls the "SPIRIT OF THE LAWS." He continues by writing that he has "not treated the laws, *but the esprit of the laws*, and that this *esprit* consists in the diverse relations that the laws can have with diverse things" (I.3.238; emphasis added). He thus places his notion of *esprit* at the heart of his project. His political science requires that political actors work to understand and operate in the context of the *esprit* of a people. Montesquieu puts forward the notion that peoples have a general character or ethos that legislators must identify, assess, and then accept or try to change. In order to recognize the appropriate way of dealing with a particular people, a legislator or political actor must ultimately discern the *esprit* of that people. This is one of the key aspects of Montesquieu's politics of place. As such, it requires a more extended examination. It is this threefold process that will permit someone to "penetrate with a stroke of genius the entire constitution of a State" (Preface.230).

The passages from I, 3 we have examined about the need for particularity in lawmaking and *esprit* shed further light on the definition of laws with which Montesquieu opens book I. "Laws," we recall, "in the most extended signification, are the necessary relations which derive from the nature of things." The nature of things, though, changes to a significant degree across time and place. Societies are not static, and variables do not function the same way everywhere. Still, the relations that derive from the nature of things are "necessary," which implies some degree of continuity regarding how variables function across time and place. As such, Montesquieu studies how variables function generally, as well as how they relate to each other. At the same time, he emphasizes that religion, for example, does not impact all societies the same way, even the same religion. The nature of religion has changed greatly in America over the past centuries. Laws, then, derive from the relations that are necessary, and yet vary. The key to unlocking the relations, and the nature of things, in a particular society is the *esprit* because it defines and is defined by the variables.

Defining *Esprit*

Esprit is the single most important word in Montesquieu's political and philosophical vocabulary. Political actors must discern the *esprit* of a society if they want to attain and maintain a secure, free, and prosperous society, in part because it shapes the conception of these terms in the society. We only can understand important concepts in Montesquieu's vocabulary such as "liberty" by first comprehending what he means by the term *esprit*. If political actors do not properly identify the *esprit*, they will be much less likely to work effectively with it and within the confines it presents. The contours the *esprit* creates impact greatly the ways and means a legislator has at his disposal to make a society secure, free, and prosperous. I will discuss the differences between Montesquieu's two key formulations of *esprit*—the *esprit des lois* and the *esprit général*—later. They have much in common, though. As such, throughout the discussion I will use the broader term *esprit*.

Despite the importance he attaches to the term *esprit*, most scholars who have mentioned it have done so only in passing. This is surprising, considering first that the word appears in the title of the work. The book is about the *esprit* of the laws. It is not titled "On laws," for example. Second, Montesquieu makes clear at the end of book I that it is his very purpose in *EL* to examine the relations that form the *esprit des lois*. The concept warrants much greater treatment than it has received. What's more, Montesquieu actually is using the word in a different way than it was used in his time. One of his innovations was helping to give the word *esprit* new meaning.

If we analyze the *Dictionnaire de l'Académie française*, in editions published in the seventeenth and eighteenth centuries,[51] we do not find any usages of *esprit* that correspond to how Montesquieu employed the term. It was not until the 1832–35 edition that there is a definition that corresponds to his usage: "*Esprit national*, Les opinions, les dispositions qui dominent dans une nation" [*national esprit*, The opinions, the dispositions that dominate in a nation]. This definition corresponds closely with the one Montesquieu presents of the *esprit général* in XIX, 4, to which we will turn shortly. If we examine the 1694, 1762, and 1798 editions of the *Dictionnaire de l'Académie française*—the one published before Montesquieu began writing, the one published shortly after *EL* came out, and the one published fifty years after *EL*'s publication—we see that none of the entries correspond to Montesquieu's usage of *esprit*. From this we can surmise two things. First, Montesquieu used *esprit* in an uncommon way. Second, it is possible, given the immense influence of *EL*, that Montesquieu's usage was a factor in *esprit* gaining the meaning seen in the 1832–35 edition, after enough time to effect a real change in how the French understood and used the term *esprit* had passed.

In the 1694 edition, the first four entries are religious. They speak of God as a "pure *Esprit*," of angels, and of the Holy Spirit. The next set of entries relate to topics like the soul and one's character. For example, one entry refers to "the faculties of a reasonable soul. *Great esprit. active esprit. strong, solid esprit . . . apply, put, exert, occupy, employ his esprit with something. cultivate his esprit.*" *Esprit* also could refer to the "humor of persons. *Gentle Esprit. Supple esprit . . . moderate esprit . . . turbulent esprit.*" One definition speaks of *esprit* in terms of "the aptitude one has for something. This man has the *esprit* of the game." Another entry concerns one's character: "*This is a good esprit. this is a beautiful esprit. this is one of the best esprits in the kingdom. . . .* One calls, *beautiful esprits*, that which distinguishes itself from the common by the politeness of their discourse and of their works." The only new entry in the 1762 edition is a scientific one, which notes, for example, that "*ESPRIT* in Chemistry, is a very subtle fluid, or a very volatile vapor. One says, *Esprit of wine, Esprit of sulphur, of salt, of vitriol. Volatile esprit.*" In the following edition, that of 1798, the same thing is true—essentially the same entries appear as in the previous editions. None of the entries in the 1694, 1762, or 1798 editions correspond to how Montesquieu used the term, namely as a mode of analyzing a society and a way of characterizing a people.

Esprit's conceptual importance in Montesquieu's thought runs throughout his oeuvre. In an unpublished essay entitled *De la politique*, composed in 1725, he explains:

> In all societies, which are only a union of *esprit* [*qui ne sont qu'une union d'esprit*], a common character forms. This universal soul takes on a manner of thinking that is the effect of a chain of infinite causes, which multiply and combine from century to century. As soon as the tone is given and received, it is this alone which governs, and all that the sovereigns, the magistrates, the peoples can do or imagine, or that they seem to shock this tone, or follow it, is related to it always, and it dominates until its total destruction. (OCI.114)[52]

Many of the insights found here make their way into *EL*. Montesquieu identifies *esprit* with a common character, and asserts that all societies have one. There are some cohesive traits that hold a society together and cause it to form a "union." This common character is unified, and yet is extremely complicated, being the result of "infinite causes" over centuries. Montesquieu portrays the *esprit* as an extremely powerful force in society. It "alone" governs a society, and political actors and the people either can follow the *esprit*, or try to "shock" it. The *esprit* or "tone" dominates a society, until either the *esprit* or the society is destroyed. Montesquieu portrays the *esprit* as both a defining and dominating aspect of all societies. Spector describes Montesquieu's usages here as referring to a "collective result."[53] His later discussions of *esprit* also portray it as touching all spheres of society.

Montesquieu's two explanations of the *esprit général* in the *Considérations sur les causes de la grandeur des Romains et de leur décadence* (1734) point us toward formulations he will use in *EL*. First, in chapter 21, he explains: "Many received examples in a nation form there an *esprit général*, and make the *mœurs*, which reign as imperiously as the laws" (OCII.193). Montesquieu will adopt similar wording in *EL*. We see that the *esprit général* is the product of numerous things, and that it is key to shaping the *mœurs* of a society. In the next chapter, Montesquieu further highlights the centrality of the *esprit*: "There is in each nation an *esprit général*, on which power itself is founded; when it shocks this *esprit*, it shocks itself, and it necessarily stops" (OCII.203). Montesquieu makes a significant universal claim, that *each nation* has an *esprit*. And legislators must note well that all power in the state is founded on this *esprit*.

Understanding precisely what Montesquieu means by the term *esprit*, especially in his magnum opus, *EL*, is complicated by the fact that he uses the term in numerous ways. He does so, in part, because *esprit* has different meanings in French.[54] An *homme d'esprit* is a witty man, for example. In *Mes Pensées* (*MP*) he often uses *esprit* with respect to the *esprit* of a person, referring to character, or in other ways that do not relate to the *esprit des lois* or *esprit général* (OCI.1295–99). Montesquieu clearly is juxtaposing the *esprit* of the law against the letter of the law. Indeed, this is a critical and long-analyzed distinction.[55] He speaks of the *esprit* of moderation, the *esprit* of monarchy, and the *esprit* of the legislator.[56] While these usages are undoubtedly important, the *esprit des lois* and *esprit général* are foundational to his thought.

Montesquieu defines the *esprit des lois* in the lengthy passage quoted above from I, 3. He identifies a host of variables that form the spirit of the laws, including the physical appearance of the country, its size, the religion of the people, their commerce, and the order of things on which they are established. These variables relate to one another; they interact. Their interaction forms the *esprit des lois*. Here, though, Montesquieu does not suggest how we might distinguish between the importance of the variables that comprise the *esprit des lois*. He does that later, in book XIX.

In a chapter entitled "What the General Spirit Is," Montesquieu explains: "Many things govern men: climate, religion, laws, the maxims of government, examples of past things, *mœurs*, manners; from this, it results that a general spirit [*esprit général*] is formed" (XIX.4.558). Building on his thoughts from I, 3, Montesquieu provides a key insight into how the variables relate to the *esprit général*: "To the extent that, in each nation, one of these causes acts with more force, the others give into it that much. Almost alone nature and climate prevail over savages; manners govern the Chinese; laws tyrannize Japan; in another time *mœurs* set the tone in Lacedemonia; the maxims of government and ancient *mœurs* set it in Rome."[57] We see, then, that it can be the case that one variable becomes especially important, indeed dominant, in a particular society.[58] When this occurs, the other variables become less important. Based on his analysis elsewhere of contemporary societies he studied, he would have identified religion as dominating life in Persia, and commerce dominating life in Holland, for example. He also notes, though, that two variables can dominate in a society, as happened in Rome where the maxims of government and ancient *mœurs* dominated. So numerous factors can exert significant force on a society. When one factor does not "dominate," political actors must nonetheless determine the "relative force or the proportion that prevails between the components."[59]

By arguing that one factor of the *esprit général* usually acts with more force, Montesquieu draws an important link to an earlier chapter, in book XI. There he notes that while "all States have in general an identical goal, which is to maintain themselves, each State has, however, one that is particular to them" (XI.5.396). He proceeds to identify, for example, expansion as Rome's goal, war that of Lacedemonia, commerce that of Marseilles, public tranquility that of China, and liberty as England's goal.

Montesquieu complicates his discussion here when he notes goals not just for specific countries, but also for forms of government. Monarchy has glory as its goal, and despotism has the delights of the prince. Be that as it may, the important point for our discussion is that one factor can be especially important as input for driving the *esprit général*, or as output, that is, as something toward which the state does or should strive. All factors are not of equal import.

It is true that Montesquieu usually refers in *EL* not to the *esprit* per se, but to the *esprit des lois* or the *esprit général*. I acknowledge differences between these two concepts. The *esprit général* is broader. It refers more fully to the character of the people. The *esprit des lois*, on the other hand, refers more specifically to how the variables impact the laws, and the product of that impact. While one or a few factors dominate the *esprit général*, Montesquieu at least does not explicitly say that one or some factors dominate or define the *esprit des lois*. The *esprit des lois* must be viewed as the more important formulation, for the obvious reason that Montesquieu titled the book *De l'Esprit des lois*, and not *De l'Esprit général*. Still, the terms are closely related.[60] Both form based on the interaction of and relation between essentially the same variables.[61] Because the terms have much in common, throughout my study I refer to the *esprit*.

For Montesquieu, the *esprit* is the ethos or (national) character of a particular people or society.[62] The *esprit* constitutes the union and common understanding of a people. It forms based on how the different variables in a society interact to make a people unique and gives each people an identity. By introducing his notion of *esprit général*, Montesquieu shows that one of his primary concerns is to see how the identity of a community, state, or nation forms, changes, and maintains itself, and how a legislator can understand it. Montesquieu thinks that to discern the *esprit*, legislators must analyze all the factors we noticed above that interact to form the *esprit* of a society. Montesquieu puts forth that all peoples have an *esprit*; this is a universal claim. But each people will have a different *esprit*, ethos, or character. In *MP* he writes, for example: "An Englishman, a Frenchman, an Italian: three *esprits*" (OCI.1327). It is possible, however, for peoples to have *esprits* that are similar if the variables operate in a similar way in both societies. The *esprit* will change over time, because the factors contributing to form the *esprit* are not themselves static. Accordingly, the character of a people can change substantially over time. Such changes occur for a wide array of reasons, in many ways. Sometimes the change in an *esprit* is abrupt, as in a revolution (e.g., France, Russia, or China). Even in these cases, many components of the *esprit* do not change immediately. In the short term, the *esprit* of a society is a relatively stable characteristic that gives a nation its particular identity. Changes in that identity, in the *esprit*, tend to occur gradually, over many years. An *esprit* can change, for example, if the religion(s) a people practices change, or if the nature and extent of their worship changes. If a society becomes significantly more—or less—religious, the *esprit* will change. Change can be intentional, as in a revolution, but more often change is largely indirect or even unintentional. It is difficult to identify a threshold at which a society's *esprit* is distinct from an earlier one.

Esprit is a way to consider a people holistically. Montesquieu suggests that we look at all the factors that constitute a society and not limit our analysis to only a few of them. Each factor impacts the character of a society, and the whole is more than the sum of the parts. With his holistic analysis, Montesquieu offers legislators a much more robust, nuanced understanding of societies, and helps them understand why his politics of place is a more effective approach. Montesquieu impels legislators to consider a people not only as a totality, but as a potentially *coherent* (or incoherent) totality.[63] Indeed, this is one of the most crucial aspects of *esprit*: a society ought to come together in a sensible, meaningful manner. A people's *esprit* should have sufficiently clear content.

Scholars have offered helpful insights into Montesquieu's usage of *esprit*. Diana Schaub, in her careful analysis of the *Lettres Persanes* (*LP*), writes, "*Esprit* is one of the most significant words in Montesquieu's political vocabulary." She notes further, "Montesquieu's discovery of the general spirit represents an epoch in the art of legislation."[64] Pangle identifies *esprit* as "national character."[65] Rahe notes that in book I Montesquieu briefly discusses kinds of laws and his typology of forms of governments and that his "stated purpose for doing so was to trace *esprit*—the spirit, the mindset, the motive, the impetus, the purpose, the intention, the object, as well as the logic—behind the 'infinite diversity of laws & *mœurs*' which are to be found in the larger world."[66] Anne Cohler writes that Montesquieu "offers spirit as an encompassing category for political life." This category revolves around the fact that spirit "has something to do with what we can hold in common with some others."[67] Judith Shklar writes that *esprit* "is like a natural fact, which an intelligent legislator must understand fully."[68] James Ceaser explains that the *esprit* places some limits on the "potential use of general political science."[69] Paul Carrese says Montesquieu has a "new politics of spirit" and that *esprit général* is a "comprehensive predecessor to the term 'political culture.'"[70] Michael Mosher highlights the dynamic between the universal and particular in "ordering thoughts about society" and shaping the *esprit*.[71]

Esprit is central to Montesquieu's philosophy. Legislators disregard it or take insufficient note of it not only at their own peril, but at the peril of their state. Spector explains how *esprit* is key to the achievement of moderation:

The theory of the *esprit général* is inscribed in this way at the heart of the philosophy of moderation extolled in *L'Esprit des lois*. The multiplicity of factors that form the character of a nation permits him to put into perspective the status of the juridical, insisting on the necessary adaptation of commands to usages, of 'established' laws to 'inspired' manners and *mœurs*, which depend more on the *esprit général*.[72]

By taking a multiplicity of factors into account, political actors understand where the boundaries of permissible action lie. Spector also rightly links Montesquieu's insistence on considering many factors to the attainment or abridgment of liberty. In XIX, 3, in the chapter before he defines the *esprit général*, Montesquieu explains that "tyranny" of "opinion" arises when "those who govern establish things that shock the manner of thinking of a nation" (XIX.3.557). Spector elaborates: "one does not obtain liberty as opinion of one's security simply by the legal protection of rights attached to an individual; it supposes the respect of collective customs deposited over time, and risks being obliterated by the 'tyranny of opinion' that shocks the manner of thinking of a people."[73] So political actors *must* consider the *esprit* of a people, according to Montesquieu. In the preface he explains: "One looks at all the parts only to judge everything together; one examines all the causes to see all the results" (230). Political actors must consider the bigger picture—that of society as a whole, that of the *esprit*. At the beginning of book XIX, he notes that he "will be more attentive to the order of things than to the things themselves" (1.556). If a political actor does not understand the *esprit*, then there is the potential to enact ineffective, inappropriate, or harmful policies. Is the *esprit* sufficiently malleable for political actors to mold it?

Montesquieu is skeptical about the abilities of legislators to shape the *esprit* of a people, in sharp contrast to Rousseau. According to Markovits, for Rousseau, the Legislator "is not a man but a hero. Rousseau examines the question of legislation at the intersection of the political and the theological."[74] Rousseau's Legislator has the power, right, and duty to (re)form a people. More than just being apprehensive about the negative consequences of political actors disregarding or misunderstanding the *esprit*, Montesquieu is highly doubtful that the Legislator possesses such abilities. As Markovits notes elsewhere, the very concept of the *esprit général* points us to the "diversity of things that steer the State to the unity of an order that is neither a principle of life, *nor the intention of the legislator*, but the effect of factors."[75] While Montesquieu does think that political actors can promote things like commerce that eventually will change the *esprit*, he does not think that political actors should attempt to remake the *esprit*, unless the *esprit* is ready for change.

For societies to be secure, free, and prosperous, their *esprits* must be "prepared" (*préparés*) (XIX.2.556). Not all peoples are ready to be free or to embrace representative governments, for example. "Liberty itself," he writes, "has seemed insufferable to peoples who were not accustomed to enjoying it." So too with democracy: it simply is not appropriate for all peoples everywhere.[76] Some *esprits* are not ready for democracy; it does not fit others. Peoples have different customs, and thus cannot—and should not—enjoy or embrace or even do the same things. To try to impose liberty or democracy on peoples ill-suited or ill-prepared for one or both is nothing short of tyrannical, according to Montesquieu. One sort of tyranny is that of opinion, which occurs when "those who govern establish things which shock the manner of thinking in a nation" (XIX.3.557).[77] Imposing the wrong order on a society does more than simply "shock the manner of thinking in a nation," though; it can be a kind of violence that greatly damages or even destroys a society. A revolutionary Montesquieu is not.

Montesquieu utilizes *esprit* as a normative concept, and not only as a descriptive one. He impels political actors to evaluate the goodness of an *esprit*. Not all *esprits* are similarly good. Some are categorically bad. Pangle explains that "Montesquieu's new undertaking by no means implies, then, that all national 'spirits' are equally good, or even deserving of support." It might be appropriate for political actors to attempt to change the *esprit* gradually. While some *esprits* "allow a more effective and complete satisfaction of the basic, original, and permanent, natural need for security," others "frustrate the need for security in varying degrees—often more than necessary in the circumstances."[78] But the process of evaluating is not done in black-and-white terms. An *esprit* can have undesirable elements, but still be on balance good so long as the desirable or positive elements outweigh the bad ones. As Spector explains, the "theory of the *esprit général* thus allows us to disqualify a moral or political evaluation that would take into account the *social utility* of collective qualities or flaws, identifiable *a posteriori*."[79] The normative evaluation of an *esprit* thus must be comprehensive and take all relevant matters into account.

Montesquieu's notion of *esprit* is antiperfectionist.[80] He thinks it neither possible nor desirable to steer a society toward the "best" *esprit*; indeed, he does not even think a "best" *esprit* exists, either generally or for a particular people. In a chapter entitled "To What Extent It Is Necessary to Be Attentive to Not Change the *Esprit Général* of a Nation," Montesquieu makes a point central to his political philosophy: "If in general the character is good, what importance does finding a few faults there have?" Montesquieu opposes trying to change a good *esprit*. He insists that it is up to the "legislator to follow the *esprit* of the nation, when it is not contrary to the principles of government; because we do nothing better than what we do freely, and in following our natural genius" (XIX.5.559). Trying to impose an economic, political, social, or moral order of any sort onto a society that will be unreceptive to the new order is foolhardy at best, and destructive at worst. What's more, Montesquieu thinks that faults are acceptable, perhaps even to be embraced on occasion. In speaking of the French *esprit*, he notes that one could change it by "restraining the women, making laws for correcting their *mœurs*, and limiting their [taste for] luxury; but who knows whether one would thereby lose a certain tastefulness which is the source of the nation's riches, and a politeness that draws foreigners to it?" Far from advocating the removal of so-called faults, Montesquieu notes that what some see as faults are appealing to others. By attempting to remove such "faults," the state likely will lose some of its positive attributes, and acquire negative ones. Montesquieu also thinks that some faults will correct themselves over time. In a chapter entitled "That It Is Not Necessary to Correct Everything" (*Qu'il ne faut pas tout corriger*), he contends: "Nature repairs everything" (*La nature répare tout*) (XIX.6.559). This suggests that he thinks societies have the potential to correct problems internally as long as they have sufficient chance to do so. More than just arguing against perfectionism, though, Montesquieu urges caution in changing undesirable *esprits* because the cure may be worse than the disease. In the preface he warns: "One senses the old abuses, one sees the correction to them; but one sees the abuses of the correction itself. One leaves the bad, if one fears the worse; one leaves the good, if one is in doubt of the better." Montesquieu reminds his reader that it is necessary to evaluate all of the potential outcomes when trying to change an *esprit*. An *esprit* of middling desirability might be better left alone because the risk of making it bad is sufficiently high.

Montesquieu offers further insights into how the *esprit* and character form in an earlier work.[81] In *Essai sur les causes qui peuvent affecter les esprits et les caractères*, Montesquieu distinguishes between the *esprit* of an individual and of a nation. "We know better," he explains, "what gives a certain character to a nation than what gives a certain *esprit* to an individual.... We know better what shapes the genius of societies that have adopted a given way of life than what shapes that of an individual" (OCII.39). It is easier, then, to generalize about a society and the values and practices the inhabitants have adopted than it is to know the particular *esprit* of an individual. Societies develop certain tendencies. All individuals may not embrace them, but enough do to justify making generalizations. Montesquieu then identifies two kinds of "causes" that affect the character of societies: physical causes (the physical environment) and moral causes (e.g., laws, education, *mœurs*, manners, and commerce). The moral causes, though, play a larger role in forming the "general character of a nation" and its "*esprit*" than the physical causes (OCII.60).[82] Montesquieu attributes somewhat greater importance to education as a moral cause. This education can come from many sources, including the laws and other people. Even the books of Confucius, with their moral precepts, greatly affect the *esprit* of the Chinese; so too the Talmud with Jews (OCII.58).

The nature of the *esprit* in a particular state impacts the *human* nature of the inhabitants. Montesquieu sees human nature as flexible.[83] He deems man a "flexible being" who "adapts himself, in society, to the thoughts and impressions of others" (Preface.230). Man's nature in a particular state forms in large part based on how the inhabitants impact—and are impacted by—the variables. The nature of the inhabitants is a product, in part, of the *esprit* in that society.

Montesquieu's view of man's nature as flexible contrasts sharply with other prominent views before and shortly after he wrote. Hobbes, in his *Leviathan*, offers a bleak view of human nature. He portrays man's natural state as a state of war in which life is "solitary, poore, nasty, brutish, and short."[84] Hobbes views man as selfish and ready to act against others when such opportunities arise. Montesquieu takes direct issue with Hobbes's account of man seeking to subordinate others to his wants and needs. He thinks Hobbes attributes characteristics to man in his natural state that can arise only in society (I.2.235). In his *Second Treatise*, Locke portrays man's nature in a more benign manner. People do not seem inclined, necessarily, to act against others, though they still do look out for their own interests. Still, Locke sees human nature as fixed. Rousseau, in his *Second Discourse*, written shortly after the publication of *EL*, portrays man as naturally good, and corrupted by society. Montesquieu does not find any of these depictions of human nature compelling. He does not think that human nature is uniform before entering society. Rather, human nature is flexible, though not totally breakable, like a wire bent into different shapes.

Examples of *Esprit*

Montesquieu's treatment of *esprit* will become less abstract by looking briefly at his depictions of the *esprit* of three societies where he spent time: France, Holland, and England. This will give us a taste of how he considers societies holistically, and how he captures, discusses, and evaluates aspects of their *esprits*. In these cases, his observations are based in part on his firsthand observation of those societies. We consider these cases for two additional reasons. First, he paid extra attention to these societies in his writings. Second, they represent distinct forms of government. Still, we note that our considerations here are brief, because extensive analysis of these *esprits* is the work of a separate inquiry.[85]

His treatment of the French *esprit* shows that it is possible for an *esprit* to be good without the political order in which it exists being good.

Immediately after defining what the *esprit général* is, in the next chapter Montesquieu depicts the French *esprit* as follows:

> If there were in the world a nation that had a sociable humor, an openness of heart, a joy in life, taste, an ease of communicating its thoughts; that was lively, agreeable, enjoyable, sometimes imprudent, often indiscreet; and along with this had courage, generosity, frankness, a certain point of honor, one must not seek to disturb, by laws, its manners, so as not to disturb its virtues. If in general the character is good, what importance does finding a few faults there have? (XIX.5.558–59)

This passage represents Montesquieu's crispest formulation of the *esprit* of a people, in the case he knows best. He seeks only to depict the *esprit* of French society, not of every French person.

Montesquieu portrays the French *esprit* positively here. His outlook is positive despite the problems he saw in French society. Montesquieu was not shy about criticizing his countrymen. He poked fun at the French throughout *LP*. Indeed, one could dedicate an entire extended inquiry to analyzing his discussion of the French in *LP*. Still, he speaks fondly of the French character. The French come off as pleasant, interesting, and fun. And yet, Montesquieu viewed the French political system in a negative light. He saw France under Louis XIV as absolutist. Montesquieu voiced his criticisms of Louis and French absolutism in *LP*, *Réflexions sur la monarchie universelle en Europe*, and *EL*. There was the potential, he thought, that France could become despotic. This threat diminished after the death of Louis XIV, but only somewhat. Montesquieu presented various mechanisms, such as the nobility and the *parlements* to combat these dangerous developments. In spite of the risk of absolutism turning into despotism, Montesquieu nonetheless judged the French *esprit* to be good. Since the French *esprit* is good, Montesquieu thinks that a "few faults" ought not to worry us. Indeed, evaluations of an *esprit* and a society often are mixed, as with Holland.

At first glance, Holland's treatment in *EL* and elsewhere is rather negative. After describing the (positive) *esprit* of commerce, Montesquieu explains that while commerce unites nations and leads to peace, it does not have the same effect on individuals: "We see that in countries where one is affected only by the *esprit* of commerce, one traffics in all human actions, and in all moral virtues: the smallest things, those which humanity demands, are done or given there for money" (XX.2.586). A footnote reveals that Montesquieu has Holland in mind with this remark. Some years before publishing *EL*, Montesquieu wrote a short piece entitled *Voyage en Hollande*. Here he offers an even sharper view of the Dutch *esprit*. Everything Montesquieu had heard about the "avarice, knavery, and fraud of the Dutch, is not made up, it is the pure truth" (OCI.863). It is so bad, apparently, that "a man who points out a road requests money" (OCI.863). Montesquieu recounts a number of other negative anecdotes about the Dutch in his *Voyage en Hollande*. There is more to the Dutch *esprit*, though, than these seemingly negative attributes.

The Dutch also have many positive characteristics. They are hardworking, so much so that they turned marshes into a moderate state. This state was formed "by the industry of men," and this industry makes the Dutch government moderate (XVIII.6.534). Immediately following the passage above about the effects of commerce on individuals, Montesquieu explains that the *esprit* of commerce "produces in men a certain feeling for precise justice, opposed on the one hand to highway robbery, and on the other to those moral virtues that make it such that one does not always speak rigidly about his interests and can be negligent of them for those of others" (XX.2.586). He has Holland in mind again. The effects of commerce on the Dutch *esprit* are mixed but overall positive: commerce makes them more just, a good thing, but this justice is rather precise, perhaps too much so. A few pages later he cites Mandeville's *Fables of the Bees*, which has as its subtitle *Or Private Vices, Publick Benefits*.

Despite this mixed portrayal of the Dutch *esprit*, Montesquieu still finds Holland to have overall a good political, economic, and moral order. The case of Holland will be important throughout our study. It suffices to note here that Montesquieu deemed Dutch society sufficiently good, despite its faults. The same is true with England.

England has a system of government that, while adequately protecting liberty, gives the English people a gray character.[86] Here we will survey briefly some of the undesirable traits he attributes to the English. We leave a discussion of their politics until chapter 3. Since all of their passions are free, "hate, envy, jealousy, the ardor for enriching themselves and distinguishing themselves, would appear in all their areas" (XIX.27.575). Far from identifying these features as faults, Montesquieu continues by noting that without them the state would be "like a man weakened by sickness, who does not have passions because he does not have strength." Apparently being envious, jealous, and so on serves the English rather well. Individuals follow their "caprices and fantasies." The people are "uneasy" (*inquiet*) about their situation.[87] But with a "certain object" the people's *inquiétude* also has positive effects. Rahe argues that it makes the English vigilant, which is key to maintaining English liberty.[88] English citizens seem isolated, as "hardly any citizen would depend on another citizen" there (XIX.27.582–83). Montesquieu identifies other aspects of the English character that we might find unsavory, including "extreme" opulence and being "always occupied by their interests." Some may read other remarks as mixed: "There one could hardly esteem men by their frivolous talents or attributes, but by their real qualities; and of this genre there are only two: riches and personal merit."[89] In *MP* he says the English are too "busy" to be "polite" (*polis*) (OCI.1335). They may be "rich" and "free," "but they are tormented by their *esprit*. They are disgusted by or disdainful about everything. They are miserable enough, with so many subjects to not be so" (OCI.1335). The English might be free, but that does not mean Montesquieu finds their *esprit* especially appealing.

Despite these remarks, Montesquieu is far from judging the English *esprit* to be on balance bad.[90] Indeed, he sees a number of good characteristics. The English have a politeness of *mœurs* and are a proud and "superb" nation. In some ways, their *esprit* is more desirable than that of the French. He writes, again in *MP*, about "the Difference between the English and the French": "The English live well with their inferiors and cannot support their superiors. We [the French] accommodate ourselves to our superiors and are insufferable to our inferiors" (OCI.1337). Still, I focus on the seemingly negative attributes for two reasons. First, it is not clear that Montesquieu actually thinks the traits listed above are on balance bad. Some prominent interpretations of *EL* argue that England was Montesquieu's preferred political system, despite or because of these characteristics.[91] Second, Montesquieu deems the English free and praises them for their commerce and political institutions. It is thus necessary to judge societies based on the bigger picture; and their *esprit* is but one important part of this picture. The English may not be as pleasant as the French in Montesquieu's account, but they have other positive qualities. English society overall is good.

Esprits are good for different reasons. There is no universal standard for assessing the goodness of an *esprit*. At the end of his account of the English *esprit*, Montesquieu makes an important observation: "one would find here something which approaches more the force of Michelangelo than the grace of Raphael" (XIX.27.583). *Esprits*, then, have something in common with art: what makes them beautiful, or good, differs. Evaluating the beauty or value of art has a subjective component. It is, to an extent, a matter of taste.[92] It might even be the case that a good *esprit* always will have some bad or vicious aspects: "the diverse characters of nations are mixed with virtues and vices, good and bad qualities. The happy mixes are those from which great goods result, and often one would not suspect them; there are some from which result great evils, and one would not suspect them either" (XIX.10.562). The good, Montesquieu acknowledges, is often mixed with the bad.

Montesquieu's notion of *esprit* thus points toward trying to understand the *esprit* of particular peoples. As I have argued elsewhere, his notion of *esprit* can be helpful for studying institutions like the European Union.[93] The enterprise of studying, discerning, and working within the context of an *esprit* entails evaluating how the variables function separately and in relation to one another in a particular society. These interactions form, and are formed by, the *esprit*. Indeed, the causal arrows go in both directions: the *esprit* shapes the variables, and the variables shape the *esprit*. These sort of interactions are a constant in Montesquieu's writings. By acknowledging the centrality of this concept, we also gain clarity about the order of *EL*.

On the Order of *De l'Esprit des lois*

Montesquieu emphasizes the necessity of discerning the order of *EL* if we are to understand his political project. "If," Montesquieu declares in the preface, "one wants to seek the design of the author, one can only discover it in the design of the work" (229). Montesquieu also speaks of a "chain" (*chaîne*)[94] that one must see in order to recognize the "truths" (*vérités*) found in his work. These truths are based, in large part, on his principles. Lowenthal rightly notes that the "*central issue* in the interpretation of *The Spirit of the Laws*—the issue with the widest and most profound ramifications—concerns the apparent lack of a comprehensive plan and order by which its thirty-one Books might be considered parts of an integrated whole."[95] Unsurprisingly, no consensus has emerged among scholars as to what the design might be, or what the chain is that holds the work together. Montesquieu explicitly lays out the design of the work at the end of book I. Montesquieu structures the book around advising political actors how to study societies in order to make them secure, free, and prosperous. *Esprit* is the chain that holds the work together.

Montesquieu himself acknowledges that understanding his project was not meant to be easy. Writing in *MP* about the art of reading, he explains:

> When one reads a book, it is necessary to be disposed to believe that the author has seen the contradictions that one imagines to encounter there at the first glance of an eye. Thus it is necessary to begin by being wary of one's quick judgments, going back over the passages that one takes to contradict themselves, compare them together, compare them again with what precedes them and what follows them, see if they make the same hypothesis, if the contradiction is in the things or solely in the proper manner of conceiving them. When one has done all that well, one can pronounce as a master: "There is a contradiction."
>
> Yet this is not always all. When a work is systematic, it is necessary again to be sure that one grasp the whole system. You see a great machine made for producing an effect. You see the wheels that turn in opposing directions; you would believe, at first glance, that the machine will

destroy itself, that all the cogs will stop, that the machine will come to a halt. So it goes again: these pieces, which seem, beforehand, to destroy themselves, unite for the proposed goal. (OCI.1228)

Montesquieu thus insists that one not judge the apparent disorder of his work quickly. And he may well have had *EL* in mind when he wrote this passage.

D'Alembert, for one, in his "Éloge de Monsieur le Président de Montesquieu," takes Montesquieu's exhortations here quite seriously. D'Alembert insists that there is an order to *EL*. This order, though, is not visible to "vulgar readers" (*les lecteurs vulgaires*), but rather only to "those whom the author has had in view." The apparent "obscurity" and lack of order thus vanishes when read by those who are prepared to comprehend Montesquieu's "important truths" that he was unable to present directly. According to d'Alembert, Montesquieu decided instead to "envelop" (*envelopper*) these truths, and hide them from those to whom they would be harmful.[96] Montesquieu's order is hidden to all but the "wise." Despite d'Alembert's assurance that an order exists in Montesquieu's work, many, including their contemporary Voltaire, were unconvinced. The apparent lack of order caused Voltaire to lash out:

> I'm sorry the book should be a labyrinth without a clue, lacking all method.... I have looked for a thread through this labyrinth; the thread is broken at almost every article; I was deceived: I found the spirit of the author—and he has a great deal!—but rarely the spirit of the laws; he hops more than he walks; he amuses more than he enlightens ... and he makes us wish that so noble a mind had tried to instruct rather than to shock.[97]

Others have been just as perplexed, but less bombastic.[98] Of those who have found an order present in *EL*, two theses have emerged. The first is the "design thesis." Proponents[99] assert that groupings of the books represent analyses of different causes of law. Advocates of this approach attempt "to explain the design" by arguing "that the books are grouped together as an analysis of the different causes of laws."[100] But proponents neither account for the division of the work into parts, nor do they discuss much of what Montesquieu says in the second half of *EL*.

The most compelling thesis puts forth that *EL* is a dialectic between determinism and freedom, with freedom eventually winning out. Ana Samuel contends that *EL* "is organized in a dialectical way" and argues that "the battle between freedom and determination is reflected in the way the first three parts alternate between a focus on determining forces and a focus on liberating forces."[101] Samuel's account does identify a clear tension in the work. But her interpretation is not without its problems. First, she claims that *EL* is centered on a concept—freedom (*liberté*)—that she never defines. This begs the question of what this central concept is for Montesquieu (and a precondition for considering how states might achieve it). Second, while she rightly seems to have identified a progression in the work, this progress is rather short—from determinism to freedom, back to determinism, and then concluding with freedom winning out. Finally, this movement is not the key to understanding the design, chain, or order of *EL*.[102] While Montesquieu certainly was an avid proponent of freedom, his project is more ambitious. Aurelian Craiutu argues that moderation is the chain to which Montesquieu referred because moderation "completes the transition from character trait to a fundamental constitutional principle."[103] Moderation is undoubtedly crucial to attaining a free political order for Montesquieu, but I put forth *esprit* as the key to achieving both moderation and freedom.

Montesquieu clearly states the purpose of *EL* at the end of I, 3. He explains that the laws are relative to a long list of variables we noted above, including commerce, religion, manners, and the physical environment. Montesquieu explains that it is necessary to consider all of these viewpoints. He then explicitly tells his reader the following: "That is what I undertake to do in this work. I will examine all of these relations: they form all together what one calls THE SPIRIT OF THE LAWS" (I.3.238). Montesquieu then clarifies that he does not treat the laws per se, but the "*esprit* of the laws" because "this *esprit* consists in the diverse relations that the laws can have with diverse things." He thus makes clear that his purpose is to examine the relations that form the *esprit des lois*. How, then, to understand these relations properly?

Political actors should analyze the variables in a society in a particular order. They should begin with the political variables, above all the "relations that the laws have with the nature and with the principle of each government" (I.3.238). This principle has "a supreme influence on the laws" and Montesquieu thinks that if he can "establish it at once, one will see the laws flow from it as from their source." Montesquieu begins with the political sphere because, as Pangle notes, it is the most important "sociopolitical environment."[104] After considering the other political variables, Montesquieu then moves on to "the other relations, which seem to be more particular." I call these relations the "subpolitical" variables. Indeed, Montesquieu proceeds in precisely the manner he recommends in these passages.

One must begin by looking at how rulers and ruled can and should act in each of the forms of government. The form of government defines the broadest parameters under which they will operate as legislators. Republics, monarchies, and despotisms all function differently. Montesquieu examines these forms of government and the laws that undergird them in book II. Political actors then must consider the principle of each government, that is, the motivating passion (virtue, honor, or fear) that citizens must possess for the government to work properly. He looks at the different principles in book III. Taken together, the form of government and its principle are the first source of laws.

Books IV to VIII fill out his discussion of the form and principle of a government by considering the education, laws, punishments, and economic policies that legislators must implement for these government types to function optimally. In book IV Montesquieu discusses the kind of education citizens in each form of government must receive. The focus is on how this education relates to the principle in each form of government. Book V considers the kinds of laws necessary to maintain each form of government. If citizens do not adhere to the principle and follow the laws, then the state must mete out proper punishment. Book VI addresses how each form of government should punish its citizens' wrongdoings. In book VII Montesquieu shows particular concern for the effects luxury has on the three forms of government, given that it has the potential to be acidic in some cases. Book VIII takes up how each form of government can become corrupt. Corruption begins with the principle.

The discussion turns to a consideration of security and liberty in books IX–XIII. Montesquieu considers external affairs in books IX and X, after having examined internal affairs in books II–VIII. Specifically, Montesquieu considers states' relations with other states. In book IX he takes up defensive force. He looks at whether each form of government is secure from external threats. In this discussion, he brings another form of government—the federal republic—into the discussion. In book X he addresses offensive force. He discusses when it is appropriate for one state to attack another. He concludes in these two books that each form of government—republic, monarchy, and despotism—faces an inherent insecurity that it must address. Political actors must make modifications to augment security, in part by making them more peaceful, and in part by making them more committed to protecting liberty.

Montesquieu's concern with security from external threats in books IX and X leads him to take up the issue of security from internal threats in books XI, XII, and XIII. Internal threats pose significant dangers to the security of states and individuals. If citizens cannot coexist peacefully with each other and with the state, then there is the potential for political unrest and upheaval. Even more than establishing security, though, Montesquieu is keen to see liberty blossom. He thinks that three kinds of liberty are crucial: political, personal, and economic. In order to establish political freedom, states need a separation of powers. In book XI Montesquieu elaborates on political liberty. The English constitution represents one way of providing for security and liberty. In order to secure personal liberty, Montesquieu explains in book XII that moderate criminal laws are necessary. In book XIII Montesquieu addresses economic liberty. He finds that low taxes are most conducive not only to economic liberty, but to personal and political liberty too.

Parts I (books I–VIII) and II (books IX–XIII) deal with the well-being of society, but in primarily political terms. It is necessary to deal with the political aspects of lawmaking to have a secure and free society. But it is not sufficient. Political actors also must take up "relations" that are more "particular," such as the physical environment, commerce, religion, and history. I refer to these as the "subpolitical" variables.

Montesquieu considers the environment, broadly speaking, in part III (books XIV–XVIII). He seeks to explain the effects of the physical environment on people. He does so more explicitly in books XIV and XVIII, in which he discusses climate (XIV) and terrain (XVIII). Sandwiched between these chapters is a discussion of slavery in books XV–XVII. The only potential justification for slavery is circumstance or environment (physical, political, or cultural). Montesquieu entertains the possibility that the physical environment provides a justification for forms of slavery. He shows, though, that while the environment is a cause for some things, slavery is not among them. This discussion of antifreedom serves as a continuation to his discussion of freedom in books XI–XIII. Books XIV–XVIII deal, in part, with causes over which humans seem to have little or no direct control. Book XIX deals with the moral effects of all of the variables on the *esprit général.*

Parts IV (books XX–XXIII) and V (XXIV–XXVI) are juxtaposed against one another. Part IV presents commerce as a panacea. Commerce has vast moral, political, and social benefits, on top of the obvious economic ones. Part V, by contrast, shows that religion has the potential to be a negative force in society. While religion has the potential to be a force for good, Montesquieu sees it falling short in many cases. Montesquieu directly pits commerce against religion in book XXV when he suggests that commerce can serve as a way of making people less religious.

Part VI has a somewhat curious structure because Montesquieu was forced to add books XXX and XXXI by the editor of the first printed edition of *EL*. Generally, though, part VI takes up lawmaking in the context of history. Book XXVII offers thoughts on "the origin and revolutions" of Roman laws of inheritance, while book XXVIII deals with "the origin and revolutions" of civil laws among the French. These two chapters discuss the most relevant historical examples for Montesquieu: Rome and France. Book XXIX was to have served as a tidy conclusion where Montesquieu offers a general theory of lawmaking guided by moderation. Books XXX and XXXI take up feudalism, allowing him the chance to address another kind of political and social arrangement.

There is thus a logical structure to *EL*.[105] Montesquieu explains his project in book I. He shows political actors that their focus should be on man in society. In order to secure man from other men and from the state, and to secure states from each other, political actors must adopt the particularistic methods of Montesquieu's politics of place. One must consider how the variables function separately, with one another, and to form an *esprit*. Montesquieu then explains how to analyze and act in societies: begin by understanding the political variables, and then turn to the subpolitical variables.

The Politics of Changing a Place

One of Montesquieu's primary goals in *EL* is to cure people of their prejudices. He is trying to cure a lack of self-knowledge, misguided notions of liberty, and the use of harsh punishments, among other misinformed, prejudiced practices. Montesquieu gives his reader an education on how to look at various regimes, societies, and factors within them. He shows his reader how to recognize tyranny and how to approach good or atrocious practices. Montesquieu works to educate people's understanding by providing a more nuanced view of politics. Montesquieu offers nuance with a purpose—to educate his reader's political sensibilities. Having done so, he is one step closer to achieving his deeper purpose: change.

Montesquieu develops his principles in order to promote positive change in societies. Change is a key theme in *EL*, especially in book XIX. But the moderation he praises so highly (and to which we turn in chapter 3) dictates that legislators not impose change. Effective, positive change comes about gradually, not dramatically or radically. As Jonathan Israel writes, Montesquieu sought to "counter the radical challenge in" the political, "social, religious, and moral spheres."[106] What's more, moderation would dictate that you not impose the good regime, or even an *Enlightened*, better regime, because doing so would be tyrannical. But how, then, can societies undergo positive changes? The answer is found in Montesquieu's principles.

Our study of the Introduction gives us critical insight into three of Montesquieu's principles. The first principle is that legislators should have as their goal to solve the three problems of politics from I, 3. A society cannot be secure, to say nothing of being free or prosperous, without addressing the three kinds of conflict effectively. The second principle is that legislators must take account of the *esprit* of a society. The third principle is that legislators must approach the variables in a particular order, congruent with the order of *EL*. These principles, as well as the other ones under consideration in this study, point to Montesquieu's core, overarching principle:

legislators should adopt the politics of place, rather than universalistic or relativistic approaches. Yet, as we will see in the next chapter, Montesquieu does make universal claims—for example, that all peoples have an *esprit*. Thus arise the tensions between Montesquieu's universal and particularistic claims. The political education he seeks to give to legislators centers on advancing universal goods in particularistic ways. Legislators must know when to err on the side of universalism, or particularism, to avoid being tyrannical. The next step in a legislator's education is to comprehend the import of the three goods that they should value above all else: security, freedom, and prosperity.

CHAPTER TWO

Security, Liberty, and Prosperity as Particularistic Political Goals

The politics of place affirms that all societies should be secure, free, and prosperous. These are universal goods in the sense that all states should establish and preserve them. The inclusion of prosperity in this list of Montesquieu's overarching goods is important, as scholars have barely treated prosperity in Montesquieu's thought. The three goods remain particularistic, though, because states should achieve and define them differently.[1] That states should *achieve* these goods in their own way is unsurprising, given Montesquieu's insistence that myriad variables shape societies, and that these variables change over time. The claim that states can *define* these terms differently may appear more surprising at first glance. We will see, though, that Montesquieu thinks leeway is necessary when defining security, liberty, and prosperity. Still, the politics of place is not equivalent to relativism. Montesquieu is emphatic that not all political, economic, social, and moral orders are equally good, and that some are categorically bad. Montesquieu judges a state's goodness based on the extent to which it upholds these three goods. He singles out despotic orders as especially terrible. The politics of place is not the politics of any-old-place.

In this chapter, we will examine Montesquieu's particularistic understanding of security, liberty, and prosperity. We will investigate what he means by these key terms. We will identify general institutions and practices he finds conducive to achieving these ends, both generally speaking and within certain states. Montesquieu makes some recommendations that are universal in character but not in practice. For example, he thinks that all states need structural checks on various powers so that no person or group acquires too much power, but he contends that these checks should vary across time and place based on a careful study of a state's circumstances.

Security, liberty, and prosperity are Montesquieu's highest political goods. He views them as necessary for the establishment of a good political order. Only with all three goods can individuals live well and flourish. All three are necessary because being secure and free, but not prosperous, for example, means that a state still has significant work to do before its citizens can achieve their goals. Security, liberty, and prosperity supersede other goods in importance too. Moderation is a possible good one might view as higher for Montesquieu. But Montesquieu advocates moderate government in order to establish these three goods. So too with *esprit*: while the concept is central to Montesquieu's political thought, he seeks to understand the *esprit* to know how to work within its context to establish security, liberty, and prosperity. We begin by considering Montesquieu's understanding of security: what security is, and how states can establish it.

Security

Security has two components for Montesquieu: being secure and feeling secure. Both are necessary for individuals and states to achieve security. The import of these two aspects of security ripples throughout Montesquieu's political thought, and especially his understanding of liberty. Consider first his definition of "political liberty in relation to the citizen." "Political liberty," Montesquieu proclaims, "consists in security, or at least in the opinion one has of his security" (XII.2.431). Political liberty is security. And this security consists in actually being secure, as well as being of the *opinion* that one is secure. In the midst of his earlier discussion of political liberty in relation to the constitution in book XI, Montesquieu explains that this kind of liberty "is this tranquility of *esprit* which stems from the opinion that each has of his security; and for one to have this liberty, it is necessary that the government be such that one citizen cannot fear another" (XI.6.397). This definition of liberty in relation to the citizen fills out further Montesquieu's understanding of security. For a person (or state) to be secure, she must feel secure enough to experience the right kind of tranquility. Good tranquility truly reigns when fear has been expunged from the personal and public spheres. The state and other citizens should not instill fear in citizens, and citizens and other states should not instill fear in the state. Montesquieu's concerns regarding security, as Rahe notes, "seem to be largely psychological."[2] Legislators must have as their first goal the establishment of security: "THE SAFETY OF THE PEOPLE IS THE SUPREME LAW" (XXVI.23.774).

The following scenarios will allow us to understand better the dynamics at play with being and feeling secure. Consider individual security. Imagine someone walking down the street in a low-crime, and thus seemingly safe, area, and then being mugged. This person was of the opinion that he was secure, but in fact he was not. Imagine another person walking, nervously, in a high-crime area on a regular basis. This area commonly is regarded as unsafe. And yet, this person never encounters any problems. She does not feel safe. But in perhaps the most important way, she is safe, because she experiences no actual threats to her security. Still, no matter how much someone insists that she is safe, she remains uneasy.

Consider now security for states. Ukraine likely felt safe from its neighbor, Russia, never expecting to be attacked. But Russia then invaded Ukraine in 2014, seizing first the Crimea, and then parts of eastern Ukraine bordering Russia. Ukraine now neither feels nor is secure. Russia's Baltic and eastern European neighbors might be safe in fact, but many of them cannot feel safe in light of Russia's aggression. States also can come under threat from nonstate entities like the Taliban, Al-Qaeda, the Islamic State, or FARC rebels. To achieve security, states must go to different lengths. Israel, for example, has far higher security concerns than Norway. Syria's security concerns are so great that the prospects for achieving any semblance of security are currently nonexistent. What, according to Montesquieu, are the origins of insecurity among citizens and states?

Conflict seems inherent to society. Before man enters society, he is timid. In the state of nature (*l'état de nature*), "each feels himself inferior; each one feels hardly equal. One therefore would not seek to attack, and peace would be the first natural law" (I.2.235). Montesquieu rejects what he takes to be Hobbes's claim that the desire to dominate, subjugate, and have empire over others already exists in the state of nature.[3] Rather, in Montesquieu's telling, it is only once we enter society that conflict arises: "As soon as men are in society, they lose the feeling of their weakness; the equality, which was between them, ceases, and the state of war commences" (I.3.236). Once we come together, Montesquieu contends, we sense both our individual and societal force; the product of this, as we saw in the previous chapter, is the three problems of politics: conflict between states, conflict between state and person(s), and conflict between persons. Fully aware of their strength, individuals and states seek to assert their strength at the cost of weaker parties. Feelings of weakness, in turn, can promote conflict, as the weak try to preempt aggressive acts by the strong. Insecurity appears as imminent and pervasive for both weaker and stronger parties. This insecurity springs from external and internal threats, from individuals and states. We will focus first on Montesquieu's discussion of how states experience and overcome insecurity, because Montesquieu discusses these matters in books IX and X. We then will turn to his discussion of personal security and liberty, a key theme in books XI and XII. We note, though, that Montesquieu sees the two concepts as inseparable in important ways.

Defensive Force

Book IX serves two key purposes. First, Montesquieu explores how republics, monarchies, and despotisms become (in)secure. Each form of government uses different methods and practices to achieve security. But Montesquieu ultimately expresses reservations about the extent to which any of these three forms of government can secure themselves from external threats.[4] Accordingly, each requires a modification before it can be secure. Second, the theme of security points us toward the priority of liberty.

Republics (either of the small, ancient, democratic variety or the aristocratic sort Montesquieu discusses in part I) face threats regardless of their size. "If a republic is small, it is destroyed by a foreign force; if it is large, it is destroyed by an internal vice. This double inconvenience equally infects democracies and aristocracies, whether they are good or whether they are bad. The ill is in the thing itself; there is no form that can remedy it there" (IX.3.369). Republics thus appear as inherently insecure, either externally or internally, because they are not large enough to protect themselves, or are too big to prevent internal conflict. And yet, Montesquieu also proclaims that the *esprit* of republics is "peace and moderation" (*la paix et la modération*), suggesting that after some sort of modification republics can become secure (IX.2.371). The modification he finds most promising is the formation of another "form of government" (*forme de gouvernement*): the federal republic. The federal republic combines the internal advantages of republican government with the external force of monarchical government (IX.1.369). Because federal republics are larger, they are significantly more secure from external threats. The continued existence of smaller member states within this union allows those states to tend better to local needs.

Republics need to make some modification in order to secure themselves from external threats. The formation of a federal republic represents one such modification. Montesquieu also recommends that republics (and all other states) pursue commerce. As an alternative means of acquiring, Montesquieu argues that commerce promotes peace and prosperity. The alternative to confederating or trading is attacking and conquering, as Rome and Sparta did. Attacking and conquering do promote a kind of material prosperity for the conquerors. But Montesquieu did not view this approach as tenable, because it came at the costs of the conquered. He saw Rome's expansion beyond the borders of Italy as one of the key causes of the fall of the Roman Republic and, with it, Roman freedom.[5] Republics thus need institutions and practices to prevent them from attacking others, while at the same time making them forceful enough to ward off external threats.

Monarchies' larger size should secure them from external threats. But their *esprit* of "war and expansion" (*la guerre et l'agrandissement*) endangers their security (IX.2.371). Their aggressive *esprit* does more than just prevent them from confederating; this *esprit* frequently thrusts them into conflict with other states. Monarchs seek greatness and glory through conquest. War is the obvious outlet to monarchs hoping to achieve these goals. Montesquieu clearly has Louis XIV in mind. The Sun King regularly made war in an attempt to make himself and his country "great." But Montesquieu judges a "universal monarchy"—which Louis sought—as something that would be "fatal to Europe," to the attacker and attacked alike (IX.7.375). Montesquieu proposes an alternative standard, however unlikely it is that monarchs will embrace it. A prince's power should consist not in his ability to conquer but in the difficulty of attacking him (IX.6.374). Rather than attacking and using offensive force (which almost always makes the state less secure), the prince should prioritize defensive force. Ultimately, monarchies can achieve lasting security only if institutions, groups, or individuals check the monarch's ambitions and actions successfully. Otherwise, the monarch will be able to pursue his desires with an eye to attaining glory. Despotisms, by contrast, seem inherently insecure.

Since despotisms should be large (VIII.19.363), they should be able to secure themselves from external threats effectively. But the despot has a distorted vision of security. He understands security only as his personal security; the security of his subjects is relevant only insofar as it somehow can augment his own security. A despot thus instills fear in his subjects to cement his authority. The despotic approach is to "sacrifice a part of the country, ravish the borders, and render them deserted" in order to try to secure the capital (IX.4.372). The despot seeks to distance himself from potential threats. He can, for example, establish provinces at the edges of his territory that serve as buffers against invaders, and which he is prepared to sacrifice to protect his hold on power. And yet, despotic regimes often cannot defend themselves effectively. When Persia is attacked, it takes months for the army to assemble. If the army on the frontier is defeated, Montesquieu continues, "it is surely dispersed, because its [the army's] retreats [*ses retraites*] are not imminent. The victorious army, which finds no resistance, advances by long daily marches, appears before the capital.... The empire dissolves, the capital is taken, and the conquerors dispute with the governors for [control of] the provinces" (IX.6.374). Despotisms obviously cannot confederate because they seek security either by remaining isolated or by attacking and expanding. These options are anathema to the federal republic.

And yet, Montesquieu's discussion here is riddled with a paradox: despite his depiction of despotisms as hopelessly insecure, these regimes are remarkably durable, and reigned over more citizens than any other form of government during Montesquieu's time. He fears, moreover, that despotism is an all-too-likely political outcome. One reason is that men are eternally led to abuse power (XI.4.395). Another reason is that the establishment and maintenance of free government is difficult, whereas despotic government is easy both to establish and maintain. All states, but especially despotisms, need restraints so they refrain from attacking others. Economic mechanisms represent significant, effective constraints.

Commerce, Montesquieu argues, leads to peace. "Two nations which negotiate with one another become dependent on each other: if the one has an interest in buying, the other has an interest in selling; and all unions are founded on mutual needs" (XX.2.585). Commerce provides political actors with an alternative outlet through which to satiate their desires. Rather than taking through force, rulers can acquire through trade. The institutions, practices, and individuals we will consider in chapter 3 represent other ways to check the ambitions of rulers and prevent them from brandishing their offensive force. We turn our attention to book X, on offensive force, for it is the other side of security.

Conquest and Offensive Force

The transition from discussing defensive to offensive force is complicated significantly by Montesquieu's logic: it moves quickly from natural defense all the way to justifiable conquest. Montesquieu is open to conquest under various circumstances and conditions. Mosher has argued convincingly that Montesquieu offers five potential justifications for conquest: security, violations of human liberty, regime change, enlightenment, and commerce. While each of these justifications is highly qualified, Mosher shows that they nonetheless are present in Montesquieu's thought.[6] Montesquieu thus sees a place for a kind of liberal imperialism that improves the situation of the conquered. Here we consider the circumstances in which he thinks such imperialism can be advisable.

Montesquieu begins by arguing that states, just like people, have the right to defend themselves by any means necessary, including killing the aggressor. But rather than focusing only on natural defense, Montesquieu sets forth "proper preservation"—a broader goal—as the preferred aim for states. He explains: "In the case of natural defense, I have the right to kill because my life is mine, as the life of the one who attacks me is his: likewise a State makes war, because its preservation is just like every other preservation" (X.2.377).[7] By "grounding the right to conquest in the natural right of self-preservation, Montesquieu places a set of derivative legal constraints on the manner in which the right to conquest may be exercised."[8] Preservation can entail not just the right to kill, but the right to *attack*: "between societies," Montesquieu writes, "the right of natural defense sometimes brings about the *necessity* to attack, when a people sees that a longer peace would enable another to destroy it, and that attack is in this moment the sole means to prevent this destruction" (X.2.377; emphasis added).[9] It is true that Montesquieu insists that the "right of war therefore derives from necessity and from precise rigor [*juste rigide*]"[10] (X.2.378). But what constitutes a just decision to attack is somewhat ambiguous. His aim is to present offensive force in the form of preemptive strikes as morally acceptable, even necessary, in certain circumstances. If a state is under imminent danger from another state, the threatened state can attack the threatening state. We can imagine cases in which states are under an existential threat from another state, which would justify an attack that would increase their chances of self-preservation. We also can imagine cases in which states wrongly perceive another state as a threat, thus justifying an unjustifiable attack. It is difficult to assess such situations properly. Still, were Montesquieu to stop here, and leave natural defense subject to the rules of "precise rigor," then it would not be unreasonable to interpret his analysis in a more limited manner. Instead, he expands his justification for using force to allow for conquest, thus fundamentally changing the nature of his discussion.[11]

Conquest, even temporary servitude, can be justifiable according to Montesquieu. From the right of war, he claims, flows the right of conquest. The latter is simply the consequence of the former (X.3.378). However, Montesquieu clarifies quickly that although conquest is an "acquisition," the *esprit* of such an acquisition carries with it the "*esprit of preservation and usage*" (X.3.378). Montesquieu's justification of conquest thus forbids states from conquering in order to take advantage of the conquered. Rather, the conqueror incurs many obligations, and must make amends for the evils (*maux*) he has caused. Montesquieu writes: "I define the right of conquest thusly: a necessary right, legitimate and unfortunate, which always leaves an immense debt to pay, in order to become acquitted with respect to human nature" (X.4.381). Summarizing Montesquieu's position, Mosher explains that where there is a right to go to war, "there is necessarily a limited right as well to temporary territorial conquest. Otherwise the conquering nation would never have a duty to undo the mischief it has caused."[12] States are obligated to repay these debts and improve the conquered. However, extreme means may be acceptable to achieve this end, including servitude. Although "servitude is never the *goal* of conquest . . . it may happen that it is a *necessary means* for gaining preservation" (X.3.379; emphasis added). Servitude appears, oddly, to sometimes be a precondition for making a state secure, free, and prosperous. Montesquieu's desire to promote these goods impels him to be open to "liberal imperialism."[13] That is, Montesquieu recognizes that intervention is sometimes necessary to free societies from the scourges of insecurity, unfreedom, and destitution. Montesquieu thus advocates intervention on humanitarian grounds.[14]

Anything—servitude or otherwise—that would harm the conquered remains unacceptable. Conquests must be careful. For example, conquerors should never try to change the *mœurs* of the conquered people, "because a people always knows, loves, and defends its *mœurs* more than its laws" (X.11.385). What's more, servitude must cease "when after a certain space of time, all the parts of the conquering State have bonded with the conquered state, by customs, by marriages, by laws, by associations, and a certain conformity of *esprit*" (X.3.379). It seems, then, that Montesquieu calls for the careful integration of the conquered state into the conquering state.

Montesquieu distinguishes between two forms of conquest: military and economic. Military conquest is precisely what we think of as conquest: entering a state forcefully, and taking control of the political institutions. Montesquieu theoretically accepts this form of conquest in the right circumstances. And yet, he offers a harsh assessment of some historical military conquests, such as when Spain invaded Mexico:

> What good could the Spaniards not have done to the Mexicans? They had a gentle religion to give them; they brought them a raging superstition. They could have set the slaves free, and they made freemen slaves. They could have made clear to them that human sacrifice was an abuse; instead they exterminated them. I would never finish if I wanted to relate all the good things they did not do, and all the evil ones they did. (X.4.381)

This brutal Spanish conquest reveals some of the awful ills that can result from conquest.[15] But his admiration for some of Alexander the Great's actions shows the flip side. Montesquieu admires Alexander's foreign conquests (while seeing him as an "oppressor of Greek liberties"[16]). Montesquieu holds up Alexander as a model imperialist: a conqueror who was sensitive to the differences and autonomy of those he conquered. What's more, Alexander used the empire he built as a mechanism for facilitating trade.[17] As Mosher insightfully explains: "Conquest precedes trade. The philosopher [Montesquieu] has one more reason to admire Alexander: trade routes. Alexander constituted an ancient precedent of what was coming together in eighteenth century Europe: an enlightenment inspired alliance of conquerors and agents of commerce."[18] Montesquieu admires Alexander further because the latter's "sensible" projects include getting the Bactrians to stop feeding their elders to large dogs, which was "a triumph" Alexander "gained over superstition" (X.5.382). Montesquieu thus sees conquest as a means to promote commerce and rid people of practices harmful to their society. Traditional conquest, in the right circumstances, can be beneficial. Economic conquest, though, seems to be Montesquieu's more likely goal.

In the midst of his discussion of the English *esprit*, Montesquieu raises the prospect of an "empire of the sea," suggesting it as a superior alternative to a land empire (XIX.27.579).[19] Maritime empires, Montesquieu explains, would establish colonies not to dominate them, but to spread commerce (XIX.27.578). Commercial empire is quite disruptive to the conquered state. But Montesquieu lauds this disruption not only in the economic sphere, but also in the political sphere. He explains that the conquering state "would give to the people of its colonies the form of its own government [*la forme de son gouvernement proper*]: and this government bringing prosperity with it, one would see great peoples become formed in the very forests it [the colonizing nation] would send out to become inhabited" (XIX.27.578). The conquered would have "a very good civil government" (*un très bon gouvernement civil*). Montesquieu anticipates that the "economy, as art of acquisition," will replace "war, the *esprit* of commerce" taking the place of "the *esprit* of conquest."[20]

And yet, Montesquieu is keenly aware that even commercial conquest has forceful elements. He acknowledges that the English "subjugated" the Irish ("a neighboring nation"). The conquered often are quite unwilling to receive the apparent wisdom of the conquerors. Montesquieu admits that English and Dutch commercial imperialism had a darker side. Some nations are better off remaining isolated than being under the boot of a conqueror. Despite the concerns he acknowledged, Montesquieu viewed English commercial conquest, and the foreign policy that promoted it, as "viable in a way that the Roman policy consistently followed by the continental powers was not."[21] More than just being viable, Montesquieu sees his preferred kind of conquest as promoting what we now call globalization, and the increased prosperity it brings.[22] But it must happen in the right circumstances and under the guidance of the right form of government.

Any form of government potentially could engage in conquest. Federal republics are the least likely to do so. Montesquieu states that it is "against the nature of the thing" that federal republics composed entirely of republics attack each other (X.6.382).[23] While members should not conquer each other, he never says they cannot conquer other states. Indeed, in part IV Montesquieu discusses Dutch conquest. Democracies have significantly more latitude. They can conquer (only) places that can "enter in the sphere of democracy" (X.6.382). Regime change, then, can be a goal of conquest. In such cases, "it is necessary that the conquered people can enjoy the privileges of sovereignty, as the Romans established it at the beginning" (X.6.382). Montesquieu's choice of Rome as an example is telling, though, given the criticism he levels at Rome's conquest, especially in the *Considérations*.

The guidelines Montesquieu establishes for monarchical conquest show his aversion to it. For a monarchy to conquer successfully, the monarch first must solidify his strong influence in the conquered state. Second, he must maintain aggressive relations with neighboring states. Third, he must not conquer beyond "the natural limits" of monarchy. Fourth, he must not treat the conquered too harshly. Finally, "it is necessary, in this sort of conquest, to leave things as one has found them: the same tribunals, the same laws, the same customs, the same privileges; nothing can be changed except the army and the name of the sovereign" (X.9.384). Even if the monarch follows these guidelines, the result remains undesirable: there is "frightful luxury in the capital, misery in the provinces the more distant they are [from the capital], abundance at the extremities" (X.9.385). We conclude then that this kind of conquest does not meet Montesquieu's guidelines of "precise rigor." It leaves the conquered states neither secure nor free, to say nothing of being prosperous. Although Montesquieu rejects this kind of conquest, its appeal is obvious: luxury, glory, and power are strong motivating factors. But these gains, Montesquieu thinks, will be temporary at best. And they often lead to despotic situations, because these desires are hard to moderate, control, or turn off. An "immense conquest," Montesquieu argues, "supposes despotism." For such endeavors, a prince needs a strong army and a "particularly trustworthy body" surrounding him that is "always ready to assail the part of the empire which could waver. This militia should contain the others, and make tremble all those to whom one has been obliged to leave some authority in the empire" (X.16.392). As the conqueror realizes that his hold on power is tenuous, he attempts to assert as much control as possible over the newly acquired territory. Montesquieu firmly rejects this approach in favor of returning the throne to the "legitimate prince" who will become a "necessary ally" and whose forces will complement those of the conqueror (X.17.393). This situation may be less bad, but it is unlikely, given the prince's tendencies; and undesirable, given the eventual harms that will follow. Montesquieu thus expresses grave apprehensions about conquering monarchies and rejects the acceptability of despotic conquest.

Montesquieu's discussion of offensive force causes us to consider when such force actually makes states more secure. Recall that Montesquieu speaks of a "right" (*droit*) of conquest, "right of natural defense," "right to kill," and "right of war." The usage of *droit* suggests that conquest can be morally justified. A primary justification is that conquest improves the conquered. But Montesquieu's discussion is problematic, for reasons he likely would admit. Perceived threats can be misconstrued, intentionally or not. Attacking clearly is not without risks: the attacker can lose, or can create a situation far worse for some or all involved. Even if the attacker wins, the conquered rarely look upon the conqueror favorably. The rule of the new regime in the conquered state will be tenuous, either because the rulers or the people will not support the conqueror. For reasons such as this, we know that Montesquieu would urge extreme caution when considering whether or not to attack another state.

Conquest has deleterious effects on a society's *esprit*. The *esprit* of monarchy, we saw, is that of war and aggression. This *esprit* will extend throughout the state, since the state relies on aggressive citizens to engage in attacks. The state must work to maintain the *esprit* to help maintain the culture and military readiness to attack successfully. Such an *esprit* will extend to other states that engage in conquest. The conquered obviously stands to have its *esprit* impacted. Recall Montesquieu's brutal example of the Spanish conquest of Mexico.

The tense nature of Montesquieu's discussion points out the particularistic nature of the pursuit of security from external threats. States differ on many counts. Smaller states will have a harder time than larger states defending themselves. Institutions are important, because they can moderate political actors. The federal republic is one such moderating institution. What's more, each state faces different neighbors and thus a different security situation. Two otherwise similar states might face quite different threats from neighbors or other enemies. The pursuit and achievement of external security thus requires a state to take careful account of the particularities of its own security situation while also taking Montesquieu's general observations on defensive and offensive force into account. There are many paths to attaining security from external threats, including the use of offensive force.

The discussion of security from external threats, in books IX and X, transitions into a discussion of security from internal threats, and from security of states to security of individuals. Montesquieu's identification of political liberty in relation to the citizen with security demonstrates the strong link between security and liberty. Given that he discusses liberty as security in the context of his three books on liberty, we set aside a consideration of personal security for the moment, returning to it after examining Montesquieu's discussion of liberty in book XI.

Liberty: Political, Personal, and Economic

Freedom, according to Montesquieu, consists in being permitted to do what one wants to do, and not being constrained "to do what one should not want to do." Liberty is neither license nor independence. Rather, in his celebrated definition, Montesquieu explains that "liberty is the right to do everything that the laws permit; and if a citizen could do what they forbid, he would no longer have liberty, because others would have the same power" (XI.3.395). Liberty thus exists "under the law."[24] Montesquieu's conception of liberty falls under the category of "negative liberty."[25] The particularistic nature of his definition is immediately apparent: the laws will and should permit different things across time and place. The range of permissible actions will vary depending on the makeup of a specific society, something that changes over time based on how the variables of *esprit* impact the society. Montesquieu acknowledges as much in his discussion of the "significations" liberty has taken on in various places. No other word has "struck the *esprits* in so many ways as liberty"—but it has struck them differently (XI.2.394). For some, liberty is deposing a tyrannical ruler. For others, liberty is the right to be armed. The Muscovites understood liberty as being able to have a long beard, something Peter the Great tried to forbid. Some "attach" the name of liberty to a form of government, but Montesquieu rejects doing so. Indeed, "Montesquieu takes special care to distinguish" all the "different types of liberty . . . from democratic self-rule."[26] "Finally," Montesquieu writes, "each has called liberty that which conforms to his customs or to his inclinations" (XI.2.394). The only understanding of liberty Montesquieu rejects is the notion that democracies are free by their nature. Otherwise, Montesquieu does not say the other understandings or interpretations of liberty are wrong. Instead, any of them can be a part of what liberty is in a particular society, so long as they conform to certain general standards.

A free society is founded on the rule of law, security of the individual, and institutions, values, and practices that moderate political outcomes. All free societies must have these elements. In that sense, the rule of law, for example, is a universal good. The content of the rules and laws, though, is particularistic (within the general boundaries Montesquieu sets). We note Montesquieu's critically important remark in XI, 4, where he states that political liberty "is found only in moderate governments." In order to protect liberty, power must stop power via effective institutions. Let us now examine the three kinds of liberty in part II: political, personal, and economic.

What Montesquieu calls political liberty in relation to the constitution is the product of institutions that provide checks on political actors and their power. Montesquieu's lengthy discussion of political liberty in the context of the English constitution has been enormously influential. As such, some scholars have put forth England as Montesquieu's candidate for the regime best equipped to protect political liberty.[27] We will see, in chapter 3, this interpretation of Montesquieu is incompatible with our reading of the Baron as a proponent of the politics of place. Here we explore briefly numerous checks on power Montesquieu identifies as potentially effective, while saving the broader discussion of these matters for later.

Political liberty can exist in numerous forms of government, and societies can achieve political liberty effectively in different ways. The English government checks power by distributing governmental powers into three branches: executive, legislative, and judicial. Each group has different functions that are separated so that no one branch can usurp liberty. Federal republics check power through member states helping to ensure that others do not take actions that would compromise the security, liberty, and prosperity of other members or of the union as a whole. In this "society of societies" it is difficult for any single member state to become too powerful. Religious authorities and institutions can check political actors by making rulers accountable to a higher authority, which in turn moderates the rulers. Rulers obey this "higher" authority more readily. Religious authorities also can occupy a prominent place in the regime. Along similar lines, social groups can serve as checks. "Intermediate, subordinate, and dependent powers," Montesquieu explains, "constitute the nature of monarchical government" (II.4.247). The nobility is the "most natural" intermediate power because the nobles are among the wealthiest, most influential, and most powerful people in a state. Their role is to ensure that the monarch, or those in power, follow the laws and do not abuse their power. It is in the nobles' interest to do so, lest they lose some or all of their own power. The nobles can govern directly, as in the French *parlements*, or indirectly by otherwise exerting influence over political actors. The aristocracy can serve a similar function to the nobility, though it can have different values and interests from the nobility. We will see later that the aristocracy is motivated by a kind of virtue, whereas the nobility is motivated by honor. Finally, the laws can check power so long as they are "fixed and established." This can come in the form of a written constitution, or through fixed laws upheld consistently, as in the rule of law. Effective structures that check power are necessary, though not sufficient, conditions for having liberty, because liberty goes beyond political institutions. Individuals must be and feel safe.

Personal liberty,[28] Montesquieu asserts, "is never more attacked than in public or private accusations. It is thus on the goodness of criminal laws that the liberty of the citizen principally depends" (XII.2.431).[29] The goodness of the laws depends on the rule of law, caution (in lawmaking and punishment), and moderate punishments. Moderation should thoroughly permeate the criminal code.[30] Political actors must determine which actions deserve to be punished—and then punish them fairly and not too harshly; they also must guarantee clear, transparent, fair rules. As Vickie Sullivan explains, Montesquieu's concern is for "the security of individuals, for the happiness of citizens, and for the gentlest possible approach to punishments."[31]

Montesquieu lays out his theory of how to protect personal liberty through criminal punishments in books XII and VI, with the former focusing on determining which actions to punish, and the latter advising political actors to punish moderately. Shklar has called Montesquieu's approach a "liberalism of fear" on the grounds that he asserts that the "liberty of the individual . . . depends radically on the extent of the criminal law and the kinds of punishment that it inflicts." This liberalism is "an effort to avoid oppression rather than directly to promote rights to political action or self-development."[32]

Montesquieu's recommendations regarding the right criminal code are universalistic at their core. Normatively speaking, the politics of place can never recommend a harsh criminal code. He does recognize the need for particular criminal codes that fit more closely with different societies, and he acknowledges that key parts of the *esprit*, like the form of government and religion(s) in a state, will determine some of the specifics of the criminal code. Still, Montesquieu insists that the state always must protect the "formalities of justice" because "the forms and rules of justice protect the dignity and liberty of ordinary citizens, for justice is administered according to fixed, impersonal, and certain standards."[33]

The rule of law is a necessary condition for having a good criminal code: "the knowledge that one has acquired in some countries, and that one will acquire in others, about the surest rules that one can pull from criminal judgments, interests the human species *more than any other thing in the world*. It is *only* by practicing this knowledge that liberty can be founded" (XII.2.432; emphases added). Montesquieu believes strongly that clear guidelines and fair processes that apply to all are essential to establishing and preserving liberty. He writes that a man who underwent a fair legal process and will be executed the next day is freer than a pasha in Turkey (XII.2.432). Political actors must make and apply rules clearly and fairly; and people must be absolutely sure of the nature of these laws and the consequences for breaking them.

A good legal code presumes that citizens are innocent and acknowledges the necessity of proving them guilty. When "the innocence of citizens is not assured, liberty is no more" (XII.2.432). The liberty of the citizen, Spector shows, "is founded on the justice of criminal procedures, and on the presumption of innocence."[34]

Robust standards are necessary for proving guilt. For example, laws that allow someone to be sentenced to death based on the testimony of a single person are dangerous. The testimony of the accuser and the accused cancel each other out, so another witness is necessary to protect the liberty of the accused (XII.3.432). At times Montesquieu even seems to advocate giving the accused the benefit of the doubt.

Montesquieu urges great caution when deciding what actions to make criminal and how to punish them. He spends much more time discussing what actions criminal laws should not punish, than what they should, in an effort to prevent the government overreach he seems to expect. Montesquieu is emphatic that "the laws are charged to punish only external actions" and not thoughts (XII.12.441). Laws cannot punish someone's character, beliefs, or personal practices unless they represent a clear and present danger to society. Criminalizing actions "can shock liberty extremely, and can be the source of infinite tyrannies" (XII.5.435); despotism can be the end result.[35] Montesquieu identifies magic and heresy as things that should not be crimes. But he really uses them as stand-ins for his larger point that actions, and nothing else, can be criminal. "The best conduct in the world, the purest morals, the practice of all the duties, are not guarantees against the suspicions of crimes" (XII.V.435–36). Besides, it is rather difficult to really "know" what someone believes, so punishing for thoughts or beliefs is all the more problematic. To the contrary, Montesquieu insists on protections for speech generally, and specifically for questioning the government verbally or in writing (XII.12–13.442–44);[36] hence his insistence that things like *lèse-majesté* not be made criminal.

A good criminal code has a few more important characteristics. It does not—and cannot—be developed quickly, because "criminal laws have not been perfected all of a sudden" (XII.2.431). Rather, Montesquieu recognizes the need for a good legal order to develop gradually over time in line with the particularities of a specific people. Penalties should be proportionate to the crime. "It is a triumph of liberty," Montesquieu proclaims, "when the criminal laws draw each penalty from the nature of the particular crime" (XII.4.433). This is a prescription to punish each general kind of crime appropriately, and each individual criminal action based on its circumstances and consequences. Finally, Montesquieu insists that criminalizing too many actions is counterproductive, in part because when many actions are punishable, the horror of real crimes diminishes (XII.8.440). In fact, Montesquieu identifies relatively few actions deserving of punishment.

Only actions that "shock" religion, *mœurs*, tranquility, and the security of the citizen should be candidates for being criminalized (XII.4.433). In each case, Montesquieu defines the nature of a crime that would "shock" one of the four rather narrowly. He means to narrow the range of actions that the state can deem criminal. Consider first crimes against religion. Only actions that "directly attack" religion constitute crimes against religion (XII.4.433). The only crime in this class he identifies is sacrilege, but he then sets a high bar for an action to qualify as sacrilege. The action must "consist in the deprivation of all the advantages that religion gives: expulsion from the temples; deprivation from the society of the faithful, for a time or forever; shunning their presence, the execrations, detestations, conjurations" (XII.4.433). Few actions would touch on all of these aspects of religion. We thus conclude that he thinks that relatively few crimes (if any) against religion should exist. In fact, Montesquieu's analysis seems to go further still. He is describing punishments for actions, while insisting that we cannot have state punishments, so his prescriptions are even freer than they first seem. One reason for his opposition to criminalizing actions against religion is his fear of the repercussions the "criminals" will face. He writes: "A Jew, accused of blaspheming against the Holy Virgin, was condemned to be flayed. Masked knights, blade in hand, raising the guillotine, for avenging the honor of the Holy Virgin . . . I do not want to anticipate the reflections of the reader" (XII.4.434). His discussion of religious crimes leaves room for the selective religious intolerance he advocates in part V. He does not want to deprive people of their liberty, but he is open to other mechanisms that fit the politics of a place. There can be good reason to make things illegal or dissuade certain behavior or beliefs in some situations.

Crimes against *mœurs* are the second class of crimes. They entail "the violation of public or individual incontinence; that is to say, of the police on the manner in which one must enjoy the pleasures attached to the use of the senses and to corporal union" (XII.4.434). Montesquieu's definition again leaves little room for an action qualifying as a crime against *mœurs*, since here he identifies *mœurs* with using one's senses and corporal union. The toughness of his list of penalties for these crimes, including expulsion from society, masks the fact that such penalties will never come into use.

Crimes against security occur when a citizen attempts to deprive or actually deprives another citizen of her security. These crimes seem to be the only sort of crime with which Montesquieu is really concerned. He proceeds to qualify crimes against tranquility as crimes against security, thus narrowing the sorts of crimes from four to three; the only crime against tranquility entails a "simple injury against the police" (XII.4.435). When someone threatens or harms the life, liberty, security, or property of another citizen, then Montesquieu thinks that the state ought to punish this action. When someone kills or tries to kill another, then Montesquieu is open to making the criminal pay with his life. When the criminal harms the goods of someone, Montesquieu recommends punishing the criminal by taking some of his goods, and not necessarily his life; but he is open to corporal punishment when the perpetrator has no goods.

The protection of personal liberty cannot be absolute. There are times when the state must suspend liberty to protect liberty. "There are, in the States where one has made more of a case for liberty, laws that violate it against one, to guard it for everyone. . . . I admit though that the usage of the freest peoples that have ever been on the earth makes me believe that there are cases where it is necessary to place, for a moment, a veil over liberty, as one hides the statues of the gods" (XII.19.448–49). Although this suggestion comes in a chapter on liberty in a republic, it seems to apply readily to all free states. The temporary abrogation of liberty, Montesquieu insists, is sometimes necessary to maintain a free society.

There is a real tension for Montesquieu between security and liberty. This tension goes well beyond his suggestion here that it might be necessary to temporarily put a "veil over liberty" to protect both liberty and security. This tension surrounds the notion that security and liberty are tantamount to a "tranquility of *esprit* that stems from the opinion that each has of his security." Montesquieu recognizes that tranquility has a potentially damaging side too. China has as its "goal" (*objet*), we see in XI, 5, "public tranquility." But this Chinese tranquility much more closely approximates the fear that prevents people from acting in certain ways.[37] While Montesquieu wants only a kind of tranquility that makes one secure, he recognizes the risk that tranquility can undermine liberty. Be that as it may, we turn now to see why Montesquieu recommends moderate punishments in book VI.

Montesquieu's politics of place affirms that moderate punishments promote security, liberty, and prosperity; harsh punishments impede the achievement of these goods. Montesquieu contemplates punishments from the practical perspective of how to deter crime, not from some metaphysical or ethical perspective about what justice requires. He is interested in deterring crime in the short term (criminals not breaking laws) and long term (criminals paying their debt and changing their behavior). Rehabilitation is a secondary aim of criminal laws. Montesquieu does not support retribution as a reasonable aim of the justice system in and of itself, because he does not think it decreases crime. Moreover, he rejects harsh punishments as wrong and ineffective, likely based in part on his personal experiences.[38] One iteration of Montesquieu's general philosophy of punishment is as follows: in moderate states "a good legislator will endeavor less to punish crimes than to prevent them; he will apply himself more to giving *mœurs* than to inflicting pain" (VI.9.318).

States should value individuals highly. In moderate states, "the head of the lowest citizen is considerable," and so there should be many formalities to protect the "honor, fortune, life, and liberty of citizens" (VI.2.310–11). It is acceptable to remove his "honor and goods only after a long examination." Montesquieu's reasoning on this point is both pragmatic (crafting criminal laws in this way has the best effects) and moral (individuals deserve such treatment). When the state is judging a crime, it is essential that there be either a tribunal or jury to evaluate the claims of both sides, because they serve as an objective voice that will apply the laws more fairly and seek the proper outcomes. In despotisms, by contrast, the prince judges. He generally metes out harsh punishments. They destroy the constitution and the formalities of judgments while invading all spirits with fear; security, trust, honor, and love would vanish (VI.5.314). Instead, Montesquieu insists that the state must mete punishments out carefully, and punish gently.

Moderate, gentle punishments best protect liberty and prevent crime. Montesquieu insists that in Europe "penalties have decreased or increased as one has approached or departed from liberty" (VI.9.318). More than just arguing that harsh penalties run counter to liberty, Montesquieu argues extensively that gentle penalties are more effective. "In moderate states," he explains, "love of homeland, honor, and fear of blame, are restraining motives, that can stop many crimes. The greatest penalty for a bad action will be to be convicted of it. Civil laws thus will correct them more easily there, and will not need as much force" (VI.9.318). Indeed, Montesquieu thinks that the shame people suffer for being convicted of a crime will serve as a weighty penalty, and that people will be struck by it, or other gentle penalties, as the *esprit* of a citizen is struck elsewhere by heavy punishments. It is unpunished crimes, rather than moderate penalties, that cause people to commit further criminal acts (VI.12.320–21). A wise legislator has multiple moderate means at his disposal to punish criminals or prevent citizens from engaging in criminal behavior. He can apply the rules of honor, use shame as punishment, or appeal to maxims of philosophy, morality, and religion. If a legislator is working with a people used to harsh punishments, then she will have to institute these practices more gradually for them to be effective. Montesquieu reiterates his point by recommending to the good legislator that he take a "middle way" and not always order "pecuniary" or "corporal penalties" (VI.18.330).

Harsh penalties, by contrast, are ineffective and counterproductive. They are a "source of political troubles and social disorders."[39] The following example is illustrative: "In Muscovy, where the penalty for thieves and for murderers is the same, one always murders. The dead, they say there, recount nothing" (VI.16.328). Severity in punishments might suit despotic government insofar as its principle is terror (VI.9.318), but harsh penalties can corrupt despotism itself and undermine the regime (VI.13.322). The instinct of violent governments may be to reach for weighty punishments; but as citizens become used to these techniques, the techniques lose their power, and the spring of government wears down. "The imagination gets used to this heavy penalty, as it got used to the lesser one; and, as it diminishes the fear of the lesser, one soon is forced to establish the heavier one in each case" (VI.12.320–21). Punishments must become harsher to have the desired, fear-filled effect.

While Montesquieu's recommendation of moderate penalties is universal, he recognizes the need to punish differently based on the place and subject of punishment. Within different regions, it is acceptable to have different laws or permit different customs (VI.1.308).[40] In republics, the manner of judging is "fixed" and judges follow the "letter of the law." In monarchies, by contrast, when the law is not precise, then the judge seeks to follow the *esprit des lois* (VI.3.311). Each approach has its advantages and disadvantages. In governments where there are distinctions between persons, as in monarchies, some groups should get certain privileges, such as being allowed to plead before one tribunal rather than another (VI.1.308).

What's more, different groups will receive different punishments for their crimes. Montesquieu turns to "old French laws" and sees that in "cases concerning pecuniary penalties, the non-nobles are punished less than the nobles. It is totally the contrary for crimes; the noble loses honor and a voice at court, while the villain, who does not have honor, is punished corporally" (VI.10.319). Montesquieu admits that this produces a thousand exceptions, which can be contrary to the spirit of moderate government. He attaches clear importance to consistent decisions from judges. But exceptions and variation in punishments can be necessary on account of the differences in rank, origin, and condition among the citizens. The *esprit des lois* can call for different penalties depending on the situation, whereas the letter of the law that republics follow requires stricter and clearer interpretations of the laws, leaving little or no leeway for judges. We turn now to Montesquieu's third, less celebrated form of liberty: economic.

The central issue Montesquieu addresses regarding economic security in book XIII is taxes. "Taxes" and "public revenues" are of great import to Montesquieu's political thought. For now we set aside the question of commerce. Here we focus on how taxes relate to economic liberty.

Taxes can protect, or destroy, our security:[41] "the revenues of the state are a portion that each citizen gives of his property to have the security or comfortable enjoyment of the rest" (XIII.1.458). Taxes touch not only on the security of our property, but on the extent to which we are and feel secure, because our property encompasses and defines a significant part of our existence. If we do not feel that our basic possessions like our house and income are secure, then it is difficult to imagine how we can say that someone feels or is secure. These things form the basis for building a life and thus are in many ways a precursor to being free. Secure property is a precondition for prosperity. Taxes are necessary for achieving these goods. The state should generate revenues to tend to the "necessities of the State, and to the necessities of the citizens" (XIII.1.458). One problem, though, is that political actors often tend to the imagined needs of the state rather than the real needs of the people. "The imagined needs," Montesquieu clarifies, "are what the passions and the weaknesses of those who govern demand, the charm of an extraordinary project, the sick desire of vain glory, and a certain weakness of *esprit* against fantasies" (XIII.1.458–59). There thus is a clear tension between the necessities of the people and states and the wants and desires, imagined and real, of political actors. This tension, along with the tendency for these wants and desires to manifest themselves, leads Montesquieu to have reservations about high taxes.

The state should tax based on limited and clear guidelines. Political actors should not tax people based on what they "can give" (*peut donner*) but, rather, on what they "should give" (*doit donner*). The implication is that what citizens should give is lower than what the state decides they can give.

If, however, the state taxes citizens based on what they can give, it must do so based on what they "can always give" (XIII.1.459). Montesquieu reiterates his preference for a lower common taxing denominator by suggesting that when some citizens pay too much the result is ruinous, whereas when some citizens do not pay enough the harm is not large (XIII.2.462). Indeed, his primary concerns are to protect individuals' property and to prevent political actors from being able to pursue their imagined needs or real wants and desires. One of the goals, then, is to promote fiscal moderation.[42] Montesquieu also provides practical reasons for having lower taxes. "The effect of riches in a country," he explains, "is to place ambition in all the hearts. The effect of poverty is to cause despair to be born there. The former is excited by work; the other consoles through laziness." Nature renders men industrious "because it attaches the greatest rewards to the greatest work. But," Montesquieu cautions, "if an arbitrary power removes the rewards of nature, one takes on the distaste for work, and inaction seems to be the only good" (XIII.2.459–60). Although Montesquieu does not explicitly say that taxes cause such ills, the fact that such comments come in a discussion of taxes and economic freedom is highly suggestive.

Montesquieu's principles here seem to go against what he calls a "general rule": "One can levy taxes more strongly, in proportion to the liberty of the subjects; and one is forced to moderate them so far as servitude increases. . . . One finds it in all countries, in England, in Holland, and in all the States of decreasing liberty down to Turkey" (XIII.12.466). At first glance, Montesquieu seems to suggest that taxes must be proportional to liberty. He does recognize that taxes can be of general benefit dependent on the end for which they are used. A free republic possibly can have higher taxes without necessarily threatening liberty, because liberty is, in some sense, the good for which they are trading their taxes, so long as they freely accept the taxes rather than having them imposed on them. He proceeds to explain that in republics citizens are willing to pay taxes because the citizen thinks he chooses to pay them, and because they see taxes as necessary for supporting the government. In monarchies, political actors can raise taxes because "the moderation of government there can procure riches." But his comment about taxes in despotism points us toward his reservations about high taxes. One cannot raise taxes in despotisms "because one cannot increase extreme servitude" (XIII.13.467). Montesquieu provides reasons elsewhere in book XIII to conclude that he does indeed see high taxes as promoting servitude.

Taxes, Montesquieu explains, can lead to servitude: "Liberty has produced an excess of taxes; but the effect of these taxes in their turn is to produce servitude, and the effect of servitude, to produce the reduction of taxes" (XIII.15.468–69). While free states can maintain high levels of freedom and taxation for some period of time, Montesquieu suggests that this probably is unsustainable. More than that, he claims that the one who has money "is always the master of the other," and the most powerful master of all is the state, particularly the political actors who pursue unnecessary or harmful projects (XIII.19.472). What's more, high taxes are not even strictly necessary to establish and maintain freedom. He cites Switzerland, Greece, and Rome as examples of free states without high taxes. So when Montesquieu says that states "can" levy higher taxes when there is more freedom, he certainly does not mean that they should, and he provides reasons to think that they should not. High taxes afford political actors the means to abuse their power. In his time, political actors often used taxes to amass ever-larger armies. The result was predictable: an arms race resulted among rival states, from which no one was relatively stronger but everyone was more indebted (XIII.17.470). Higher taxes and war were the inevitable consequences of such endeavors. The supposed need for redistribution among different geographical regions is another oft-used motive for instituting higher taxes. One takes from one region to pay for another that does not pay enough; but "one does not restore" the latter, while one destroys the former. "The people grow desperate between the necessity of paying, out of fear of exaction, and the danger of paying, out of fear of surcharges" (XIII.18.471). This provides a further disincentive for regions and people to strive to prosper.

Economic liberty thus arises in Montesquieu's politics of place as a key component of a good political order. As Spector explains, Montesquieu affirms that "the economy cannot develop in a context of uncertainty and insecurity of property, nor where too many hindrances on the mobility of men or capital exist."[43] People who have financial security and freedom can engage more confidently in the activities that will improve the state. What's more, economic liberty promotes the *esprit* of commerce that, as we will see later, has the potential to transform society positively in myriad ways. Just as Montesquieu emphasizes the centrality of security and liberty, he abhors the realities of antifreedom that manifest themselves in the different kinds of slavery he discusses in books XV, XVI, and XVII.

Three Forms of Slavery as Antifreedom

More than simply affirming the value of security and liberty, the politics of place also denounces all forms of slavery.[44] As Melvin Richter notes, Montesquieu "spoke out against slavery as no previous political philosopher had done."[45] In books XV, XVI, and XVII, Montesquieu sets out to refute various justifications for civil, domestic, and political slavery. He insists that all of these forms of slavery are illegitimate.[46] Only the temporary servitude he discusses in book X—that has as its goal the establishment of security, freedom, and prosperity in a particular place—possibly can be justifiable. Essentially all slavery, though, is permanent and bad for everyone involved, not only because it represents a gross violation of human freedom but also because it does not even achieve its desired ends. Let us consider his arguments against the forms of slavery, all of which he sees as forms of extreme antifreedom.

Montesquieu quickly rejects slavery as bad for everyone involved.[47] It is bad "by its nature." It is useful neither to the master nor to the slave. The slave "can do nothing with his virtue." The master develops many bad habits through his treatment of his slaves, including losing any semblance of moral virtue and becoming "proud, tough, angry, voluptuous, cruel" (XV.1.490). Indeed, slavery becomes only about craving luxury and voluptuousness while rejecting any concerns about the ills slavery causes for society (XV.9.497). Slavery is opposed to civil right and natural right, one reason being that all men are born equal; thus, slavery is never justifiable (XV.2.492; XV.7.496). Slavery also limits what a society can accomplish. While a small number of rich people benefit through the economic gains of slavery, the rest of society loses (XV.9.497). Even a small number of slaves harm society because the existence of slavery undermines liberty throughout society (XV.13.500). Montesquieu's critique of slavery is noteworthy in its context given that slavery was widely accepted in French and British colonies in his time. His home city, Bordeaux, was a major slave-trading port. Along with his general case against slavery, he refutes the grounding for different "origins" of the "right" of slavery.

Montesquieu makes quick work of the many justifications for slavery. We consider some of his more important points. Roman jurists have offered various justifications for slavery. The Romans deemed slavery permissible since it is better than being killed, which is permissible during wartime. Montesquieu insists that the right to kill is a product of strict necessity, which ends with the war, or when someone becomes a prisoner (XV.2.491). Montesquieu rejects the idea that one can sell himself into slavery because "the liberty of each citizen is a part of public liberty" (XV.2.491). Dislike for another people or even simple difference can never be a justification for slavery. Montesquieu abhors, for example, that the Spanish scorned some of those they conquered because they did not like what they found in their baskets (XV.3.493). Religion can foment slavery too. "I would just as much like to say that religion gives to those who profess it a right to reduce to servitude those who do not profess it, for working more easily for its propagation" (XV.4.493). Thinking this way brings nothing but destruction and crimes (XV.4.493). Montesquieu saves his most scathing criticisms for prejudice as a justification of slavery, in particular racial prejudice. People justify the slavery of "negroes" (*les nègres*) based on absurdities like the price of sugar, the color of their skin, and the shape of their noses. But slavery based on prejudice—racial or other—is nothing more than a gross moral and Christian injustice (XV.5.494). Some also justify slavery based on nature, broadly speaking. He targets Aristotle here, who put forth that some men are slaves based on their nature. Montesquieu responds: "But, as all men are born equal, it is necessary [*il faut*] to say that slavery is against nature" (XV.7.496). So Montesquieu appeals to nature to reject slavery. After refuting many common justifications for slavery in book XV, he takes aim at the domestic enslavement of women in book XVI.

If we retrospectively and broadly apply the modern term "feminist" to cover arguments that critically address the oppression of women on the basis of sex, we can read Montesquieu as making robust feminist arguments in book XVI. Montesquieu begins by identifying the condition of women in many countries as "domestic servitude" (XVI.1.508). This strong wording about women's unequal treatment can be seen as a clear rejection of the oppression of women, especially given Montesquieu's strong support for political, personal, and economic liberty, along with his deep aversion to all kinds of slavery. Sylvana Tomaselli describes Montesquieu's discussion of domestic servitude as a "tyrant-slave dialectic"—in which men are the unnatural tyrants and women are the unnatural slaves—that "neutralises" any conflict between the sexes through a careful balance of their distinctive social roles.[48] While book XVI is purportedly about "How the laws of domestic slavery are related to the nature of the climate," the contents of its chapters reveal that there is nothing natural about domestic servitude—it is natural neither with respect to the physical environment nor with respect to women's capabilities.

Women's enslaved condition appeared natural to some in the eighteenth century, rooted for example in the physical environment. Montesquieu observes that in hot climates women are married too early, at eight, nine, or ten years of age: "They are old at twenty: thus reason in women is never found with beauty there" (XVI.2.509). But Montesquieu finds this practice troubling. He thinks women should marry later: their "charms are better preserved," "they have children at a more advanced age," and they have "more reason and knowledge" (XVI.2.509). When women have a substantial say in household affairs, the benefits extend beyond their families and throughout society. Still, men prefer to take on multiple wives and to place women in a position of permanent servitude. Polygamy thus becomes the epitome of domestic servitude.

In countries with polygamy, women are unfree. They are totally dependent on men in many ways, particularly on their husband's "riches" (XVI.3.510). Although some writers had justified polygamy on the grounds that more women are born in certain places, Montesquieu finds no such significant disproportion. Besides, if numbers were the issue, then women should be allowed to have multiple husbands when the disproportion is reversed (XVI.4.511). Montesquieu demonstrates the unfairness of the unequal treatment of women in polygamy by turning the demographic argument on its head. He continues in this vein by arguing that there might be situations in which a woman having multiple husbands would be beneficial. For example, it might be easier for a state to maintain a military spirit if women practiced polyandry. This would prevent a man from getting too attached to his wife, allowing men to focus instead on the important affairs of the state (XVI.5.512).

Polygamy has roundly harmful consequences, according to Montesquieu. It aids or even inspires despotism (XVI.9.514–15). The servitude of women conforms to despotism because the latter requires tranquility. Confining women to the harem helps to accomplish such "tranquility."[49] Yet the segregation of women is not limited to despotic regimes: "It is a consequence of polygamy, that, in voluptuous and rich nations, one has many wives. Their separation from men, and their enclosure, follows naturally from this large number" (XVI.8.514). Muhammad may have called for the equal treatment of wives, but Montesquieu finds good, fair, and equal treatment of the sexes in polygamous relationships to be impossible (XVI.7.513). He thus judges polygamy as bad for everyone involved: "With regards to polygamy in general, independent of the circumstances that can make it somewhat tolerable, it is not useful to mankind, nor to the two sexes, either to the one who abuses, or the one who is abused. Nor is it useful to children" (XVI.6.512).

Montesquieu points to ways in which women should be freer than they were in his native France at the time. He suggests that wives should be able not only to divorce but also repudiate their husbands. A right to divorce is insufficient for women's freedom, because it requires a mutual consent that is unlikely in the context of male domination. As such, women should have the same power as men had to repudiate and exit marriages whenever they are unhappy (XVI.15.519–20). Without a way for women to exit marriage, domestic servitude is perpetual. What's more, women must have access to the financial resources that will allow them to no longer be reliant on men (XVI.3.510). The ability to earn a living and enter and exit a marriage freely are key conditions for a woman's freedom. And Montesquieu thinks that women ought to have these and other personal, political, and economic freedoms in all societies, despite the notion that domestic slavery seems somehow appropriate in regimes like despotism that enslave everyone (XVI.9.514–15).[50]

This discussion of political servitude points to two important reasons for the emergence of servitude: weak states and unenlightened actors. When powerful states oppose each other, this dynamic prevents either one from being subjected to slavery. In Asia, strong nations face weak ones; "warrior peoples, brave and active, immediately touch effeminate, lazy, timid peoples: therefore it is necessary that they are conquered, and that the others are conquerors." In Europe, by contrast, strong nations are opposed by other strong nations. This is "the big reason . . . for the liberty of Europe and the servitude of Asia" (XVII.3.526). Montesquieu advocates for strong states that can protect themselves from their neighbors, thus making their people more secure and free. Another reason why Europeans are freer is their reliance on reason. Reason is the instrument that "breaks the chains forged in the south," these chains being the reason that men, whom nature has made "equal," remain unfree in some places. Once reason enters the public and private minds of citizens, they will be hard-pressed to continue to justify enslaving human beings. The liberation of peoples is at least one reason Montesquieu declares in the preface: "It is not indifferent that the people be enlightened." Still, Montesquieu seeks more; he seeks prosperity.

Prosperity

The politics of place holds that prosperity should be an aim for all societies. This claim may seem surprising at first glance, given that scholars pay scant attention to the place of prosperity in Montesquieu's thought. This makes a certain kind of sense, since he uses the word only fifteen times in *EL*, including only six times in part IV on commerce. He does not mention prosperity as a goal of states in XI, 5. However, a careful examination of his usages reveals that his multifaceted understanding of prosperity is an essential part of his political philosophy.

Prosperity has obvious economic components for Montesquieu. He wants individuals to be able to put themselves in a situation where they can work to provide for themselves and others. He wants individuals to be able to acquire, produce, sell, and trade, with the goal being to increase the common stock of society. Marseilles used commerce (specifically, the commerce of economy), which was its goal (XI.5.396), to achieve prosperity despite living among barbarous nations. They achieved prosperity by being industrious (and supplying for themselves what nature refused), by being just and moderate, and having frugal *mœurs* (XX.5.588–89). In a sense, the inhabitants of Marseilles had no choice: "It was necessary to subsist; they pulled their subsistence from the whole universe" (XX.5.589).[51] Montesquieu commends additional attributes of the inhabitants of Marseilles that contributed to their prosperity, including being moderate and just. Montesquieu identifies Carthage as prosperous, also due to its trade (X.6.382–83). The Greeks appear as prosperous, in part due to their commerce. Greek towns "acquired prosperity, as soon as they found themselves close to new peoples" (XXI.7.612). So expanding, getting closer to, encountering, and engaging in commerce with others promoted Greek material prosperity. But then, in the next paragraph, Montesquieu suggests that Greek prosperity was broader, extending beyond economics. Montesquieu suggests other reasons for the prosperity of Greece (*de prosperité pour la Grèce*): Greek games, temples, festivals, oracles, and, above all, "taste and the arts carried to a point, that to believe one surpasses them will always be to not know them!" (XXI.7.613). We will return to the noneconomic aspects of prosperity shortly.

Certain practices, rules, and laws are critical to attaining prosperity. The most important is respect for property. Laws must protect indemnity and amortization. Indeed, Montesquieu insists that "prosperity" is due in part to "the exercise of these two rights" (XXV.5.741). While he is speaking here about France, his analysis is meant to be more general. Montesquieu thinks it is essential to be able to pay money owed over time, because it allows people to acquire more things, and to do so more securely. Should someone's property be damaged, they must legally be entitled to be paid for their damage, loss, or injury. While Montesquieu insists on extending such legal protections to citizens, he rejects mortmain as harmful. He wants to stop mortmain because of the troubling powers it gives to ecclesiastics. Montesquieu's language here is strong: "Increase these rights, and stop mortmain, if possible" (XXV.5.741). A reliable and protected means of exchange is essential to attaining prosperity. Montesquieu explains that a state has "prosperity, according to whether, on the one hand, silver suitably represents all things, and on the other, all things represent silver and they are signs of one another" (XXII.2.653). The technical point here is clear: silver, or any other means of exchange, including money, must have a consistent value in order for it to be useful for commerce. Elsewhere Montesquieu highlights the need for "letters of exchange" in order to conduct commerce and maintain it everywhere (XXI.20.640).

Moderate government promotes, and is a necessary condition for, prosperity. After discussing the difficult history of the Jews, and explaining how they nonetheless managed to promote commerce in critical ways, Montesquieu presents three short paragraphs that are central to his political thought:

> It was necessary, since this time for princes to govern themselves with more wisdom than they would have thought of themselves: for, as it happened, the great acts of authority turned out to be so inept, that experience shows that it is *only the goodness of government [la bonté du gouvernement] which produces prosperity.*
>
> One has begun to be cured of Machiavellianism [*se guérir de machiavélisme*], and one will continue to be cured of it every day. It is necessary to have more moderation in councils. What used to be called *coup d'état* would today, the horror notwithstanding, be only indiscretions.

And, happily, men are in a situation where, though their passions inspire them to the thought of being wicked [*méchants*], it is nevertheless not in their interest to be so. (XXI.20.641; emphasis added)

We learn, first, that *only* the goodness of government produces prosperity. Of what, then, does a good government that can produce prosperity consist? Here Montesquieu explains that good government is moderate: "moderation in councils" is "necessary." This moderation comes in stark contrast to the harsh immoderation and rejection of a middle way that Machiavelli presents. Indeed, this passage highlights one of the key ways Montesquieu firmly rejects Machiavelli.[52] The cure to Machiavellianism, and another aspect of good government, is controlling passions and channeling interests. We will examine the political aspects of this thought in chapter 3, and the commercial ones in chapter 4. Montesquieu further links good, moderate government to prosperity in a passage we just considered. After arguing for a consistent measure of value (especially for money), Montesquieu insists that affirming such "relative value" can happen "*only in moderate government*" (XXII.2.651; emphasis added). But, he cautions, it does not happen always in moderate government. Moderate governments respect property: "for example, if the laws favor an unjust debtor, the things that belong to him do not represent silver, and they are not a sign of it" (XXII.2.651). One goal, then, of many of the things Montesquieu prizes highly—such as moderate criminal laws, political, personal, and economic liberty, and security—is to assist in the promotion of prosperity.

And yet, prosperity can arrive via controversial means. Specifically, prosperity and conquest can be linked to one another. In his discussion of England in book XIX, Montesquieu first explains how commerce has benefited England, making it materially wealthy, even resulting in "extreme" "opulence" (XIX.27.578). "A commercial nation has a prodigious number of small individual interests; it thus can shock and be shocked in an infinite number of manners. It would become sovereignly jealous; and it would be afflicted more by the prosperity of others than it would be pleased by its own" (XIX.27.578). So commerce has made the English prosperous, and yet they have difficulty enjoying that prosperity. Still, they seek to spread their commerce and prosperity to their colonies. As we noticed above, England has colonies more to expand its commerce than its domination (XIX.27.578). To do so, it must thrust its form of government upon its colonies: "As one likes to establish elsewhere what one finds established at home," they "would give to the people of its colonies the form of its own government: and this government bringing prosperity with it, one would see great peoples become formed in the very forests it [the colonizing nation] would send out to become inhabited" (XIX.27.578). We see, again, that the form of government is tied closely to prosperity. But it seems potentially acceptable to force a form of government on a people in order to promote the prosperity both of the conquerors and conquered. Montesquieu then almost immediately acknowledges the problematic nature of this enterprise. While the "conquered state would have a very good civil government," it nonetheless "would be overwhelmed by the rights of nations; and one would impose on it the laws from nation to nation, which would be such that its prosperity would only be precarious and solely on deposit for a master" (XIX.27.579). The imposition of good government, and the subsequent promotion of prosperity, is uncertain at best. Montesquieu's discussion of conquest and prosperity is complicated further by his remarks on Alexander.

Through his genius, Alexander sought to increase the prosperity of the peoples he conquered by leaving only a light footprint. "He did not only leave the vanquished peoples their *mœurs*, he also left them their civil laws, and often the same kings and governors he had found" (X.14.390). Rather than sweeping away the customs and traditions of the conquered, he respected them. He sought to be the "first citizen of each town" (X.14.390). His main goal in all this was their prosperity: Alexander "wanted to conquer all to preserve all; and whatever countries that he crossed, his first ideas, his first designs were always to do something that could augment prosperity there" (X.14.390). Montesquieu's discussion suggests that he thinks Alexander had more than a modicum of success, due in part to his frugality and economy, and his focus on public expenditures. The relationship between prosperity, liberty, and security remains complicated for Montesquieu.

Inequality and participation also promote prosperity. In Montesquieu's discussion of democracy in book II, he explains that classes and groups in society should not be equal, because such equality would thwart prosperity: "In the popular State, one divides the people into certain classes. It is in the manner of making this division that the great legislators distinguish themselves; and it is on that that the duration of democracy and its prosperity have depended" (II.2.241). This quotation comes in the context of Montesquieu explaining the need to slow down the people (*le peuple*), lest they move too quickly and damage the state and the interests of its inhabitants. But the point is clear: a certain amount of inequality is key to promoting prosperity. And if this is true in democracies, which are based on equality, then it holds true in other forms of government as well. Still, it is important for the people to have some say. In the next chapter, while discussing laws in aristocracies, Montesquieu notes that the people should have some say in affairs. In Genoa, for example, the Bank of St. George was administered by the people, which gives the people "a certain influence in the government." The consequence is significant: this influence "makes all of their prosperity" (II.3.245).

However, material wealth that is not coupled with the requisite good government can undermine security, liberty, and prosperity. Rome became prosperous by giving the people legislative say and allowing them to confirm the decisions of the kings, consuls, or Senate. But the people, "in the drunkenness of prosperities [*dans l'ivresse des prospérités*] ... augmented its executive power" (XI.17.421). This contributed to the fall of the Roman Republic. And it occurred because of a breakdown in Roman institutions that resulted from a problematic spread in material prosperity. The Roman people became increasingly well-off materially, and this improvement in their condition led to the "drunken" condition that made them want more power still. Material prosperity thus has the potential to disrupt general prosperity if it does not occur in the context of good governance.

The implications of defining prosperity in more than just economic terms are significant. We generally associate prosperity only with economic and financial matters.[53] Montesquieu uses the term in a way closer to that found in the 1762 edition of the *DAF*: "Happy state, happy situation, either of general affairs, or individual affairs." Such a positive situation cannot arise, Montesquieu insists, unless the government and laws are good.

Montesquieu's definition of prosperity in these broader terms is significant. A state is prosperous based not only on the extent of its material wealth, but on political and social standards as well. We thus can return to the English and French cases to understand his notion of prosperity more fully. The English have much, but they do not seem to enjoy what they have. They focus much more on what others have, and on gaining still more. Their *esprit* is uneasy, partisan, isolated, dour, and generally undesirable. The French, by contrast, are happy and enjoy life. The French have "a sociable humor, an openness of heart, a joy in life, taste, an ease of communicating its thoughts; that was lively, agreeable, enjoyable, sometimes imprudent, often indiscreet; and along with this had courage, generosity, frankness, a certain point of honor" (XIX.5.558–59). Might happiness be a part of Montesquieu's notion of prosperity? We certainly do not see this kind of joy in the ancients, although they do focus on harmony. Montesquieu offers a different kind of harmony where we deal with each other in a relaxed manner, absent of fear. The English and the Dutch do not live this way. Still, Montesquieu says that England brings its prosperity to its colonies. So the happiness and joy Montesquieu sees in France is not a necessary condition for being prosperous.

Montesquieu's remarks on France also highlight that a prosperous society is not a perfect one. "If," Montesquieu writes, "in general the character is good, what does it matter that some faults might be found there?" (XIX.5.559). In this same chapter, Montesquieu certainly seems to depict French society as prosperous.

Over the next two chapters we will explore in greater detail more of Montesquieu's general prescriptions as well as some of his specific policies that he thinks promote prosperity, liberty, and security. Before we do so, though, we must examine how he thinks that states should define and achieve these goods differently.

The Particularism of Security, Liberty, and Prosperity

Security, liberty, and prosperity are universal goals insofar as all societies should seek to attain them. However, these goals remain particularistic. Reason being, states can define *and* achieve these goals differently, within the framework of the politics of place. The suggestion that states should achieve security, liberty, and prosperity through different policies, practices, laws, and institutions may not be remarkable. After all, the great variation among states makes this suggestion quite reasonable. The claim that states may *define* these goals differently will appear, at first glance, as more surprising.

The necessity of particularism is most obvious regarding security. It is significantly more difficult to be and feel secure in dangerous states like Honduras, Venezuela, Iraq, Syria, and Somalia than it is in places like Sweden, Switzerland, and Canada. Reasons for insecurity include history, religion(s), neighboring countries, and lawlessness. Among the dangerous states listed, their reasons for insecurity differ greatly. Iraq faces a threat from the Islamic State, and is on the verge of a sectarian civil war. Honduras is riddled with rampant crime. We thus have no reason to think that a policy that augments security in Iraq necessarily will do so in Honduras.

The definition of security also can vary. Individuals define security partially in the context of personal and societal values. Citizens in Singapore or South Korea, for example, will define security in the context of their (similar but not identical) East Asian values.[54] Their understanding of society focuses more on the collective. Citizens in the United States and the United Kingdom, by contrast, tend to be more individualistic. They tend to define security in the context of protections for the individual. The result is diverging policies that have the same goal, security, but understand it differently. For example, Singapore has tighter restrictions on free speech than does America, which tends to reject such restrictions.

There is no single way, the politics of place maintains, to achieve a free society. In the next chapter we will explore the institutions, laws, practices, and values that can promote liberty. Here, our focus is on how the politics of place allows for a flexible definition of liberty. To illustrate this, we study the French and English definitions of liberty Montesquieu presents. Stated simply, the Frenchman acts from duty and out of honor. The Englishman acts from will; his "extreme" freedom is independence. The two experience freedom differently.

Consider first Montesquieu's discussion of honor. Montesquieu certainly sees honor as a defining feature of French society and the French *esprit.* Honor is a kind of "art," which can inspire "the most beautiful actions." Honor does this by demanding "preferences and distinctions" (III.7.255–57). Honor impels the French to judge actions based on whether they are beautiful, not good; great, not just; and extraordinary, not reasonable (IV.2.262). Honor enters into "all the ways of thinking and all the manners of sensing, and directs the principles themselves" in the direction of the common good (IV.2.264; III.7.257). Honor helps accomplish this when each person pursues her individual interests—burnishing her honor—and undertakes difficult actions without being deterred by others if duty or honor requires the action (III.7.257). Montesquieu's example of Crillon is illustrative. Crillon's honor impelled him to defy the king's order to kill Huguenots because, as he told his sire, "I have found among the inhabitants and people of war only good citizens, brave soldiers, and no executioners; thus, they and I, beg your Majesty to employ our arms and our lives to doable things." "This great and generous courage," Montesquieu continues, "regarded cowardice as an impossible thing" (IV.2.264). Education establishes the "supreme rules" of honor's moral code. No one—king, priest, or parent—can require us to act dishonorably. If someone tries to get us to act dishonorably, it is our duty to refuse such invitations and conform to the education and principles of an honorable person.

French freedom must be understood in the context of honor, Montesquieu insists. The morality of honor thus serves as a higher force than the laws or religion. Honor is a central component of maintaining a free government in monarchies because of the critical check it provides against the ambitions of the monarch. Thus individual Frenchmen, and French society more generally, are free in the context of their honor. English freedom is different.

The English constitution has as its "goal" political liberty (XI.5.396). The English maintain their freedom by being independent, having a "proper will," being "uneasy" (*inquiet*), and focusing on their self-interest in a way that seems vigilant and effective yet somehow undesirable, at least when compared to the French *esprit* from XIX, 5 (XIX.27.575, 580). By "independent" Montesquieu means, at least in part, that "no citizen" depends on "another citizen," and consequently "each would make more of a case for his liberty than for the glory of other citizens, or of one alone" (XIX.27.575). He also means that each individual "would follow his caprices and fantasies a lot, one would change party often; one would abandon one and would leave all of his friends, to bind with another in which one would find all his enemies; and often, in this nation, one could forget the laws of friendship and those of hatred" (XIX.27.575). Another taste of Montesquieu's bleak portrayal of English passions comes when he writes that "all the passions being free there, hate, envy, jealousy, the ardor to enrich oneself and to distinguish oneself, would appear in all their extents." Lest one think this is somehow unnecessary, Montesquieu continues by explaining that "if this was otherwise, the State would be like a man knocked down by a sickness, who does not have passions because he does not have force" (XIX.27.575). Uneasiness pervades society. The English believe themselves in danger even in those moments when they are more secure (XIX.27.575–76). Lowenthal explains that English "liberty is not only of actions and thoughts but of passions. To be free is mainly to follow one's appetites for money, prestige, and power. England is capitalistic: the moral limits on endless competitive acquisition have been removed."[55]

The contrast between how the French and English experience freedom is stark indeed. Montesquieu seems to allude to it when, at the end of his discussion of the English *esprit*, he says one finds there something that approaches "the force of Michelangelo" rather than "the grace of Raphael," this grace something one presumably finds in France. France's graceful freedom is distinct from England's forceful freedom. And yet, both are free (and remarkable) in their own particular ways.

There are many contemporary examples that illustrate the need for a flexible understanding of liberty. Consider how different states understand the relationship between religion and liberty. The French banned religious symbols in schools and burqas on the streets because they find that devout Muslims pose a threat to their strictly secular liberal democracy. The Swiss passed a referendum banning the construction of minarets out of the same concerns as the French. The same laws in Turkey or Jordan would deeply offend the vast majority of the citizenry. These societies all understand freedom differently. The French and Swiss at least can make arguments about how these laws conform to their notions of liberalism. That said, opponents of these bans would retort, "liberty for *whom*?" They argue that these bans are anti-immigrant measures that violate the liberties of these nations' Muslim minorities, rather than just a product of a different and equally valid understanding of liberty.

Having established the need to define and achieve security and liberty differently in particular societies, it is easy to see why the same is the case for prosperity. When we examine Montesquieu's discussion of commerce, we will see that he insists that while states generally should pursue commerce, they should pursue it in different ways and degrees depending on their circumstances. Holland is extremely commercial, but an extreme approach to commerce will not be effective in many other places. What's more, few countries will embrace commerce in the extreme way Montesquieu observes in Holland. Practically, landlocked countries like Austria cannot center their pursuit of economic prosperity on sea trade and fish exports, for example, in the same way that Ireland and Iceland can. In political terms, prosperity is linked to the goodness of government. But what constitutes a good government will vary across time and place. The form of government and the institutions that advance security, liberty, and prosperity vary. The options Montesquieu identifies for advancing these goods come to the fore in chapter 3.

Since the politics of place understands prosperity in economic and political terms, the need to define prosperity differently becomes apparent. A prosperous political order will look different across time and place; so too with a prosperous economic order. For example, while commerce is necessary for economic prosperity, the mode and manner of that commerce will differ based on the goals and values of a society. Today, France and Italy do not embrace free markets to the extent that Britain and the United States do. American economic prosperity is tied more tightly to capitalism and the free market. French economic prosperity, by contrast, is tied more closely to statism and social democracy. It would be indefensible for anyone to maintain, though, that either France or America is not prosperous.

The Universalism of Security, Liberty, and Prosperity

It is necessary to consider more carefully the role of universalism in Montesquieu's politics of place. He rejects universalism of institutions. He refuses to say that any one regime is universally valid. Indeed, no set of institutions can fit diverse peoples across time and place. Instead, as we will see in the next chapter, he identifies numerous institutions that can advance security, liberty, and prosperity, depending on the context. But even Locke concedes that no one regime is universally valid.[56] How, then, is Montesquieu's thought distinct from Locke's? The answer lies in the nature of their universalisms regarding principles.

Locke's universalism is grounded in natural rights. The assertion that all persons have a moral claim to life, liberty, and property is universal. What's more, Locke's understanding of these terms allows for little if any leeway in how we define these goods. Locke does not allow for significant variance in defining what liberty is, for example. On other key points, like the necessity of consent, Locke also is unwavering. Locke means his philosophy of natural rights to be applicable across time and place. Locke can make such claims because he views human nature as fixed. His philosophy offers a clear rubric for determining whether or not a government is legitimate.

As discussed above, Montesquieu is not a natural rights thinker. He deems appeals to natural rights unnecessary and potentially problematic. Philosophies of natural rights are too rigid. Some societies might attain security, liberty, and prosperity by incorporating natural (or even positive) rights into their institutions and social fabric; but in many other places, natural rights will be ineffective in achieving security, liberty, and prosperity. Montesquieu also does not have a fixed view of human nature; he views it as flexible. As such, his ability to make natural rights claims seems limited at best, and perhaps nonexistent.

Still, Montesquieu's politics of place is universalistic regarding its core principles. All states should establish and maintain security, liberty, and prosperity. This is a universal claim. But Montesquieu differs from Locke, for example, because he does not offer one rubric for defining and achieving these goods. Instead, he offers flexibility in how we define and achieve these goods. This is what makes Montesquieu's appeal to these goods particularistic; still, he is no relativist. He has clear standards.

Moderation is Montesquieu's benchmark for a good government. In the next chapter we will examine the centrality of moderation to the politics of place. Montesquieu recommends moderation universally. But because moderation inherently is a middle point between two extremes, and what the extremes are will vary, moderation itself varies across time and place. A course of action that might indeed be moderate at one point in time, or in one place, may not be moderate in another time or place. So while moderation is universally good, its content cannot be universal; the moderate course of action is between two extremes. As such, the content of security, liberty, and prosperity, the goods legislators seek to achieve by embracing moderation, is particularistic.

On the Relationship between Security, Liberty, and Prosperity

How do security, liberty, and prosperity relate? Does Montesquieu prioritize one over the others? Do they always go together? If not, what does Montesquieu recommend in cases of conflict? Does their relationship depend on the circumstances? There is no simple answer to these questions.

At a foundational level, security, liberty, and prosperity are related. In some cases, Montesquieu's understanding and definitions of these terms overlap. Personal liberty exists only when one feels and is secure. To have economic liberty, and especially to feel the power of its full effects, property must be secure. Economic liberty propels prosperity, material and otherwise. Political liberty relates not only to the other kinds of liberty (economic and personal), but also to security and prosperity. It relates to security because the distribution of powers Montesquieu recommends helps to prevent rulers from abusing their power, as such abuse often leads to the destruction of security, other kinds of liberty, and prosperity. Indeed, Montesquieu thinks these goods flourish when governmental power is limited and controlled. Political liberty also contributes to establishing prosperity. It is "only the goodness of government," we saw just above, "that produces prosperity."

In practice, though, security, liberty, and prosperity may not always go together for a period of time. That is, it might be necessary for states to prioritize one or two of these goods, at the short-term expense of the other(s). Security is the most likely candidate for prioritization. Suppose that a state (e.g., Honduras) is riddled with crime. It might be necessary for the state to deemphasize certain freedoms, or utilize temporary measures, to establish security. As already noted, Montesquieu says that "the usage of the freest peoples that have ever been on the earth makes me believe that there are cases where it is necessary to place, for a moment, a veil over liberty, as one hides the statues of the gods" (XII.19.448–49). One reason to put a veil over liberty could be to establish physical security. Such measures must be only "for a moment," though, and states must return as quickly as possible to prioritizing all three goods. Security is not the only good that might warrant prioritization. It might be reasonable for a state to focus on economic liberty and economic prosperity in order to raise living standards, leaving improvements in political liberty for later. Singapore has followed this model, to seemingly good effect. It simply is not always possible for states to treat each of these goods as equally important, as desirable as it may be for them to do so in some theoretical sense.

Circumstance undoubtedly plays a role in how security, liberty, and prosperity relate. This must be so, since states have different understandings and definitions of these goods. States achieve, and even prioritize, them in diverse ways. More than that, variation across time and place necessitates that the relationship among security, liberty, and prosperity differs. How could circumstance *not* impact the relationship of these three goods? Societies change regularly. Why would we expect the relationship between security, liberty, and prosperity to remain static, when the society, and its conception of these goods, does not? Besides, practices and policies that advance security at one point in time may not do so later. With circumstances constantly changing, societies must recalibrate on a regular basis their approach to achieving security, liberty, and prosperity. Over the course of the next two chapters we will investigate in greater detail the various ways in which diverse states can pursue these goods, beginning with the political factors.

CHAPTER THREE

The Political Variables

Moderation is the key to establishing and maintaining a secure, free, and prosperous society.[1] Montesquieuian moderation is not the same, though, as the moral moderation we find in theories of virtue ethics. Montesquieu does not recommend that political actors embrace the moral or philosophical moderation found in Plato or Aristotle, for example. Montesquieu certainly does not think that political actors should attempt to inculcate citizens to adopt this kind of moral virtue. Rather, Montesquieu advises legislators to develop institutions and laws to produce moderate *outcomes*. Institutions should be structured such that different powers in the state check each other. The effect of these interactions and relations should be the establishment of security, liberty, and prosperity. Crucially, Montesquieu does not insist that only one form of government is capable of achieving a good, that is, free and moderate, political order. To the contrary, Montesquieu's politics of place presents four forms of government—aristocratic republics, federal republics, monarchies, and mixed regimes—as having the potential to produce moderate outcomes.[2] Montesquieu also would have approved of liberal democracies had he had the chance to study them. Of all the forms of government Montesquieu studies, he only rules out despotisms and (ancient) democratic republics as incapable of producing a moderate political order.

This chapter will provide a deeper understanding of the institutions and practices Montesquieu thinks advance—or hinder—the establishment of moderate, free political orders. Here the focus is on what I call the "political variables." The focus shifts to the "subpolitical" variables in chapter 4.[3] We begin with the political variables because Montesquieu discusses them first, in parts I and II. He then moves, in parts III, IV, and V, to issues that are more particular, the subpolitical variables. Montesquieu's particularism comes out in his manner of proceeding. In the final sentence of book I he writes: "Then I will move to the other relations, which seem to be more particular" (I.3.238). Analytically, it makes sense to move from the more universal to the particularistic, and so we will proceed in this manner.

We set out first to examine Montesquieu's understanding of a moderate political order because this frames his analysis of different forms of government. All good political orders are moderate. So we must be clear on his conception of moderation. We then turn to the various structures he thinks can promote moderate government. We treat the structures as part of a menu of options, so to speak. Legislators must take careful account of the circumstances of a place, especially the *esprit*, to determine which institutions and practices can promote moderate government in their context.

Montesquieuian Moderation

Montesquieu's primary purpose in *EL* is to promote moderate government. In book XXIX, which originally was to conclude the work, Montesquieu explains: "I say it, and it seems to me that I have made this work only to prove it: the *esprit* of moderation should be that of the legislator; the political good, like the moral good, is found between two limits" (XXIX.1.865).[4] Montesquieu calls loudly and clearly for moderation elsewhere in *EL* too. In VI, 12 he writes: "Men must not be led to extremes." In XXII, 22 he insists: "I will always say it, it is moderation that governs men, and not excesses." Citing Ovid approvingly, Montesquieu later advises to "go the middle way: it is the safest" (XXX.10.893fn). Montesquieu advises against going too high or too low, too far to the left or right.[5] Montesquieu is wary even of an "excess of reason," which he views as "not always desirable." He continues by noting, "men accommodate themselves almost always better in the middle than the extremities" (XI.6.407). Craiutu, in his study of moderation, thus rightly notes that Montesquieu "made the concept of political moderation the keystone of his liberal political philosophy."[6] Rahe describes political moderation as Montesquieu's "cause."[7] Here we consider key features of Montesquieuian moderation that will allow us to understand better how political actors can embrace the *esprit* of moderation with an eye to establishing a good political order.

Legislators should proceed with caution when considering if and how to effect change. The approach should be, in this sense, conservative. Montesquieu advises caution because he is rightly concerned about the undesirable and potentially disastrous consequences that can follow from inappropriate attempts to "improve" societies. Indeed, Montesquieu frames his political philosophy with the following essential point in the preface of *EL*:

> In a time of ignorance one has no doubt, even when one does the greatest evils; in a time of enlightenment, one trembles again when one does the greatest goods. One senses the old abuses, one sees the correction; but one sees the abuses of the correction itself. One leaves the bad, if one fears the worse; one leaves the good, if one is in doubt of the better. One looks at the parts only for judging everything together; one examines all the causes to see all the results. (Preface.230)[8]

Montesquieu does not reject political change. He is neither an archconservative nor a reactionary. His purpose in this passage, and in *EL*, is different. He rejects radical change, however seemingly rational, in part because it is likely to go off the rails.[9] He also cautions that "deliberate change is not always for the better."[10] He is concerned about "corrections that leave problems, which themselves need correction."[11]

We see this in many revolutions since his time, especially the French and Russian cases. Rash action is antithetical to moderate government, and thus cannot be part of a formula for establishing a good political order. His concerns go deeper, though. He rejects the notion that a legislator possesses some sort of special knowledge, or even can attain an omnipotence that will allow him to correct societal ills easily and quickly. Montesquieu insists, to the contrary, that bad consequences often arise out of the best of intentions. One seeks the better, so one discards the good. One abhors the bad, but makes things worse.

Moderation is neither the product of a particular form of government nor the result of virtuous political actions. Montesquieu insists, "democracy and aristocracy are not free States by their nature" (XI.4.395). In the case of democracies, he elaborates that many have "confounded the power of the people with the liberty of the people" (XI.2.394). There is nothing inherent in any form of government, including republican government, that guarantees or even promotes a free or moderate political order.[12] Individuals prove themselves even more unreliable. It is not simply that the good character of some legislators cannot always achieve a good end. Montesquieu's apprehensions run much deeper. Men often work *against* the achievement of the good ends Montesquieu seeks. He argues that "it is an eternal experience that all men who have power are carried to abuse it; he goes until he finds limits. Who would say it! virtue itself needs limits" (XI.4.395). Later, Montesquieu claims that "great men who are moderate are rare" (XXVIII.41.858).[13] Instead of relying on such rare men, Montesquieu wants to channel our tendency to abuse power to harness the good potential of this tendency.

Immoderate actions, channeled through institutions, produce moderate outcomes. Effective institutions pit political powers against one another. "Political liberty," Montesquieu explains, "is found only in moderate governments. But it is not always in moderate governments; it is only there when one does not abuse power" (XI.4.395). But as we just saw, men are eternally led to abuse power! How then to stop these abuses? In order to prevent abuses of power, "it is necessary that, by the disposition of things, *power stops power*" (XI.4.395; emphasis added). This phrase—"power stops power"—is one of the most important in all of Montesquieu's writings.[14] His entire political project is centered on the notion that power stopping power is necessary to achieving security, liberty, and prosperity. This idea also is central to his theory of a distribution of powers. Crucially, though, one stops power in different ways based on the situation.

A certain kind of *im*moderation is, seemingly paradoxically, the key to achieving moderate outcomes. It is the power of the different actors, not their gentleness, care, virtue, morality, or good intentions, that stops the power of other actors. Their desire to protect their own powers and prerogatives encourages them to stop other political actors from infringing on their powers. Montesquieu thus encourages channeled immoderation to achieve moderate outcomes. Importantly, though, this moderation must operate within clear institutional confines; it must actually promote a moderate political order, rather than lead to its destruction.[15] This occurs when political actors have the power to forcefully and (sometimes) aggressively protect their interests and prerogatives while not usurping the powers of other institutions. The goal is to "transform discordant passions and interests into social harmony. In such governments, political liberty results from the 'agitation' and friction that is produced when diverse social groups and interests collide."[16] Montesquieu explains that in order to form a "moderate government, it is necessary to combine powers, regulate them, temper them, make them move; give, so to speak, a ballast to one, to place it in a state to resist the other" (V.14.297).[17]

Moderate outcomes arise when powers are distributed, not separated. This distinction is important. As Craiutu rightly notes, "Montesquieu in fact favored a blending rather than a strict separation of powers and referred in his book to *pouvoirs distribués* and not to *pouvoirs séparés*."[18] Indeed, Montesquieu never uses the phrase *pouvoirs séparés*. "It is precisely because the powers should be in a position to oppose each other," Spector explains, "that they cannot be separated or isolated."[19] Montesquieu seeks to distribute and balance powers, not separate them.[20] And to good effect:

> Montesquieu's theory of the balance of powers achieved in the end something that a strict separation of powers would never have been able to accomplish on its own. For the principle of the separation of powers does not actually determine how powers ought to be composed; it merely separates their functions and spheres of competence and is common to several types of commonwealths. Montesquieu understood this

point better than anyone else. In his eyes, moderation as a constitutional principle combined the horizontal separation of powers among various branches of government with the vertical diffusion of power among several layers of authority.[21]

James Madison thus rightly channels the spirit of Montesquieu's analysis here when, in *Federalist* No. 47, he insists that powers among branches and between the state and federal governments should not be totally separated.

Montesquieu's emphasis on moderate government represents a significant development. Craiutu identifies two important things Montesquieu achieved by drawing a dichotomy between moderate and immoderate government. Montesquieu "shifted the focus of inquiry from the ethical to the *institutional* aspects of moderation, paying special attention to the architecture of constitutional government in which political moderation is embedded." Perhaps more importantly, "he extended the scope of the concept of *gouvernement modéré* by applying the label not only to republican regimes, whose main principle is political virtue ... but also to monarchies, whose underlying principle is honor."[22] As our analysis proceeds, we will see that Montesquieu thinks different iterations of these forms of government can produce moderate outcomes.

One of Montesquieu's primary targets in his discussion of moderation is Machiavelli. We saw in the previous chapter that Machiavellianism is a disease of which we are gradually being cured. The cure, you may recall, is "moderation in councils" (XXI.20.641). The wicked Machiavelli rejects the middle way in favor of extremes. Machiavelli insists that immoderate, awesome deeds, to be committed at least once every ten years, are necessary to bring states back to their good, founding principles. Montesquieu, by contrast, eschews Machiavelli's harsh recommendations in favor of gentle ones.[23]

We find a universal lesson in the approach to moderation Montesquieu presents: a simple government is likely to be a bad government. Simple governments have insufficient checks on power. The more complex the government, the more likely it is to approximate the political good. But this argument, while tinged with universalism, retains particularistic elements, because complex governments come in different shapes and forms, some better than others. Legislators therefore must determine how to promote an effective kind of complex government in their state.

Montesquieu's philosophy of moderation is a philosophy of change. Montesquieu is deeply concerned about discerning ways to improve societies. He seeks to proliferate knowledge of preferable systems, because he knows that the knowledge he shares has the potential to dramatically improve mankind's lot. Montesquieu believes that he is creating knowledge that is distinct from other approaches. Montesquieu seeks to give future legislators the proper knowledge to achieve security, liberty, and prosperity. Still, the claim that Montesquieuian moderation is all about change might be striking in light of his remarks in the preface we just examined. Montesquieu seems wary of change. But he is offering a warning against immoderate change, not rejecting change altogether. One problem potential legislators often face when seeking to improve societies is overestimating their own capacities. They mistakenly come to be under the impression that they are capable of penetrating with a stroke of genius the entire constitution of a state. This hubris often leads to damaging though often unintended consequences. These are the men who lose the good while seeking the better, or make things worse than they already are. In order to effect positive change, legislators must follow Montesquieu's method for analyzing societies. This method is grounded in the politics of place and centers on studying the variables separately and in relation to one another. It culminates in discerning how these interactions form an *esprit*. Such analysis will reveal to legislators that in almost all cases, change must take place gradually, over time. Moderation requires as much. Over the next two chapters we will study the mechanisms Montesquieu identifies for undertaking moderate change. We begin with institutions, in the context of his discussion of the forms of government.

Rulers and Ruled: Nature and Principle in Montesquieu's Forms of Government

The establishment of moderate government is in large part the product of who rules and how, and who is ruled and how. Montesquieu considers how those in power (should) act, and how inhabitants of a society (should) act. That is, he is interested in what he calls the "nature" and the "principle" of each form of government: democratic republic, aristocratic republic, monarchy, and despotism. In this section we consider the contours of his discussion of these key concepts before examining his analysis of the different forms of government.

Montesquieu defines the various forms of governments based on their institutions and laws. He understands their "nature" based on the "particular structure" of a government, which is what "makes it what it is" (III.1.250–51). Broadly speaking, Montesquieu identifies three potential structures: "Republican government is that in which the people themselves, or only a part of the people, have sovereign power; monarchical, the one where one alone governs, but by fixed and established laws; whereas, in despotic, one alone, without law and without rules, drags everything along by his will and by his caprices" (II.1.239). The key features of the nature of a government are who holds power and how they (can) wield it.[24] There are two categories of governments: lawful and unlawful. Monarchies are lawful because they operate based on "fixed and established laws." Republics become lawful through the people having sovereign power. Despotisms, by contrast, are wholly unlawful. There are two kinds of rule: by many and by one. And rulers can rule in two ways: moderately or immoderately. The three general forms (republic, monarchy, despotism) are not inherently distinct. The English regime, for example, mixes elements of a monarchy and a republic. Nor are the categories uniform. In his definition of republics, two types emerge: democracies and aristocracies. In democracies the people rule; in aristocracies, ruling is limited to a part of the people. Later, the federal republic enters the discussion. We see that other institutional structures further expand the potential configurations of states. A federal republic brings together numerous republics to establish another distinct "form of government."

The nature of a government provides an evaluative rubric for states in a few ways. One is factual—does the state meet the criteria Montesquieu identifies? For example, does a single ruler uphold the fundamental laws, thus making the state a monarchy? Or is he despotic, ruling based on will and caprice? The second is normative: if a monarch does not follow the fundamental laws, then he is a bad monarch, or no monarch at all. The third is prescriptive: the form of a government dictates, generally speaking, how it ought to function.

Each form of government, Montesquieu suggests, needs the rulers and inhabitants to act in certain ways to function optimally. Each state requires a "principle" (*principe*) or "spring" (*ressort*). The principle is what makes the government "act." It consists of the "human passions that make it move" (III.1.250–51). Samuel describes the "spring" as the "emotional motor" that "keeps the machinery of government in motion."[25] The development of the spring was undoubtedly an important innovation.[26] Montesquieu identifies a passion[27] necessary in four types of governments: political virtue in democracy, moderation in aristocracy, honor in monarchy, and fear in despotism. Inhabitants must embrace the principles in their public and private lives. Montesquieu compares the principle to the gear that makes a watch tick, suggesting that a state cannot function at all without it. He also notes that it is possible for more than one principle to shape citizens in a particular state. Honor, for example, can be present in republics.[28] Importantly, Montesquieu does not identify a specific principle for federal republics and mixed regimes. The principles require an education, the laws of which prepare people to be good citizens (IV.1.261). People must be taught to be fearful or virtuous by the state. By contrast, society educates people to be honorable. The principle is of the utmost importance. "The corruption of each government begins almost always with that of its principles" (VIII.1.349).[29] When the principles become corrupt, "the best laws become bad, and turn against the State; when the principles are sound, the bad have the effect of the good; the force of the principle brings about everything" (VIII.11.357).[30]

On this point Montesquieu echoes and diverges from Machiavelli, who argues in his *Discourses* that in republics virtuous individuals have to set in motion public trials or themselves commit awesome deeds that arouse the fear that supports the laws in the hearts of their fellow citizens.[31] Machiavelli judges such actions necessary to rekindle attachment to the founding principles of a state. While emphasizing the importance of returning a state to its principles, Montesquieu would disagree with the desirability of arousing fear, which leads to despotism. Montesquieu approves only of moderate means for (re)attaching people to a principle.

The nature and principle are important variables that impact, and are impacted by, the *esprit*. Montesquieu thought that the principles function in conjunction with, and in the context of, the *esprit* of each particular nation. So what is honorable or moderate will differ somewhat based on the particulars of each society that embraces that principle. Honor is not identical in France and Japan. What's more, states that have the same form of government often have different *esprits*. Two monarchies might share a form of government, and a spring, but they may have different modes of commerce, environments, religions, and so forth. The nature and principle are neither universal nor universalizing. Rather, they fit into the politics of place framework.

In what follows, our purpose is not to examine every detail of Montesquieu's discussion of each form of government. Many scholars have offered excellent extended analyses of such matters. Rather, we are interested in how Montesquieu's discussion of the six forms of government sheds light on the question of what politics is appropriate for a place. In particular, we seek to understand better how various institutions, practices, and beliefs can serve the central role of having power stop power.

Montesquieu's Rejection of Two Immoderate Governments: Despotism and (Ancient) Democracy

Before examining the four forms of government Montesquieu looks upon favorably, we first must consider briefly the two he rejects as incapable of establishing a secure, free, and prosperous political order: despotism and democracy.

Despotism is, by far, the worst potential political outcome according to Montesquieu. He summarizes the idea of despotism as follows: "When the savages of Louisiana want to have fruit, they cut down the tree, and collect the fruit. Voilà despotic government" (V.13.292). Despots follow nothing but their immediate, voluptuous desires, without any regard for the consequences of their decisions (II.5.249). Fear should permeate all spheres of society for the despot to maintain control effectively.[32] Fear should define public and private existence. This fear will dispose people to provide the "extreme obedience" the despot needs and accept their sad situation (III.10.259). Man must be transformed into "a creature who obeys a creature who wants" (III.10.260). Shklar rightly explains that for Montesquieu the "politics of fear" always "remained the supreme enemy."[33] The ultimate goal of despotic practices is to depoliticize the state, making politics impossible.[34] All aspects of life under despotism are insecure. There is no real freedom. Property is unprotected. There is no sense in speaking of prosperity, because any gains are fleeting and easily lost. Power is wholly unchecked. Despite its terrible nature, despotism is a powerful enemy. It is easy to maintain, "since only passions are necessary for establishing it, [and] everyone is good enough for that" (V.14.297). Despotism is, as Spector remarks, a "perpetual menace."[35] Montesquieu's intention, Pangle rightly notes, is to "contribute to preventing its encroachment into Europe—and, wherever possible, his hope to help mitigate its deplorable proclivities in the vast portions of the world where it prevails."[36]

Montesquieu's critique of democracy is more nuanced. But sharply critical he is. At first glance, ancient democratic republics seem to hold promise for Montesquieu. When the force of democratic virtue was felt sufficiently throughout society, one "did things that we no longer see today, and that shock our small souls [*nos petites âmes*]"[37] (II.4.266). The ancients, with their great souls, appear to be superior to the lowly moderns. Accordingly, some have interpreted Montesquieu as preferring the (ancient) democratic republic to all other forms of government.[38] But Montesquieu judges the ancient democratic republic undesirable and untenable.

Democratic virtue is totalizing and deeply problematic. Citizens must embrace it, and allow it to permeate their heart and soul. To be politically virtuous, citizens must love the laws, homeland, equality, frugality, and the republic (Author's Foreword.227; V.2.274; V.3.274). This virtue, which "is singularly connected to democracies" (IV.5.267), is not tantamount to moral or Christian virtue. It does not consist of the wisdom, justice, moderation, or courage one traditionally associates with virtue. This is not the virtue of Plato or Aristotle.[39] But democratic virtue is deeply unnatural. Political virtue is "a renouncement of oneself [*un renoncement à soi-même*], which is *always* a *very painful thing*" (IV.5.267; emphasis added). Numerous scholars have shown why Montesquieu rejects this "repression of the self-expressive and humane passions that are natural and that are basic to the happiness of humankind living in society."[40] Citizens must be continuously educated—inculcated—to believe in the correctness of such "virtuous" beliefs. The laws must establish the requisite love of homeland and equality (V.4.276). Citizens must embrace setting aside, or sacrificing, their individual interests and prioritize those of the state. The laws are most forceful when they require "the extreme subordination of the citizens to magistrates" (V.7.283). To achieve equality, the state must (re)distribute property equally, and keep portions small (V.5.276; V.6.279). But doing so can be "impractical," "dangerous," or even run "counter to the constitution" (V.7.281). Political, personal, and economic freedoms run counter to the goals of ancient democratic republics. As Spector explains, constant surveillance is necessary to maintain democracy's "extraordinary institutions."[41] "Privacy," Pangle notes, "is all but eliminated."[42] Acceptance of the doctrine of political virtue is absolutely necessary because when "this virtue ceases, ambition enters into the hearts that can receive it, and avarice enters into all. The desires change goals: that which one loved, one loves no longer; one was free with the laws, one wants to be free against them; each citizen is like a slave escaped from the house of his master" (III.3.252). In this remarkable passage Montesquieu equates repressive ancient democratic freedom with slavery![43] Indeed, ancient democratic republics needed to enslave other populations to exist, something that goes against nature.[44]

Even one of democracy's potentially most appealing features, that it gives the people "sovereign power" (II.2.239), is deceptive. Montesquieu proclaims that the laws "that establish the right to vote are . . . fundamental in this government" (II.2.239–40). They are, indeed, fundamental, but not in the way one initially might expect. The people actually play a rather minor role. Democratic republics only permit a small number of citizens to vote and engage fully in politics.[45] The state should divide people into classes in a way that gives little if any say to the people, as was done in Rome and Athens (II.2.241–42). Real power is reserved for the ruling classes or the citizens who are not poor. Such divisions appear to be necessary because the people do not make good decisions. The people always want to go too quickly or too slowly; they are immoderate (II.2.240–41). In Montesquieu's portrayal, democracy "thus does not signify the integral power of the people, government by the people and for the people, nor the absolute sovereignty of the people."[46]

Montesquieu's presentation of democratic republics founded on virtue shows them to be incapable of allowing their citizens to be free and thus secure. By banning inequality and rejecting luxury, prosperity is out of reach too. More than just rejecting the end of political virtue, Montesquieu wholly rejects the means of achieving it, including the constant surveillance of citizens. Montesquieu thus rejects democratic republics as a viable option for political actors considering how to establish and maintain a good political order.

Monarchy

The contrasts between despotism and monarchy begin to demonstrate why Montesquieu viewed monarchy favorably. While despotism and monarchy both are rule by one, two key features distinguish them: lawful checks on the monarch's power and honor. Where despotism is lawless, monarchy is lawful. Where despotism has no checks on the ruler's power, monarchy has numerous checks. Where fear in despotisms seeks to beat everyone down, honor raises people up in monarchy. A distribution of power makes power apply itself "less immediately" and more carefully (V.16.299). Montesquieu thus identifies monarchy with moderate government explicitly.[47] While some scholars argue that Montesquieu viewed monarchy negatively,[48] sufficient evidence shows that Montesquieu thinks monarchical governments can protect security, liberty, and prosperity. At the same time, Montesquieu grew up under Louis XIV. This experience made Montesquieu keenly aware that monarchies could become absolutist. At times, he even suggests that Louis XIV's regime risked becoming despotic. In this section we will study first how an effective distribution of powers among various institutions is necessary to keep monarchy lawful and moderate. Once we have established that Montesquieu thinks monarchy can promote security, liberty, and prosperity, we will consider when it might fit the politics of a place.

Monarchy is superior to republican and mixed governments in certain ways. "Monarchical government has a great advantage over republican: affairs being led by one alone, there is more promptness in execution" (V.19.289). The presence of a single executive in the form of a monarch allows states to respond quickly to problems that arise. Speedy responses can be critical to protecting a state, especially when a state is under attack. When a monarch makes errors, or when he ceases to execute the laws, he "can easily repair the evil [*le mal*]: he only has to change the Council, or correct this negligence himself" (III.3.251–52). Republican government, by contrast, can sometimes move too slowly, thus jeopardizing the effectiveness of the response and the well-being of the state. Montesquieu viewed the loss of Holland's executive, the stadholder, as problematic.[49] The flip side, however, is that "this promptness could degenerate rapidly." For an example of such degeneration, he turns to one of his villains: Cardinal Richelieu. Richelieu dislikes the "thorns of the countryside, which make difficulties of everything. When this man did not have despotism in his heart, he had it in his head" (V.10.289). The actions of this mighty minister demonstrate the proclivity powerful actors have to augment their authority. Richelieu rejected checks on his power.

But it is generally insufficient, even dangerous, to rely on monarchs to always follow the laws, or enact good laws. Monarchs have a tendency to seek to augment their power. If one alone governs, the ruler needs guidance, prodding, and resistance to do so by fixed and established laws. Montesquieu thus explains that "intermediate, subordinate, dependent power constitutes the nature of monarchical government." The prince may be "the source of all political and civil power." But the fundamental laws suppose necessarily additional mediums through which power must flow "because if there is only the momentary and capricious will of one alone in the State, nothing can be fixed, and by consequence there is no fundamental law" (II.4.247). Intermediary powers have a "special role . . . in preserving moderation and liberty in monarchical regimes. The importance of these *corps intermédiares* derives mainly from their ability to successfully restrain and temper the momentary and potentially capricious will of the monarch."[50] Intermediary powers prevent the monarch from becoming despotic, and help him maintain his legitimacy.[51] The key intermediate powers include "political and juridical bodies (*parlements*, towns, seigniorial and ecclesiastical jurisdictions), social orders (nobility, clergy)," and the laws.[52] We focus on how four intermediaries are especially important for checking power and moderating outcomes: the nobility, the laws, alternative political bodies like the *parlements*, and religion. These institutions have the potential to check political power effectively.

A robust nobility is a necessary condition for a moderate monarchy. Nobles are "the essence of monarchy, of which the fundamental maxim is: *no monarchy, no nobility; no nobility, no monarchy*. But one has a despot" (II.4.247). The nobility therefore is inherent to the idea of monarchy; without the nobles, the state likely will become despotic. The nobility is a "more natural" intermediate power (II.4.247). Montesquieu thus thinks that the laws should "work to support this Nobility, of which honor is, so to speak, the child and the father" (V.9.288). Nobles have the incentives and ability to protect their powers and prerogatives and prevent the monarch from augmenting his power. The nobility can play this role effectively until it renders itself, or is rendered by the monarch, toothless and irrelevant. Let us consider the nobility's motivations and mechanisms for checking the monarch's ambition.

Nobles' powers and privileges originate, in large part, from their land and the wealth it provides them; their very dignity, Montesquieu suggests, is attached to these things. The nobility wants to protect the power it exercises over a region and more generally. Nobles have an obvious incentive to protect their power in their spheres of influence against attempted usurpations by the monarch or anyone else. In order for the nobility to serve as an effective check against the monarch, the privileges that nobles receive must be particular to them, otherwise one would "diminish the force of the Nobility and of the people" (V.9.288). The notion of nobility requires a kind of exclusivity; otherwise noble powers and privileges easily could be watered down, as by issuing more titles of nobility. Because noble privileges are deeply embedded, the nobility has a longer horizon regarding power. Nobles are protecting power that has been passed down in their family for generations, and that they will pass to their progeny. Montesquieu approves of the nobility being hereditary. It allows the nobility to serve as a critical "link" (*le lien*), or intermediary, between the monarch and the people (V.9.288).

The nobility remains, nonetheless, unreliable. Montesquieu is skeptical about the degree to which the nobility reliably will fulfill these functions. The nobility may be an intermediate power, but it also is a *subordinate* power. The nobility might not check the monarch, either by choice or circumstance. Montesquieu explains:

> It does not suffice that there are, in a monarchy, intermediate ranks; it is still necessary to have a depository of laws [*dépôt des lois*]. This depository can only be in the political bodies, which announce the laws when they are made and recall them when one forgets them. The natural ignorance of the nobility, its inattention, its disdain for civil government, require that there is a body that ceaselessly removes the dust from the laws where they would be buried. The Council of the prince is not a suitable depository. It is, by its nature, the depository of the momentary will of the prince who executes, and not the depository of fundamental laws. (II.4.249)

The nobles can be disinclined to protect the state from the monarch's advances on various spheres of society. They can see their position in society as secure and comfortable. They do not always understand themselves to have an immediate incentive to oppose the monarch. Rather, the monarch often entices the nobility to work with him and against other groups in society. As a group, it becomes subservient to the monarch, and loses the ability to restrain him. Montesquieu certainly has in mind how this scenario played out at Louis XIV's court at Versailles. The best remedy for reinvigorating the nobility is honor, to which we turn shortly, because it motivates the nobles to act to protect their powers and privileges. Without honor, they all too often do the monarch's bidding.

The depository of laws is tantamount to a kind of constitution. This depository, which consists of a set of codified laws that protect basic liberties, must reign supreme. The rule of these good laws is necessary to establish security and make citizens be and feel safe. These laws must ensure moderate punishments for crimes. They must uphold the three forms of freedom Montesquieu prizes. And they must allow people to become prosperous. The laws themselves are insufficient, though, without intermediate powers to ensure they are enforced and respected. For this, entities like the *parlements* are necessary.

Political bodies like the French *parlements* are crucial to preserving fundamental laws.[53] Montesquieu was intimately familiar with such institutions, as he inherited the position of *président à mortier* (though he eventually sold the office). The united nature of these bodies allowed them to speak with a stronger voice by agreeing on a position vis-à-vis the monarch. Many power brokers together opposing the monarch could serve as a more robust check than individual nobles acting alone. Mostly nobles populated these assemblies. French kings often tried to suppress the *parlements*, because of the clear threat these bodies posed to his power. The role of religious institutions, by contrast, appears more mixed.

The clergy can be a bulwark against creeping monarchical powers. As in despotism, religion can serve as a higher law to which the monarch must submit. More than that, religion and the clergy can erect small barriers to stop the monarch. Montesquieu explains, "monarchs, whose power could seem without limits, stop themselves by the smallest obstacles, and submit their natural pride to complaint and prayer" (II.4.248). Still, Montesquieu's portrayal of the clergy is quite mixed. He identifies the clergy as an "evil" (*le mal*), but suggests that an evil that limits "dreadful evils" is a "good" (*un bien*). While the clergy has the potential to be good, or to cause good effects, Montesquieu points to many examples showing how it simply promotes evil. We saw already his disdain for Richelieu. Mazarin certainly was another powerful cleric at the front of Montesquieu's mind. These two figures demonstrate the potential for the clergy to rule in tandem with the monarch against society and against the fundamental laws. Montesquieu pointedly highlights the dangers the clergy—and religion—can cause. "Where would Spain and Portugal be since the loss of their laws, without this power [the clergy] which alone stops arbitrary power?" (II.4.248). This is the specific context in which Montesquieu calls the clergy an "evil" that can limit "dreadful evils." Further consideration of Montesquieu's perspective on Spain and Portugal shows that he was quite critical of these states, especially with respect to the role religion played in them. Specifically, he was horrified by the Inquisition that raged in these countries, and he criticizes the Inquisition in sharp terms later in *EL* (XXIV.13.723). While Montesquieu suggests that the clergy occasionally can check the monarch, the proclivity of clerics to work with him toward bad ends leaves them unreliable at best, and dangerous at worst. Ultimately, the most important institutions for checking the monarch—the nobility, the *parlements*, and the towns they oversee—need honor to effectively check the monarch and institutions and individuals like the church and clergy that can pose threats to the fundamental laws.

Honor is the lifeblood of monarchies. Monarchy supposes "preeminences, ranks, and even a nobility of origin. The nature of *honor* is to demand preferences and distinctions; it is therefore, by the thing itself, placed in this government" (III.7.257). Individuals crave preferences and distinctions as ways to set themselves apart from others. At one level, they are tied directly to the status of being a part of the nobility, as well as to the benefits with which such a status is associated. At another, higher, and for Montesquieu more important level, preferences and distinctions result primarily from the "most beautiful actions" that honor can inspire. Ultimately, Montesquieu thinks that honor, when "joined with the force of the laws," can drive "towards the goal of government," which is the moderate rule of one by fundamental laws and with the advice of intermediary groups (III.6.256). But the honor that produces this beneficial dynamic is not what we might expect.

We generally associate honor with "high moral standards of behavior," "good quality or character as judged by other people," and with "respect that is given to someone who is admired."[54] On this understanding, honor seems to be associated with someone who does something simply because it is the right, proper course of action; this makes it honorable. Rather than being driven by the pursuit of the right action per se, Montesquieu insists that honor often is driven by ambition. While "ambition is pernicious in a republic" (for reasons we will examine shortly), it "has good effects in monarchy; it gives life to this government; and one has this advantage there, that it is not dangerous there, because it can be ceaselessly repressed" (III.7.257).

Ambitious honor encourages citizens to prize their own, particular interests above other interests. Honor-seeking citizens are keenly interested in basking in the admiration of others. And this admiration flows their way only when they perform good actions for the entire world to see. Honor does not manifest itself away from others. That individuals seek honor in this way is not detrimental to the state. Montesquieu insists, instead, that this pursuit of honor is beneficial for the state. "Honor," he explains, "makes all the parts of the body politic move; it ties them by its action itself; and it finds that each works for the common good, believing that he works for his individual interests" (III.7.257). Honor-seeking citizens advance general political goods by pursuing what is good for them, namely being and being perceived as honorable. "Ambition for distinction on the part of all classes and individuals elicits conduct that redounds to the public benefit while aiming only at private or selfish good."[55] This pursuit of self-interest might strike us as immoral and thus undesirable. As Spector explains, Montesquieu demurs: "Monarchical society prospers not thanks to the morality of its subjects, but thanks to their *immorality*, regulated by the laws of honor. Sovereignty should neither repress the passions nor attempt to make the austerity of a moral order reign."[56] Here, as elsewhere, Montesquieu demonstrates an affinity for Mandeville's argument regarding how private vices produce public benefits. The good outcome outweighs the potential undesirability of the seemingly crass nature of these selfish motivations.

It is essential to emphasize the morality that arises from honor, lest it get lost in Montesquieu's focus on honor's selfish nature. "And is it not impressive to obligate men to do all the difficult actions which require force, without any other reward than the renown of these actions?" (III.7.257). The desire to take difficult actions, such as opposing the monarch, is what gives the code of honor its force. Honor forms "an unconditional obligation with regard to its code that imposes the refusal of doing degrading actions."[57] The upshot, then, is that "the code of honor sets unofficial limits to the arbitrariness of king and subjects alike."[58] The code of honor is powerful because of the selfish motive it imposes. It gains still more force when one considers the other kind of honor Montesquieu celebrates, that found in the case of Crillon.

Crillon acts honorably in the noblest sense:

> Crillon refused to assassinate the Duke of Guise, but he offered to Henry III to fight against the Duke. After St. Bartholomew's Day, Charles IX having written to all the governors to massacre the Huguenots, the Viscount of Orte, who commanded in Bayonne, wrote to the king: "Sire, I have found among the inhabitants and men of war only good citizens, brave soldiers, and not a single executioner; thus, they and I, beg Your Majesty to employ our arms and lives to something doable." This great and generous courage regarded cowardice as something impossible. (IV.2.264)

Sharon Krause has discussed the paramount importance of this example to Montesquieu's political philosophy.[59] Crillon does not appear to be acting from crude self-interest. He does not refuse to kill because it would be harmful to him or his reputation. Rather, he seems to be driven by honor in the highest sense in which we might imagine it. The key effect of this honor is that "the prince can never prescribe an action that dishonors us, because it would render us incapable of serving him" (IV.2.264). Montesquieu thus includes a kind of honor inspired by the desire to do beautiful actions to his understanding of monarchy's spring.

There are therefore two distinct motives that promote honorable actions: self-interest and ambition, and a desire to engage in beautiful actions. These two forms of honor unlock the nobility's power-checking potential. While some men will want to act as Crillon does, most will need selfish motives to be honorable. The nobility has a proclivity to become subservient to the monarch, either because nobles do not protect their prerogatives effectively, or because they choose to work with the monarch rather than opposing him when necessary. The nobility can only serve as a check if it does indeed represent a significant power in a state. Nobles therefore must be motivated by one of these two kinds of honor, because their pursuit of honor is the firmest guarantee against acquiescing to the monarch and his ambition. By offering different avenues by which to produce honorable actions, Montesquieu's principle of honor as a check on the monarch becomes more robust. The reasons for acting honorably are more extensive still.

Honor and its pursuit are natural and pleasant, according to Montesquieu. For this reason, it is not necessary for the state to "educate" people to be honorable. Instead, "it is when one enters into the world that the education commences in some way" (IV.2.262). This education has three core tenets: "it is necessary to place in the virtues a certain nobility, in the *mœurs* a certain frankness, and in the manners a certain politeness." People should judge actions not as "good [*bonnes*], but as beautiful [*belles*]," not as "just [*justes*], but as great [*grandes*]," not as "reasonable [*raisonnables*], but as extraordinary [*extraordinaires*]" (IV.2.262).[60] This metric for acting and for judging actions appears easy to embrace, for who would not want to be—and be seen as being—great, beautiful, extraordinary, frank, polite, and thus noble? Again, Montesquieu does not suggest that people necessarily act out of a certain moral goodness. Rather, one wants to be seen as being frank because he likes to seem "hardy and free." And one wants to be polite because we are born to please ourselves and others (IV.2.263). Above all of this, though, Montesquieu identifies honor's three "supreme rules." First, one is allowed to give importance to his fortune but is "sovereignly forbidden" from giving any to his life. Second, our social rank must serve as a minimum guide to our actions, so that we do nothing unworthy of that rank. Finally, honor and the things it defends are protected best "when the laws do not contribute to proscribing them"; moreover, the actions that honor demands "are more strongly demanded when the laws do not require them" (IV.2.265). When the code of honor reigns supreme, society benefits at many levels.

The promulgation of honor results in an aesthetically pleasing worldview, pleasant actions, and potentially an aesthetically pleasing world. The yearning for aesthetic pleasure is another important motivating factor in doing honorable deeds. Even Crillon certainly deemed his actions great, beautiful, and extraordinary. It was on account of viewing his actions as such that he took them. Thus we might rightfully say that he took a certain kind of pleasure in his actions. Far from decrying this aesthetic approach, Montesquieu lauds its value. We recall that he considers the French *esprit*, which is founded on honor, to be good. He identifies it with being sociable, open, lively, agreeable, generous, and frank, among other positive attributes. And the French would not be this way without "a certain point of honor" (XIX.5.558–59). Honor is a powerful motivating force.

And yet, this honor is not without its problems. For one, Montesquieu calls it "false": "it is true that, philosophically speaking, it is a false honor that drives all the parts of the state; but this false honor is as useful to the public, as the true one would be to individuals who could have it" (III.7.257). Based on this formulation and other aspects of his discussion, some commentators interpret Montesquieu to be critical of honor.[61] Montesquieu certainly does not see honor as an unqualified good. He even sees it as false in some way. Montesquieu nonetheless was undeterred in his general support of honor. He cares most—maybe only—about the practical and political benefits of honor; and we have demonstrated that it proves effective on these counts. Other, more significant problems surround honor, though.

War and conquest are two prominent means to act "honorably." The battlefield represents perhaps *the* primary means for nobles to distinguish themselves. Crillon, Montesquieu's emblematic honorable man, did so, while setting the terms for just combat. Honor and war are tied closely together. "Honor," Montesquieu explains, "permits chivalry when it is united with the idea of sentiments of the heart, or the idea of conquest" (IV.2.262). The pursuit of honor thus seems to support, perhaps even promote, conquest. The gaze toward acquiring honor in this way can become singular. In monarchies men of war might "only have glory as their goal," rather than simply honor or fortune (V.19.304). Nobles' status often necessitated that they lead men to and in war. Because of the force they wield, Montesquieu insists that nobles who pursue honor in this manner should not be able to hold civil offices at the same time. Indeed, civil magistrates must contain the nobles. The nobles, who check the king, also must be checked. Montesquieu certainly does not want the state going to war to attain glory. This was one of his most significant critiques of Louis XIV's France. Glory and conquest can destroy honor's good effects.

Honor becomes corrupt when the nobility loses its independence and becomes attached or subservient to the monarch. The monarch can diminish the nobility's power through the offer of offices and honor. This attaches the nobility to the monarch, thus making it unable to check the king, because its power is attached to his. What's more, nobles increasingly pursue titles and status rather than engaging in honorable actions. They begin to act with "infamy," while cloaking such action in "dignities" (VIII.7.355). Rather than checking the monarch, these dignities thrust them into a position of "servitude." The nobles lose the respect of the people, and become nothing more than "vile instruments of arbitrary power" (VIII.7.355). Such behavior, Montesquieu insists, is contrary to the needs of one's "homeland" (*patrie*). It therefore is imperative that the nobles see themselves as a check on the monarch, and not as his underlings who must be subservient to his will. Otherwise, the state risks becoming absolutist or even despotic.

Monarchies risk devolving into despotism (VIII.17.364). The threat is real, and the transition can occur quickly and in various ways. The general cause is the monarch's desire to increase his power. To do so, he judges that he must change the order of things. He removes the "natural functions" of groups and institutions that check his power and arbitrarily gives these functions to others. He pursues these ends by destroying honor and the powers of the nobility. He also works to remove the powers, prerogatives, and privileges of the towns (VIII.6.354). By rendering local power, especially the *parlements*, largely irrelevant, one more check on his power dissipates. At the same time as he destroys these other power centers, he works to locate power exclusively in his capital and, eventually, in himself. The effect of this shifting of power is to "call the State to his capital, the capital to his court, and the court to his person" (VIII.6.355). This allows the monarch to become infatuated with his "fantasies," and the situation becomes grim. Montesquieu clearly has Louis XIV in mind here. Louis's governing philosophy was "*L'État, c'est moi.*" He worked to locate as much power as possible in his person, palace and court in Versailles. Montesquieu also discusses these concerns at length in his *Réflexions sur la monarchie universelle*. Monarchy can devolve into absolutism, which in turn devolves into despotism. The difference between absolutism and despotism is that the former seeks primarily to control the public, political sphere; it leaves some space in the private sphere. It does not try to instill fear in everyone. Despotism is totalizing in its attempts to make inhabitants fully fearful. It is precisely because of the potential for monarchy to slide into despotism that Montesquieu insists on strong bulwarks against the monarch's powers. Do the people have a role to play in any of this?

Montesquieu encourages the people—but not the nobility—to embrace the bourgeois virtues. They represent, first and foremost, the best way for individuals to provide for themselves and their families. Commerce and trade are powerful mechanisms through which the people can advance themselves. Indeed, as we will see in chapter 4, commerce is necessary for monarchies to prosper. "It is necessary," Montesquieu explains, "that the laws favor all the commerce that the constitution of this government can give it; so that the subjects can, without perishing, always satisfy the reemerging needs of the prince and his court" (V.9.289). We see here the mixed nature of the commercial enterprise. The monarch sees the riches that emerge as a means of increasing his own wealth and power. Even still, commerce remains the most effective way the people can advance themselves not only economically, but politically too. Commercial success eventually can open the door to them gaining a say in political affairs. If they become rich enough, they can purchase a title of nobility. In so doing, they choose to stop their pursuit of commercial wealth. Instead, they embrace luxury.

Can the people embrace honor? On one reading, the answer would seem to be no, they cannot. Montesquieu describes honor as being attached to privileges and distinctions, which are reserved for the nobles. If honor is inaccessible to non-nobles, then the sphere of politics in monarchies shrinks markedly. Krause has, however, suggested a more inclusive and more robust reading of Montesquieuian honor. She has described the actions of actors like Martin Luther King Jr. as being driven by honor.[62] Her compelling reading of honor, traced back to Montesquieu, significantly opens up the sphere of politics in monarchies and elsewhere.

Let us consider one final point about maintaining the balance of power in monarchies. Monarchies must be of medium size. If one were too small, it would become a republic. If it were too large, the "principal men of the state, great by themselves, not being under the eyes of the prince, having their court outside his court, assured moreover against the prompt executions by the laws and by the *mœurs*, could cease to obey" (VIII.17.363). The concern is that these principal men will become separate power centers divorced from the state. They become, in turn, interested in pursuing only their own interests, even if those interests clearly are against those of the state.

Legislators must determine whether and how the structures and practices of monarchy can promote security, liberty, and prosperity in their particular place. Certainly, a legislator can do this most completely if the state already is a monarchy. The key then becomes making institutions robust enough, and making honor powerful enough, to promote moderate governance. One possible model of such balanced monarchy may have been the old French Estates General sharing legislative power with the monarch.[63] "In addition to fixed and fundamental laws, various customs, social codes, religious norms, and political forms protect the honor, fortune, life, and liberty of citizens by moderating the ambitions of princes and ensuring that things are rarely carried to excess."[64] If a state is not a monarchy, then all of the politics of monarchy will be hard to implement, because establishing a monarchy, in Montesquieu's time or today, is rather difficult. However, many of the other structures beyond the person of the monarch remain available to legislators as they seek moderate political outcomes. For example, Krause has shown that Montesquieu's honor is compatible with liberalism.[65] The nobility have a role to play in Montesquieu's account of aristocratic and federal republics, as well as in mixed regimes. The value of monarchical institutions thus goes well beyond the confines of monarchical regimes. The means monarchy provides for checking power can improve the politics of many places.

Aristocracy

Generally speaking, scholars overlook Montesquieu's discussion of aristocracy.[66] To the extent that they have treated aristocracy, scholars judge Montesquieu to be negatively disposed toward this form of government.[67] David Carrithers, in the only extended treatment of this theme in Montesquieu's thought, focuses on the city of Venice to show that Montesquieu was critical of aristocratic republics.[68] Carrithers is right that Montesquieu expresses important reservations about Venice, both in *EL* and earlier in his *Voyage de Gratz à la Haye* (OCI.544–93). There are, however, three key reasons why Montesquieu judges aristocracies as able to promote security, liberty, and prosperity. First, they have moderation as their spring. Second, numerous aristocratic republics, or states with strong aristocratic elements, like Rome, Geneva, and Venice, survived—and thrived—for a long time.[69] Third, and crucially, Montesquieu's usage of the term "aristocracy" is not what it first seems in *EL*; instead, it is closer to what we might characterize as meritocracy.

Elsewhere I have discussed the concept of aristocracy and some of its developments.[70] The term "aristocracy" derives from the Greek *aristokratia*, with *aristos* meaning "excellent" and *kratos* meaning "power." An important debate has centered on how to define the *aristoi*. Historically, one usually attained aristocratic status through birth, though it also was possible to purchase noble titles. In Montesquieu's discussion of aristocracy, he turns instead to a more philosophical understanding of the "best." Aristotle, in his *Politics*, defines the best in aristocracy as those who either are best at ruling, or those who rule "with a view to what is best for the city and those who participate in it."[71] One can interpret Plato's recommendation that philosopher kings rule as arguing for the same political structure.

Montesquieu's understanding of how an aristocracy should function follows in this philosophical vein. He seeks to identify a natural aristocracy comprised of those men and women who are best at ruling. The key virtue they must possess is moderation. By associating the *aristoi* with merit, in contrast to the hereditary nature of this group in his native France, Montesquieu works to get the natural aristocracy to rule. Montesquieu understands that selecting good legislators dramatically increases the chances of having a good political order. As long as political power is not hereditary but is, instead, earned through merit, aristocracy can comprise a good political order. To be sure, he sees a place for hereditary nobility, especially in monarchy.[72] In aristocracies, though, the "best" leaders generally are those chosen based not on birth but on their merit.

Initially, Montesquieu seems to offer a traditional understanding of who rules in aristocracy. He writes that in an aristocracy, "sovereign power is in the hands of a part of the people" (II.2.239). A "certain number of persons

... make the laws and execute them; and the rest of the people is nothing more in their regard than, in a monarchy, the subjects are with regards to the monarch" (II.3.244). It seems that the people who rule are "certain families" who have sovereign power. Elsewhere he references "aristocratic families" who rule (II.4.247).[73] These unsurprising remarks suggest a traditional understanding of aristocracy, in line with historical examples like Venice. However, Montesquieu explicitly states that "extreme corruption" arises in aristocracies "when the nobles become hereditary." When this occurs, the noble rulers cannot embrace moderation (VIII.5.353). Montesquieu's goal is to promote a moderate political order. The hereditary transfer of power is destructive to this end. As such, Montesquieu cannot support aristocratic rulers acquiring their office by hereditary means. Instead, he offers an alternative understanding of aristocracy as rule by the best few.

Aristocracies should strive for higher levels of inclusion regarding who participates in politics.[74] "The best aristocracy is that where the part of the people who does not have a part of the power, is so small and so poor, that the dominant part has no interest in oppressing it" (II.3.246). Montesquieu wants the number of people excluded from having any kind of power to be small.[75] He accepts excluding some people because he questions the extent to which they can contribute sufficiently.[76] But those who partake in politics should protect the interests of the excluded few. Montesquieu affirms fairly broad participation because he thinks it helps bring better rulers to power. More than just allowing a broader swathe of the people to help select leaders, Montesquieu advocates for allowing the people to take up elected office. He explains that aristocracies become more perfect when the rulers—the "aristocratic families"—are "of the people as much as possible" (II.3.247). By contrast, the "most imperfect" aristocracy of all is that in which "the part of the people who obeys, is in civil slavery to those who command, like the aristocracy of Poland, where the peasants are slaves of the nobility" (II.3.247). To avoid not only this kind of "civil slavery," but the establishment of a corrupt aristocratic political system, Montesquieu proposes opening up significantly who can hold office in aristocracies. Rather than passing power on through generations, Montesquieu wants rulers to come from the people and acquire office through elections.

Elections check the rulers. This represents one of the more important differences between aristocratic and monarchic nobles.[77] The people should get to vote to select the best people based on merit. Voting is the only legitimate means for coming to power. Senators, for example, cannot simply replace departing colleagues with people of their choosing (II.3.245). It is true that their choices are constrained to those who are capable of ruling, but Montesquieu means to open this group up substantially. Voting represents an important check. And this check is regular, as the law should mandate term limits of one year (II.3.246). The people therefore get a regular say in political affairs, which produces better outcomes. In his *Voyage en Hollande* Montesquieu writes: "The city of Amsterdam is an aristocracy, but the most sensible kind of aristocracy: the people are governed by a small number of persons, but they do not get there via jure hereditario, but by election" (OCI.872). Election through merit thus is a key mechanism for aristocracies to flourish. Still, the aristocrats need moral and external checks.

Aristocracy's principle is different from political virtue, which is "singularly connected with democracies" (IV.5.267). Aristocracies rely, instead, on moderation. Moderation is a "lesser virtue . . . that renders the nobles at least equal to each other, and allows for their preservation. *Moderation* therefore is the soul of these governments. I intend that which is founded on virtue, not that which comes from a cowardice and a laziness of soul" (III.4.254). That this virtue is "lesser" is preferable, because the seemingly "higher" virtue of democracies is undesirable and unattainable. Montesquieu elaborates on this moderation:

> But as it is rare to find much virtue where men's fortunes are so unequal, the laws must tend to give, as much as they can, a *esprit* of moderation, and they must seek to reestablish the equality necessarily taken away by the constitution of the state.
>
> The *esprit* of moderation is what is called virtue in aristocracy; there it takes the place of the spirit of equality in the popular state.
>
> If the pomp and splendor surrounding kings is part of their power, modesty and simplicity of manners are the strength of nobles in an aristocracy. When the nobles affect no distinction, when they blend with the people, dress like them, and share all their pleasures with them, the people forget their own weakness. (V.8.284)

Aristocratic moderation is robust. The very identification of moderation as aristocracy's principle is significant, given the central importance of moderation for Montesquieu. Anytime Montesquieu speaks of something in relation to moderation in such terms, we must pay special attention to it. Aristocratic moderation seems to be founded on a kind of virtue associated more closely with the cardinal virtues—moderation, wisdom, justice, and courage. The rulers' rejection of "cowardice" and "faintheartedness" resembles courage. The embrace of modesty and simplicity of manners, along with rejection of "pomp and splendor," approximates moderation. Rejecting "laziness of soul" in favor of physical and intellectual industriousness helps the rulers become wiser. Since the achievement of this aristocratic virtue is "rare" when men's fortunes are so unequal, rulers favor outcomes that benefit others too. When aristocratic rulers act in accordance with these principles, they are wiser, and their actions and outcomes are more just. By masking the superiority of the nobles over the populace, the *esprit* of moderation also can make the common people more supportive of the government, "thereby enabling aristocratic republics to avoid substantial friction between rulers and those who are ruled."[78] While an important check on the rulers, this moderation remains insufficient for containing them. Additional checks are necessary.

The government needs checks on the aristocrats: "It is necessary that there is, for a time or always, a magistrate who makes the nobles tremble, as the ephores did in Lacedemonia, and the inquisitors did in Venice, magistracies that are not submitted to any formalities. This government needs sufficiently violent springs" (V.8.287).[79] Since aristocrats will not always check themselves, other institutions like the ones Montesquieu mentions here are necessary. Other options exist. External enemies can refocus the rulers on being virtuous and moderate. An aristocratic republic must "dread" (*redoute*) something. Fear of the Persians maintained the laws in Greece; mutual intimidation between Carthage and Rome served the same purpose. "Singular thing!" Montesquieu remarks: "The more security these states have, the more, like water that is too tranquil, they are subject to becoming corrupt" (VIII.5.354). The aristocrats must feel insecure in various ways in order to remain vigilant and work more effectively toward good political outcomes. Moderate virtue alone does not establish the strong culture of accountability necessary for aristocracies to function and flourish.

While aristocratic rulers must remain moderate and virtuous, the same is not true of citizens. "It is true," Montesquieu remarks, that virtue "is not absolutely required" in aristocracies (III.4.254). This is primarily true of the people, who need not embrace this moderation. They have "less need of virtue" (III.4.254). Instead of striving to be virtuous, the people should focus their energy on commerce.

Commerce allows citizens in an aristocracy to better themselves materially, thus promoting prosperity. In an aristocracy it is "necessary that the laws defend commerce." The rulers must not be allowed to engage in commerce, because they would establish monopolies to benefit themselves. This gives significant power to the people. "Commerce is the profession of equals; and, among despotic states, the most miserable are those where the prince is merchant" (V.8.286). Those who do not rule are the economic engines of the society. This critical role affords them great power. What's more, Montesquieu insists here on the distribution of power between rulers and ruled: the rulers wield political power, while the ruled wield economic power. The distribution of resources arises as a vital check on power.

Certain kinds of inequality can derail an aristocratic republic. The "two principal sources of disorder" in aristocracies are inequality between rulers and ruled, and inequality among those who govern. "From these two inequalities result the hates and jealousies that the laws must prevent or stop" (V.8.284). The first inequality arises from the privileges of the rulers that bring shame to the people. His example is a Roman law that prohibited patricians from marrying plebeians. It had the effect of making patricians both haughtier and more odious. It is harmful for aristocratic rulers to try to separate themselves from the people. The second inequality, between rulers and ruled, arises when the rulers make different financial laws for themselves. Examples include when the aristocrats give themselves the privilege of not paying various charges, when they are fraudulent, and when they take from the people (V.8.285). Montesquieu concludes therefore that it is "above all essential, in aristocracy, that the nobles not levy taxes. . . . The nobles would be like the princes of despotic states, who confiscate the goods that please them" (V.8.286). Montesquieu's suggestion here implies that aristocratic rulers will not be making all of the laws, at least not those related to taxation. It is thus necessary to have additional institutions that fulfill the functions aristocrats cannot or should not.

Aristocratic rulers need to feel and be distinguished in some way. But this cannot be in economic terms. It would be destructive to the state if they were to enrich themselves financially through their office. The state should ensure that the rulers have only moderate financial wealth. Rulers should not be extremely poor or wealthy. If they were extremely wealthy, they would have too much power. If they were extremely poor, they would have an incentive to use their office to their personal benefit. Mechanisms like paying their debts can help prevent them from becoming too impoverished (V.8.287). An aristocracy is "poorly constituted," Montesquieu thinks, when the rulers control wealth. Luxury "is contrary to the *esprit* of moderation and should be banned there" (VII.3.335). The rulers should not be allowed to acquire too much wealth (though Montesquieu does not specify how to prevent this). Rather than distinguishing themselves through financial largesse, Montesquieu thinks that aristocratic rulers become distinguished through the honors they receive from ruling well.

In contrast to the three previous forms of government, Montesquieu does not identify a specific kind of education necessary to get political actors to adopt the principle of the government, in this case moderation. A state does not need to indoctrinate citizens with this kind of virtue, in contrast to the political virtue of democracies. It seems that aristocratic education most closely resembles the social education nobles acquire in monarchies. Aristocratic nobles must develop qualities that show them to be part of the natural *aristoi*.

Our discussion here has established that Montesquieu viewed aristocratic republics as capable of supplying good politics to a place. Carrithers does rightly point to some of the concerns Montesquieu had about aristocratic republics, above all Venice. But Carrithers also identifies and acknowledges various good characteristics Montesquieu found in aristocratic republics, even Venice.[80] Not the least of these features was the Venetian Republic's longevity and relative stability, both praiseworthy attributes.

Aristocratic republics, understood in the sense we have presented here, have broader appeal and more to offer our discussion about establishing a good political order than do traditional aristocracies. The establishment and maintenance of traditional aristocracies is limited to states that have an aristocracy, or where one could be established. Meritocratic aristocratic republics, by contrast, are available as options to a wider swathe of states because the key pillar of these regimes is the existence of a class of people capable of ruling well. Thomas Jefferson would later argue that there is a "natural aristocracy among men. The grounds of this are virtue and talents.... The natural aristocracy I consider the most precious gift of nature for instruction, the trusts, and government of society."[81] The reliance on merit also found in Montesquieu injects a heightened sense of the need for quality rulers into the equation of selecting political actors. The best, understood as the most competent and capable, should rule. Meritocratic aristocracies have more to offer various states than readers of Montesquieu might be inclined to think. The federal republic appears as more promising still.

The Federal Republic

Montesquieu holds the federal republic up as an especially promising way for states to organize themselves.[82] His discussion of this "form of government" centers on determining whether federal republican institutions can form a good political order.[83]

Montesquieu is sanguine about the federal republic as a form of government because it can secure states from external and internal threats effectively, maybe even more so than republics, monarchies, and despotisms. "If a republic is small, it is destroyed by a foreign force; if it is large, it is destroyed by an internal vice" (IX.3.369). No matter its size, a republic seems to face a grave problem. Democracies and aristocracies alike are afflicted: "the evil is in the thing itself; there is no form that can remedy it there" (IX.3.369). Monarchies are large enough to secure themselves against external threats, but their *esprit* of "war and expansion" endangers their security (IX.2.371). Despotisms provide neither internal nor external security to citizens, as they instill fear in all their subjects and "sacrifice a part of the country, ravage the frontiers, and leave them deserted" in order to try to secure the capital (IX.4.372). By contrast, a federal republic allows states to have "the internal advantages of republican government, and the external force of monarchy" (IX.1.369).

Federal republics gain protection from external threats because they are larger and more forceful than republics, and from internal threats because smaller member states can tend better to local needs. Montesquieu's investigation and examples of ancient (Greece and Rome) and modern (Holland, Germany, and Switzerland) federal republics show that he considered them unified societies, not mere defensive arrangements. We will pay particular attention to Montesquieu's analysis of the case of Holland because it allows us to see more clearly why he developed a positive opinion of this form of government.

Federal republics are durable, and can achieve and maintain security and freedom. Three modern federal republics—Holland, Germany, and the Swiss Leagues—"are regarded in Europe as eternal republics" (IX.1.370). Montesquieu does not tell us who regards them as such; perhaps he is repeating a commonplace.[84] This is the only place in *EL* where he speaks of a state potentially being eternal, in his or anyone else's view.[85] Even if Montesquieu does not share this opinion, simply stating it is significant. At a minimum, we know that he views federal republics favorably. "This sort of republic, capable of resisting external force, can maintain itself in its size without corrupting itself internally: the form of this society *prevents all inconveniences*" (IX.1.370; emphasis added). This statement refers to more than just the inconveniences related to size. He explains: "if some abuses introduce themselves into one part, they are corrected by the healthy parts" (IX.1.370). This claim is significant indeed. Member states can correct the errors of other members. This decreases the chances that a federal republic becomes corrupt.

A "federative constitution," Montesquieu writes, "must be composed of states of the same nature above all republican states" (IX.2.371). The *esprit* of republics, according to Montesquieu, is "that of peace and moderation," whereas the *esprit* of monarchies is "that of war and expansion" (IX.2.371). In his study of German states, Montesquieu sees problems emerging when republics and small states "subject to princes" unify. When a federal republic consists of monarchies and republics, the union "can only subsist by a manner of force in a federal republic" (IX.2.371). This fundamentally undermines the peaceful nature of the union. "Experience has shown" that Holland and Switzerland, both composed entirely of republics, have a superior approach (IX.2.371). Montesquieu posits that members will interact peacefully with one another. However this may be, it is not necessarily true in their relations with other states. The Dutch frequently were at war (though often not by their own choosing), and the Swiss served as the mercenaries of Europe for a long time. Perhaps he means that the Swiss and Dutch were more peaceful and less aggressive than monarchical counterparts like France. In the Dutch case, Montesquieu does identify particular structures that made Holland (more) peaceful and secure.

The Dutch promote peace by requiring that one province obtain the consent of all the others before making an alliance.[86] This preventative mechanism is another reason Montesquieu prefers the Dutch model to the German. Montesquieu considers this a "very good law, and necessary all the same in the federal republic. It is missing in the German constitution, where it would prevent the misfortunes that can happen to all the members, by imprudence, by ambition, or the avarice of one" (IX.3.371–72). By requiring all member states to approve the formation of an alliance by one member, each member state has the power to prevent others from acting contrary to its interests or the interests of the federation. This structure seems to flow from the deep nature of the Dutch political union, in which all members seek to act in the interest of the union. A republic like Holland "that unites itself by a political confederation has given itself entirely, and has nothing else to give" (IX.3.372). The Dutch make this union more effective through their schemes of representation among members and between citizens and the state.

Federal republics must separate power among themselves effectively. This requires multiple mechanisms. One such mechanism is a federal assembly, which allows members to discuss, vote on, and adjudicate matters. They must determine whether to assign an equal or unequal number of votes. In Holland, all seven provinces had one vote.[87] In Lycia, an ancient federal republic, the twenty-three towns each had one, two, or three votes depending on their size. Montesquieu elaborates:

> The towns of Lycia paid the expenses according to their votes. The provinces of Holland cannot follow this proportion; they must follow that of their power.
> In Lycia, the judges and the magistrates of the towns were elected by common council, and according to the proportion that we have said. In the republic of Holland, they are not elected by common council, and each town names its magistrates. If it was necessary to give a model of a beautiful federal republic, I would take that of Lycia. (IX.3.372)

Montesquieu prefers the Lycian scheme. One reason is his apparent approval of the council of the confederation appointing the magistrates of the towns. Another reason is their proportionate distribution of votes. He finds it problematic that Holland does not assign votes based on the power of each province, especially in the case of Amsterdam, which is more powerful and much wealthier.[88] The Dutch political system is, in this sense, out of whack. Despite this, Montesquieu's politics of place impels him to refrain both from condemning the Dutch system and from recommending significant changes. His reservations about Amsterdam being underrepresented notwithstanding, the Dutch system seems to function well enough at a basic level.

A federal republic must form a significant yet carefully calibrated union in order to be successful. It is a political order in which "many Body politics consent to become citizens of a larger state that they want to form. It is a society of societies, that makes a new one, which can grow by new associates that unite with it" (IX.1.369). "A republic," Montesquieu explains, "that unifies itself through a political confederation has given itself over entirely, and has nothing more to give" (IX.3.372). In order to form this significant union, the federal republic needs a similar *esprit* and a strong political leader.

Member states need to share an *esprit* to confederate successfully. Montesquieu never states this explicitly. But his examples, and the nature of his discussion, confirm it. The Dutch shared *mœurs*, religion, a language, history, and commercial interests before formally forming a federal republic in the sixteenth century. Much the same is true for the Swiss, with the exception of language, and for the Germans, except that Germany did not exist formally until later. While Rome stayed inside Italy, member states also shared a similar religion, *mœurs*, history, and language, even before sharing political institutions. In Greece two alliances in the Peloponnesian War tended to divide (though not perfectly) between oligarchies with Sparta and democracies with Athens, so each alliance shared a political system. If the *esprits* of member states are too different—if their values, priorities, laws, institutions, and so on conflict—then the viability of the confederation comes into question and under threat. As I have argued elsewhere, this remains true today. We need only look at the problems facing the European Union to see that when states differ on these important issues, it is more challenging to form and maintain a cohesive and effective political union.[89] While sharing elements of an *esprit* might almost be a necessary condition, it is not sufficient. It assists in the formation of a functioning political union, but it does not serve as a guarantee. Other factors also are key.

Federal republics need an effective executive, because arriving at decisions collectively can prove quite difficult. Member states sometimes have divergent interests. Policymaking can become a tempestuous affair. Moreover, some members are bigger and stronger than others, which presents the possibility that they will strong-arm weaker members. Some issues, such as making war and bringing in new members, should require unanimous consent. These sorts of problems highlight the need for a political leader to help guide the federal republic. Despite its problems, the German federal republic "subsists because it has a leader [*chef*], who is in some way the magistrate of the union, and in some way the monarch" (IX.2.371).

Montesquieu's early discussion of the Dutch stadholder illustrates the utility of an executive to lead a federal republic.

The stadholder was an executive head of state with limited though important authority. Technically, each Dutch province had its own stadholder. But the provinces often elected the same person to be stadholder over multiple or all provinces. Stadholders were central figures in Dutch history. The first stadholder, William I of Orange, led the revolt against despotic Spanish rule in 1581 (when the Act of Abjuration was issued). William III of Orange countered Louis XIV's aggression until William's death in 1702, but he was the last stadholder for nearly fifty years.

Montesquieu shows, in both *MP* and *Voyage en Hollande,* that the stadholder serves a crucial executive function and checks other powers within and beyond the state.[90] The office is so important that, according to Montesquieu, the Dutch "republic will never rise again without a stadholder" (OCI.872).[91] The stadholder's absence from 1650 to 1672 and from 1702 to 1747 was problematic because he provides leadership, commands the army, and checks various powers. In *MP* Montesquieu contends that the stadholder helps preserve freedom in Holland by checking local magistrates: "'If there were not a king in England, the English would be less free.' This proves itself with Holland, where the peoples are more enslaved since there is no longer a stadholder: all of the magistrates of each town, small tyrants" (OCI.1402).[92] Montesquieu notes that the "leader of republics is a civil magistrate. Chance and necessity gave a stadholder to Holland, and it [Holland] did great things" (OCI.1435).

The stadholder was a crucial component of the separation of powers in Holland. And this office was distinct from other executive institutions like those in France and England. The stadholder helped promote a free political order. The stadholder was an important decision-maker. Masterson suggests that Montesquieu thought the stadholder made the republic more efficient, protected liberty, and prevented exploitation from the oligarchs.[93] The stadholder corrected the oppression of the mercantile oligarchs by mitigating their harmful actions. Masterson also shows that Montesquieu viewed the stadholder "more as a republican magistracy than as a monarchic institution."[94] The electoral competition to become executive, which did not exist in other European states, fostered a kind of virtue among the stadholders, making them better rulers and making them serve the interests of member states and citizens. The stadholder made the state more moderate by discouraging "abuse of power by the magistracy."[95] Montesquieu views local magistrates negatively, as they give little to the public (OCI.872); hence the importance of the stadholder checking the magistrates of each town. The stadholder combats these various harms and is a key player in the Dutch system of checks and balances.[96]

Montesquieu continued to think that Holland could never rise again without a stadholder. But a surprising turn of events in April 1747 caused him to remove all mention of the stadholder from *EL*. A little more than one year before Montesquieu published *EL* (after nearly twenty years of work and reflection), the Dutch restored the stadholderate in response to the French invasion of Holland. Montesquieu feared that his pages on the stadholder could jeopardize his safety in France. In a letter to Guasco, in July 1747, he writes: "I will tell you that I have judged by the way to remove, for the present, the chapter on the stadholderate; in the present circumstances it perhaps would have been poorly received in France" (*Œuvres complètes de Montesquieu*, 1093–94). No record remains of what Montesquieu intended to say about the stadholder. But the content must have been weighty and positive enough to cause quite a stir; brief or negative comments were unlikely to be "poorly received."[97] The stadholder frequently defeated France on the battlefield. The office represented a real rival to the French king. Montesquieu therefore deemed it prudent to remove all mention of the office, especially because its restoration ameliorated one of Holland's main institutional faults. He therefore had to make his point about the importance of an executive in other ways. He did so in his brief discussion of the executive in the German federal republic, and in his considerations of the executive in monarchies and England's mixed regime.

Federal structures can improve the politics of various places. The most natural fit for federal structures is among republics with similar *esprits*. Contemporary examples include the United States, Germany, Switzerland, Canada, and Holland. But Montesquieu's discussion offers much more to legislators seeking to promote moderate political orders. Even if a country cannot form a confederation out of its different regions, it can benefit greatly by dispersing power across the country. This option has appeal to a wide range of states. Consider his critical remark about France: "In the past each village of France was a capital; today there is only a great one: each part of the State was a center of power; today everything is related to a center; and this center is, so to speak, the State itself" (XXIII.24.709–10). Montesquieu sees this development as deeply problematic. He prefers the time in France when regions, with their *parlements*, had significant power over local affairs; he laments the centralization of power that occurred especially during the reign of Louis XIV. Centralized power often becomes unwieldy and dangerous. Montesquieu thus thinks that prying power from the grip of the capital and dispersing power to different regions helps check the powers of the national government. Legislators have additional reasons to find the establishment of federal structures appealing. The deliberation and consent required to make decisions promote careful, moderate outcomes. The election of the executive opens up the possibility of bringing deserving candidates into this office. Holland's specific executive, the stadholder, clearly is quite different from other European executives in Montesquieu's time.

But not all states can make good use of federal structures. Despotisms never can confederate because they maintain their security by war and expansion, or by walling themselves off from outsiders. They are too repressive and aggressive to form a deep, permanent union with another state. Monarchies cannot confederate because their *esprit* is that of war and expansion.[98] Their proclivity to make war would draw in other members to conflicts. And since each monarchy would have its own executive, cooperation would prove difficult. Tensions among the members might eventually lead them to attack each other. States with republican elements therefore are the only candidates for confederating successfully. But not all republican states. Ancient democratic republics can confederate only when the larger state they form shares the same values they have been inculcated to embrace since birth. It already is a painful thing to be indoctrinated to love a particular homeland; learning to love another, different homeland would be harder still. The republic also cannot be warlike. The *esprit* of a republic should be that of peace and moderation. But warlike republics such as Rome and Sparta acquired through conquest. Holland, by contrast, was commercial, which helped that federal republic endure.

Although he does not discuss them explicitly, local governments represent an additional means to protect liberty. The distribution of power between the central government and member states helps to protect liberty by making sure neither the central government nor the states become too powerful. Further vertical distribution of powers can provide another layer of protection for liberty. Towns and cities, for example, can act as a bulwark against state power in particular, but also centralized power. In some cases this additional layer will be effective and important.

Montesquieu's discussion of the federal republic also opens up the politics of place as a mode of analysis. His discussion proceeds in a different manner than his considerations of despotisms, monarchies, democracies, and aristocracies. He identifies neither a nature nor a principle for the federal republic; citizens of these states thus may not be required to embrace a particular spring for that state to be secure, free, and prosperous. Subsequently, Montesquieu does not suggest that a certain kind of education is required in federal republics; nor does he point to certain criminal laws to reinforce such an education. He does not specify how federal republics become corrupt either. So they at least do not seem to have one clear path to corruption. Montesquieu thus makes his politics of place broader and less rigid. The categories from part I remain useful, but they also have clear limitations. Those categories certainly do not apply to all societies. Instead, the politics of place must maintain a crucial element of flexibility.

Montesquieu's discussion of England, which also does not fit into his analysis from part I, further confirms this need for flexibility.

The Mixed Regime

Many scholars interpret Montesquieu as judging the English (mixed) regime to be the best. These scholars see his discussion of England in books XI and XIX, along with his other, scattered comments about England, as proof that he thought the English had discerned and implemented the best political order. Paul Rahe and Thomas Pangle powerfully present these interpretations.[99] On their readings, Montesquieu is a kind of universalist. Pangle proclaims, for example, that Montesquieu thought the "English constitution affords the *best guarantee*" for protecting liberty and security "through a system of checks and balances among king, nobles and populace, each embodied, or represented in separate institutions that are defined by distinct if overlapping governmental functions."[100] On this interpretation, Montesquieu recommends that other states adopt the English model so far as possible. To the extent that they do not resemble this model, they are inferior, perhaps even bad.

There are good reasons for reading Montesquieu as preferring the English model. He says the English constitution has political liberty for its "direct goal." He will "examine the principles on which it [the constitution] founds it [liberty]. If they [the principles] are good, liberty will appear there as in a mirror" (XI.5.396). He notes later that the English are "the people of the world who have known best how to let three great things prevail at once: religion, commerce, and liberty" (XX.7.590).

And yet, the position that Montesquieu views the English regime as best ultimately is untenable.[101] Montesquieu certainly holds up England's political order as good. But he does not hold it up as unquestionably good. He expresses deep concerns about English politics and society. Montesquieu, who is a proponent of moderation in all things, calls England's political liberty "extreme"; that is, immoderate (XI.6.407). He even predicts that this nation "will lose its liberty, it will perish" one day. In his other extended discussion of England, in XIX, 27, Montesquieu presents a dim, critical understanding of the apparently dour English and their society. Rahe insightfully investigates the grim nature of the *inquiétude* that Montesquieu thinks permeates English society.[102] In light of Montesquieu's numerous reservations about England, coupled with his particularism, we cannot conclude that he viewed England as best. He certainly did not think the English model was universally applicable. Rather, he viewed England's mixed regime as one example of a good political order that distributed powers successfully, allowing it to protect security, liberty, and prosperity. As such, we will consider how English practices can be useful to legislators working in diverse places.

Montesquieu's discussion of the English constitution establishes firmly the need to distribute power among political institutions in order to protect liberty. Recall that Montesquieu seeks to distribute, not separate, power. In book XI he offers a new way to distribute power: among three branches of government. He also holds up elections and the military as other institutions that check power. As we explore these institutions, our focus will be on what is "free" and good about them, rather than what is "English" about them.

Distributing political power among three branches can protect political liberty effectively. The legislative branch makes the laws, "for a time or forever, and corrects or repeals those which are made." The executive branch is tasked primarily with managing security from external and internal threats. This branch "makes peace or war, sends or receives ambassadors, establishes security, prevents invasions." The judiciary "punishes crimes, or judges the disagreements of individuals" (XI.6.396.397).[103] Each branch helps address multiple "problems of politics." The executive addresses conflict between states, and between state and person. The judiciary adjudicates conflict between persons, between person and state, and potentially between states, if the conflict goes through the legal system. The legislative branch makes the laws that govern relations between persons, between states, and between state and person.

Liberty comes under threat if one branch usurps the distinct powers or responsibilities of another branch. If legislative and executive powers are united, "there is no liberty" because political actors could make tyrannical laws, and then execute them tyrannically. If judicial and legislative powers are not separate, "power over the life and liberty of citizens would be arbitrary: because the judge would be legislator." By joining the judiciary with the executive, "the judge could have the force of an oppressor" (XI.6.397). "Everything would be lost," Montesquieu continues, "if the same man, or the same body of principal individuals, or nobles, or people, exercised these three powers" (XI.6.397). Montesquieu's general point is clear: the three powers must remain separate. But tucked inside this quotation is an important expression of his particularism, which shows he does not intend to speak only of England. Montesquieu opens power up to more groups in society. He identifies numerous people or bodies that can exercise power: the monarch, a legislative body, nobles, or the people. Each of these groups is capable of wielding political power in some of the branches. Montesquieu provides further proof that he has more than just England in mind. He speaks in the conditional voice throughout the chapter and rarely mentions England by name (except, admittedly, in the chapter's title). The same is true in XIX, 27.

THE POLITICAL VARIABLES   113

Montesquieu's insistence here on distributing power among the three branches does not appear to be absolute. He proceeds to note that in "the majority of kingdoms of Europe, the government is moderate, because the prince, which has the first two powers, leaves to his subjects the exercise of the third," that of judging (XI.6.397). This further reveals the particularistic nature of Montesquieu's recommendations. Preferably, the three branches should remain distinct. It is possible, however, for moderate government to exist when two powers are united.

The judicial branch must be built around the notion that one's person is "sacred" (*sacrée*), and therefore warrants rigorous protection. The judiciary is the place where the state guarantees or threatens an individual's security most immediately. Proceedings and procedures must be fair, and must be structured to protect liberty. Montesquieu therefore recommends dividing judicial power between judges and the people. Judges oversee proceedings and determine punishments. Penalties should be fixed so that judges work within clear confines when assigning punishments. But judges should not determine guilt. The power of judging should be given, instead, to "persons pulled from the people, in a certain time of the year by the manner prescribed by law, to form a tribunal that can last only as long as necessity requires" (XI.6.398). We call these tribunals juries. The formalities Montesquieu identifies here increase the chances that the judicial process is fair. Most importantly, juries must be composed of people of the same condition as the accused: "It is necessary that the judges be of the same condition as the accused, or his peers, so that he cannot be placed into the *esprit* that he has fallen into the hands of people inclined to do violence to him" (XI.6.399). Fairness again is the issue here. For example, the people are unlikely to judge the "great" (*les grands*) fairly, because the former harbor jealousy and envy toward the latter. The "great" therefore should judge the great.

The judiciary best protects liberty by not making its presence known in citizens' everyday lives. The power of the judiciary must not be felt or seen. "In this manner," he explains, "the power of judging, so terrible among men, being attached neither to a certain fact nor profession, becomes, so to speak, invisible and null. One does not have the judges continuously before their eyes; and one fears the magistracy, and not the magistrates" (XI.6.398).[104] The most effective way to build a legal system on the sanctity of the person, Montesquieu argues, is to have the judiciary wield its power carefully. Citizens cannot feel the gaze and power of the judiciary watching or hovering over them, waiting to punish them for alleged wrongdoings.

The notion that the judiciary should constitute a separate branch represents Montesquieu's most important contribution to theorizing about the separation of powers. John Locke, for example, earlier distinguished legislative from executive functions. Montesquieu, however, is the first political theorist to detail the benefits of separating the judiciary from the other two branches.[105]

The legislative branch wields the most power of the three branches, because it makes the laws the other branches must execute, interpret, and apply. The legislature thus needs additional checks on it. Montesquieu identifies two: elections and the separation of the legislature into two branches that operate differently.

Montesquieu argues that free states ought to provide individuals with representation and a say in affairs. Because each man has a "free soul," the "body of the people" should have "legislative power." "But as this is impossible in large states and is subject to many inconveniences in small ones, it is necessary that the people do through its representatives everything that they cannot do by themselves" (XI.6.399–400).[106] Rather than advocating direct democracy, Montesquieu argues for letting the people "give their voice" by choosing a representative in the lower house. He finds this to be a more effective way of managing political affairs, in part because representatives know best the needs of their home region and are more capable of discussing affairs (XI.6.400).[107] Elections serve as a check on rulers, as the people have the opportunity to remove underperforming officials. All citizens should be able to share their voice, except "those who are in such a state of baseness [*bassesse*], that they are reputed to not have a proper will" (XI.6.400). Montesquieu does not define "baseness," and so he does not clarify how restrictive he means his suggestion to be. A high bar would result in real restrictions on who can vote. However this may be, the people can vote for one branch, the lower house of the legislature. Only the lower branch can make, correct, or overturn laws, which he calls the "*faculty of enacting*" (XI.6.401).

The Dutch approach to individual representation gives people a voice, but less directly and less effectively than the English system. Montesquieu compares the two: "When the deputies, says Mr. Sidney very well, represent a body of the people, as in Holland, they must be accountable to those who have commissioned them; it is different when there are deputies by boroughs, as in England" (XI.6.400). "All the citizens," he continues, "in the diverse districts, must have the right to give their voice for choosing a representative themselves." In England, representatives should exercise independent discretion when representing a separate population within a state. In Holland, by contrast, a representative takes instructions from a distinct republic, including the republic's magistrate. Montesquieu appears to prefer the English approach. After all, in the same chapter he says that England's representatives are able to discuss the public business better than the people themselves.

Nevertheless, Montesquieu does not reject the Dutch approach. Rather, in the context of his politics of place it seems to be effective enough not to warrant significant changes. The Dutch should not adopt the English system, because the English system would not transfer properly. The English system does not fit the Dutch *esprit*. Montesquieu accepts that different models of representation are appropriate depending on the circumstances. A carefully selected lower branch may not be enough, though. An upper branch can play a critical role in adopting good laws.

A second, hereditary legislative branch can promote a good political order. Certain groups bring an alternative voice into the conversation about lawmaking:

> There are always in a State persons distinguished by birth, riches, or honors; but they were mixed among the people, and if they had only one voice like the others, common liberty would be their slavery, and they would have no interest in defending liberty, because the majority of resolutions would be against them. The part that they have in legislation thus should be proportionate to the other advantages they have in the state: that will happen if they form a body which has the right to stop the enterprises of the people, as the people have the right to stop theirs. (XI.6.400–401)

The second, upper legislative branch (which corresponds to England's House of Lords, as the first, lower branch corresponds to the House of Commons), gives a voice to intellectual and financial elites, as well as nobles and possibly other interests and groups. Because the nobles have neither the same interests nor the same passions as the people, "the legislative power should not be switched back to a simple organ, individual or unique assembly: it is necessary to entrust it in a complex organ, formed from heterogeneous and contentious elements and embodying the diversity of social positions."[108] Positions in this branch should be hereditary (XI.6.401). Montesquieu does not open this branch up to possibly being elected. This branch only has the faculty of preventing (*faculté d'empêcher*) or vetoing, which is the right to render resolutions "null." If the legislative institutions function properly, then they sometimes will work together to make laws, whereas in other instances they will have to work against the other to temper or stop its misguided policies and passions, as well as those of the executive.

Given that Montesquieu is speaking of the English constitution, we might easily conclude that he intends for the executive to be a monarch. Indeed, he specifically says, "executive power should be in the hands of a monarch" (XI.6.401). However, Montesquieu opens the possibility of an elected magistrate being the executive. At the beginning of XI, 6, when he defines the broad roles of each power, he specifically speaks of both a prince and a "magistrate" potentially filling the executive function.

When he explains the nature of the executive, his reasoning clearly supports numerous options. Consider what follows the previous quotation: "Executive power should be in the hands of a monarch, because this part of the government, which almost always needs momentary action, is better administered by one than by many" (XI.6.401–2). An executive needs to be able to act quickly and forcefully, especially when tending to security from external threats, as in the case of invasion. The executive's primary function is to establish security from external and internal threats. But Montesquieu never says that a monarch is the only person suitable to do so. He only insists that the executive be capable of providing for security. Whereas he maintains that the upper house of the legislature should be hereditary, he never mentions the executive being hereditary. Montesquieu's early discussions of the stadholder in *MP* and *Voyage en Hollande* reveal that he recognizes that elected executives can rule effectively too. We can understand quite well, then, why he chose to remove his potentially dangerous discussion of the stadholder: it presented a rival to the French method of selecting executives. Montesquieu clearly had to be careful about offering up the prospect of electing heads of state. His primary concern is that the executive can meet the security needs of the state, and he thinks monarchs and elected executives both can serve that function.

The executive is tasked with maintaining security and protecting liberty. He must be able to defend the state against external threats and so is responsible for conducting foreign affairs. But he also must be a bulwark against internal threats to liberty, especially the advances of the legislature. "If the executive power does not have the right to stop the enterprises of the legislative body, the latter will be despotic; because, as it will be able to give itself all the power that it can imagine, it will ruin all the other powers" (XI.6.403). The executive can check the legislature both by vetoing its laws and by deciding how to execute the laws. However, the reciprocal power of stopping the executive should not extend to the legislature. Execution has natural limits, so "it is useless to restrict it; besides, executive power always is exerted on momentary things" (XI.6.403). While the legislative power cannot stop the executive, the former retains the right to "examine in what manner the laws that have been made are executed" (XI.6.403). The relationship between the executive and legislative powers is much more confrontational than any involving the judiciary and either power. The executive determines when the legislature assembles. The legislature must be regularly, but not always, assembled; always being assembled would burden the representative unreasonably (XI.6.402).

Montesquieu describes a dynamic between the three powers that can be tense and cantankerous. Each branch seeks to augment its power, usually at the expense of the other two. Montesquieu argues, though, that the proper institutional structures will have the effect of preventing bad decisions, and of moving the state in a better direction: "These three powers would need to form a rest [*un repos*] or an inaction [*une inaction*]. But as they are constrained to move by the necessary movement of things, they will be forced to move in concert" (XI.6.405). The powers, on this understanding, need to work together, almost as a team, while also checking each other. Still, Montesquieu acknowledges that the mechanisms he discusses here are insufficient to protect liberty in this mixed constitution. Other political actors are necessary.

The army and the people also must safeguard liberty. "So that the one who executes cannot oppress, it is necessary that the armies that one entrusts to him are of the people, and have the same *esprit* as the people" (XI.6.406). The army is important for stopping oppression. It must balance its role of serving the executive as he attempts to protect the state, and its duty to protect the state against harmful actions on the part of the executive. The army therefore appears as another institution that can check powers. It does so, however, only if it is comprised of the people. Armies made up of mercenaries, or people loyal to either an army officer, noble, or the king, are less likely to have the interests of the people and the state in mind. Any army comprised of the people, however, will be less inclined to oppress the citizenry.

Montesquieu's reservations about this mixed constitution do not end with his call for additional checks, such as those provided by the army. As we noted above, he is concerned about the very nature of this form of government. He predicts that it will come to an end, just as Rome, Lacedemonia, and Carthage did. And he calls its political liberty "extreme." "How can I say," Montesquieu wonders, that such extreme liberty is appropriate, "I who believe that the excess even of reason is not always desirable, and that men almost always accommodate themselves better in the middle of two extremes?" (XI.6.407). The English mixed regime is not without its defects. Coupled with this, it is not appropriate to most other places. Almost always, transferring the English model is impossible because the other society is too different. While it technically is possible to force the English model on other societies, the outcome would be worse than the status quo because the society would resent and reject the model. More importantly, we have identified other political options Montesquieu deems suitable to secure liberty in particular situations. Montesquieu therefore does not recommend the English mixed regime universally.

Montesquieu does universally recommend establishing checks on power. But he does not universally recommend the checks found in the English constitution. To be sure, he sees great value in them. But in the following chapter (XI, 7) he emphasizes that monarchies establish an *esprit de liberté* without having political liberty as their direct goal. Glory—of the state or prince—is their direct goal. "But from this glory results an *esprit de liberté* that, in these States, can make as great things, and perhaps contribute just as much to happiness as liberty itself" (XI.7.408). Monarchies should pursue political liberty; otherwise they devolve into despotisms. Montesquieu therefore directly says that states can be free even if they do not adopt the English constitution.

As with the federal republic, Montesquieu does not identify the nature or principle of the mixed regime. Rahe has insightfully shown the importance of *inquiétude* to Montesquieu's discussion of England, suggesting that vigilance is the principle of England. We will be better equipped to understand the passions required of citizens in these states once we investigate commerce in the next chapter, because Montesquieu specifically identifies a number of traits that citizens in states founded on commerce should adopt. We thus set this matter aside until then.

Montesquieu's discussion of the English constitution makes his politics of place more robust. First, it places yet another option on the table for legislators as they work to discern the most appropriate political order for a given people. Second, it brings numerous means of checking power into the discussion. The most important is the distribution of three powers. Voting is another important mechanism. By pointing to the military as yet another check, Montesquieu encourages us to think more broadly about the institutions, groups, and individuals that can help secure liberty. Montesquieu thus emboldens legislators to think more broadly in their pursuit of security, liberty, and prosperity.

The Particularism of Power Stopping Power

Montesquieu's political project has as its central goal to establish and maintain security, liberty, and prosperity. Moderate government is the key to achieving this end. The theoretical innovation the politics of place offers is not merely that "power stops power." This is certainly important, and America's Founding Fathers, especially James Madison, founded the American republic and crafted its institutions based on this notion. Madison suggests, in *Federalist* No. 51, that "ambition must be made to counteract ambition." The politics of place is truly innovative, though, because it offers legislators numerous practices, policies, and institutions by which power can stop power effectively. The goal is universal, but the means for achieving and defining it are not. Power-checking practices, policies, and institutions include distributing governmental powers into three (executive, legislative, and judicial), the federal model, moderate laws, the rule of law (including protection of property), a constitution or depository of laws, education, the principles of a form of government (especially honor), religion and religious authorities (e.g., the clergy), social groups (especially the nobility and aristocracy) that have the power to check others, the military, and commerce.

There is no universally commendable model. Instead, Montesquieu identifies four forms of government that can produce free and moderate states: monarchy, aristocracy, a federal republic, and a mixed regime. Montesquieu emphasizes, though, that there are a great many and variety of cultures; and these cultures change over time. The complicated nature of cultures arises in part from the other important political variables Montesquieu considers, including representation, classes, and the military. Legislators thus need to analyze their society in the context of all the political variables Montesquieu studies, along with the subpolitical variables. They must conduct this analysis in the context of the principles Montesquieu lays out throughout *EL*. These principles center on his understanding of a good political order, and of the universal or particularistic approaches to establishing this order. But this is not all. Montesquieu seeks to diffuse knowledge. His goal is to promote positive political change. Such change can occur only when legislators conduct their analysis at three levels. They first must discern how each of the political variables functions independently. Second, they must study how each variable interacts with all the other variables, political and otherwise. Finally, legislators must understand how the variables interact to form an *esprit*. It is this process that allows them to understand what approach may or may not be effective in their state.

Chapter Four

The Subpolitical Variables

The politics of place holds that, in order to establish and maintain a good society, it is necessary to examine the geographical, economic, and moral makeup of a society. Montesquieu demonstrates in parts III, IV, and V of *EL* that these are central aspects of any society; as such, it is necessary to consider how these factors function in a particular society in order to promote the ends Montesquieu identifies. I call these variables "subpolitical" because they are not necessarily directly political; but they impact politics and are critical components of any society. Physical factors such as climate and terrain inevitably influence the lifestyle of the inhabitants of a given place. Economic activity in the form of commerce has wide-ranging effects including the promotion of peace among nations. The religion(s) or beliefs of a people play a large part in determining how political actors can and must maneuver. Studying only the political issues will leave a political actor woefully unequipped to establish or maintain a good political order.

Legislators must consider the effects of the physical environment on the inhabitants of a place. Montesquieu argues that climate and terrain do more than simply impact a people's way of life; they change people biologically. Admittedly, some of his biological claims warrant skepticism. Turning next to commerce, Montesquieu sees it as a mechanism for effecting positive change in societies. Commerce helps make societies more secure, free, and prosperous. However, Montesquieu's approach to commerce remains particularistic insofar as he did not think that all states should engage in the same amount or type of commerce. Moreover, Montesquieu saw a darker side of commerce that some commentators tend to overlook. The case of Holland is illustrative, and so I examine the Dutch republic's commerce extensively. In the final part of the chapter I investigate Montesquieu's particularistic treatment of moral beliefs, or what he calls "religions." He was an advocate of what I call "selective religious intolerance." He thinks that there are instances when it is appropriate for a state to find nonviolent ways to marginalize, weaken, or remove a religion from a society. Montesquieu bases his judgments about the effects of a religion, and how the state ought to relate to it, on a deep consideration of how a particular religion fits into a particular place.

The first subpolitical variable under consideration is the physical environment, which Montesquieu treats as a fact to be managed. Commerce, which holds tremendous promise, is next; and finally religion, which can be a potential problem. Throughout our discussion, the focus remains on how each factor impacts the politics of a place, and how that impact relates to the prospects for positive change.

Geography Matters: The Physical Environment

"The empire of climate," Montesquieu claims at the beginning of his discussion of this theme in *EL*, "is the first of all empires" (XIX.14.565).[1] Montesquieu explains elsewhere in *EL* his understanding of climate's impact: "if it is true that the character of the *esprit* and the passions of the heart are extremely different in the diverse climates, the laws should be relative to the difference of these passions, and to the difference of these characters" (XIV.1.474). This claim also relates to our investigation because he states emphatically that the physical environment shapes the *esprit*. Montesquieu even suggested that the environment changes people biologically. He certainly was not the first to analyze the effects of the environment on humans.[2] His statements have caused some to interpret Montesquieu as being a climate determinist.[3] Montesquieu claims, these scholars argue, that the physical causes overrule the moral causes. However, as Rasmussen rightly notes, "throughout his career Montesquieu was consistent in according a far greater role to moral than to physical causes."[4] While Montesquieu certainly thought the environment influenced men and societies in significant ways, he nonetheless insisted that political actors were capable of overcoming the effects of climate. Political actors must learn to navigate the literal (and figurative) terrain of a society if they are to establish and maintain a secure, free, and prosperous political order.[5] His purpose, as Rahe notes, "is to elucidate the degree to which nature stands in liberty's way."[6] Legislators must learn how to manage the environment.

What biological changes does Montesquieu claim result from differences in climate? He suggests, for example, that cold air "tightens the extremities of the exterior fibers of our bodies; this augments their spring, and favors the return of blood from the extremities to the heart." By contrast, hot air "loosens the extremities of the fibers, and extends them; therefore it diminishes their force and their spring" (XIV.2.474). Montesquieu continues by considering other effects of climate such as reaction time and blood flow. To corroborate his claim that the climate changes beings biologically, Montesquieu conducted an infamous experiment with a sheep's tongue. He froze the tongue and observed the papillae retreating; he then defrosted it and saw them become visible again. He concludes: "This observation confirms what I have said, that, in cold countries, the tufts of nerves are less open: they sink into their sheaths, where they are to cover the action of exterior goals. The sensations thus are less lively" (XIV.2.476). Montesquieu certainly was trying to utilize the best science available at the time.[7] It seems obvious, though, that his claims about the biological effects of climate are mistaken.[8] Accordingly, I will set these claims aside and focus on his second set of observations about the climate, which warrant more attention.

Montesquieu's more reasonable claim is that different climates produce different characteristics in people; this, in turn, impacts the politics of a place. The harder it is to live in a particular place, the more effort the people have to exert to provide for themselves, the more positive attributes they acquire through their hard work. Summarizing Montesquieu's claims, Lowenthal explains: "Temperature, by influencing the human body, influences the mind and the passions."[9] Cold climates require hard work from inhabitants, Montesquieu thinks, whereas hot climates seem to discourage hard work and thus the development of the industrious virtues Montesquieu values. In cold climates, living requires more effort. These efforts make people more vigorous, confident, courageous, and less sensitive to pleasures. "You will find in climates of the north peoples who have few vices, enough virtues, much sincerity and frankness" (XIV.2.477). Society becomes more secure through the fostering of these virtues and the improved morality they bring. Hot climates, by contrast, have bad effects on people. The heat reduces people's desire to work, and the fertile terrain means that people do not have to work hard to provide for themselves. In hot places, people "will fear everything, because they will sense that they can do nothing [*rien*]" (XIV.2.475). Thus, inhabitants are timid. As one approaches hot climates, "you will believe that you are moving away from morality itself" (XIV, 2). In fact, the hotness of the climate can be so excessive that the body will be "absolutely without strength." Exhaustion "will pass to the *esprit* itself." The heat will take away the "curiosity," "enterprise," and "generous sentiment" of the people. The people will be more passive and lazy, and thus more susceptible to servitude and despotism (XIV.2.477).[10] Montesquieu believes that the effects he notes are so certain that if you transport a man to a hot, extreme climate, he will lose the good attributes he acquired previously and almost lose the ability to engage in "beautiful actions" (XIV.2.475).[11] Let us now turn to terrain to understand more fully the effects Montesquieu thinks the environment has.

Legislators must pay special attention to two aspects of Montesquieu's discussion of the terrain of a place: the extent to which the people must work the soil to sustain themselves, and what kinds of strategic (dis)advantages people get from the nature and location of their terrain. Fertile soil decreases the chances that people will learn important habits of industriousness. "The sterility of the earth," he argues, "renders men industrious, sober, hardened by work, courageous, ready for war." These peoples have to procure for themselves "that which the earth refuses them" (XVIII.4.533). Countries with less fertile terrains are more "cultivated" (*cultivés*) in two senses: their lands potentially can produce more because of how hard the people work to cultivate them, and the people themselves are more cultivated in the sense that their hard work improves their morality. Fertile lands, by contrast, tend to make people too dependent on the land (XVIII.1.531). Three negative consequences result. First, when people do not cultivate the land, they tend to quarrel with each other more frequently (XVIII.12.538). Second, people in fertile countries are less concerned with protecting their freedom because they are consumed with individual affairs (XVIII.1.531). Third, and most importantly, the government of one alone is found more often in fertile countries (XVIII.1.531). Legislators in fertile countries thus must work hard to combat these negative consequences through legislation and other mechanisms to promote the development of good habits and values.

Different kinds of terrain confer various advantages and disadvantages on a people. Montesquieu focuses on plains, mountains, and islands. Plains appear as particularly problematic because "one cannot dispute anything with the stronger [person]; one therefore submits to him, and when one is submissive, the *esprit* of liberty would not know how to return there; the goods of the country are a testimony [*gage*] of fidelity" (XVIII.2.532).[12] Montesquieu's thought here is that plains provide no natural protection for a people; rather, they leave the people open to being attacked more easily by other, stronger states. Mountains and islands, by contrast, provide natural defenses and, in doing so, better governments. "Mountain dwellers retain a more moderate government, because they are not as greatly exposed to conquest; they defend themselves easily, and they are attacked with difficulty" (XVIII.2.532). What's more, liberty "is the sole good" that warrants defense in mountainous countries, so the people defend it ferociously (XVIII.2.532). Switzerland is his prime example. Island nations are even more conducive to liberty. The sea separates the inhabitants from enemies, so they are naturally more protected from conquest (XVIII.5.534). England[13] certainly is on Montesquieu's mind, but Ireland, England's long subjugated island neighbor, shows that Montesquieu provides generalizations and not universal rules or assessments. Indeed, Montesquieu's entire discussion of the climate and terrain is meant merely to highlight the potential problems the physical environment can cause in an effort to help political actors work around or within their contours.

Wise legislators can overcome many of the challenges posed by what Montesquieu calls the "physical causes."[14] "The more the physical causes carry men to resting, the more the moral causes must divert men away from it" (XIV.5.480). The physical causes—climate and terrain—are not insurmountable. Rather, a legislator can, by addressing the "moral causes" (which include religion, morals, commerce, and laws) mitigate, if not fully overcome, the problems a particular environment presents. By diminishing the effects of the physical causes, the moral causes can prepare "the workspace of man and of the legislator."[15] Laws can counteract the effects of the environment, as by promoting a good education: "As a good education is more necessary for children than for those whose *esprit* is mature, likewise peoples from these [hot] climates have more of a need for a wise legislator than the peoples of the north" (XIV.3.478). As Craiutu explains: "Bad legislators favor and encourage the vices caused by the climate of a country, while good ones try to enact measures that mitigate and limit their nefarious effects, such as laziness, indifference, and apathy."[16] Legislators accomplish this by implementing laws that "remove all the means of living without working" (XIV.7.481). Done properly, the people are far from subject to the general effects of the environment; rather, they can reshape the environment and the way it impacts them.

People can overcome, or even change the effects of, the physical environment. Men can make seemingly uninhabitable places habitable through hard work, care, and good laws (XVIII.7.535). People can do this by reshaping the earth, as through canals. In many other cases, like Holland, the "industry of men" has made places habitable (XVIII.6.534–35). More than just allowing the people to provide for themselves, Montesquieu thinks that when men have to work hard to provide for themselves, it promotes moderate government and liberty (XVIII.3.532; XVIII.6.534). Montesquieu thus holds out the promise of physically overcoming the environment.

Montesquieu is not an environmental determinist. Instead, he makes a basic claim about the physical environment that seems hardly objectionable: "different needs in the different climates have formed different manners of living; and these different manners of living have formed diverse sorts of laws" (XIV.10.483–84). The physical environment affects the lifestyle of a people. He does think that the environment tends to have certain effects on people. However, he offers various ways legislators or people can mitigate or overcome these effects, most notably though laws, education, and industriousness. We certainly can acknowledge that there are differences among peoples on account of the climates in which they live. Regardless of whether or not we agree with all of the details of Montesquieu's analysis, it seems true that people in Sweden, Siberia, Sicily, Singapore, and Sri Lanka all have different lifestyles based in part on their physical environments. Consider that contemporary experts in global development like Paul Collier have identified the importance of access to water for shipping purposes. Collier notes that being landlocked represents a "trap," especially for lesser-developed states.[17] Numerous technological developments have played a significant role in mitigating the impacts of the physical environment across the world. For example, air conditioning has made previously harsh climes comfortably habitable. Accordingly, we must be careful not to follow Montesquieu's analysis too closely, since technology has rendered it increasingly less applicable.

Montesquieu concludes that the environment need not determine the politics of a place. Legislators must take the physical causes into consideration when attempting to establish a good political order. The climate and terrain are important factors in a society, and they do help shape the *esprit* of a people, such as by making them industrious (or not). But rather than giving in to environmental determinism, Montesquieu insists that legislators, laws, people, and technology can overcome the ill effects of the environment. The environment thus appears as a less important factor in determining the politics of a place. It certainly is rarely as transformative as commerce, which can change radically the political, social, moral, and economic climate and terrain of a state.

Commerce as a Particularistic Agent of Change

Commerce has the power to transform the politics, morals, and economics of a place. Given the immense import Montesquieu attaches to commerce, some scholars have interpreted Montesquieu as recommending commerce with few or no reservations. English commerce in particular appears as universally desirable. In this vein, Pangle writes: "*All nations*, even those with a commerce of luxury, should try to emulate the *universality* of English international trade."[18] Montesquieu certainly admires English commerce. He undoubtedly sees commerce as transformative. And he thinks that commerce makes states more secure, free, and prosperous. Be that as it may, he does not view commerce as an unqualified social, moral, political, and economic good. He sees commerce as a mixed bag that results in some unfortunate consequences. He recommends commerce despite certain reservations. What's more, he does not recommend commerce to all peoples in the same way. Instead, he demonstrates that diverse peoples should pursue different types of commerce, and to different degrees; commerce should not be uniform around the world. Legislators must fit commerce to the politics of their particular place. They must discern what modes of commerce will promote security, liberty, and prosperity. After examining his general views on commerce, we will study the illustrative case of

Holland to better see the positive and negative aspects Montesquieu associates with commerce. To frame our discussion appropriately, we consider first Montesquieu's understanding and usage of the term "commerce."

Today, we associate "commerce" primarily, or solely, with economic matters. We think of financial transactions and trade. Commerce tends to be about buying and selling commodities, making profits, and promoting economic growth. Commerce retains this aspect for Montesquieu. He writes, for example, that the "effect of commerce is riches" (XXI.6.605). Commerce promotes prosperity. Commerce cannot flourish if the material goods that one acquires are not secure, and if those who engage in trade cannot do so relatively freely.[19] But commerce is not only an economic matter for Montesquieu. When he proclaims that commerce "is the thing in the world the most useful to a state" (XX.14.633), he means that commerce is useful because of the ways it also permeates the social, moral, and political spheres.[20]

"The history of commerce," Montesquieu writes, "is that of the communication of peoples" (XXI.5.604). Commerce, for Montesquieu, is about social interactions.[21] It involves the exchange of diverse ideas, opinions, products, and lifestyles. This exchange happens in many ways and on many levels, like the direct exchange of customs, habits, and beliefs among traders and travelers, or the exchange of art, literature, or philosophy. "Commerce introduces into a country different sorts of peoples, a great number of agreements, types of goods, and manners of acquiring" (XX.18.596). Commerce for Montesquieu, as Larrère explains, is a "history of civilization, a history of enlightenment, a history of technological progress."[22] These interactions and advancements are among the reasons Montesquieu values commerce highly.

Commerce can be destructive. Montesquieu proclaims: "[The people's] diverse destructions, and a certain ebb and flow of populations and devastations, form them for the greatest events" (XXI.5.604). He then remarks: "Commerce, sometimes destroyed by conquerors, sometimes bothered by monarchs, wanders the earth, flees where it is oppressed, rests where one lets it breathe: it reigns today where one only saw deserts, seas, and rocks; there where it reigned, there are only deserts" (XXI.5.604). But commercial destruction usually is positive, he thinks. To be sure, the destruction of *mœurs*, customs, beliefs, practices, and institutions occurs. And such destruction often is not received warmly by many of the people it impacts. The invasive spreading of commerce, by permeating all aspects of society, can fundamentally reshape the politics, morals, and economics of a place. Commerce also can be destructive in a more primitive sense. Commerce often is linked with empire, commercial or territorial. Even in cases like Holland that Montesquieu views on balance favorably, he still voices concerns about imperialism that we will consider later.

Historically, nations had satiated their desire to acquire through war and conquest. It is one of Montesquieu's great hopes—and expectations—that commerce can provide states and individuals a way to acquire peacefully rather than violently. This would augment states' security, because they would not come under threat or endure an invasion at the hands of another country. "The natural effect of commerce," Montesquieu theorizes, "is to lead to peace. Two nations that negotiate together render themselves reciprocally dependent: if the one has an interest in buying, the other has an interest in selling; and all unions are founded on mutual needs" (XX.2.585). The reasoning here presents itself as descriptive: two nations need things from each other, so they should trade with one another to acquire what they desire or require. Montesquieu explains later that "all nations" have "reciprocal needs" and suggests that money is an easy medium to mediate their commercial interactions (XXII.1.650). Nations should, in theory, have something to offer one another, and thus be able to engage in commerce. When a disagreement arises, "commercial social relations encourage the formal adjudication of rival claims rather than violent conflict."[23] Eventually, Montesquieu sees nations' economic interests becoming so entangled that stopping commerce will be too destructive, thus making the use of force much less likely. Cooperation should ensue.[24] Commerce substitutes "the interdependence of interest for war and negotiation for predation." At the same time, commerce breaks down "xenophobic prejudices and nationalistic passions."[25] Commerce also "encourages peace by developing more genteel characters in men and by creating a structure for international trade which demanded regular relations and an atmosphere of trust among merchant classes."[26] Pacification occurs, according to Pangle, as a result of "a commercialization of the manner of thinking."[27] Yet Montesquieu's reasoning here is aspirational in important ways. He realizes that the story is much more complicated.

Montesquieu acknowledges two complications to his story of commerce leading to peace. First, while individuals, merchants, companies, and businesses are the primary participants in trade, states (particularly powerful political actors) are the primary participants in war. So while commerce may unite the economic interests of nations, it does not necessarily unite the leaders of nations that trade with one another. As such, legislators may determine that it is in their interest to attack a nation with which it trades, even if negative economic consequences ensue. The problem is more acute when a country is ruled by one alone; the *esprit* of monarchy, we remember, is that of war. War-loving monarchs like Louis XIV certainly were at the front of Montesquieu's mind. Second, commerce and empire can go hand in hand, as they did in the cases of England and Holland.

Commerce also promotes peace by softening the harsh *mœurs* that increase the chances of war. Commerce, Montesquieu observes, "cures destructive prejudices; and it is almost a general rule, that everywhere where there are gentle *mœurs*, there is commerce; and that everywhere where there is commerce, there are gentle *mœurs*" (XX.1.585). Commerce accomplishes this by making it such that "the knowledge of the *mœurs* of all nations has penetrated everywhere: one has compared themselves with others, and significant goods have resulted" (XX.1.585). The upshot is the perfecting of *mœurs* through the corruption of "pure *mœurs*" (*les mœurs pures*), since commerce "polishes and softens barbarous *mœurs*" (*les mœurs barbares*).[28] Commerce as communication and interaction thus fundamentally disrupts the moral order of societies in a positive way. As Montesquieu injects himself into the *doux commerce* debate in favor of commerce's softening effects, we gain a clear understanding of how he can say that commerce promotes peace and security. People encounter different *mœurs* and new beliefs. Often, they find aspects of these *mœurs* or beliefs appealing, enough to incorporate them into their own, sometimes along with or in addition to, and sometimes instead of, their old beliefs and *mœurs*. Montesquieu elaborates: "The more people communicate[29] with one another, the more easily they change their manners, because each is more a spectacle for another; one sees better the singularities of individuals" (XIX.8.560). "Precisely because commerce promotes communication across national boundaries," Rahe notes, "it is quasi-medicinal."[30] These benefits of commerce flow into the political sphere too, as "commerce promotes gentle governments and tempers excessive political passions, such as ambition and the desire for power and domination, by channeling them into peaceful and benign activities that aim at material gain and wealth rather than power and domination."[31] This general picture of commerce's effects might look appealing. But the relations Montesquieu describes among individuals appear as anything but.

While commerce can unite nations, it does not have this direct effect on individuals:[32] "We see that in countries where one is affected only by the *esprit* of commerce, one traffics in all human actions, and all moral virtues: the smallest things, those which humanity demands, are done or given there only for money" (XX.2.586). A footnote reveals that Montesquieu is referring to Holland. Commerce also impacts justice and morality: "The *esprit* of commerce produces in men a certain sentiment of exact justice, opposed on the one hand to robbery, and on the other to those moral virtues that make it such that one does not always discuss his interests with rigidity, and that one can neglect them for those of others" (XX.2.586). At first glance, it appears that Montesquieu views this side of commerce negatively. Far from uniting individuals, it seems that commerce promotes disunity through unsavory actions. Commerce may at times be an affront to humanity, a quality Montesquieu unquestionably values. But Montesquieu came to see that commerce ultimately advances morality, virtue, and maybe humanity, effectively, when people come to exude what we can call commercial virtue.[33]

Commercial states need a certain, modern kind of moral virtue to flourish. We saw earlier that the "political virtue" that makes republican government move is insufficient, unviable, and problematic, because it is a "renouncement of oneself, which is always a very painful thing" (IV.6.267). Modern states need a very different kind of virtue to subsist, one based on commerce and self-interest rather than self-renunciation:

> It is true that, when democracy is founded on commerce, it can very well be the case that particular citizens have great wealth, and that the *mœurs* are not corrupt. The *esprit* of commerce brings with it the *esprit* of frugality, economy, moderation, work, wisdom, tranquility, order, and rule. Thus, while this *esprit* continues to exist, the wealth it produces has no bad effects. The trouble arises, when the excess of riches destroys this *esprit* of commerce; one sees, all of a sudden, the disorders of inequality come into existence, which had not been sensed.
>
> For maintaining the *esprit* of commerce, it is necessary that the principal citizens engage in it themselves; that this *esprit* must reign *alone and not be crossed by another; all the laws must favor it.* (V.6.280; emphasis added)

Commercial virtue does not require self-sacrifice; citizens should affirm, not renounce, themselves. This self-affirmation is more natural, since people do not seem inclined to fall on their swords. As Spector shows, "the good merchant can therefore be a good citizen."[34] And this is so in various modern states, because Montesquieu insists that the *esprit* of commerce has these good effects in different forms of government and places, and not only in one particular form or place. In making this argument, Montesquieu is following closely the reasoning of Bernard Mandeville's *Fable of the Bees*, which has as its subtitle *Or Private Vices, Publick Benefits*. Montesquieu endorses what appears to be a "paradox"—"that private vices can promote the public good and that the progress from barbarism to civilization is grounded in moral corruption."[35] This line of thinking—that commerce, and the private vices it fosters, promote morality—comes out again in an important remark in book XXI. After revealing that the world is being cured of Machiavellian immoderation, Montesquieu writes: "And it is fortunate for men to be in a situation where, while their passions inspire in them the thought of being wicked [*méchants*], they have, however, an interest in not being so" (XXI.20.641).[36] Commerce thus provides men with compelling and durable reasons to reject being wicked and, instead, be moral.

Private vices benefit individuals and society, thus producing virtues of the bourgeois variety. To promote these bourgeois virtues, "all the laws" must favor commerce; so allowing people to be affected *only* by the *esprit* of commerce is on balance a good thing. I say "on balance" because Montesquieu does not see the moral effects as completely positive. The "exact justice" Montesquieu references in XX, 2 is precisely what one would expect from people who have the bourgeois virtues listed in V, 6. Trafficking in all moral virtue cannot be seen as a good thing, because Montesquieu sees humanity as a major virtue. Even though we lose something, this path remains desirable, regardless of which type of commerce one practices.

Commerce can take two primary forms. There exists the commerce of economy and the commerce of luxury.[37] Montesquieu explains:

> In the government of one alone, it [commerce] is ordinarily founded on luxury, and although it is founded on real needs, its principal goal is to procure for the nation that does it everything that serves its pride, delights, and fantasies. In the government of many, it [commerce] is more often founded on economy. Traders, having their eyes on all the nations of the earth, carry to the one what they take from the other. It is thus that the republics of Tyre, Carthage, Athens, Marseilles, Florence, Venice, and Holland, have engaged in commerce. (XX.4.587)

Commerce of economy consists of trading widely and frequently. This conforms more closely to how we tend to conceive of commerce. The commerce of luxury, by contrast, primarily entails servicing "pride, delights, and fantasies."[38] Montesquieu associates the commerce of economy more with republics, because it "is founded on the practice of gaining little, and even gaining less than any other nation and of being compensated only by gaining continually" (XX.4.587). The commerce of luxury is found more often in monarchies. He insists, though, that monarchies are not excluded from the commerce of economy, only that they are less carried to it; and that the commerce of luxury can be present in republics, even though it has less of a "relation to their constitution" than the commerce of economy (XX.4.588). Scholars disagree about whether Montesquieu prefers one of these forms of commerce, and about whether he sees a place for both in various societies.[39] We find sufficient evidence in *EL* to show that he thinks both forms of commerce contribute to promoting security, liberty, and above all, prosperity. The two kinds of commerce, it turns out, are much more closely intertwined than Montesquieu initially suggests.

The commerce of economy accomplishes great things by focusing on achieving many small gains. States founded on this type of commerce can enact "great enterprises" because of the desires this continuous trading and gaining promote. "One commerce," Montesquieu explains, "leads to another; the small to the medium; the medium to the large; and he who had so much desire to gain little, places himself in a situation where he does not have less of a desire to gain a great deal" (XX.4.587–88). These great enterprises are possible in part because of the greater certainty one has in the security of her property. Because people believe that what they acquire is secure, they "undertake everything" and dare "to expose" their property "in order to acquire more." Men "expect much more of their fortune" (XX.4.588).

What's more, the commerce of economy seems to be especially good at promoting industry, which advances prosperity.[40] "Riches," Montesquieu writes, "suppose a great deal of industry" (XXIII.29.713).[41] In a chapter on "peoples who have engaged in the commerce of economy," Montesquieu uses the example of Marseilles to show how this commerce promotes hard work and other bourgeois virtues. In order to survive, let alone flourish, the people of Marseilles had to be industrious, just, moderate, and frugal (XX.5.588–89). Once property is secure, the desire to gain blossoms, and industriousness takes hold among the people; societies find themselves becoming increasingly prosperous. The commerce of economy, Howse explains, is "the commerce of the impoverished, the powerless, and the oppressed" because people must "work to create something of value to others, which can then be traded to meet the basic needs of self-preservation."[42] By contrast, Montesquieu thinks that someone generally is poor "because he does not work" (XXIII.29.712); so too with societies. In many ways, this commerce appears quite different from that of luxury.

The commerce of luxury, we saw, has as its "principal goal to procure for the nation that does it everything that serves its pride, delights, and fantasies." Rather than looking to build on many small gains, regimes like that of Louis XIV "see only grand goals," and do whatever they can to attain them. Fundamentally, the two types of commerce seem appropriate for different types of political systems. Montesquieu's discussion of luxury in book VII appears, at first glance, to confirm the suggestion that a state must choose one type of commerce. There he declares that luxury is "singularly proper to monarchies" (VII.4.336). A closer look at his discussion of luxury—which is not necessarily the same as the commerce of luxury—in books VII and XX reveals that his prescription is less straightforward.

Luxury, Montesquieu explains, is always proportionate "to the inequality of fortunes. If, in a state, riches are equally divided, there is no luxury." To establish the equal division of goods, "it is necessary that the law only gives to each the physical necessities. If one has more than that, some will spend, others will acquire, and luxury will establish itself" (VII.1.332). But the only political system that works to establish equality—a democratic republic—is undesirable, precisely for this reason.[43] So Montesquieu thinks that the establishment of luxury is both inevitable and desirable. He embraces the dynamic that luxury produces: "The more men are together, the more they are vain and feel arise in them the desire to distinguish themselves with small things." This desire is wholly compatible with the bourgeois virtues discussed above; and it becomes even stronger when men are together in large numbers, and they work harder to distinguish themselves. "But by dint of wanting to distinguish oneself," he explains, "everyone becomes equal, and one no longer distinguishes himself: as everyone wants to be looked at, one notices no one" (VII.1.333–34). The inequality of luxury encourages people to acquire more to increase their relative situation, which benefits everyone.[44] Montesquieu argues that relative luxury is a key component of states becoming and staying rich, and that commerce is key to this process (VII.5.338). "Luxury, vanity, *can* stimulate work and economic vigor. . . . The luxury of the idle nobles stimulates industry and commerce in the lower classes."[45] Once people become rich, their luxury obliges them to help others in need; otherwise "the poor will die from hunger" (VII.4.336). Luxury thus has moral benefits to different groups in society. Those who have more are in a better position to help others, not only directly, but also indirectly through the creation of more wealth. Indeed, luxury "vastly increases the number of objects desired and thereby stimulates a broader commerce."[46] Luxury, more than being inevitable, actually can benefit everyone. This is true not just in monarchies, but in other forms of government as well.

Luxury should be present in free political orders.[47] Montesquieu writes that in nations where servitude reigns, "one works more to conserve than to acquire. In a free nation, one works more to acquire than to conserve" (XX.4.588). Since monarchies and republics can be free states, the desire to acquire reigns in both. Specifically, people desire riches, superfluous things, and, eventually, luxury.[48] "The effect of commerce," Montesquieu explains, "is riches; that of riches, luxury; that of luxury, the perfection of the arts" (XXI.6.605). Montesquieu wholly supports all of these things, as they are features of a prosperous society. Crucially, luxury thus appears as a natural consequence of commercial society. It is in this light that we must understand Montesquieu's statement that "it is hardly possible that it [the commerce of economy] can be done by a people among whom luxury is established, that spends a lot, and only sees great goals" (XX.4.587). The final phrase is important: when states *only* see grand goals, they cannot engage in the commerce of economy. Montesquieu shows that in all free states many people focus on small and medium-sized goals.

Still, not everyone should engage in commerce: "it is against the *esprit* of commerce, that the nobility does it [the commerce] in monarchies" because that "would remove between the merchants and the plebeians the facility of buying and selling."[49] The nobility thus would endanger the livelihood of merchants and commoners. It also is contrary to the "*esprit* of monarchy, that the nobility engage in commerce there" (XX.21.598).

Montesquieu turns to England and contends that the nobility's engaging in commerce weakened the monarchy. But the solution here is simple: have merchants, traders, and others engage in commerce. Indeed, these groups plant the seeds of luxury.[50] Commerce can be robust in monarchies, so long as it is not carried out by nobles or by the regime. As such, industry can be an engine of growth in free governments.

Montesquieu thus qualifies his earlier statement, that the "great enterprises of commerce are not for monarchies, but for the government of many," in an important way. The two types of commerce are not as distinct as he initially suggests. A state that pursues commerce of economy also can pursue luxury. He even blurs the distinction himself throughout his discussion. He speaks almost always of "commerce" without specifying that he is referencing one type or the other. More than that, though, he speaks of a monarchy, a mixed regime, and a republic all as engaging in "commerce" in the positive sense he describes: "Europe engaged in commerce and navigation from the other parts of the world; France, England, and Holland carry out almost all the navigation and commerce in Europe" (XXI.21.645).[51] Montesquieu thus blurs the lines between the different types of commerce. He does so in part because all states should engage in the commerce of economy, and also embrace at least some luxury.[52] Societies thus can benefit from the goods that both forms of commerce offer. These goods accrue most readily when commerce is free.

Montesquieu encourages trade liberalization, while allowing for restrictions in various instances. Consider the grounds on which he chastises the Japanese:

> The true maxim is to not exclude any nation from its commerce without substantial reasons. The Japanese engage in commerce only with two nations, the Chinese and the Dutch. The Chinese earn a thousand percent on sugar and sometimes as much on the return. The Dutch make profits of about the same amount. Every nation that conducts itself on the maxims of the Japanese, will be necessarily deceived. It is competition that places a just price on merchandise, and that establishes the true relations among it [merchandise]. (XX.9.591)

But competition does much more than simply set a just price for goods. Competition encourages traders to try to acquire goods for the best price, and sellers to find the right buyer for their goods. Competition also incentivizes those who engage in the commerce of economy, such as merchants and traders, to work hard to produce better products at lower prices. What's more, the "capitalist merchant ... must be cautious, always concerned with prudent investments with an eye toward long-range profit."[53] Montesquieu's robust support for competition does not, however, lead him always to support completely free trade. Rather, he is open to various restrictions on commerce.

Some restrictions on commerce actually can help commerce flourish. "The liberty of commerce," Montesquieu suggests, "is not an ability accorded to merchants to do what they want; this would, instead, be commerce's servitude" (XX.12.593). Commercial freedom, like political freedom, is not license. "What disrupts those who engage in commerce," he continues, "does not disrupt commerce. It is in countries of liberty that the trader finds innumerable contradictions; and he is never less thwarted by the laws than in countries of servitude" (XX.12.593). To show that restrictions are necessary for commerce, he turns to England. England prohibits the export of English wool and requires ships from its colonies to anchor in England. The English "disrupt the trader, but it is in favor of commerce" (XX.12.593). Montesquieu's conclusion here is significant, because it demonstrates that he is not a proponent of commerce without any restrictions. In light of this, there is reason to think that a tension exists between two strands of Montesquieu's thought: promoting the needs of the state and promoting the needs of commerce. Allowing ships to bypass England certainly would lower their costs and promote competition, both goals Montesquieu supports. Nonetheless, Montesquieu insists that such restrictions on commerce can promote commerce. While it would be going too far to identify Montesquieu as a mercantilist, he certainly allows for more restrictions on trade than we would expect from one of the great modern supporters of commerce.

Montesquieu's theory of commerce has a long time horizon. This is a key feature of his discussion of commerce. His argument is not that commerce immediately leads to any of the beneficial outcomes he identifies. Rather, he understands that changes in habits, *mœurs*, manners, and practices, to say nothing of the economic, political, and social conditions in diverse states, almost always occur gradually. Montesquieu expects, though, that commerce will come to flourish, and that prosperity will increase.

Montesquieu universally recommends that all societies engage in some commerce (understood in the robust, multifaceted conception he presents). Commerce is a necessary condition for achieving prosperity.[54] We know that he thinks that commerce benefits societies that engage in it economically. Yet the majority of his discussion does not focus on the economic benefits commerce produces, contrary to what we might expect. His discussion of themes like the benefits of competition is fairly short (though unquestionably significant). Montesquieu focuses, instead, on the moral and political benefits of commerce, even at a time when the economic benefits were not widely acknowledged or accepted. He does so because a prosperous society is not merely one that is rich, but one that is good in the other ways he describes throughout his analysis of commerce. Examples include being industrious and peaceful toward other states. Moreover, states will attain commercial prosperity in different ways. This is one key reason he defines such prosperity broadly. Such an understanding also fits naturally into his flexible politics of place. Consider his discussions of commerce in diverse states.

Still, Montesquieu's approach to commerce remains particularistic because he does not think that the same amount and type of commerce can, should, or will fit the politics of all places. The Romans and the Arabs did not engage in commerce, but for different reasons. The Romans' lifestyle led them to move far away from commerce: "their genius, their glory, their military education, the form of their government, took them away from commerce" (XXI.14.632). They focused, instead, on war and politics in the cities, on agriculture in the country, and on promoting "a tough and tyrannical government [that] was incompatible with commerce" in the provinces (XXI.14.632). Their political constitution was opposed to commerce, they rarely thought about it, and their *esprit* was against it (XXI.14–15.632–33). The Arabs, for their part, were "destined" by "nature" to be commercial, not warring and aggressive. But they became belligerent nonetheless. The first step was their unfortunate situation. They were between the Romans and Parthians, "and they became auxiliaries of both." Islam was the crucial second step: "Mohammed found them warriors; he gave them enthusiasm, and they became conquerors" (XXI.16.634). In the case of Poland, Montesquieu contends that the Poles would be better off if they did not engage in commerce, because a few powerful lords control all of the resources, which harms the people greatly. The lords, who "possess entire provinces," "squeeze the laborers" in order to get even more grain, which they in turn will "send to strangers, and procure for themselves what luxury demands." Montesquieu concludes that if "Poland did not engage in commerce with any nation, the people would be happier" (XX.23.600). When a small group of people controls most goods and the means of production, and when they abuse their power by manipulating the system, commerce is against the interest of the state and the interests of the people as a whole. Just as countries forgo commerce for various reasons, nations that engage in commerce do so in different ways.

Commerce is a powerful tool for legislators. We have seen that commerce deals not just with political economy, but morality as well. Legislators seeking to improve the harsh, barbarous, pure, or otherwise undesirable *mœurs* of their country can turn to commerce to soften these *mœurs*, for example. Legislators can make their countries safer from external threats by trading with countries that might otherwise attack their country. To improve the political and moral economy of states, though, legislators are permitted variation regarding how much commerce a society pursues, and what kind. For example, a society need not engage in the two forms of commerce equally, or in the same way as another state. Instead, states are capable of handling different degrees and types of commerce. All societies need not be as extremely commercial as the Dutch.

The Case of Dutch Commerce

Readers of *EL* often interpret England as Montesquieu's model commercial regime.[55] After all, at one point Montesquieu does seem to suggest that England practices commerce better than any other country: England "has always made its political interests cede to the interests of its commerce." The English are "the people in the world who have best known how to let prevail at once these three great things: religion, commerce, and liberty" (XX.7.590). As we saw, though, England did not let commerce prevail by making it fully free; rather, the English state imposed taxes, tariffs, and other restrictions on commerce. This approach, Montesquieu thinks, helped England prosper. But it certainly is not the only approach to commerce a country can embrace. In this section we examine the illustrative case of Dutch commerce. We will see that Montesquieu considered Holland's approach beneficial yet distinct from England's. Rather than finding one mode superior, he held up different models as praiseworthy. The consequence of my argument is to show that Montesquieu did not have one model commercial regime, but numerous models, of which England and Holland are two. Dutch commerce also points to the darker side of commerce; namely, commerce can harm some while benefiting others. Commerce can lead to conquest, unfair practices, and imperialism. Holland serves as a fascinating case study on how Montesquieu thinks that commerce can fundamentally shape a society. While Montesquieu initially had a rather negative opinion about Dutch commerce, his mature view, in the context of his politics of place, was generally positive. We consider first those early views.

The early Montesquieu, in *Voyage en Hollande* and *Mes Pensées*, paints a bleak picture of how commerce and high taxes corrupt Dutch *mœurs*. "The heart of the inhabitants of countries which live on commerce is entirely corrupted: they do not render you the least service, because they hope that you will buy it" (OCI.864). "In Holland," he observes, "all services are sold."[56] Montesquieu found such behavior reprehensible, because it removes humanity, care, and compassion from transactions. High taxes deserve some blame. The Dutch pay endlessly, since everything is taxed.[57] Montesquieu deems Dutch finances "totally lost" as they impose new taxes every day (OCI.873). He finds many of these taxes "ridiculous": "your chair pays for sitting on the pavement of the street. Everyone pays; everyone requests; regardless of what you do, you find a tax" (OCI.864). Seemingly seedy *mœurs* ensue: "Since they are overwhelmed by taxes, they must have money by any course. There are two such courses, avarice and robbery. The base people will ask you for your purse for having carried your coat rack. . . . A man who shows you a street comes to ask you for money" (OCI.863). These harsh observations about Dutch commerce lead Montesquieu to an unforgiving conclusion about Dutch *mœurs*: "Everything that one had told me about the avarice, knavery, and fraud of the Dutch, is not made up, it is the pure truth" (OCI.863). The end result of Holland's problematic politics and commerce is dreary indeed: "Finally, the republic falls into corruption" (OCI.867).

On the one hand, Montesquieu's early views on Holland are so negative that it is difficult to imagine him developing a positive opinion about the Dutch. On the other hand, it is surprising that one of the great proponents of commercial society could have expressed such negative opinions on, above all, Dutch commerce. How can we reconcile these divergent views? There are two key explanations for the new perspective he gained.

First, we must consider the art of writing in published works versus private notes. At the beginning of *MP* Montesquieu explains: "There are ideas that I have not dealt with in depth, and that I keep for thinking about them on occasion. I refrain from answering for all the thoughts that are here. I have placed most of them there only because I have not had the time to reflect on them, and will think about them when I make use of them" (OCI.974). Montesquieu emphasizes that such unpublished remarks like those on Holland in *Voyage* and *MP* are not thoroughly thought-out ideas. Rahe elaborates: "To rely on the material in Montesquieu's notebooks to any great degree, to treat it as more than a supplement sometimes useful for fleshing out themes prominent already in his published works, is to court error."[58] We thus must be careful about how much weight we assign them. Second, Montesquieu's politics of place helped him gain new perspective on the Dutch and their commerce over time. He came to have a generally positive opinion about Dutch commerce and its effects.

The Dutch pioneered commercial activity in Europe. The Dutch "almost alone engaged in commerce from the south to the north" of the continent (XX.6.589). The Dutch conducted commerce in order to be able to engage in more commerce. In another example of Dutch commercial exceptionalism, Holland appears as one of three commercial leaders (with France and England). These three states "carry out almost all the navigation and commerce in Europe" (XXI.21.645).[59] Commerce made Holland more secure and powerful. In a section in *MP* called "Cause of Dutch Power," Montesquieu explains that Holland's power derives from it being "master of all the navigation of these rivers and streams [in and near Holland], by means of places that they have had by treaties, and those that they have had demolished" (OCI.1406). Their commerce also helped them "shake the yoke from Spain." "The land," he explains, "has been given to monarchies; the sea, to free peoples"—like the Dutch (OCI.1108). Their particular approach to commerce is the key to their success.

Holland appears as exemplary in its practice of the commerce of economy. It is worth quoting Montesquieu at length:

> Sometimes . . . a nation that engages in the commerce of economy, needing a product from a country to serve as a basis for procuring the products of another, contents itself with gaining very little, and sometimes nothing, on the one, in the hope or certainty of gaining much in others. Thus, when Holland almost alone engaged in commerce from the south to the north of Europe, the wines of France, that they carried to the north, only served, in some manner, the funds for engaging in commerce in the north.
>
> . . . Often, in Holland, some kinds of merchandise come from far not to be sold there more expensively than they cost from the place itself. Here is the reason. . . . : a captain who needs ballasts for his vessel will take on marble; he needs wood for packing his cargo, he will buy it; and provided he loses nothing on it, he will believe he has done well.
>
> . . . Not only can commerce that gives nothing be useful, but so can disadvantageous commerce. I have heard that in Holland whale hunting . . . almost never returns what it costs; but those who have been employed in building the ship, those who have provided the rigging, the gear, and the provisions, are also those who take the principal in the hunt. Even if they lose on the hunt, they have come out ahead on the equipage. This commerce is a kind of lottery, and each one is seduced by the hope of a lucky number. Everyone loves to play, and the most sober people willingly enter the play. (XX.6.589–90)

The metaphor of the lottery is important here, as it ties into the debate on the morality of commercial societies. It also highlights the *esprit* of *inquiétude* that tends to permeate commercial societies. The Dutch engage in commerce because they embrace risk-taking and trying to gain, so much so that they trade even when they do not benefit monetarily from a particular transaction. Their long-sighted approach makes them richer because they evaluate their interests in the aggregate and over the long term. "Riches," Montesquieu explains, "consist in real estate or moveable property. . . . The State that possesses the most of this moveable property in the World is richest; Holland and England have an immense quantity of it" (OCI.1488). Mason thus interprets Montesquieu as especially favorable toward Dutch commerce: "Holland was for him the outstanding modern exemplar of the economico-political type of trading republic, the state practicing 'commerce d'économie'; and this type . . . with its commitment to industry, enterprise, and the constant dissemination and exploitation of wealth, fixes most of the parameters in his book on trade."[60] Montesquieu's depictions suggest that he may have viewed Holland to be quintessentially commercial. Recall that for a state to maintain the *esprit* of commerce, "it is necessary that the principal citizens engage in it themselves; that this *esprit* alone reigns; ... that all the laws favor it" (V.6.280). Holland is the sole nation affected *only* by the *esprit* of commerce, and his depiction of how the Dutch engage in the commerce of economy supports his contention.

The Dutch need to be industrious and to trade, work their lands, and develop technology in order to prosper because they cannot procure many goods from their land.[61] What they lack in materials, tools, and equipment they make up for in industry. "It was necessary to subsist; they pulled their subsistence from the whole universe" (XX.6.589). Their industriousness helps them trade widely and effectively as they scour the globe pursuing commerce in spite of having inferior ships (XXI.6.609). Their industriousness also promotes moderate government. Montesquieu identifies Holland as one of three countries "formed by the industry of men" (Egypt and two provinces in China are the others). He writes: "The countries that the industry of men has rendered habitable and that need, to exist, the same industry, call us to moderate government" (XVIII.6.53). Montesquieu continues by explaining that it was "necessary that power was moderate" in Holland, which "nature has made so that attention was on herself, and not abandoned to nonchalance or caprice" (XVIII.6.535). Montesquieu's claim here is significant, given that he wrote *EL* to prove that the *esprit* of moderation should be that of the legislator (XXIX.1.865), and that he thinks institutions should be a moderating force that prevents anyone from having excessive power.[62]

The Dutch benefit from their commerce and communication domestically as well as with peoples around the world. We saw above why Montesquieu thinks such communication is beneficial. The Dutch embrace these benefits. For example, Dutch sailors go to the Indies to trade and then decide to "establish themselves" (XXIII.25.710). However, Dutch interactions appear as decidedly one-sided.

Holland's aggressive commerce, which sometimes resulted in imperialism, often disadvantaged the other parties involved. Consider first Montesquieu's discussion of Dutch trade with Japan. Holland was one of only two nations (with China) that traded with Japan, and the Dutch made profits of about 1,000 percent. Montesquieu says little directly about Dutch engagement in Japan. He notes that the Dutch "were told that they could not spend nights on benches without being assassinated" so they departed (VI.13.324). Elsewhere, though, Montesquieu is critical of Dutch involvement. The Dutch helped the shogun put down a rebellion of Japanese Christians. As a result of this rebellion, the shogun expelled all other European nations. Montesquieu refers to these particular events in Japan:

"The [Japanese] magistrates regarded the firmness inspired by Christianity as very dangerous when it was a question of renouncing the faith; one thought one saw audacity increase.... One was ordered to renounce the Christian religion ... one saw a horrible combat between the tribunals who condemned and the accused who suffered, between civil laws and those of religion" (XXV.14.749).

Dutch practices in the East Indies were mixed. The Dutch negotiated exclusive trading rights with Indian kings, mainly for spices. Whenever possible, the Dutch removed competitors. For example, Portugal had established dominance in various regions. "But the other nations of Europe did not let them enjoy their division tranquilly: the Dutch chased the Portuguese from almost all of the East Indies, and diverse nations set up establishments in America" (XXI.21.642). After chasing the Portuguese out, the Dutch continued many of their harsh practices in Asia: "The Portuguese deal with the Indians as conquerors. The cumbersome laws that the Dutch impose today on small Indian princes regarding commerce, the Portuguese had established before them" (XXI.21.642). Montesquieu does not hesitate to point out the harms of Dutch imperialism.[63] He does not turn a blind eye to the imperial harms that can result from commerce. He acknowledges similar problems with English commerce. His hope, however, is that over time the Dutch will become fairer and less harsh when dealing with other peoples. Montesquieu thinks that such positive changes will occur gradually, over time.

Commerce may be a mixed bag for Montesquieu. It can be an affront to humanity, and it can lead to imperialism and conquest. But Montesquieu is unambiguous that the moral changes commerce effects are, on balance, good. This is never more evident than in how it impacts religion. In the final chapter of part IV, on commerce, directly before he begins his discussion of religion in part V, Montesquieu writes:

> Henry VIII, wanting to reform the Church of England, destroyed the monks, a lazy nation itself, and one that maintained the laziness of others, because, practicing hospitality, an infinity of idle people, gentlemen and bourgeois, spent their life running from monastery to monastery. He removed again the poorhouses where the common people found their subsistence, as the gentlemen found theirs in the monasteries. Since these changes, the *esprit* of commerce and industry became established in England. (XXIII.29.713)

Commerce and politics can be in tension with religion, depending on the politics of a place. We turn, now, to examine Montesquieu's analysis of religion, the final subpolitical variable.

Montesquieu's Case for Selective Religious Intolerance

Is it appropriate for all states to advocate religious toleration? Scholars generally interpret Montesquieu in one of two ways: either as a proponent of religious toleration, or as hostile to revealed religion and seeking, so far as possible, to detach souls from religion. I offer an alternative perspective. Rather than favoring or opposing religious toleration per se, Montesquieu judges a religion in the context of a particular state. Sometimes he views a given religion (e.g., Christianity) favorably; other times, unfavorably. He thinks that there are instances when it is appropriate for a state to find nonviolent ways to marginalize, weaken, or remove a religion from a society. This makes Montesquieu a proponent of what I call "selective religious intolerance." By intolerance I mean more than simply abrogating religious "freedom" or practice. I mean a concerted effort by the state to directly or indirectly curtail a religion's effectiveness and, when necessary, remove it from the state. Montesquieu bases his judgments about the effects of a religion, and how the state ought to relate to it, on a deep consideration of how a particular religion fits into a society.

Both camps contain notable scholars. Consider those who view Montesquieu as a proponent of religious toleration. Binoche sees Montesquieu's support for religious tolerance stemming from a desire to maintain civil peace.[64] Spector interprets Montesquieu as opposing religious intolerance in *EL* because of its violent nature and since intolerance is an abridgment of liberty (she also notes that he recommends subordinating theology to the needs of the state).[65] Casabianca views Montesquieu's toleration as a balancing act, "a principle of adaptation that must assure at once the tranquility of the state, of religions, and of citizens."[66] Larrère, Kingston, and Shackleton make extended cases that Montesquieu supports religious toleration. Larrère thinks Montesquieu strongly supports tolerance but notes that tolerance does not necessarily imply religious liberty, and that Montesquieu is much less effusive when it comes to this liberty.[67] Kingston pays attention to Montesquieu's historical context, especially the papal bull *Unigenitus*. She sees Montesquieu as part of "a moment in the development of modern political thought when toleration was beginning to be advocated as a public virtue."[68] Shackleton asserts that Montesquieu's support for religious tolerance was "the belief to which he clung more tenaciously than any other, and in support of which he engaged to the limit his powers of eloquence."[69] Numerous others have interpreted Montesquieu as favoring religious tolerance.[70] Schaub sees Montesquieu supporting religious tolerance and pluralism but criticizing Christianity.[71] Samuel suggests that Montesquieu views religion positively because "religion, and especially Christianity, advances political order."[72]

A second group of scholars interprets Montesquieu as hostile to revealed religion. They contend that Montesquieu wants to detach man's soul from religion and attach it, instead, to commerce and liberal republicanism. They think he deems revealed religion pernicious—it is bad for individuals and society; on this reading, Montesquieu lacks any sincere basis for toleration. In his first book on Montesquieu, Pangle notes that because Montesquieu discusses religion last among the major topics of *EL*, religion is not especially important to Montesquieu. For Montesquieu "religion makes no contribution to political theory."[73] In his recent analysis of religion in *EL*, Pangle contends that Montesquieu views revealed religion negatively. In despotisms "the will of God comes to sight as a kind of higher despotic will, superimposed on the human despot, and thus constraining—even while, and precisely by, reflecting—the nature and the principle of the regime."[74] Pangle sees Montesquieu "as a prophet of the religion of reason."[75] Bartlett argues that Montesquieu thinks "religion is responsible for greater ills than benefits, at least in well-governed polities, and that it can safely be demoted if the task of politics becomes the pursuit of such goods (e.g., liberty understood as security)."[76] Pangle and Bartlett see Montesquieu as a partisan of a different kind of religion—liberal, commercial republicanism. Shklar argues that Montesquieu ascribes little, if any, "social merit" to Christianity, and notes, "religions tend to support despotism, because belief in an after-life makes people fatalistic, passive, and ready to endure oppression."[77] Lowenthal interprets Montesquieu as critical of Christianity: it "makes people poor citizens, opposes commerce, discourages marriage and propagation, among other ill effects."[78]

Both camps offer valuable insights on Montesquieu's views on religious toleration. However, the issue for Montesquieu is not toleration per se, but rather whether a particular religion has overall positive or negative political, economic, social, and moral effects. When a religion has overall negative effects, it is a candidate for selective intolerance. I say "candidate" since even if a religion has negative effects, removing or trying to remove it could have worse consequences.

Here I elaborate on Montesquieu's framework for *judging* religions with regard to their *political* effects. I explain his case for and against religion, and show when a religion is a candidate for not being tolerated. I provide a theory of *why* he is selectively intolerant.

Introducing Religion into *De l'Esprit des lois*

Early parts of *EL* highlight the political, not religious, character of Montesquieu's analysis. His first point, in the "Author's Foreword," is to clarify that republican virtue "is love of homeland, that is to say, love of equality. This is neither a moral virtue, nor a Christian virtue, it is *political* virtue." This is the first of many times he defines matters in primarily or solely political, not religious, terms.

In book I, Montesquieu explains that politics holds more promise than philosophy or religion for addressing societies' problems. Montesquieu says men are subject to three kinds of authority—religion, morality, and law. God "has called" men back to their creator with religion, and philosophers "have informed" men of morality, but neither appear successful in their endeavors.[79] Legislation, not philosophy or religion, has the greatest potential to establish a good political order: "Made for living in society, there they could forget others; legislators have returned them to their duties through political and civil laws" (I.1.234). Religion can help establish a good political order only if it conforms to a political situation. Montesquieu reinforces his insistence on viewing the world in principally political terms in part V.

Religion: Political, Not Metaphysical or Theological

Montesquieu defines religion broadly as a coherent set of beliefs that can be grounded in, among other things, a holy text, the texts of Plato, the practices of the Stoics, a particular moral structure, or tradition. The roots of a religion can be "in heaven" or "on the earth" (XXIV.1.714). The "various sects of philosophy among the ancients could be considered as kinds of religion" (XXIV.10.721). Montesquieu received criticism for this broad definition in France;[80] but it lays the groundwork for his strictly political consideration of religion. He does not study religion "in relation to the more sublime truths" (XXIV.1.714) because "here we are political men and not theologians" (XXV.9.744). Instead, he examines "the various religions of the world only in relation to the good to be drawn from them in the civil state" (XXIV.1.714). Accordingly, Spector notes that Montesquieu "subordinates the City of God to the City of Man."[81] His considerations of religion are therefore political and psychological,[82] not metaphysical[83] or theological. Montesquieu's primary interest is in religion's civic and political utility.[84] Montesquieu thus injects himself into the dialogue in the history of political philosophy surrounding civil religion.[85]

Religion's function for Montesquieu is quintessentially political: to "make good *citizens* of *men*" (XXIV.14.724; emphasis added). His standard for judging the social and political utility of a religion is the extent to which the religion contributes to making people good citizens, not good human beings per se.[86] He does not identify a single set of beliefs as "good." Judaism is appropriate in some places, not in others. Generally, though, religions should make a state more secure, free, and prosperous. Legislators should encourage citizens to adopt the proper public beliefs to foster these ends. Montesquieu is not the only political philosopher to employ this standard; Machiavelli did so earlier in his *Discourses*, and Rousseau later in his *Social Contract*.[87] But Montesquieu is one of the first *liberals* to argue that a religion is not good if it does not help create good citizens.

Montesquieu rejects any religion that makes citizens worse off. Consider some of his remarks on Islam.[88] In despotic states, people are driven by fear, the spring of such regimes. In Islamic states like Persia, where "religion has more influence than in any other" (V.14.294), there is "fear added to fear.... [In] Mohammedan empires the peoples derive from religion a part of the astonishing respect they have for their prince" (V.14.294).[89] The people are lazier (and thus less commercial), partially because of the "dogma of predestination" (XXIV.14.724). Muslims are bad citizens since they "turn their backs on all that belongs to this world" five times a day (to pray) (XXIV.11.722). Women are enslaved domestically (XVI.10.515): "In Mohammedan states, one is not only the master of the life and goods of the female slaves, but also of what is called their virtue or their honor.... [In] these countries ... the larger part of the nation exists only in order to serve the voluptuousness of the other. This servitude is rewarded by the laziness that such slaves are given to enjoy, which is yet another misfortune for the state" (XV.12.499).[90]

If a religion undergirds despotism in a particular state, for example, the religion is bad. Within these broad parameters, a religion's acceptability varies according to the *esprit*—the essence, ethos, or character—of a particular people, of which the religion is a key component.[91]

On the Function and (Im)Proper Content of Religion

Religion's most crucial function, Montesquieu thinks, is to advance morality and moderation. A good religion helps restrain people from engaging in bad actions (XXIV.2.715–16). Religion is not perfect in restraining men, but to "say that religion gives no motive for restraint because it does not always restrain is to say that civil laws are not a motive for restraint either" (XXIV.2.715).

Religion can make men more moral: "religion, even a false one, is the best warrant men can have of the integrity of men" (XXIV.8.720). Montesquieu justifies this claim with examples of the religions of the people of Pegu and the Essenes. The people of Pegu are exemplary because the principal tenets of their religion "are not to kill, not to steal, to avoid immodesty, to cause no displeasure to one's fellow man, and instead, to do him all the good one can." Moreover, "they believe that one will be saved in any religion whatever; this makes these peoples, though ... proud and poor, show gentleness and compassion to unfortunates" (XXIV.8.720). The Essenes "took an oath to observe justice toward men, to do no harm to anyone ... to hate unjust men, to keep faith with everyone, to command with modesty ... and to flee all illicit gain" (XXIV.9.721). For Montesquieu, such notions had real and beneficial effects.

Religion moderates rulers, especially despotic rulers. "Even if it were useless for subjects to have a religion" (which it is not), Montesquieu remarks, "it would not be useless for princes to have one and to whiten with foam the only bridle that can hold those who fear no human laws." He continues, "A prince who loves and fears religion is a lion who yields to the hand that caresses him or the voice that pacifies him; the one who fears and hates religion is like the wild beasts who gnaw the chain that keeps them from throwing themselves on passers-by; he who has no religion at all is that terrible animal that feels its liberty only when it claws and devours" (XXIV.2.715–16). Religion thus can serve as a force of resistance against despotism by moderating rulers, something Spector identifies as an important aspect of the originality of Montesquieu's analysis of religion.[92] But not all religions do so equally well. Consider his contrast of Christianity with Islam.

Christianity "is remote from pure despotism," unlike Islam (XXIV.3.716). Moreover, "the gentleness so recommended in the gospel stands opposed to the despotic fury with which a prince would mete out his own justice and exercise his cruelties." Cohler thus notes that in Montesquieu's view Christianity's gentleness makes it appropriate for moderate governments, seems "to offer the possibility that that community is all mankind," and "engenders to find a motive for restraint that is not dehumanizing."[93] Consider Montesquieu's comparison of rulers influenced by Christianity and Islam: "Whereas Mohammedan princes constantly kill or are killed, among Christians religion makes princes less timid and consequently less cruel. The prince counts on his subjects, and the subjects on the prince. Remarkably, the Christian religion, which seems to have no other goal than the felicity of the other life, is also our happiness in this one!" (XXIV.3.716). Christianity softens harsh *mœurs*. For example: "In spite of the size of the Ethiopian empire and the vice of its climate, the Christian religion has kept despotism from being established there and has carried the *mœurs* and laws of Europe to the middle of Africa" (XXIV.3.716). These European *mœurs* are gentler and grounded in Christianity. Scholars disagree on Montesquieu's views on Christianity. Pangle sees his praise of Christianity as "rather weak": "Christianity is praised only as preferable to the modern alternative, Islam, and especially because of its restraining effect in despotic regions."[94] Conversely, Shackleton argues that Montesquieu thinks Christianity opposes despotism and improves "the lot of human beings in many parts of the world."[95] Montesquieu does seem to suggest that by establishing a higher authority or belief set to which rulers are accountable, Christianity fosters desirable values among rulers like gentleness and moderation.

Let us now examine his portrayal of Islam. "Mohammedan princes," we saw, "constantly kill or are killed," and Montesquieu judges Islam the cause of their violence. This violence permeates the political culture, because Muhammad gave his followers enthusiasm that manifested itself in them becoming conquerors (XXI.16.634). Barrera suggests that Montesquieu sees Islam as a conquering religion, or a religion of conquerors.[96] Montesquieu contends that it was through this force alone that Muhammad acquired followers (XXV.13.747), but this force eventually destroyed the Persian Empire (XXIV.11.722). Schaub argues that Montesquieu's criticism of Islam serves a double purpose, as he criticizes Islam "to gain a hearing that will eventually lead the audience to indict its own [Christian] beliefs as much as those of Islam."[97]

Religions, Montesquieu thinks, can rescue a state from dire circumstances: "religion can sustain the political state when the laws are powerless" (XXIV.16.726). Richter explains that for Montesquieu religion "can even save a state, which left to its own police power, would be overturned."[98] As we consider some particular ways religion can improve a state, we remind ourselves that for Montesquieu the political usefulness—not truth—of doctrines is central. The "truest and most saintly dogmas," he writes, "can have very bad consequences when they are not bound with the principles of society" while "the falsest dogmas can have remarkable consequences when they are made to relate to the same principles" (XXIV.19.728–29).

Montesquieu finds believing in a god useful. Montesquieu engages Bayle, who claimed "it is better to be an atheist than an idolater" because it is "less dangerous to have no religion at all than to have a bad one.... [Bayle] should prefer ... for one to say of me that I do not exist, than for one to say that I am a wicked man" (XXIV.2.715). Montesquieu deems this sophistry, arguing that "the fact that it is of no use to mankind for one to believe that a certain man exists" does not mean that it is not "quite useful for one to believe that God exists." To contradict Bayle,[99] Montesquieu does not insist that God exists,[100] but only that it is *useful* to believe in God or idols. This is important first since a "good" religion can include belief in an idol(s), god(s), or God. Second, he emphasizes the utility of believing in God, partially because it attaches men to the religion.

Adhering to a religion is more crucial than merely "believing" in it. In a chapter entitled "On the Motive for Attachment to the Various Religions," Montesquieu identifies numerous practices that facilitate this attachment. When a religion "gives us the idea of choice made by the divinity, and of a distinction between those who profess it and those who do not profess it," it becomes more effective (XXV.2.736). Distinguishing between believers and nonbelievers gets people to adhere to a religion more readily.[101] Subsequently, there should be a stigma attached to not believing in a religion and thus not being a part of this essential community. This social form of religious intolerance could justify pressuring people into following a religion, and excluding them from the community if they do not follow it.

A religion should require followers to display their belief in it regularly and in various ways to increase its effectiveness. Hence, Montesquieu contends that a "religion burdened with many practices attaches people to it more strongly than another one that has fewer; one is attached to the things that continually occupy one" (XXV.2.736). Staying engaged reminds practitioners of their attachment and commitment to the religion.

Religions are more effective with a place of rewards. "Men are exceedingly drawn to hope and to fear, and a religion that had neither hell nor paradise would scarcely please them." He elaborates:

> The idea of a place of rewards necessarily brings with it the idea of a region of penalties, and when one hopes for the former without fearing the latter, civil laws no longer have any force. Men who believe in the certainty of rewards in the next life will escape the legislator; they will have too much scorn for death. How can one constrain by the laws a man who believes himself sure that the greatest penalty the magistrates can inflict on him will end in a moment only to begin his happiness? (XXIV.14.725)

Entrance into a place of rewards must come with conditions (i.e., good behavior) and people must suffer for not adhering to religious doctrine sufficiently. People need to earn their place in heaven, and must know they will pay dearly if they do not. While I interpret Montesquieu's remarks as potentially positive, Shklar offers a sharper reading: for Montesquieu, "generally religions tend to support despotism, because belief in an afterlife makes people fatalistic, passive, and ready to endure oppression."[102] Shklar seems to go too far. We can imagine Montesquieu observing that belief in an afterlife has good consequences in a particular society, or that trying to remove the belief would be worse than letting it remain.

Montesquieu identifies "pure morality" as another way to attach men to a religion. But instead of explaining what it means for a religion or morality to be pure, he writes: "Men, rascals when taken one by one, are very honest as a whole; they love morality, and if I were not considering such a serious subject, I would say that this is remarkably clear in theaters: one is sure to please people by the feelings that morality professes, and one is sure to offend them by those that it disapproves" (XXV.2.737). The fact that people react this way to fiction says a lot about our feelings toward reality, according to Montesquieu: people generally want the right outcome, particularly when watching other people, and even more so when in groups. Social pressure helps encourage "rascals" to have purer morals.

His final point on how men become attached to religion relates to external displays: "When the externals of worship are magnificent, we are flattered and we become very attached to the religion. Wealth in the temples and the clergy affects us greatly. Thus, the very poverty of peoples is a motive attaching them to that religion, which has served as a pretext for those who have caused their poverty" (XXV.2.737). People seem to be attached to magnificent displays, especially of wealth and beauty. A gorgeous place of worship impresses followers and draws them in. Yet there is a darker point: church authorities keep people impoverished to make them more attracted to the wealth and beauty of church displays, and thus to the religion. Shklar elaborates: "Magnificent objects of veneration both bind believers deeply to the faith and make them love those who are most responsible for their misery. . . . Compulsory gifts to the clergy, as well as clerical celibacy and idleness, contribute to the poverty of an already poor population."[103]

Montesquieu insists that religious advice should not be as binding as laws: "Human laws made to speak to the spirit should give precepts and no counsels at all." Religion, by contrast, is "made to speak to the heart, [and] should give many counsels and few precepts" (XXIV.7.719). Precepts are laws, whereas counsels are "highminded suggestions."[104] Laws are binding. Religion, made to speak to the heart, should provide advice but rarely command (at least in good societies; it might be appropriate for a religion to give precepts to improve a bad situation). Bartlett considers this distinction antireligious: "all the teachings of Christ that Montesquieu deems compatible with 'moderate government' become Christ's orders, whereas those he deems incompatible become mere 'counsels.'"[105] Whatever the case, Montesquieu certainly suggests that religious advice ought to be limited, and the state should not enforce it. When a religion tries to give rules "not for the good but for the better, not for what is good but for what is perfect, it is suitable for these to be counsels and not laws, for perfection does not concern men or things universally." Religion is more effective when its advice is narrower and more limited.

Religion must not interfere with citizens' eagerness to act regularly to help the state flourish. Montesquieu explains, "Men, being made to preserve, feed, and clothe themselves, do all actions *in society*, religion should not give them an overly contemplative life" (XXIV.11.722; emphasis added). He is concerned about religions that cause people to withdraw from the public sphere and focus exclusively on private spiritual matters. His named culprit is Islam: "Mohammedans become speculative by habit; they pray five times a day, and each time they must do something that makes them turn their backs on all that belongs to this world: this forms them for speculation" (XXIV.11.722). Merry contends that "the real target is the ascetic and monastic aspects of the Catholic Church."[106] The general message is clear: men who contemplate do not act.

Finally, Montesquieu argues that religions should not interfere with citizens' ability to support the state. Addressing the Sabbath as a day of rest, Montesquieu writes: "When a religion orders that work come to an end, it should have more regard for the needs of men than for the greatness of the being that it honors" (XXIV.23.731). Montesquieu provides multiple examples demonstrating the importance of prioritizing the needs of men. In Athens, the excessive number of religious festivals frequently prevented business from being conducted. When Constantine ordered that one rest on Sunday, he "made this ordinance for the towns and not for the peoples of the countryside; he felt that the useful work was in the towns and necessary work in the country." Montesquieu would proscribe religious rites that interfere with the needs of a state, be they in international affairs, agriculture, or anything else. "In other words, human contracts have precedence over divine covenants, including that of the Sabbath."[107] In a chapter entitled "That One Must Not Decide by the Precepts of Religion When Those of Natural Law Are in Question," Montesquieu points out other religious practices that did or could jeopardize a state's safety:

> The Abyssinians have a harsh fast for fifty days, which so weakens them that they cannot act for a long time; the Turks do not fail to attack them after this fast. To favor natural defense religion ought to put some limits on these practices. The Jews were ordered to observe the Sabbath, but it was dull-witted of this nation not to defend itself when its enemies chose that day to attack.... Who can fail to see that natural defense is of a higher order than all precepts? (XXVI.7.757–58)

Religion must cede ground to political and civic matters.

Montesquieu's Subtle Intolerance

Montesquieu initially seems supportive of toleration in XXV, 9–12. Kingston and others hone in on these chapters to support their reading of Montesquieu as a proponent of liberal toleration.[108] I see reasons for an alternative interpretation. Montesquieu notes that there is "much difference between tolerating and approving a religion." Disliking a religion is not necessarily grounds for not tolerating or accepting its existence. He continues, "When the laws of a state have believed they should allow many religions, they must also oblige them to tolerate each other. The principle is that every religion that is repressed becomes repressive itself; for as soon as, by some chance, it can shake off oppression, it attacks the religion that repressed it, not as a religion, but as a tyranny" (XXV.9.744). One might interpret this statement as favoring tolerance, since intolerance can cause problems throughout society. Kingston notes, "This commitment to religious pluralism in Montesquieu's work is protected and promoted precisely through a policy of non-intervention."[109] Instead, I think we see Montesquieu's first qualification on toleration at the beginning of this passage: we are obligated to tolerate religions "*when* the laws of a state have believed they should allow many religions." Montesquieu does not think that the state always should allow many religions, because some religions have bad effects. Otherwise he would have said that states should allow and tolerate multiple religions. Thus begins his case against toleration.

Montesquieu continues by explaining his peculiar notion of toleration: "It is useful therefore that the laws require of these various religions not only that they not disturb [*troublent*] the state, but also that they not disturb each other. A citizen does not satisfy the laws by contenting himself with not agitating the body of the state; it is also necessary that he not disturb any citizen whatsoever" (XXV.9.744). Much hinges on how Montesquieu means "disturb." "Disturb" could entail not violating the rights of other citizens. "Disturb" might mean producing bad outcomes or having unwanted effects; if so, perhaps a religion could participate in political life if doing so has no bad effects. There is reason for a stronger reading, though, based partially on the context of these four chapters. Montesquieu might use "disturb" broadly to mean bother by negatively impacting or interfering in the affairs of others or the state.[110] Montesquieu acknowledges this stronger reading of his "tolerance" in *Défense* but avoids taking it on because he knows he is susceptible to this critique (OCII.1146–47). Consider how some commentators interpret his opinion of Christianity. Dos Santos suggests that Montesquieu thinks Christianity breeds intolerance.[111] Schaub contends that according to Montesquieu "Christianity is itself a form of despotism."[112] Lowenthal writes, "Montesquieu is critical of the social and political effects of Christianity. . . . Christianity opposed commerce and money-lending in the Middle Ages; by fostering conventional chastity, it discouraged marriage and propagation; it was hostile everywhere to polygamy and divorce; it promoted civil disobedience in the name of a higher law; it turned Christian against Christian and Christian against non-Christian through an intolerant zeal for universality."[113] These scholars provide evidence suggesting Montesquieu thinks Christianity can "disturb" the state. By contrast, Samuel argues: "Montesquieu is not anti-Christian nor is he against religion generally in *Spirit*. The first theme of Book XXIV is a defense of the way in which religion, and especially Christianity, advances political order."[114]

Religions not endorsed by the state should not interfere with public affairs or other citizens with different beliefs. Adherents of unsanctioned religions certainly should not proselytize. Montesquieu's conception of toleration might open the door to a kind of legally enforced isolation from the state, adherents of other religions, and other citizens. XXV, 10 offers more evidence of his selective intolerance.

Montesquieu finds religions that try to spread problematic: "there are scarcely any but intolerant religions that are greatly zealous to establish themselves elsewhere, for a religion that can tolerate others scarcely thinks of its propagation" (XXV.10.744) Most religions, but especially Christianity and Islam, have worked vigorously to establish themselves elsewhere, even violently through Inquisition, jihad, and so on.[115] When practiced this way, Montesquieu judges these prominent religions intolerant and therefore candidates for intolerance.

Montesquieu proceeds to argue for limiting the number of religions: "[It] will be a very good civil law, when the state is satisfied with the established religion, not to allow the establishment of another. Here, therefore, is the fundamental principle for political laws in religious matters. When one is the master of the state's accepting a new religion, or not accepting it, it must not be established; when it is established, it must be tolerated" (XXV.10.744).[116] One might emphasize that once a religion is established, it *must* be tolerated. For example, Larrère finds two principles in this passage, which she thinks Montesquieu brings together in support of toleration: "do not establish, tolerate" (*ne pas établir, tolérer*).[117] But his suggestion that "when the state is satisfied with the established religion," it should "not allow the establishment of another" provides basis for a stronger reading.[118] Montesquieu thinks it is reasonable, sometimes preferable, that states decide whether religions are satisfactory. Once the state finds a religion that fits the *esprit*, the state should not allow in any other religion. This is an argument for *in*tolerance toward nonestablished religions. Kingston contends, "Montesquieu offers a somewhat eclectic defense of toleration. Still, all these arguments are rooted in the more general notion that religious diversity is not a threat and that toleration in fact may be more conducive to the good of the society."[119] But a proponent of toleration and religious diversity plain and simple would not permit limiting the number of religions, especially not to one.[120] Montesquieu thinks religious diversity and liberty can threaten the state; his support for religious toleration is further qualified.

We gain added support for this view when we read this passage alongside another where Montesquieu explains that when religions "give us the idea of choice made by the divinity, and of a distinction between those who profess it and those who do not profess it," they become more effective (XXV.2.736). It is easier to distinguish between believers and nonbelievers, and to exert sufficient pressure on people, when only one religion is permitted in the state.

We must pause to address an alternative reading of XXV, 9–10. Might Montesquieu defend toleration in general, or prefer a state that tolerates other religions, within a general liberal framework, while sanctioning intolerance only of *in*tolerant or persecuting religions? He seems to make such a qualification when he speaks of there being "hardly any but intolerant religions that have a great zeal for establishing themselves elsewhere"

(XXV.10.744). Notwithstanding his apparent qualification in XXV, 10, on my reading, Montesquieu's selective intolerance goes further. First, a religion can have harmful beliefs regardless of whether the religion persecutes others. What's more, even if a religion itself is tolerant, Montesquieu is open to not tolerating it; so his intolerance is more general. Second, one religion could be a central factor to a state's goodness, and a core component of its *esprit*. Since another religion could disrupt the primary religion's good effects by giving people an alternative religion to follow, the state reasonably could decide to block the spread of (seemingly) disruptive ideas. The state need not even view another religion as inherently harmful to be "satisfied with the established religion" and thus not allow in other religions. Montesquieu finds many reasons for religious intolerance beyond the religion being intolerant.

Still, Montesquieu rejects religious intolerance becoming violent. He uses the Inquisition to argue against using violence in religious matters. Comparing Christians to the Japanese, Montesquieu has a Japanese emperor observe: "We treat you [Christians], you who do not believe as we do, as you yourselves treat those who do not believe as you do; you can complain only of your weakness, which makes it so that we exterminate you" (XXV.13.746–47).[121] Violent intolerance provokes violent intolerance. Christians who persecute seem more violent than the Japanese emperor because they kill Jews who "follow a religion that you [Christians] yourself know to have been formerly cherished by God; we think that God loves it still, and you think that he does not love it any longer, and because you judge it thus, you have afflicted with iron and fire those who are in the quite pardonable error of believing that God still loves that which he loved" (XXV.13.747). The persecution of Christians comes across as unjust, unreasonable, and unenlightened. XXV, 13 confirms that intolerance should never be violent. It does not reverse calls for a certain kind of intolerance. When a state needs to be intolerant, it should do so in a subtler manner. Montesquieu specifies slow, careful ways to change religions, rather than abrupt, coercive approaches.

If a religion is not a positive force in a particular society, then Montesquieu is open to the state carefully trying to change, marginalize, or remove it. After two chapters on "toleration," the next chapter is entitled "On Changing Religion." The topics are closely linked. Montesquieu urges caution when trying to change a religion:

> A prince who undertakes to destroy or to change the dominant religion in his state is greatly exposed. If his government is despotic, he runs a greater risk of seeing a revolution than he would by any tyranny whatever, which is never a new thing in these sorts of states. The revolution results from the fact that a state does not change religion, *mœurs*, and

manners in an instant, or as soon as the prince publishes the ordinance establishing a new religion. (XXV.11.745)

Changing a religion is difficult and complicated. Because people usually are attached to their religion, they normally do not take kindly to attempts to change it, especially open and confrontational ones. If done improperly, the risk of unrest or revolution increases. The proper way to change religions, *mœurs*, and manners is slowly; in proceeding this way, people's passions are not as easily inflamed.

Some have seen Montesquieu's caution in this paragraph as evidence of him opposing the state trying to change religions. Durkheim writes that Montesquieu "held that customs and religion were beyond the power of the lawgiver and that even laws relating to other measures had to be compatible with customs and religion."[122] But Durkheim then acknowledges that there "are even societies in which not only the laws but the religion and customs as well can, to some extent, be fashioned by the prince."[123] Our discussion suggests an alternative interpretation, namely that Montesquieu is open to lawmakers changing religions when necessary, by proper means. Rahe notes that Montesquieu had always "been perfectly prepared to censure laws and practices rooted in harmful prejudices, and ... in his *Spirit of Laws* he did so with some abandon—presumably because he regarded himself as someone ... able to penetrate with a stroke of genius the entire constitution of a state."[124] In a short but crucial chapter—XXV, 11—Montesquieu demonstrates the complicated nature of this enterprise:

> the former religion is linked with the constitution of the state, and the new one is not attached to it; the first one is in accord with the climate and the new one often resists it. Furthermore, the citizens find their laws distasteful; they scorn the government already established; suspicions of both religions are substituted for a firm belief in one. . . . One gives the state, at least for some time, bad citizens and bad believers. (745)

Religion is integral to the state's *esprit*, and often is a force for good. Even if a religion is bad, the inhabitants have embraced it, and it persists for a reason; it is a fundamental part of the state's makeup. This is one major reason why we cannot conclude, as Pangle and others do, that Montesquieu simply wants to eradicate revealed religion. Doing so is often impossible, and normally destructive.

The Mechanisms of Intolerance

Montesquieu suggests ways to change undesirable religions. He also identifies alternative beliefs to embrace. The most provocative method entails demonstrating that commerce can offer more moral and material goods than religion. A more certain way of detaching the soul from religion is not by having laws mandate certain new beliefs but "by favor, by the comforts of life, by the hope of fortune, not by what makes one indignant, but by what leads one to indifference when other passions act on our soul and when those that religion inspires are silent." It should be pleasant and desirable for someone to change their religious beliefs and embrace comfort instead. From this follows a "general rule": "in the matter of changing religion, invitations are stronger than penalties" (XXV.12.746). Invitations come primarily from commercial activity, which encourages people to set new priorities.

Montesquieu sees commerce—the interaction of peoples, states, and cultures—as powerful. We saw earlier in this chapter that commerce cures destructive prejudices, fosters gentler and softer *mœurs*, spreads knowledge of the *mœurs* of all nations everywhere, and produces in men a certain feeling of exact justice (XX.1–2.585–86). Commerce makes men ambitious and industrious (XIII.2.459), and states (more) democratic (XX.4.587–88). The *esprit* of commerce "brings with it the *esprit* of frugality, economy, moderation, work, wisdom, tranquility, order, and rule. Thus, as long as this *esprit* continues to exist, the wealth it produces has no bad effect . . . this *esprit* must reign alone and not be crossed by another; all the laws must favor it" (V.6.280). Bartlett writes, "to be concerned above all with the tangible goods of this world is necessarily to be less concerned with the intangible, perhaps ineffable, and certainly more controversial goods of the next."[125] Perhaps this is what Montesquieu means with invitations being stronger than penalties. Pangle suggests that commerce leads to the overcoming of Christianity: "All that is required . . . is to show the way to an understanding of Christianity which is not in conflict with devotion to commerce and comfort; the inherent attractions of these things will do the rest."[126] On these readings, commerce would replace (or at least heavily marginalize) revealed religion. We would focus on promoting trade and interaction, which increase individual and societal prosperity. Engaging in beneficial economic and cultural interactions from which people profit financially and morally can help them recognize the goods commerce provides as superior, though Montesquieu's remarks on Holland (XX.2.586) show that he does not see all aspects of commerce as unqualifiedly good.

Montesquieu offers other ways to detach someone's soul from a religion. We saw that religion should not give men an overly contemplative life, because it hinders work. If a state gets people to be less contemplative, they should be less attached to their religion, because they are not as committed to it psychologically. The state can also encourage people to focus on their present concerns and not look for rewards in the afterlife. It might be appropriate for a state to try to mitigate the importance of heaven in a religious doctrine. This can help ensure that its citizens focus on this world. Once a state is satisfied with a religion, it need not permit other religions into the state, and can try limiting the number of religions in a state to one. Montesquieu contends that religions should neither seek to expand nor bother nonmembers. These prohibitions can marginalize religions: if they cannot work to increase their number of followers, their existence might be jeopardized.

We must note that Montesquieu advocates minimizing the influence of religion only when two conditions are met: when the religion is on balance harmful and when possible. Montesquieu believes that religions can benefit states, for example by improving morality and integrity. Religions fit some societies better than others. Montesquieu argues that Catholicism matches up better with monarchy, while Protestantism better fits republics (XXIV.5.718). Skrzypek notes that Montesquieu considered Protestantism "more favorable to economic activity—an essential source of prosperity for the state and its citizens."[127] A state can only act against a religion under the right conditions. Religion can be an integral part of the *esprit*. It is one of the many things that govern men and form an *esprit général*. Montesquieu does not advocate a complete elimination of religion, because doing so is undesirable and improper.

Ultimately, Montesquieu recommends selecting a religion for intolerant treatment only when it does not make a state more secure, free, and prosperous; that is, when it does not fit the politics of a particular place. To determine this, we must comprehend how the religion functions somewhere by analyzing many factors, including the form of government, laws, commerce, climate, and *mœurs*, that form a society's *esprit*. Accordingly, Montesquieu largely refrains from generalizing too broadly about a religion's effects, with the possible exception of Islam. Selective intolerance could do more harm than good. "One leaves the bad, if one fears the worse; one leaves the good, if one is in doubt about the better" (Preface.230). Caution is necessary, even with Islam, since it is such a key component of the *esprit* in various states. Removing it may do more harm than good. We must read Montesquieu's selective religious intolerance in the context of the flexibility he seeks to give legislators to act in diverse conditions across time and place.

Montesquieu's politics of place insists that robust analysis of a society must include a study of subpolitical factors. Physical, economic, and moral factors are essential components of any society. Just as political actors must understand that the input, so to speak, of the subpolitical factors differs across time and place, so too, therefore, will the "output." Reasonable variation or unchangeable features necessitate different political, economic, social, and moral outcomes. To avoid including them in their calculus is to court not just error but potential disaster. Montesquieu acknowledges that legislators must work within the context of the physical environment of their country because it impacts the inhabitants and their practices in significant ways. Legislators all should pursue commerce, but the extent and type should vary across time and place. And while religions can have significant benefits in societies, it also is quite possible that a set of beliefs is detrimental to some societies (though not others). In such situations, it might be appropriate for legislators to use methods of selective intolerance to reduce or remove the negative effects of a religion.

CHAPTER FIVE

The American Founding as a Particularistic Achievement

Montesquieu offers his readers a political education. This education teaches that both great and small *esprits* should favor particularism over universalism. Montesquieu intends for this framework to be useful for legislators as they seek to refound or enact changes in a state. Legislators gain tools to promote security, liberty, and prosperity. The politics of place also helps us evaluate better the nature and outcome of political events. We gain tools to judge the actions of legislators. Here we use the politics of place to evaluate a pertinent case: the American founding.

Montesquieu was undoubtedly the most influential philosopher during the American founding period. Recall that no other thinker was cited more from 1760 to 1805 in America;[1] Montesquieu leads by a wide margin in the 1780s, the time when the founders were constructing institutions. Montesquieu is the only political philosopher delegates cited during the Constitutional Convention, according to James Madison's *Notes on Debates in the Federal Convention of 1787*.[2] The founders turned to Montesquieu to develop the principles and structure of their government. They explicitly adopted Montesquieu's theory of a distribution (or, as they would call it, separation) of three powers, and then made it more republican. The American founding was a successful affair. Many subsequently hail the writing and ratification of the Constitution as a "great rehearsal" for the "end of history." The American founding and its principles then appear as universal and, even, exceptional. And since Montesquieu was the philosopher to whom they turned more than anyone else, it seems that his teachings may be universal too.

In this chapter I use Montesquieu's politics of place to consider whether the American founding was exceptional. How are we to assess the accomplishments of America's Founding Fathers, above all the United States

Constitution? To what extent, if any, should America—and its founding in particular—serve as an example to other countries? Might the founding be universally exceptional?

The question of whether or not America is exceptional goes back to the early colonists, and continues through today. America might be exceptional in religious, economic, or empirical terms. Christianity's central influence throughout America's history has led some to view America as religiously exceptional. America is exceptional because it embraces and exemplifies true, noble Christian principles in its society and government, and does so better than any other country. The most prominent early expression of this came from the Puritan John Winthrop, who famously suggested in his "Modell of Christian Charity" that Puritan colonists consider themselves to be a "city upon a hill."[3] Tocqueville later identified America's Christian character as the most important causal factor that maintains America's democratic republic.[4] Today, America remains religiously exceptional from an empirical perspective.[5]

Another iteration of American exceptionalism focuses on economics. The founders certainly favored commerce.[6] Many Americans continue to view capitalism favorably.[7] America has worked to open markets and spread capitalism across the world, with the expectation that both parties will benefit from the exchanges.[8] America thus appears to many to be the standard-bearer for capitalism and free markets. Others have presented evidence that America is a statistical outlier on a wide range of issues, including the size of government, commitment to certain conceptions of personal freedom, number of voluntary associations, and rates of private philanthropic activity.[9]

In this chapter I focus on historical and philosophical ways of evaluating America as exceptional. I readily acknowledge that America was a true historical exception. My focus then shifts to three forms of political and philosophical exceptionalism: universal, unfortunate, and particular. Many interpret the Founding Fathers' accomplishments as universal: the founders discerned the true, right, or best political principles and form of government. The principles found in the Declaration of Independence certainly appear universal. None other than Alexander Hamilton, in *Federalist* No. 1, claimed that the framers of the US Constitution were "establishing good government from reflection and choice." Alternatively, some view the founding as unfortunately exceptional—that is, as a *bad* exception. For example, the Constitution allowed slavery to continue, and may have condoned it. But the universal and unfortunate interpretations are narrow and misguided readings (in quite different ways) of the founding—and of Montesquieu. They cause us to misinterpret what the founders really accomplished.

The founders discerned one good way to apply (and adapt) Montesquieu's politics of place. For this we can applaud them. But they did not discover the one "right" approach to politics. Indeed, there exist numerous political, economic, and moral paths states can take to achieve goodness. This is the core teaching of Montesquieu's political education. We should not view the American founding as the apex of "American exceptionalism," nor should we hold up the US political system as a model for all peoples. What's more, such notions of American exceptionalism actually hinder many peoples from achieving what really makes America exceptional—that the founders established a political, economic, and moral system that made a particular people more secure, free, and prosperous. The American founding is exceptional in particularistic terms. We turn to Montesquieu, the Constitutional Convention, and Tocqueville to support this interpretation.

Before proceeding, we must pause and consider our usage of the term "exceptional." This is crucial to providing the clarity needed to discern if a state, situation, or historical event qualifies as exceptional. *Merriam-Webster*'s offers two kinds of definitions for exceptional. Exceptional can mean "not usual; unusual or uncommon; deviating from the norm."[10] As noted, America does appear as empirically different.[11] This sense of exceptional is not noteworthy because, as Joyce Appleby argues, "all nations are different," so "exceptionalism cannot simply mean different."[12] We are interested, instead, in an alternative, normative conception of exceptional: "unusually good: much better than average."[13] As Hilde Restad explains, "American exceptionalism itself entails the belief in the special and unique role the United States is meant to play in world history, its distinctiveness from the Old World, and its resistance to the laws of history."[14] Tami Davis and Sean Lynn-Jones remark, "American exceptionalism not only celebrates the uniqueness and special virtues of the United States, but also elevates America to a higher moral plane than other countries."[15] Ceaser notes that exceptional means special. But the most important senses of special are normative. Special can refer to being in "possession of a certain quality." A country also can be special by "being charged with or embracing a task or mission." This latter understanding suggests that, at least in the American case, some Americans think America is called on to fulfill its mission.[16] We consider later what this mission might be. Throughout our inquiry we use "exceptional" in the normative sense.

Historical Exceptionalism

America unquestionably is a historical exception. It was the first modern, commercial, democratic, federal republic with a written constitution.[17] The written Constitution that the founders produced during the Constitutional Convention in Philadelphia in 1787 is truly exceptional in historical terms.[18] It did much more than merely replace the flaccid Articles of Confederation and the mostly dysfunctional republic the Articles governed during the 1780s. The Constitution represents the first written constitutional document enshrining a form of government and institutions.

America is founded on a novel philosophical claim: men have rights that precede government, and men form governments to protect these rights. Before America, rulers, usually kings, determined the extent of citizens' liberties. No more, said the Americans. Drawing on Locke for inspiration, America's founders asserted that our rights derive from nature, not from a king or a legislature or any other institutions, political or otherwise. Rulers cannot take away or infringe on these rights arbitrarily. If they do, their rule may become illegitimate and subject to revolt. Other documents like the Magna Carta (1215) and the English Bill of Rights (1689) established parameters within which rulers had to operate, and guaranteed certain rights, privileges, or liberties to citizens. The Declaration of Independence asserted that fundamental natural rights exist. America's Constitution was the first political document to cement and protect rights and liberties by establishing the institutions, practices, and rules that were to govern the institutions, those who ran them, and the citizens more generally. Because of the importance the founders attached to our rights, they enshrined critical ones in the Bill of Rights, the first ten amendments passed in 1791. These begin, importantly, with freedom of speech and religion. England, by contrast, still has no written constitution. The American Constitution has made the written constitution a hallmark of most contemporary states, liberal democratic and otherwise.[19] We have come to see a written constitution almost as a necessary condition for establishing a good political order, thanks in large part to America's example. One primary reason the founders created a written constitution was to clearly outline the role of each branch and to help prevent abuses of power and protect rights and freedoms.

America was exceptional for devising various schemes to separate powers and protect the liberties and rights established in the Constitution.[20] The idea, James Madison wrote in *Federalist* No. 51, was that "ambition must be made to counteract ambition." In this, the founders were following a number of important thinkers. The most relevant is Montesquieu, whom Madison quotes at length in *Federalist* No. 47 when discussing the theory of a separation of powers. Madison's maxim on ambition is nearly identical to Montesquieu's recommendation that political actors structure institutions such that "power stops power."[21] Like Montesquieu, the founders were unwilling to rely on political actors having altruistic motives or prioritizing (their conception of) the common or public good. The founders deemed this approach uncertain and insufficient at best, and deeply dangerous at worst. Rather, the founders followed Montesquieu and asserted that the best way to protect life (security), liberty, and the pursuit of happiness (prosperity) was to rely on political actors pursuing their self-interest and the interest of their institutions. For example, a member of Congress should protect Congress's powers against encroachments from the executive and judicial branches. As such, the founders structured institutions to pit their interests against those of other actors and institutions. The founders instituted various schemes to separate powers, including federalism, representation, and separating the legislative, executive, and judicial branches, with an eye to establishing as many effective checks on power as possible.

The United States was not the first federal republic. Holland and Switzerland were well-functioning federal republics long before the United States became an independent country; indeed, the founders looked especially to the Dutch model (as well as Montesquieu's analysis in book IX) when theorizing about their own federal republic. Still, they gave this form of government heightened legitimacy and prominence because federalism seemed to be an important ingredient to America's success; James Madison argued as much in *Federalist* No. 10. The American states were true governing entities with real powers. They remained distinct from the federal government in important ways. The American states had the power to check each other and the federal government. They also had the power to innovate and create different environments in which citizens might choose to live. Federalism assigns responsibility to local, state, and national institutions. The United States thus far has provided evidence for Montesquieu's supposition that federal republics potentially could be "eternal."

The founders established the first fully democratic republican modern state.[22] The English model was only partially democratic. America's founders asserted, instead, that a state could—perhaps should—be based primarily on democratic institutions. The American people were to choose representatives. In this way the people would serve as a check on those in power. America's innovation opened up new democratic possibilities to the entire world. America was the most extensive experiment in democracy, in terms of the size of the country, the inclusiveness of its democracy, and the extent to which participation and representation permeated the institutions and culture. As observers like Tocqueville noticed, local institutions like townships were in many ways the lifeblood of the United States because of how they kept citizens democratically engaged.[23]

It is clear that America is a historical exception. Here we have touched on only some of the main ways it is such. Yet the historical perspective does not necessitate normative assessment. Normative assessment arises out of the consideration of American exceptionalism in political, moral, and philosophical terms.

Universal Exceptionalism

In this section we will examine how one might judge America to be universally exceptional. We pay special attention to the American founding period, from 1776 to 1789, because it was during this time that the founders developed the principles that define America. We will focus on the Declaration of Independence and Constitution, as well as documents like *The Federalist* and personal correspondences that serve to illuminate the purposes of the two key documents. Our goal is to discern what the core ideas and values in these documents are and how one might consider them universal. Claims about the universality of America's political, moral, and philosophical principles certainly differ in nature. But they generally all advance the claim that America's founders established the "right" or "true" principles of a good political order.[24] Therefore, the arguments run, other societies ought to emulate America's principles so far as possible, because these principles are universally applicable.[25] Some iterations maintain that America should try to spread or impose its values and practices on others. We will consider different versions of universal exceptionalism, with an eye to pointing out the drawbacks of such approaches. Montesquieu's politics of place makes these drawbacks more apparent.

The Declaration of Independence is of course one of the key sources for those who consider America's exceptionalism to be universal. Michael Zuckert, for example, in his excellent analysis of the Declaration, refers to the "natural universal principles of the Declaration" that govern "the political sphere."[26] In this Lockean document,[27] we see Jefferson and the other authors of the Declaration hold up core universal truths that should define and shape politics: "We hold these truths to be self-evident, that all men are created equal, that they are endowed by their Creator with certain unalienable Rights, that among these are Life, Liberty, and the pursuit of Happiness."[28] These rights appear not simply as American rights, but as natural, human rights;[29] everyone possesses these rights by virtue of being human. *All* men and women—not just Americans—are endowed with these rights. Humans have these rights before they enter government. These rights cannot be taken away arbitrarily or without our consent. Men institute governments to "secure these rights." Governments are just and legitimate only when they protect these rights and derive "their just powers from the consent of the governed."[30] And whenever government "becomes destructive of these ends, it is the Right of the People to alter or to abolish it, and to institute new Government."[31]

The Declaration sets forth a (brief) universal theory of legitimate government. It asserts that everyone everywhere has these rights, regardless of whether the government protects or respects those rights; the rights therefore appear as universal. Anyone has the moral authority to assert her claim to these rights. Any government that does not protect these rights is illegitimate. The Declaration bases its universal theory of legitimate government on these rights claims; as such, this theory is prescriptive.[32] The Declaration, Zuckert explains, was meant to be a broad "statement about the origins and ends of legitimate public authority."[33]

Jefferson certainly understood the Declaration to be universal and forward looking. At one level, Jefferson thought he was expressing the "American mind." But the American mind was, in turn, expressing universal truths. In a letter to Henry Lee in 1825, Jefferson explained that the "object of the Declaration" was to "place before mankind the common sense of the subject"—"the rights of man"—"in terms so plain and firm as to command their extent, and to justify ourselves in the independent stand we are compelled to take."[34] Jefferson did not mean to suggest that only Americans had these rights, though. Rather, he explained to Roger Weightman in 1826 that the document and act of declaring independence was meant to be an example for the whole world:

> May it be to the world, what I believe it will be, (to some parts sooner, to others later, but finally to all,) the signal of arousing men to burst the chains under which monkish ignorance and superstition had persuaded them to bind themselves, and to assume the blessings and security of self-government. That form which we have substituted, restores the free right to the unbounded exercise of reason and freedom of opinion. All eyes are opened, or opening, to the rights of man. The general spread of the light of science has already laid open to every view the palpable truth, that the mass of mankind has not been born with saddles on their backs, nor a favored few booted and spurred, ready to ride them legitimately, by the grace of God. These are grounds of hope for others.[35]

Jefferson thus attempts to remove any doubt about his understanding of the Declaration. It was meant to assert man's rights, and then inspire others to take up the cause of protecting those rights, just as the Americans did. We see that Jefferson is drawn over time toward a universalistic understanding. He goes from expressing the "American mind" to viewing the Declaration as a world-historical event.

Not everyone has understood the Declaration in universalistic terms. John Adams thought that only the act of declaring independence—and not the Declaration itself—would be remembered.[36] Other scholars also reject the universalistic interpretation. Pauline Maier reads the Declaration as backward, not forward, looking. She sees the Declaration as explaining and justifying the American colonies' separation from Great Britain.[37] Justin Litke, in his work on American exceptionalism, also denies the universality of the Declaration. Litke finds the "most striking feature of the

Declaration" to be "its fundamental particularity."[38] Litke goes so far as to argue that the "questions of universality or theories of history may be dealt with quickly." While the claims are said to be "truths," it cannot be said that the claims of the second paragraph serve any purpose but to legitimate the thirteen former colonies' separation from Britain and to recognize their dignity as sovereign states. The Declaration is a concrete document of political action, and the universalistic tone is subordinated to particular aims. Thus, interpretations of the Declaration of Independence as a charter of rights for all nations are not in keeping with the understanding of the founders. Long cited as one of the grandest and most universalistic documents of the American political tradition, Litke argues that the Declaration is, to the contrary, one of the most limited and concrete, even in its most rhetorically memorable passages.[39] But Zuckert convincingly explains the problems with this line of interpretation of the Declaration: "the Declaration by its very nature was more than a mere explanation and justification for the Revolution; it explained and justified the Revolution in terms of a general theory of legitimate, rightful, and just government."[40]

Even if one is not convinced that the Declaration originally was meant to be universal, it certainly has come to be read and understood as being universal by many, maybe most, people. The document has had the *effect* of promulgating universal notions about rights and legitimate government. The famous notions in the second paragraph have inspired people for over 240 years to pursue these goods and goals. The Declaration certainly influenced the French Declaration of the Rights of Man and the United Nations Declaration of Human Rights.[41] We therefore must understand that many people have read the Declaration as universal.

Montesquieu's politics of place has numerous objections to the Declaration. The politics of place is not a rights framework. Generally, it deemphasizes the language of rights. But the deeper problem, from the standpoint of the politics of place, is the Declaration's universalism. It is possible that Montesquieu could accept rights language if it were truly limited to being an expression of the "American mind." On this reading, the language of rights could be effective for a particular place and context. And he almost certainly would deem it effective in the American context. So the authors of the Declaration may have been operating in a Montesquieuian fashion. But Jefferson and others push much further. They treat the Declaration as a document that holds true over time and place. Montesquieu's politics of place does not accept the notion that all nations always must be founded on the goal of protecting the *rights* to life, liberty, and the pursuit of happiness (or property). The politics of place recognizes these are universal goods. But the politics of place does not accept that the language of rights is necessary to protect these goods. And insofar as the Declaration presents a universalistic understanding of these goods, the politics of place would find this problematic. America's Declaration marks, in key ways, the beginning of the universal political and philosophical exceptionalism that has been so influential in America and beyond. This universal exceptionalism flows into the founding period that immediately followed.

Many view the American founding as universalistically exceptional because the founders developed a concrete, generally successful scheme for embracing and protecting life, liberty, and the pursuit of happiness.[42] The Constitution of the United States of America set forth that scheme.[43] *The Federalist* then served to explain and justify the right theory of government. All states, the argument runs, should adopt a written constitution that at least resembles (if not completely mirrors) that of the United States, and that embraces all of its core principles and institutions. That includes protections for the rights set forth in the Bill of Rights, including freedom of speech, assembly, and religion. It also includes the kinds of institutions the founders established for the American republic.

Many of the founders viewed their accomplishments as exceptional, universal, and of world-historical importance. Consider that the Great Seal of the United States, created a few years before the Constitutional Convention, reads *novus ordo seclorum*—"a new order for the ages." This new order was based in reason. Alexander Hamilton, writing in 1787 as Publius in the first paragraph of *Federalist* No. 1, states that it "has been frequently remarked, that it seems to have been reserved *to the people of this country*, by their conduct and example, to decide the important question, whether societies of men are really capable or not, of establishing good government from reflection and choice, or whether they are forever destined to depend, for their political constitutions, on accident and force."[44] Given Hamilton's role as Publius, and his task of getting Americans, and especially New Yorkers, to understand, adopt, and embrace the new Constitution, we must recognize elements of drama, propaganda, and self-aggrandizement in such statements. But at its core, Hamilton's statement was meant to be entirely truthful, and was embraced by many of the founders, who thought they had used "reflection and choice"—reason—to devise the best institutions to establish and maintain a secure, free, and prosperous political order. These institutions were superior to those found anywhere else in the world. In this sense the founders were working squarely in the part of the Enlightenment tradition that found its bearings in reason.[45] If the Constitution was based simply in reason, then other political actors, lawmakers, and statesmen who sought to use reason and reflection to (re)shape a society would choose the same kind of government the founders chose. The institutions and practices thus appear as universal.

The founders did not lose or move away from their understanding of their accomplishments as both exceptional and universal. Consider Thomas Jefferson's remarks in an 1801 letter to John Dickinson: "A just and solid republican government maintained here, will be a standing monument & example for the aim & imitation of the people of other countries." He continued by expressing his "hope and belief" that others "will see, from our example, that a free government is of all others the most energetic; that the inquiry which has been excited among the mass of mankind by our revolution & it's consequences, will ameliorate the condition of man over a great portion of the globe."[46] Jefferson clearly viewed America's republican government as an exemplary model, one to which others should turn for guidance. Read alongside his remarks about the Declaration made long after its publication, we see that his belief in American universal exceptionalism was strong. John Adams, despite his above remarks about the Declaration, also voiced similar thoughts on the influence of the American Revolution.[47] Influential later statesmen made this exceptionalism more prominent still.[48]

More than any other person outside the founding era, Abraham Lincoln played a decisive role in universalizing America's founding principles.[49] Lincoln, in a letter declining to speak at a birthday celebration honoring Thomas Jefferson in 1859, praised Jefferson's "capacity to introduce into a merely revolutionary document [the Declaration of Independence], an abstract truth, applicable to all men and all times, and so to embalm it there, that to-day, and in all coming days, it shall be a rebuke and a stumbling-block to the very harbingers of re-appearing tyranny and oppression."[50] Lincoln leaves no doubts about how he interprets the Declaration.[51] The "abstract truth" that Jefferson introduced was that "all men are created equal," and that they have certain natural rights that governments must uphold if they are to be legitimate. This truth is "applicable to all men and all times"—even slaves—so it is universal. It has the force of a supreme moral law.[52] And it is the key to fighting against tyranny and oppression. Lincoln's immediate sights were set on his southern political adversaries like John Calhoun, but he viewed the Declaration as a powerful force for improving humankind's lot.[53] In this fight in favor of freedom and against oppression, Lincoln saw America as playing an exceptional, world-historical role. He judged that it was up to America, after having established these principles, to protect them for all mankind. Rather than seeking to "escape history," Lincoln embraced the world-historical nature of his decisions and the import of American principles. Lincoln boldly proclaimed that America represented the "last best hope of earth" to assure freedom for everyone. The way of the universal, abstract truths against oppression (especially slavery) "is plain, peaceful, generous, just—a way which, if followed, the world will forever applaud, and God must forever bless."[54] Lincoln thus holds up America's universal principles as a model for the world. He shares his belief that America is positioned better than any other nation to espouse, extend, and protect these principles. Having discovered these universal truths, America seems to have a *responsibility* to bring them to others. Be that as it may, it remains true that not all the founders embraced this universal exceptionalism.

In his Farewell Address George Washington advocated for individual liberty and economic prosperity while insisting on a defensive military stance toward the world. He warned, for example, against entangling American foreign policy with European politics and military endeavors.[55] Washington clearly expressed misgivings about America seeing its politics as universal and expansionist. Patrick Deneen calls Washington's approach "liberal isolationism," which he contrasts to the "communal perfectionism" of John Winthrop and the "liberal expansionism" of later actors.[56] John Quincy Adams's speech on the Fourth of July, 1821, appears as the "second high water mark of liberal isolationism."[57] Still, most others did not hold opinions like those Washington and Adams expressed. Let us now consider the nature of the universal exceptionalism that has come out of the American founding, paying attention to notable general expressions of this exceptionalism. We do this through the work of four scholars who have presented compelling analyses of American exceptionalism: Charles Dunn, James Ceaser, Hugh Heclo, and Charles Murray.

Charles Dunn argues that "America is the only nation in the world that is founded on a creed. That creed is set forth with dogmatic and even theological lucidity in the Declaration of Independence."[58] Dunn identifies ten core values of the creed of American exceptionalism: equality, liberty, respect for property and ownership, opportunity, democracy, duty, efficacy, community, religion, and meritocracy.[59] In making this list, Dunn explicitly draws on Seymour Martin Lipset, who "said that five words describe American Exceptionalism: 'liberty, egalitarianism, individualism, populism, and laissez-faire.'"[60] Dunn insists that American values have a "magnetic appeal" to people across the globe.[61] Dunn finds these values to be universally exceptional.

James Ceaser identifies the notion of a "mission" as central to understanding what the founders accomplished. Ceaser contends that the aims of *The Federalist* are twofold. Its arguments explain how the Constitution secures "liberty into a republican form of government." But the founders had much loftier goals. They sought not only to "be an example to the world."[62] The founders had an extensive, and potentially expansive, mission: they sought to show others how to be secure, free, and prosperous. Ceaser claims that the founders specifically thought their values, institutions, and the mission that derived from them would change "the course of the modern world."[63] But Ceaser acknowledges a potentially troubling trajectory of this sense of a mission. Since its inception, "America has lived on the verge, so to speak, of a crusade, although a few have interpreted this mission as being properly promoted by setting an example and without the exercise of an assertive foreign policy."[64] We return to this problematic expansionist trend in universal understandings of American exceptionalism later.

Hugh Heclo distinguishes between numerous kinds of exceptionalism. We focus on four iterations of American "exceptionalism of mission." "Mere providence" sees America as exceptional "in the sense that divine protection is bestowed on Americans' efforts to pursue righteous causes." This does not mean, though, that America "is uniquely chosen for God's purposes."[65] A second variety sees America as chosen, but not special.[66] The next two varieties are most important for our study of universalism in the founding. America might be "a 'sanctified' nation—not just one country among others, but rather one set apart for achieving transcendent purposes."[67] America's exceptional mission is superior to other approaches. Other societies can improve themselves by more closely approximating the American system. America is supposed to lead others by holding up "the light of liberty."[68] America's values and practices are universal. But only the final notion insists that America try to spread these values. America also might be a "redeemer" nation. "America's mission is to redress evil and fulfill the purpose of history—variously identified as freedom, or equality or individual rights, or some other human view of the Good."[69] America might be called to go to great lengths, and make significant sacrifices, to "redress evil and fulfill the purpose of history." America should help, even force, other societies to embrace the right political principles and practices. Indeed, redeemer nations "are necessarily proactive in going out to save others."[70]

It is possible, as Charles Murray and others demonstrate, to consider American exceptionalism in primarily historical terms. Murray treats America's exceptionalism as a fact acknowledged by observers around the world.[71] American exceptionalism can refer to "qualities that were first observed in the opening century of our history" that may or may not remain today.[72] One need not insist that America is excellent or superior. But it remains true that a notion of mission often creeps into discussions of American values and practices, to say nothing of American exceptionalism. Gordon Wood explains: "Our beliefs in liberty, equality, constitutionalism, and the well-being of ordinary people came out of the Revolutionary era. So too did our idea that we Americans are a special people with a special destiny to lead the world to liberty and democracy."[73] Indeed, the thought that America has a special role to play in world history seems to be at the core not just of notions of American exceptionalism, but of analyses about the very idea of America.

Francis Fukuyama's thesis about the "end of history" seems to be a kind of culmination of notions of American exceptionalism. Drawing on notions of a philosophy of History presented by G. W. F. Hegel and Alexandre

Kojève, Fukuyama argues that History is directional, and that we have arrived at a final historical and philosophical endpoint: liberal democracy, the only ideology with universal validity.[74] The liberal part of the ideal centers on a rule of law "that recognizes certain individual rights or freedoms from government control."[75] The democratic side of that notion affords all citizens the universal right to share in political power by voting and participating in politics. The sovereignty of the people, on which the ideal of liberal democracy is grounded, represents a "universal principle of legitimacy."[76] Fukuyama acknowledges "peaks and troughs in" the development of liberal democracy as the only universal, legitimate political order. But when considering the "*whole scope of history*," he finds the trend to be undeniable.[77] And America plays a special role in this process of pushing History toward its end. He explains, for example, that "the meaning of the 'Spirit of 1776'" was "not the victory of yet another group of masters, not the rise of a new slavish consciousness, but the achievement of self-mastery in the form of democratic government."[78] This victory has continued to send ripples throughout history and History. Prominently, the list of rights Fukuyama identifies as fundamental both to liberalism and to democracy is "compatible with those contained in the American Bill of Rights."[79] America has not simply defined and shaped our understanding of liberal democracy. More than that, America has shaped how liberal democracy has been practiced around the world, particularly during two world wars and the Cold War. Fukuyama's notion of the end of History, with America in the driver's seat, has clear appeal. It gives a prominent historical and contemporary place both to the nation and to its ideals. At its core, the thesis represents an iteration of universal American exceptionalism. However, many of these iterations are deeply problematic, especially because they link up to notions of empire that have currents throughout American political thinking, perhaps beginning with the founding.

The seeds of America's imperial universalism can be found, according to some scholars, in America's founding. John Jay, in *Federalist* No. 4, while discussing the importance of America being able to expand its commerce, writes: "Spain thinks it convenient to shut the Mississippi against us on one side, and Britain excludes us from the St. Lawrence on the other; nor will either of them permit the other waters." Jay continues by insisting that "we are not to expect they [Spain and Britain] should regard our advancement in union, in power and consequence by land and by sea, with an eye of indifference and composure."[80] Deneen argues that this is where the "American expansionist project was announced. . . . Jay in fact argued that such a strong defensive posture would be necessary due to the inevitability of American continental expansion."[81] There are reasons to doubt this interpretation. The quotation's context shows that Jay is concerned with America's ability to engage in commerce in waters adjacent to the new country. The Mississippi and St. Lawrence would be crucial for America's economic prosperity; hence Jay's reasonable insistence on being able to use the rivers for trade.[82] Jay acknowledges that war might result from this expansion. But he recommends "advancement in union" specifically to *prevent* war. Jay's focus is for America to be able to pursue "mutual intercourse and traffic." Whatever the case may be, Jay's statement is not the only one to raise concerns about the intentions of those who developed America's universal principles, especially Thomas Jefferson.

Jefferson, first a few years after penning the Declaration, then weeks after leaving the presidency, spoke about America establishing an "empire of liberty." In a 1780 letter to George Rogers Clark, discussing military strategy in the ongoing war, Jefferson suggests that America might seek to "add to the Empire of liberty an extensive and fertile country [Canada] thereby converting dangerous Enemies into valuable friends."[83] The context is important: Jefferson is here speaking about how to defeat Britain, and establish peace. Read, however, with his later remarks, we can understand why Deneen thinks Jefferson offers a "vision of continental expansion."[84] Writing to his successor as president, James Madison, Jefferson raises the prospect of bringing Cuba into the American union, and going north of the border to expand further. The result would be "such an empire for liberty as she has never surveyed since the creation; & I am persuaded no constitution was ever before so well calculated as ours for extensive empire and self-government."[85] In this problematic formulation, Jefferson expresses grand visions for a future "empire of liberty." Rather than establishing this empire simply through reason and choice, America would forcefully build this empire. Restad argues that expansionism "was an integral part of the building of this empire and ... is intimately connected to the rejection of an isolationist-internationalist dichotomy. The fact that the Americans did not see themselves as invaders, aggressors, or occupiers is a testament to the powerful exceptionalist identity that was expressed through its manifest destiny version during the nineteenth century."[86] The appeal of spreading the ideal of American freedom has persisted throughout American history.[87]

The mid-1800s period of manifest destiny and the "defense of so-called imperialism at the end of the nineteenth century" represent two key historical moments during which America has sought to spread its principles.[88] Manifest destiny, in Ceasar's view, refers to "a political program, popularized from the 1830s through the 1850s, to acquire more territory on the American continent on which to implant democracy and open the door for massive European immigration." It represents the "first critical moment when the idea of mission influenced the conduct of foreign policy."[89] America understood its mission to include spreading its form of liberal democracy across the continent. This mission continued to develop into the imperial policies of later decades, principally involving the Spanish-American War.

This imperial ambition became prominent again in the early twenty-first century. The presidency of George W. Bush thrust universal American exceptionalism back onto the stage (though some would argue it never left). The United States and its allies attempted to help first Afghans, and then Iraqis, overthrow tyrannical regimes and replace them with liberal democracies. The United States sought to advance the cause of liberty around the world by "exporting" democracy. Policies such as the "Freedom Agenda" were central to this cause. There were numerous justifications for these endeavors. One was the belief that all people everywhere should live under free government. Everyone, the thought goes, has a universal claim to life, liberty, and the pursuit of happiness. These ideals are universal, not just American. Deneen identifies a second justification. A lack of freedom in some places represents a threat to freedom everywhere. So the United States should expand freedom to promote peace.[90]

America's universalistic exceptionalism can manifest itself in the world in numerous ways. America might simply be an exemplar. States can try to emulate the American model to improve their political order. Proponents of this view debate how much leeway states should have in defining and achieving these universal human freedoms and rights. But experiences and policies from the past two centuries point to a more ambitious understanding of America's universalistic exceptionalism. The notion that American values are universal has persuaded political actors to try to impose these values on other societies. If America has discovered, and exemplifies, the "right," "true," "best" political principles, then is it not America's role to help others embrace these principles? The appeal is apparent: why not lead other societies out of the darkness of their undesirable situations by guiding them with the light of American ideas and ideals? Rather than simply being exceptional within its own borders, America should help other countries demonstrate exceptional commitment to securing rights and freedoms through the adoption of American-style practices. It is America's *mission* to guide other peoples to these values. Sometimes America's guidance will be forceful, as in Afghanistan and Iraq. Given the stakes, the argument goes, it is acceptable, perhaps necessary, to sometimes use force. Thus arises what Litke calls "imperial exceptionalism," the idea that "America is supposed to have a mission to civilize, educate, or otherwise dominate the world politically or economically."[91]

The goal of helping various societies become free(r) is laudable insofar as all states should be secure, free, and prosperous. But the reality of America's actions has been harsh. One justification for the military interventions in Afghanistan and Iraq was to replace tyrannical regimes with liberal democracies.[92] These experiences have shown the difficulties of instituting new and better regimes. These policies have proved terribly ineffective, and effectively terrible. Iraq remains on the threshold of war, perhaps a civil war, perhaps with the so-called Islamic State. Security, liberty, and prosperity are nowhere to be found more than a decade after the two invasions. America's efforts to impose its values on other cultures have met fierce resistance.

These forays highlight the problems with trying to universalize, and then export, America's apparently exceptional principles. The goal of such endeavors is to shape a state into something "better," with an eye to making it "good." This goodness is grounded in America's universal ideals. But the actual consequences of these forays have done more than simply leave these states in terrible situations. They have revealed the near impossibility of imposing "something better," generally defined as Western-style liberal democracy, on societies.[93] These failures make us rethink how political, social, economic, and moral change within the varied societies of the world today might be effected.

Asserting America's "exceptional" founding principles as universal has not only been ineffective; it has been damaging and dangerous. The objects of American actions remain in disarray. The peoples have not wanted what America is selling. Deep problems are evident with the universalistic approach, and point us to the politics of place as an alternative framework. There is no reason to think that American principles should or will fit a particular place. The *esprit*, and all the variables that comprise it, vary significantly across time and place. So too should the means necessary to establish and maintain a secure, free, and prosperous society. To the extent that it is sensible to talk about changing a specific society, the inhabitants of that society must be prepared, and must want, to change. Montesquieu's politics of place therefore brings a healthy dose of skepticism to the belief that US or Western-style liberal democracy is best for everyone, and that proponents of this form of government should "assist" others in adopting it.

Unfortunate Exceptionalism

Our discussion of American exceptionalism has presupposed that America's exceptionalism is positive. But not everyone sees it that way. Scholars have pointed to the existence of slavery in the American republic and the undemocratic nature of the Constitution. On this reading, to the extent that America is exceptional, it is a *bad* exception. Despite being the first liberal, democratic, commercial, constitutional republic, the argument goes, America had key moral failings that call some of its core principles into question. It is important to consider this angle, because it bears directly on the politics of place framework. The politics of place acknowledges that societies always are imperfect: the bad comes with the good. Sometimes, the bad outweighs the good. Does the bad outweigh the good in the case of America? If it does, then the bar for the kinds of politics that are acceptable in a particular place will be higher.

The institutional support for slavery that permeated the early American republic raises serious questions about the extent to which America's founding principles are universal, exceptional, good or even desirable. For more than two hundred years, most African Americans were held as slaves in America. They were denied all political, personal, and economic liberties. They were forced to work for their masters. Paul Finkelman argues that this calls the very universality of the principles the founders espoused into question. Finkelman puts forth that more than simply doing little or nothing to mitigate slavery as an institution, in many cases the founders actively supported slavery. Many of the founders themselves were slaveholders—among them George Washington, James Madison, and, most infamously, Thomas Jefferson.

Support for and perpetuation of slavery was systematic during the founding, according to Finkelman. He points to five provisions in the Constitution that dealt directly with slavery, as well as numerous other indirect protections of slavery, to argue that "slavery was sanctioned throughout the Constitution."[94] These provisions included the Three-fifths Compromise and the fugitive slave clause.[95] The Constitution's system of limited powers meant that "Congress lacked the power to interfere in the domestic institutions of the states"—above all slavery.[96] The Constitution provided significant protections for slavery at little, if any, cost to the South. Southern delegates thus left the Convention perfectly content. More than that, delegates from slave states were convinced "that slavery would be a permanent part of their culture and society. No one who attended the Philadelphia Convention could have believed that slavery was 'temporary' in the South."[97] Even northerners who expressed qualms over the justice of slavery justified their compromises. For them, the political and economic gains outweighed the ills of slavery.

The founders' support for slavery calls the universality of the principles of the founding, especially the Declaration, into question. Finkelman's criticism is harshest with respect to Jefferson. Finkelman holds Jefferson to the highest standard because he was a leader of the American Enlightenment. Finkelman concludes that Jefferson was unable to transcend his economic and regional interests "to implement the ideals he articulated."[98] Finkelman points, in part, to the fact that Jefferson owned more than 150 slaves when he wrote the Declaration and manumitted less than 2 percent of his slaves during his lifetime.[99] Reason being, Jefferson "did not in fact believe that blacks were entitled to the same rights as other Americans."[100]

Finkelman thus attaches no real weight to Jefferson's antislavery passages in an earlier draft of the Declaration.[101] Jefferson apparently took other actions that illustrated his disdain for blacks, including advocating for "harsh, almost barbaric, criminal punishments for slaves or free blacks" and proposing "expelling from Virginia the children of white women and black men solely because they had 'corrupt'—mixed—blood."[102] To the extent that Jefferson thought blacks might have natural rights, he did not think they could exercise them in the United States.[103] Finkelman draws harsh conclusions about Jefferson: "time and again, Jefferson sided with slavery and against freedom."[104] "The history of Jefferson's relationship to slavery is grim and unpleasant. His words are those of a liberty-loving man of the Enlightenment. His deeds are those of a self-indulgent and negrophobic Virginia planter."[105]

Finkelman's critique of Jefferson raises some important questions about the extent to which the American founding was exceptional. Was it exceptional in primarily negative terms? Was it exceptional at all, given that the founding seems to have perpetuated slavery? Is it sensible to speak of doctrines as universal if they did not apply to people of all races? Can we continue to view American ideals as exceptional in light of significant failings in practice? One way to set aside these difficult questions is to adopt Lincoln's understanding of the principles of the Declaration, and embrace Lincoln's (and others') actions to bring equality to the races. For those who want to uphold the founders' ideals as positive (universal or not), this is a sensible path forward. Another approach would be to suggest that the Constitution was deliberately designed to be ambiguous because it was hoped that the tensions over slavery at the time would be resolved later as the country progressed as a democracy. But questions surrounding the universality of the founding principles linger.

A second major line of critique comes from concerns about the undemocratic nature of the American Constitution. Many scholars such as Sanford Levinson have criticized the Constitution as insufficiently democratic.[106] Here we take as representative Robert Dahl's critique in *How Democratic Is the American Constitution?* If we hold democracy to be a core value, and the US Constitution is either undemocratic or insufficiently so, then we might not be able to view the founders' accomplishments as universally exceptional.

Dahl puts forth democracy as the core political standard. A constitution is legitimate, at least for a democratic people, only when it is "crafted to serve democratic ends. Viewed from this perspective, an American constitution ought to be the best that we can design for enabling politically equal citizens to govern themselves under laws and government policies that have been adopted and are maintained with their rational consent."[107]

Dahl sees the Constitution as failing the democracy test on many counts. Numerous American institutions allegedly inhibit democracy. Federalism is one. America's federal system "was not so much a free choice as a self-evident necessity imposed by history."[108] This necessity has the effect of inhibiting what the central government can do, often to bad effect, according to Dahl. The democratically elected national legislature should have ultimate say over laws and policies, something the federal model prevents. America's strong bicameralism also hinders democratic processes by making it significantly more difficult for the legislature to pass laws. Getting things done becomes more challenging when different parties control the two chambers. Dahl sees bicameralism as unnecessary at best, especially given that numerous countries do fine without it.[109] Second chambers, in turn, necessitate "unequal representation," by which Dahl means "that the number of members of the second chamber coming from a federal unit such as a state or province is not proportional to its population [or number of citizens or eligible voters].... The main reason, perhaps the only real reason, why second chambers exist in all federal systems is to preserve and protect *unequal* representation."[110] The upshot is that two senators from North Dakota represent less than a million people, while two senators from California represent nearly 39 million. More than just being undemocratic, Dahl suggests that this system has led to injustice, because "unequal representation has sometimes served to protect the interests of the *most* privileged minorities," such as slaveholders.[111] Dahl also questions the strong judicial review of national legislation. He poses a straightforward question: "If a law has been properly passed by the lawmaking branches of a democratic government, why should judges have the power to declare it unconstitutional?"[112] On this understanding, judicial review serves to undermine the democratic lawmaking process.

Dahl saves some of his harshest criticism for America's electoral system. Dahl strongly prefers a system of proportional representation to America's first-past-the-post system because the former allows for representation of more parties; more democratically elected voices thus come into the conversation. Dahl sees the multiparty system arising from proportional representation as clearly beneficial, and much more appropriate for democratic countries. As mistaken as our way of electing legislators is, Dahl finds the US system of electing the president all the more troubling. The electoral college has three undemocratic features on which Dahl focuses. First, the candidate with the greatest number—or even a majority—of popular votes may not win the election. Second, in eighteen elections the winner has emerged without a majority of overall votes cast.[113] Third, representation in the electoral college is unequal because representation in the Senate is unequal. The winner-takes-all system also is problematic because it reduces the importance of most states and disincentivizes third-party candidates from running.[114]

The negative consequences resulting from the undemocratic features of America's Constitution call America's exceptionalism into question. If we accept even parts of Dahl's critique, this supposed bastion of liberal democracy is insufficiently democratic. Two and a half of three branches—the presidency, the Senate, and the judiciary—wield the power to impede democratic decision-making. To the extent that America is an exception, Dahl suggests that it is an unfortunate, bad exception. America should try, instead, to more closely approximate European (social) democracies.

There are many persuasive responses to Dahl's critique. We need turn only to *The Federalist* to find some of them. Publius, especially James Madison, specifically crafted America's institutions with an eye to cooling the embers of democratic passions. This certainly was, on balance, to good effect.

The purpose here has not been to adjudicate these debates, or analyze and critique Finkelman's or Dahl's arguments. Instead, the purpose has been to identify another relevant strand of American exceptionalism and to point toward the final type of exceptionalism—particularistic—that is more compelling.

Particularistic Exceptionalism

Montesquieu's politics of place provides grounds for critiquing the universal and unfortunate strands of American exceptionalism. It also provides a more fruitful framework. The politics of place interprets the American founding to be exceptional on particularistic grounds. Here we examine the Constitutional Convention, as well as Alexis de Tocqueville's *Democracy in America*, because each helps us think about American exceptionalism in particularistic terms. We consider first Montesquieu's critique of this universalistic project.

Thomas Paine, in *Common Sense*, boldly exults: "We have it in our power to begin the world over again."[115] Paine seeks radical action based on clear ideas about the best political order and the "rights of man."[116] Paine and many others during the founding period felt the draw of universalism and uniformity. Montesquieu warns against this sort of ambition. Recall the grave concerns Montesquieu expresses about great and small *esprits* being seized by "certain ideas of uniformity" (XXIX.18.882). Men are drawn to seek "perfection." Montesquieu advises against legislators falling into the trap of seeking uniformity. He has a deep concern about imposing approaches on others. Indeed, this line of thought can lead all the way to conquest, as great *esprits* attempt to impose political institutions and systems on other nations or cultures. Montesquieu advises legislators to think and talk about politics in a different manner. Legislators should not think in strictly universal terms; therefore, we ought not universalize the founding. There is notable irony in the fact that the founders were bringing in Montesquieu to construct their institutions and philosophy of government. To the extent that the founders who favored universalism thought Montesquieu promoted this universalism too, they misinterpreted and misused Montesquieu. Indeed, it goes directly *against* Montesquieu's teaching. Montesquieu taught that legislators should proceed with caution, and not seek to (re)make the world anew. He taught legislators to favor particularism over universalism.

There also is a way, however, in which the idea of American exceptionalism actually turns toward particularism. An exception, by definition, goes *against* uniformity. Merely to think about exceptions begins to call universalism into question. Exceptional cannot mean we have reached an ideal. This is one way exceptionalism can lend itself to Montesquieu's ideas. We consider now another.

The politics of place offers an alternative understanding of the founders' accomplishments: what the founders achieved is exceptional in *particularistic* terms. The American founding was exceptional insofar as it developed principles, institutions, and practices that made *America* secure, free, and prosperous. Indeed, the United States does well on these performance metrics; it found an unusually effective way to achieve these three goods. This exceptionalism is particularistic, though, because the American model, while suitable for America, is not necessarily workable for other societies; the American model therefore is not universal. Montesquieu would highlight that "American" values might not fit another people or, still worse, could be inappropriate for and damaging to them. If one tries to universalize principles and practices and apply them to societies where they will not function how one envisions, there is the potential to do great harm. The politics of place warns precisely against such action. The founders' achievements are remarkable. But we should be reluctant to try to apply them to other peoples and places. What, then, does an interpretation of the American founding through the lens of the politics of place look like?

America's founders deserve significant praise. In the wake of a war against their former rulers, they managed in 1787 to devise a political system that successfully established and maintained security, freedom, and prosperity. This alone makes their accomplishments normatively exceptional. What's more, the system they implemented has proved extraordinarily durable. The US Constitution has met the test of time. America's founders invigorated our understanding of separation of powers theory. They developed new ways to make power stop power or, in Madison's words, have ambition counteract ambition. One such development was separating the executive, legislative, and judicial powers into three branches. Another such development was having a written constitution that included protections for rights both within the document and in a Bill of Rights. They expanded our understanding of other ways to distribute power. They showed that federalism could work on a much larger scope than many had thought. In all of these ways, they were building on Montesquieu. They founded America on certain theories of rights. This approach has become prominent, and seems to have been effective in promoting better political orders in some places. These are some of the founders' more significant achievements.

There is no need to hail these achievements as universal, however remarkable they may be. Instead, the politics of place puts us on much firmer footing by understanding the achievements as effective in the American context, but not necessarily applicable in others. Rather than insisting that other states adopt America's conception of (natural) rights put forth in the Declaration, the focus should be on determining the extent to which rights language might be effective in achieving the desired goals in a given society. Even if rights language will be effective, American rights language may not be effective in or appropriate for diverse societies. The same line of reasoning applies to other key aspects of America's supposedly universal exceptionalism. Why would it be the case that America's institutional structures are necessarily the most effective at promoting security, liberty, and prosperity across time and place? Instead, we should examine the extent to which any given institution, like the presidency or federalism, will be effective in a particular place. If a state adopts the presidency, it may or may not resemble America's executive. Why must we accept that the principle of legitimacy set forth in the Declaration is the one all societies should adopt? Can a government be legitimate, for example, if it protects life, liberty, and the pursuit of happiness without recognizing notions of "rights"? Certainly. These queries demonstrate that asking whether or not America's principles are universal is asking the wrong question. The question must be, instead: what practices and principles will promote security, liberty, and prosperity in a particular place? And this does seem to be the question the delegates asked at the Constitutional Convention.

The American founding, viewed through the lens of the Constitutional Convention of 1787, was actually a particularistic moment. Is it not more important to look at the substance of the debates during which the delegates crafted the US Constitution, rather than the rhetoric used in *The Federalist* to justify the Constitution? A study of the debates reveals that rather than appealing to universal notions of the best political order, the delegates from diverse states worked to arrive at compromises that could be acceptable to all the states. It is true that all of the delegates came to the Convention committed to a republican form of government with some kind of distribution or balance of powers. But there was remarkable disagreement on a wide range of issues.

The Convention involved arguments between big states and small states. The Virginia Plan favored strongly the large states, allotting them more seats in Congress through proportional representation in both branches.[117] The small states, by contrast, favored the equal representation found in the New Jersey Plan.[118] Only after weeks of debate did they arrive at the Connecticut Compromise, which provided for equal representation in the Senate and proportional representation in the House.[119] The issue of representation also divided northern and southern states. The latter wanted slaves counted in full or, at a minimum, in part toward their representation. Some in the North rejected counting slaves at all. Eventually, the infamous Three-fifths Compromise arose as the solution. Other issues like the nature of the executive divided the delegates. Many worried about giving the executive too much power. They differed over the best length of presidential term. Should it be seven years? Perhaps four? Should the president be one person? Or should multiple people comprise the executive? Pennsylvania had a multiperson executive. Should the president be eligible for reelection? Should he, as Alexander Hamilton proposed, be an elected monarch?[120] The biggest issue was the scope, size, and powers of the federal government. The Anti-Federalists, led by Luther Martin of Maryland, voiced grave concerns about the power of the national government the delegates were constructing. Even after four months in Philadelphia, a sizable number of delegates—sixteen—did not sign the Constitution. Many went home to oppose it. There was nothing inevitable or obvious about many of the compromises the delegates reached. There certainly was nothing universal about them. The delegates were working to found a political order that would make the states secure, free, and prosperous. And they had to do so with the consent of the other parties involved. Without compromises, there may have been no union. Hamilton's remark in *Federalist* No. 1 about "establishing good government from reflection and choice" can only be understood properly if we acknowledge that that reflection and choice happened in a particular context. Understood in this way, we can say that the delegates of the Convention used the methods of Montesquieu's politics of place. The delegates had a kind of Montesquieuian sensibility. The process that founded the political order and institutions of the United States was anything but universal.

The American founding was not universally exceptional because American institutions will not promote good political orders everywhere. These institutions simply are not appropriate for or accessible to many peoples. Tocqueville, in *Democracy in America*, provides a particularistic analysis of America. He demonstrates that many singular features allowed America to perpetuate its democratic republic. Tocqueville identifies three causes that primarily were responsible for maintaining America's democratic republic: "The Particular and accidental situation in which Providence has placed the Americans forms the first; The second comes from the laws; The third flows from habits and *mœurs*."[121] Among the "accidental or providential causes" Tocqueville names are that America has no neighbors (and thus no great wars, in contrast to Europe), no great capital, an "empty continent" throughout which to expand, and a beneficial physical environment (climate and terrain).[122] America's "point of departure" also was decisive. We have unique insight into American history because we know its genesis: the arrival of the Pilgrims from England. Tocqueville thinks that the Puritans brought over beneficial values, especially the equality of conditions, and a common language.[123] Throughout his discussion of these factors, Tocqueville shows that Americans had little if any control over them. They could not change their physical environment. They did not choose to have a common language. Other societies thus face significantly different, more challenging historical, cultural, social, and linguistic situations than America did.

American legal structures are not transferable to other societies; attempts to transfer them directly will not yield the desired results, and there is a good chance doing so will yield undesirable ones. Tocqueville considers how four specific institutions are fit for America: the federal form, townships, the "constitution of judicial power," and the Constitution.[124] Tocqueville's remarks about the Constitution are especially pertinent. The case of Mexico shows that American laws are nontransferable. Mexico was as "happily situated" as America, with good terrain and no neighbors. Mexico "appropriated" American laws. And yet, rather than prospering, Mexico was unable "to become habituated to the government of democracy."[125] One reason is the marked differences between Mexican and American *mœurs*.

America's Christian *mœurs* have allowed Americans to perpetuate their democratic republic and made the country prosperous.[126] America's mix of Protestantism and Catholicism has proved fortuitous. Protestantism brings men to independence. Catholicism promotes the equality of conditions. Because Catholics are in the minority, "they need all rights to be respected to be assured of the free exercise of theirs."[127] Tocqueville concludes that in America "the spirit of religion and the spirit of freedom ... [are] united with one another: they reigned together on the same soil."[128]

Tocqueville's analysis is especially relevant here because his framework for analyzing America is fundamentally Montesquieuian. Tocqueville considers the factors forming America both separately and in relation to one another, and he considers also how they form an *esprit*. He studies how many of the factors that allow America to maintain its security, freedom, and prosperity were particular to America. States seeking these goods cannot simply adopt American laws or *mœurs*. In some ways, Tocqueville understood America better than the universalistic founders did.

The American founding is not so much a single event as a period in time during which Americans worked through the politics of their particular place. One of the most remarkable features of the founding is that it took thirteen years from the onset of the Revolution and the issuance of the Declaration of Independence to establish a stable federal government. It took a significant amount of time to write, ratify, and seat a government under the Constitution. Political actors from across the world should draw a few important lessons from this fact. First, although Americans found themselves in a fortunate situation—geographically, culturally, and politically—it still took a significant amount of time to agree on durable political institutions. Why, then, would we expect political actors in countries that have experienced recent upheavals like Egypt or Iraq to be able to adopt good political orders quickly? We expect states to establish a good political order in increasingly short periods of time. But we would do well to remember the extensive amount of time it took the founders to resolve enough of their differences to establish America's political order.

One key ingredient of the founders' success was the moderation with which they proceeded. One way they were moderate was through the construction of moderating political institutions. But more than that, the founders demonstrated crucial commitment to compromise throughout the founding period. During the Constitutional Convention, no group of delegates left with everything they wanted, but almost everyone left with an agreement with which they could live, and under which the republic could prosper. The founders' remarkable commitment to proceeding carefully, in a way that would garner wide public support, was exceptional indeed. This inquiry into the founding has shown that interpretations of the founding as universally exceptional are problematic. The politics of place offers a more fruitful alternative by understanding the founding as exceptional in particularistic terms.

This interpretation of the founding has crucial implications for political actors today, particularly those seeking to (re)shape and (re)found a society. Without question, many societies are in need of better political orders. Billions of people around the world suffer because they lack sufficient security, liberty, and prosperity in their lives. The question we should ask is how we best can guide them to establish security, liberty, and prosperity in their particular place. Instead of insisting on the supposed universality of American values, we would do much better to point them to the founding as one exceptional instance of a people discerning what principles and practices would promote good political order in their society. This approach offers political actors the flexibility they need to navigate their particular societies and define and achieve security, liberty, and prosperity.

Conclusion

The core claim of the politics of place is that the politics, economics, and morals of a society must fit a particular place and its people. All states must commit to pursuing security, liberty, and prosperity. But they must have leeway in how they define and achieve these goods. This is a key reason why Montesquieu's particularism is more appealing than universalism. His claims are descriptive and normative. They are descriptive because factors differ significantly across time and place. The factors on which we have focused include laws, institutions, the environment, commerce, religion, and morals. These factors in turn form, and are formed by, the *esprit* or character of a society. Consider France and South Korea. Descriptively, they differ on many of these factors; consequently, they have distinct *esprits*. The politics of place assists us in understanding better how societies actually operate. This fundamental context defines the parameters of a society. What's more, it is dangerous to disregard the particularities of a place when attempting to make policies there. Legislators who do so often make undesirable, inappropriate, or harmful changes. The politics of place recognizes the fact that "one size does not fit all"; that is, the same regime (however good) is neither possible nor desirable in all times and places for all peoples. The politics of place is useful for analyzing and describing states independent of normative analysis. The framework allows us to understand better how societies operate. But it is the normative component that makes the framework more compelling.

The politics of place also tells us how societies *should* operate. By establishing that all societies must pursue security, liberty, and prosperity, the politics of place is useful for evaluating whether societies are "good," "bad," or somewhere in between. While some cases are clear-cut, the politics of place recognizes that there are many shades of gray when attempting to evaluate the goodness of states. A state might score well on some fronts, and not on others. For example, a state could be secure and free, but not prosperous. Rather than condemn the society in toto, the politics of place insists on a more nuanced evaluation. The politics of place thus is a mix of descriptive and normative analysis. But then, compelling political analysis necessarily combines these two elements. Montesquieu does so with an eye toward instructing legislators on how they can implement positive changes in a society, and avoid making negative changes.

While Montesquieu was prescient in many ways, his framework is not without its limitations. Three limitations are notable; considering them highlights the need at times to go beyond his work to achieve a more comprehensive approach. We note these limitations here; a full investigation of them is the work of a separate inquiry. First, Montesquieu sometimes was mistaken in his empirical observations. The most obvious instance is his contention that the environment changes people biologically. Since this is not accurate, the sensible way forward is simply to set aside this part of his teaching, as we did in chapter 4. On this matter, there was a clear way to do so. Or consider commerce. Is it the case, for example, that commerce tends to promote peace? The answer appears to be in the affirmative, but the question warrants careful study for confirmation. Whenever possible we should test empirically the validity of as many of his observations as possible; indeed, this is one of the next steps in solidifying the soundness of the politics of place. The focus here is on empirically testable matters. Value judgments are a separate matter. For example, the query "Is commerce on balance beneficial for a society?" is distinct from "Empirically, does commerce tend to have a particular effect?" To understand the limitations of Montesquieu's approach, the focus first should be on descriptive matters. Then we can assess.

Second, while *EL* is a fairly comprehensive work, it does not address everything. An expectation that it would is unreasonable. But in cases where Montesquieu is silent, or speaks little, it is necessary to study the matter and discern how it fits into the politics of place framework. Consider again commerce. Montesquieu focuses on the social, moral, and political outcomes of commerce. His focus on these aspects makes sense. But he speaks rather little of the economic effects of commerce. To make the politics of place more comprehensive, we must investigate questions like "What are the economic effects of commerce?" and "How do these economic effects impact other parts of society?" It is necessary to address these questions given the significant impact they clearly have on society. For the politics of place to be comprehensive, it must address all core matters thoroughly. A good place to identify the core matters is in Montesquieu's definition of the *esprit des lois* in book I, and his definition of the *esprit général* in book XIX. Does Montesquieu discuss all matters sufficiently? In some cases, his discussions are brief or indirect. For example, what of the "way or life of the peoples" or the "maxims of the government" that he mentions in I, 3? Montesquieu's analysis in *EL* is an excellent starting point, but it certainly is not an endpoint.

Finally, the world obviously has changed since Montesquieu wrote *EL*. The most significant development is the arrival of forms of government distinct from the ones Montesquieu was able to consider: liberal democracy, communism and socialism, and totalitarianism.[1] How might he have compared these forms of government with the (good) regimes he discussed? Regarding communism, socialism, and totalitarianism, Montesquieu would have rejected these forms of government, just as he did despotism. Totalitarianism is more extreme than despotism. Totalitarianism's spring is terror. In no way does totalitarianism protect security, liberty, or prosperity. To the contrary, it obliterates each of these goods. Nor do communism and socialism measure up to the standards of the politics of place. Montesquieu would have rejected communist and socialist ideals like equality and destruction of private property. Individuality and private property are central to his framework. But he also would have looked at the realities of communist and socialist rule in the twentieth century and rejected them on account of their failure to establish security, liberty, and prosperity anywhere.[2]

In the case of liberal democracy, Montesquieu would have judged this regime type positively. Looking at examples like the United States, Britain, and Germany, Montesquieu would have seen that liberal democracy can establish and maintain security, liberty, and prosperity. It has effective moderating institutions. Yet the politics of place does not necessarily judge liberal democracy to be superior to the other forms of government Montesquieu identifies as potentially good—the federal republic, mixed regime, aristocracy, and monarchy. Liberal democracy is not appropriate for all societies. Recall the discussion in chapter 5 of the unsuccessful attempts by the United States and its allies to bring this form of government to Iraq after the invasion in 2003. Rather, Montesquieu would continue to ask the question "Which form of government best promotes security, liberty, and prosperity in a particular context?" The answer to this question will not always be liberal democracy, in part because of how diverse societies are across time and place. As with liberal democracy, he likely would have seen the social democracy that exists in Nordic countries as an effective approach in these places.

One of the key contributions of Montesquieu's political theory is to help revive the study of national character. In the nineteenth century, G. W. F. Hegel played a key role in mutating the notion of *esprit* with his concepts of *Geist* and *Volksgeist*. History, Hegel put forth, marched toward the realization of the *Geist* that was supposed to be at the end of History. Then, nineteenth-century nationalist movements made the notion of a "people" that had a "spirit" increasingly pernicious, as the "us versus them" dynamic continued to develop. Twentieth-century fascism made the notion of a "people" violent. The ethical community that constituted the people came to be one that rejected "others" from its community, and sought to fight against those outside the "people."

But there is nothing inherent in Montesquieu's notion of *esprit* that necessitates the march toward a pernicious understanding of a people. The politics of place accepts that most peoples have an *esprit* or character. We can leave it as an open question whether all peoples have an *esprit*, for perhaps we can imagine a situation in which a people could lack one. Some societies might have multiple *esprits*, based on the diverse makeup of a given populace. Still, it is important to identify and understand the nature of the *esprit* of a people in order to interact with that people more fruitfully. Americans, Angolans, Argentines, Armenians, and Austrians are different in fundamental ways that we can attribute, in part, to their differing characters. Neighboring countries like Germany and France have different *esprits*. Rather than arguing against the existence of *esprits*, the politics of place treats the existence of *esprits* as a basic fact of societies. We must understand this basic fact, because if legislators attempt to implement policies that run contrary to the *esprit*, then they risk damaging the well-being of the society. The notion of *esprit* centers on the observation that peoples differ on a wide range of political, economic, social, moral, environmental, and historical matters. What's more, these things are not static over time. The example of the European Union, which I have discussed elsewhere at length, is illustrative.[3]

Many European leaders seek to form an "ever closer union" among the EU's members. They want the idea of "Europe" to supersede that of European nation-states. They seek to suppress national institutions, practices, and identities through the European Parliament and other transnational institutions. These leaders want to unite members more closely on political, economic, social, and moral issues. They seek to form what I call a "tight" European spirit. And they do so undemocratically.[4] This enterprise is mistaken. The differences between countries are too great to bring countries together as closely as EU leaders desire. There exist significant differences between southern European countries like Greece, Italy, Spain, and Portugal, and more northern countries like Germany, Sweden, Denmark, and the Netherlands. To the extent that the EU should seek to form an *esprit*, it should try to form a "loose" *esprit*, not a "tight" one. EU members should not seek extensive levels of agreement on political, social, economic, and moral matters. Instead, it suffices for EU members to identify a baseline of values, policies, and practices that can hold them together as one loose union of federal republics with an eye to advancing security, liberty, and prosperity throughout the continent.

The politics of place provides insight into other contemporary issues. Consider immigration. What effects does the arrival of new members to a society have on the *esprit* of a people? Can the change in the *esprit* from immigration be either negative or positive?

These challenging questions do not have clear-cut answers. For Montesquieu, as with many other things, the effects of immigration—descriptive and normative—may differ depending on the situation. These effects can be positive or negative, and they can change over time, even in a specific society. Montesquieu recognized that the movement of peoples would alter the *esprit*. He thought that, in many cases, the benefits of these interactions were positive; he praises commerce precisely because it makes *mœurs* softer, gentler. Yet immigration represents a different degree of interaction and change, since it is people who are moving, rather than just their ideas or practices, and the move is usually permanent.

The arrival of new members can significantly alter the *esprit*—or not. One factor to consider is the number of immigrants that arrive. How many immigrants are coming each year? Thousands? Hundreds of thousands? How do these numbers compare to the overall size of the population? Another matter to examine is whether the immigrants are mostly from one region, or whether they come from diverse areas. Are they, for example, mostly from eastern Europe? Or are they from many regions, like Latin America, East Asia, and the Middle East? The larger the proportion of immigrants from a specific region, the greater impact they will have on society. One also must study the *esprits* of the immigrants and the host society. What is the nature of the immigrants—their character, beliefs, practices, values, and so on? What are their reasons or motives for immigration? And how does it compare and contrast with the makeup, values, and *esprit* of the host society? Is the host society homogeneous? Or is it heterogeneous? How might we expect the different groups to interact? Today we see tensions arising from Muslims entering societies where Islam is not a part of the *esprit*, like France and Germany. The reception of Muslim immigrants in these countries has been mixed. Another factor to consider is the location of the host society. Where is it? What is the makeup of neighboring countries? What is the general political, economic, and social climate in the region? Ultimately, one must examine all of the variables Montesquieu identifies as forming the *esprit* of the laws with respect to the immigrants and the hosts. The goal is to try to determine how the groups would relate to each other. Undoubtedly, immigration can shape the factors we have considered in this investigation. Immigrants can bring with them a new religion, new *mœurs*, alternative views of commerce, experiences with different institutions, and different understandings of security, liberty, and prosperity, to name but a few potential points of divergence. The descriptive element entails identifying the reality of these matters. The normative aspect prompts us to make evaluative judgments about them.

Changes in the *esprit* resulting from immigration (or anything else, for that matter) can be positive or negative. There are numerous ways one might evaluate changes to the *esprit*. I focus on two. First, do changes to the *esprit* from immigration make the state more—or less—secure, free, and prosperous? To answer this question, we would need to focus on how such changes impact variables like institutions and commerce. If the *esprit* becomes hostile to commerce, for example, the society would be less secure, free, and prosperous. So this change would be negative. Certainly, the effects of such changes are difficult to measure. Or immigration might bring various economic benefits.[5] Second, how does immigration change the character of a people? This question is even more challenging to answer. It is difficult enough to discern the character of a people. It is more challenging, though, to come to agreement about how we *evaluate* that character. Recall Montesquieu's description of the French *esprit* in XIX, 5, or of the English *esprit* in XIX, 27. Immigration has the potential to alter these *esprits*. Supposing we agree with Montesquieu's descriptions of these two *esprits*, two people still might reasonably disagree about whether and to what extent these *esprits* are good, and whether the changes that could result from immigration would be positive or negative.

Once a society has achieved a good *esprit*, should it reject the arrival of immigrants that might disrupt this good *esprit*? Can people be right to perceive immigration as a threat to a native place and *esprit*? These are perhaps the most challenging questions in considering immigration. The latter question is slightly easier to answer. At a basic level, the answer appears to be yes: immigration can sometimes be a threat to a native place and its *esprit*. How then should a society respond? In some instances, the *esprit* of a given place, its accrual, so to speak, of its own history, is open to internal transformation in part because its constitution can sustain change. In such cases, it would be inadvisable to reject completely the arrival of immigrants. In other places, however, the *esprit* is not open to internal transformation. In such cases, the society may have a stronger case for rejecting immigrants that can disrupt the *esprit*. In America, traditionally we have addressed these issues with the idea of a "melting pot" as a durable metaphor for the successful assimilation of immigrants into American culture. The idea itself has been a force for acceptance of immigration as nonthreatening. It also is important to note that the *esprit* Montesquieu analyzes is first an *esprit* of laws, which is not necessarily attached to a specific place.

The politics of place helps us understand, investigate, evaluate, critique, and make recommendations about diverse places. The framework does not pretend to offer easy or clear solutions to difficult problems. But Montesquieu's political theory remains relevant for us today because the particularism it presents is a more compelling means of analyzing and improving societies. Montesquieu thus appears as a valuable interlocutor as we work toward the achievement of security, liberty, and prosperity in the context of particular places.

Notes

Introduction

1. I speak of universalism in the normative sense that a code of morals and politics is considered to be true everywhere.
2. Here I follow Dennis Rasmussen, who places Locke and Bentham in the Enlightenment. See, for example, Rasmussen, *Pragmatic Enlightenment*, 2, 6, 9–10.
3. As Rasmussen explains, the thought of these two philosophers is "highly idealistic in character" and grounded in "transcendent or a priori first principles." It aimed to satisfy "abstract standards of right derived from God, Nature, or Reason" and pursued "perfection or the imposition of strict requirements for legitimacy" (*Pragmatic Enlightenment*, 2). Rasmussen also rightly categorizes Immanuel Kant's thought as universalistic. Kant's deontological moral code centers on the need to act from duty; that is, the necessity to take an action (or not) based on respect for the moral law. We must do what the law requires *because* the moral law requires it. And what should we do? Kant states, "Act only in accordance with that maxim through which you can at the same time will that it become a universal law" (*Groundwork*, 31). The categorical imperative is universal: it applies to everyone everywhere. It always must guide our actions. We are never permitted to lie or kill, for example.
4. Van Doren writes that while the "supporters of the Convention in 1787 knew they were planning a government only for the United States . . . they believed their experiment would instruct and benefit all mankind. Their undertaking might be . . . a rehearsal for the federal government of the future" (*Great Rehearsal*, x). He presents the Constitutional Convention as a rehearsal for contemporary statecraft and nation building. Francis Fukuyama argues in *End of History* that the endpoint of "History" looks distinctly American, because America ushered in this new, final era.
5. Lutz, "Relative Influence," 193.
6. Hamilton, Madison, and Jay, *Federalist*, 262. In No. 78 Hamilton refers to the "celebrated Montesquieu."
7. See esp. Rahe, *Montesquieu and the Logic of Liberty*; and Pangle, *Montesquieu's Philosophy* and *Theological Basis*. See also Zuckert, "Natural Rights and Modern Constitutionalism"; and Israel, *Dutch Republic*.

8. See esp. Ehrard, *L'esprit des mots*; and Mosher, "Monarchy's Paradox." Consider also de Dijn, "Montesquieu's Controversial Context." However, de Dijn's arguments in this essay seem to contradict her work elsewhere where she argues Montesquieu is a proponent of aristocratic liberalism. See *French Political Thought*.
9. De Dijn, *French Political Thought*.
10. Nelson, *Greek Tradition in Republican Thought*.
11. Ford, *Robe and Sword*; Cox, *Montesquieu*.
12. In other academic literature, and especially anthropology, the term the "politics of place" refers to the local, particular, and identity politics that emerge in opposition to global or universalizing politics and tendencies. The politics of place seems to concern the activities, issues, and identities that emerge on a local level and are often in conflict with totalizing and universalizing national or international politics. The term is closely associated with minority and multicultural concerns. Consider, for example, Amin, "Regions Unbound"; Dirlik, "Place-based Imagination"; Escobar and Harcourt, "Women and the Politics of Place"; Kemmis, *Community and the Politics of Place*; Moore, "Subaltern Struggles"; Yung, Freimund, and Belsky, "Politics of Place." The politics of place of today is more concerned with political activity and policy. The "politics" of place refers to political groups, actors, and movements relevant to particular issues. My usage of the term is distinct. Montesquieu's politics of place is fundamentally concerned with thought and analysis, description and proscription. Here, the notion of *esprit* is important. Contemporary scholars would disregard it in favor of political action. What's more, Montesquieu is addressing entire nation-states and peoples rather than particular minority groups or identities. Although there are similarities, contemporary scholars do not seem to say that the politics of place occurs at a national level.
13. Ceaser notes that Montesquieu gives "weight to the unique elements of each place" (*Liberal Democracy*, 61). Ceaser also emphasizes the importance of "knowledge of place" to political science more generally (42).
14. Previously I referred to Montesquieu's approach as "political particularism." See Bandoch, "Forming a European Spirit." While I continue to identify Montesquieu as a particularist, the language of the "politics of place" more precisely captures Montesquieu's thought because of the attention he pays to the peculiarities of places. Accordingly, I have implemented the terminology of "politics of place" here and elsewhere. See Bandoch, "Montesquieu's Selective Religious Intolerance."
15. Indeed, throughout the nineteenth century French writers thought about how different countries have different ways of implementing their values; this gave rise to sociology. Aron, in *Main Currents*, thus identifies Montesquieu as a forerunner of sociology.
16. Consider Spector, *Montesquieu: Liberté, droit, et histoire*, e.g., 77–78; Larrère, *Actualité de Montesquieu* and "Montesquieu and Pluralism"; Binoche, *Introduction*; and Manin, "Montesquieu et la politique moderne."

17. Dallmayr argues that Montesquieu "was sufficiently endowed with common sense to appreciate the role of history and culture, and hence to resist an abstract rationalism operating deductively from first principles" (*Good Life*, 240). See also Rasmussen's account of why Montesquieu is not a universalist in *Pragmatic Enlightenment*.
18. Berlin, "Montesquieu," 148.
19. As a matter of interpretation, I rely on a fairly wide range of Montesquieu scholarship. My purpose is not to align strictly with one interpretive school; rather, my goal is to use varied accounts to outline Montesquieu's framework.
20. A recent article by Keegan Callanan, "Liberal Constitutionalism," argues that Montesquieu is a proponent of liberal constitutionalism and political particularism. My account differs from Callanan's in important ways. In contrast to Callanan, I acknowledge universalist elements in Montesquieu's thought, most importantly in his universal recommendation of security, liberty, and prosperity. I propose that Montesquieu's concept of *esprit* is central to his particularism, whereas Callanan mentions the concept only in passing. I present an extended definition and explanation of the politics of place, whereas Callanan does not provide a clear definition of what he means by "political particularism."
21. Montesquieu does not describe the different factors as variables. I adopt the term because it is consistent with his project. The matters he considers as part of the *esprit* vary and have differing impacts across time and place.
22. For another account of *esprit* in Montesquieu see Mosher, "Particulars of a Universal Politics." Mosher's article (along with the work of other scholars) marks the beginning of a shift in thinking about Montesquieu's notion of *esprit* regarding the relations between universality and particularity. Technically, Montesquieu never invokes the contrast "particular-universal." While this contrast certainly is at work in Montesquieu's thinking, the origin of this peculiar vocabulary lies with the German idealist appropriation of Montesquieu. Mosher insightfully illustrates this.
23. Spector, in "Montesquieu était-il libéral?," questions whether it is appropriate to identify Montesquieu as a liberal.
24. Craiutu explains that for Montesquieu, since "there can be no recipe for good legislation in general, legislators must be flexible in order to avoid the misfortune of becoming tyrannical" (*Virtue for Courageous Minds*, 59).
25. Burke, *Reflections*. He continues,

> Abstractedtly speaking, government, as well as liberty, is good; yet could I, in common sense, ten years ago, have felicitated France on her enjoyment of a government (for she then had a government) without inquiry what the nature of that government was, or how it was administered? Can I now congratulate the same nation on its freedom? Is it because liberty in the abstract may be classed among the blessings of mankind that I am seriously to felicitate

a madman, who has escaped from the protecting restraint and wholesome darkness of his cell, on his restoration to the enjoyment of light and liberty? Am I to congratulate an highwayman and murderer, who has broke prison, upon the recovery of his natural rights? This would be to act over again the scene of the criminals condemned to the gallies, and their heroic deliverer, the metaphysic Knight of the Sorrowful Countenance.

26. For more on the relationship between Montesquieu and Burke, see Courtney, *Montesquieu and Burke*; and Chaimowicz, *Antiquity* and *Freiheit und Gleichgewicht*.
27. Tocqueville, *Correspondance*, 418.
28. Tocqueville, *Democracy in America*, 265.
29. Consider Carrithers treatment of these notions ("Montesquieu's Philosophy of History").
30. Carrithers notes, "Unlike political philosophers prone to abstract, theoretical arguments, Montesquieu developed his political theory by means of careful study of actual governments, both past and present" ("Not So Virtuous Republics," 248).
31. I follow Montesquieu's usages in referring to England and Holland rather than Great Britain and the Netherlands.
32. Some scholars do interpret Montesquieu to be part of the social contract tradition. See, for example, Waddicor, *Montesquieu*.
33. We will see in chapter 1 that Montesquieu discusses the state of nature principally to dispense with the construct.

Chapter One

1. Spector explains that for Montesquieu "there is not a best in politics [*de meilleur en politique*], solely a plurality of goods relative to the situations" ("Montesquieu était-il libéral?," 63).
2. All translations are my own, though I have consulted the Cohler translation on occasion. I have used the Pléiade edition of the *Œuvres complètes*.
3. Montesquieu explicitly offers two understandings of political liberty—in relation to the constitution (book XI) and in relation to the citizen (book XII). He mentions philosophical liberty in book XII only to express his disinterest in it.
4. Montesquieu explains, "I thus will examine the various religions of the world only in relation to the good to be drawn from them in the civil state; whether I speak of that which has its root in heaven, or those that have theirs on earth" (XXIV.1.714).
5. Consider, for example, the Author's Foreword where Montesquieu explains that virtue is political virtue, not Christian or moral virtue (*Avertissement de l'auteur*.227).
6. Consider, for example, Pangle, *Montesquieu's Philosophy*, 11–19.

7. Carrese argues that Montesquieu thought prejudices and passions could dominate even great minds like Plato, Aristotle, Machiavelli, More, and Harrington ("Montesquieu," 2435).
8. Montesquieu refers to "nature" on numerous occasions throughout *EL*. For more on the role of nature in Montesquieu's thought, see Goyard-Fabre, *Montesquieu*.
9. Carrese discusses the importance of Montesquieu's poetry citations in "Montesquieu's Complex Natural Right," 238–39.
10. For an analysis of this line, and what it means for Montesquieu's usage of "law," see, for example, Spector, *Montesquieu: Liberté, droit, et histoire*, 39–49.
11. See, for example, Pangle, *Montesquieu's Philosophy*, 24–28; Pangle, *Theological Basis*, 15–19; see also Lowenthal, "Book I"; Lowenthal, "Montesquieu"; and Shklar's discussion of book I (*Montesquieu*, 70–72).
12. For more on Montesquieu's discussion of the state of nature and how it relates to Hobbes, as well as a broader consideration of book I, chapters 2–3, see Pangle, *Montesquieu's Philosophy*, 30–42; Pangle, *Theological Basis*, 19–27; Zuckert, "Natural Law"; and Zuckert, "Natural Rights and Modern Constitutionalism." Consider also how Spector, *Montesquieu: Liberté, droit, et histoire*, 24–26, juxtaposes Montesquieu's thought against Hobbes. She discusses book I, chapters 2–3, on 49–75.
13. For a more general comparison of Montesquieu and Rousseau, consider Rahe, "Enlightenment Indicted."
14. When citing *EL* in text, I will use the following format: book, chapter (e.g., I, 3). I will provide page numbers only with quotations.
15. See esp. Lowenthal, "Book I"; Pangle, *Montesquieu's Philosophy*, 24–28; and Pangle, *Theological Basis*.
16. Montesquieu calls "intelligences superior to man" "particular intelligent beings." The latter could include both the divinity and man.
17. For a more extended discussion of the laws of nature in this context, see Krause, "Laws, Passion, and Right Action."
18. Though Montesquieu identifies "the desire to live in society" as the fourth natural law, it actually is the fifth he names.
19. Spector, in *Montesquieu: Liberté, droit, et histoire*, compares Montesquieu to Aristotle on the subject of man's natural sociability:
> Montesquieu seems to join the classical tradition which defines man as a political animal or a social animal (the tradition to which Hobbes, precisely, was opposed). But this justification for sociability is very different here: for Aristotle, man is more sociable than herd animals because he possesses *logos*, the instrument of knowledge which permits him to differentiate not solely between the helpful and the harmful, but also the just and the unjust that is related to communal affairs. Yet in *L'Esprit des lois*, the desire for society is understandable starting from animal instinct, which then refines itself intellectually in permitting the establishment of justice and right. (61)

See also Rasmussen, *Pragmatic Enlightenment*, 252–58, for more on Montesquieu's views of man's sociability. See Dallmayr, *Good Life*, for more on Montesquieu's affinities with Aristotle.

20. Pangle, *Theological Basis*, 22. Making a similar point, Pangle writes elsewhere, "Following Hobbes, Montesquieu teaches that the state of war is the *permanent* state of man's relation to man insofar as *civil* society of the 'State' does not intervene to impose peace" (*Montesquieu's Philosophy*, 33).
21. Throughout this discussion at the beginning of I, 3, Montesquieu uses "*nation*" rather than "*état.*"
22. Lowenthal offers a different interpretation of this passage. He writes, "In chapter 3 Montesquieu explicitly rejects the idea that any one form of political society is most in conformity to nature." He continues by arguing,

> Thus, the particularity of the political problems and solutions of each people does not by itself imply that no form of political society is best for man. It did not imply this for Aristotle, and there are innumerable indications in *De l'Esprit des Lois* that the debits and credits of the various regimes—as judged by some general and unchanging standard independent of them—are in the forefront of Montesquieu's attention. Democracy based on virtue, for example, is clearly superior to both monarchy and despotism. ("Book I," 497)

Lowenthal thus argues that despite the particularity in this passage, Montesquieu continues to affirm the superiority of certain forms of government over others, beyond denying the acceptability of despotism. Alternatively, Spector argues, "the government 'the most conforming to nature' is not that which deduces itself from the rational nature of man but that which accords itself to the nature of peoples" (*Montesquieu: Liberté, droit, et histoire*, 67). And this nature, Spector shows, differs across time and place.
23. Spector, *Montesquieu: Liberté, droit, et histoire*, 68. She continues, "It is henceforth the propriety of laws, their adaptation to circumstances, which is judged primordial."
24. "Law, in general, is human reason, as it governs all the peoples of the earth; and the political and civil laws of each nation should only be the particular cases where one applies this human reason" (I.3.237).
25. Craiutu, *Virtue for Courageous Minds*, 63. This observation has important implications for our understanding of how we should draw the line between the ancients and moderns. Craiutu continues by arguing that the line between the moderns and the ancients should not be traced purely along chronological lines (as is commonly done by historians of political thought), but must be rethought in light of the monist-pluralist dichotomy. This line separates, in fact, advocates of pluralist polities such as Aristotle, Machiavelli, Montesquieu, and Burke, who believed in the essential indeterminacy of the political good and endorsed moderation, from philosophers such as Plato, Hobbes, Rousseau, and Marx who

advocated monist theories of the political good and embraced forms of radicalism.

26. See Manin, "Montesquieu et la politique moderne," 193. Manin also speaks of the political good as indeterminate and finds it rooted in Montesquieu's philosophy of moderation (201).
27. Rasmussen, *Pragmatic Enlightenment*, 21.
28. Ibid., 20. Rasmussen explains later that for Montesquieu "there is simply no such thing as a perfect, single best, or uniquely legitimate form of government or set of political institutions and practices" (82). He notes, moreover, that "given his lack of a single standard for judgment and his insistence on the importance of context, it is unsurprising that Montesquieu refuses to single out any one regime or set of institutions as universally the best, and instead outlines the various benefits and drawbacks of each" (92).
29. Ibid., 1–2.
30. Condorcet, *Observations*, 274.
31. Ibid.
32. Ibid. We must note that these quotations from Condorcet show him at one of his more extreme rationalist moments. Emma Rothschild, in *Economic Sentiments*, and David Williams, in *Condorcet and Modernity*, have argued that Condorcet was a far more pragmatic thinker. Nonetheless, we cannot imagine Montesquieu having written these lines; indeed, they provide a clear contrast between his approach and Condorcet's.
33. Craiutu, *Virtue for Courageous Minds*, 55; see also 58. For more on Condorcet and Montesquieu, see Baker, *Condorcet*, 260–63, 353–54.
34. Manin, "Montesquieu et la politique moderne," 201–2.
35. Rasmussen explains clearly why Montesquieu is not a relativist; see *Pragmatic Enlightenment*, 65–66. Vickie Sullivan, in "Against the Despotism," also shows that Montesquieu is not a relativist, in her discussion of his views on criminal laws. Sullivan explains, moreover, that Montesquieu seeks to identify and root out the sorts of prejudices that lead to inhumane criminal laws and punishments. Consider also Spector, *Montesquieu: Liberté, droit, et histoire*, 279–83. Shklar, by contrast, identifies Montesquieu as a cultural relativist (*Montesquieu*, 26). Berlin, "Montesquieu," 143; Curtis, *Orientalism and Islam*, 77; and Israel, *Enlightenment Contested*, 288, also identify Montesquieu as a kind of relativist.
36. Many thinkers do not self-identify as relativists. One figure commonly held up as a relativist, though, is Protagoras, who appears in a Platonic dialogue by that name, and expresses relativistic views while in dialogue with Socrates. Some have identified Thomas Kuhn, Joseph Margolis, and Paul Feyerabend as relativists.
37. Locke, *Two Treatises*, 350.
38. Pangle, for example, argues, "As his teaching unfolds, Montesquieu introduces, in a gingerly fashion, certain universal principles of rational or 'natural,' human rights and laws, defining basic constituents of personal

and familial liberty or security" (*Theological Basis*, 26). Carrese also argues that Montesquieu is a natural rights thinker, in "Montesquieu's Complex Natural Right" and "Montesquieu."

39. Rahe argues that "the way of thinking about constitutionalism that Montesquieu bequeathed to the American Founding Fathers was based on an understanding of the state of nature, of objective natural right, and of subjective natural rights fundamentally similar to but not identical with that found in Locke's book" ("Montesquieu's Natural Rights Constitutionalism," 65). See also 61.
40. Zuckert, "Natural Rights and Modern Constitutionalism." See also Zuckert, "Natural Law."
41. Zuckert, "Natural Rights and Modern Constitutionalism."
42. Zuckert, "Natural Law," 249.
43. Rousseau, *Emile*, 458.
44. Lowenthal, "Book I," 495.
45. For more on Montesquieu's critique of Hobbes, see Zuckert, "Natural Law."
46. Craiutu, *Virtue for Courageous Minds*, 42.
47. Rasmussen, *Pragmatic Enlightenment*, 86. Consider also Spector: "No longer does he [Montesquieu] defend the individual conceived as a rights-bearing owner and property as a sacred and inviolable natural right" ("Montesquieu était-il libéral?," 69).
48. Rights claims are not always universalistic. For example, rights can be associated with a group or class, and thus applicable only to a subset of a population.
49. Consider also Pangle, *Theological Basis*, 23; Spector, *Montesquieu: Liberté, droit, et histoire*, esp. chap. 1; and Rasmussen, *Pragmatic Enlightenment*, 82, 85.
50. Markovits, "Montesquieu," 214. She makes her point further by quoting a passage from *MP* 645: "These things all have a mutual relation with each other. If you change one, the others only follow slowly; that places a type of dissonance everywhere" (214).
51. All editions of the *Dictionnaire de l'Académie française* (hereafter *DAF*) from which I cite are available as part of The ARTFL Project of the University of Chicago and the Analyse et Traitement Informatique de la Langue Française, http://dictionnaires.atilf.fr/dictionnaires/ACADEMIE/index.htm. All entries on *esprit* are available also through the Analyse et Traitement Informatique de la Langue Française, http://portail.atilf.fr/cgi-bin/dico1look.pl?strippedhw=esprit&headword=&docyear=ALL&dicoid=ALL&articletype=1.
52. The *Œuvres complètes* (1951) is cited as follows: OCI for vol. 1, and OCII for vol. 2.
53. Spector, "*Esprit général*," para. 1.
54. Consider the thirteen distinct entries in the *Larousse French Dictionary*, s.v., "esprit," accessed June 7, 2017, http://www.larousse.fr/dictionnaires/francais/esprit/31059?q=esprit#30979.

55. While it is separate from our current inquiry, we must note that Montesquieu clearly is playing on the distinction between the *esprit* and the letter of the law, between the essence and the particularities. The distinction between the letter and *esprit* of the law goes back at least to the New Testament of the Christian Bible. Consider Romans 2:29 and Mark 2:3–28, 3:1–6 for examples.
56. Lowenthal also discusses the various potential meanings of *esprit*:
    > An inspection of the use of the term "esprit" within the work itself permits us to go a step further. It has a diversity of meanings. Almost all refer to some element of man's constitution: thus "esprit" as mind of intellect, as character; temperament or disposition, as spiritedness (a specific disposition), and even as animal spirits (certain bodily fluids). When the "esprit" of laws rather than of men is mentioned, it signifies their specific character or meaning in the context within which they exist. The French language also permits *esprit* to apply (though Montesquieu did not apply it) to the substance of God and to the Holy Ghost. ("Book I," 497–98)
57. The movement is from people without a state (savages), to people living under despotism, to a nation, to an oligarchy, to a republic.
58. Markovits compares the way one variable dominates to the way a passion dominates someone: "Book XIX develops the idea that these causes which determine the *esprit général* are in a relation of force between themselves; just as, in a man, there is a character, a dominant passion" (*Montesquieu*, 111).
59. In "*Esprit général*" Spector writes, "The *esprit général* (synonym of the *esprit* of a nation, of the character or genius of nations) *results* from the influence conjoined of different causes which give place to the existence of a dominant feature. In the absence of *a priori* hierarchies between these causes, the *esprit* is determined by a sum of forces or a chemical mélange, by the relative force of the proportion which prevails between its components."
60. Spector suggests that it is the relation between these two terms that "forms the true heart of the work": "One will see, it is precisely the relation of the *esprit des lois* and the *esprit général*, to know the question of the totality of relations of right with the different moral and physical principles that govern men (together with the physical and moral causes which constitute themselves this totality that is the *esprit général*) which forms the true core of *L'Esprit des lois*" (*Montesquieu: Liberté, droit, et histoire*, 73).
61. Although the lists of variables that form the *esprit des lois* and the *esprit général* are different, Montesquieu certainly would not have said that commerce, for example, cannot impact or dominate the *esprit général*, even though he does not list commerce in XIX, 4. His analysis of Holland in *EL* and his remarks in his *Voyage en Hollande* show that he thought commerce could dominate the *esprit* of a people.
62. In XIX Montesquieu seems to use "*esprit*" and "character" interchangeably.

63. Originally, I thought it best to speak of only "coherent" totalities. But there are many states that are incoherent in numerous ways, because they were constructed arbitrarily, or include groups that are disparate from one another. Spector contends, by contrast, that a coherent totality forms: "The *esprit des lois* relates to all the factors of the *esprit général*, which themselves relate to each other in forming a coherent totality" (*Montesquieu: Liberté, droit, et histoire*, 73). Spector also speaks of the *esprit des lois* as totalizing: "The originality of this project reflects the notion that totalizes the relations, to know the notion of the *esprit des lois*" (ibid., 70).
64. Schaub, *Erotic Liberalism*, 98, 138. On the relationship between the *esprit* and laws Samuel writes, "A legislator is to take his or her cues from the general spirit. When the spirit is not harmful to the principles of government, one must respect and preserve this spirit as part of the very liberty of the people" ("Design," 313).
65. Pangle, *Montesquieu's Philosophy*, 184. He also suggests that the "general spirit provides the social bond of habit that welds men into a cooperative community." Still, Pangle completely skips over Montesquieu's discussion of *esprit* in I, 3. He discusses only Montesquieu's usage in book XIX.
66. Rahe, *Montesquieu and the Logic of Liberty*, 11.
67. Cohler, *Montesquieu's Comparative Politics*, 12, 38. In opposition to the contention that *esprit* is an important or even sensible category for Montesquieu, Judith Shklar asserts that "Montesquieu simply did not have a coherent theory of psychological development or of education to explain how the enormous differences between individual members of a society could be compatible with the notion of a discernible, single, politically meaningful, collective spirit" (*Montesquieu*, 102). Yet while she contends that Montesquieu did not have a coherent conception of spirit, she is forced to incorporate spirit into her analysis only a few pages later when she speaks of spirit in ways that seem to suggest that the concept is intelligible. She writes, for example, that "all law manifests a purposeful will, that is its spirit" (109). See also 104, 105, and 109 where she speaks of spirit as if it is an intelligible concept.
68. Shklar, *Montesquieu*, 103.
69. Ceaser, *Liberal Democracy*, 66.
70. Carrese, "Montesquieu's Complex Natural Right," 234, 236; see also 246.
71. Mosher, "Particulars of a Universal Politics," 182.
72. Spector, "*Esprit général*." See also Spector, *Montesquieu: Liberté, droit, et histoire*, 236–37, for more on the link between *esprit* and moderation; and see 230–37 for a discussion of *esprit*.
73. Spector, "*Esprit général*."
74. Markovits, "Montesquieu," 208.
75. Markovits, *Montesquieu*, 118; emphasis added. She continues, "General maxims of government as well as *mœurs* or manners, religion, and particular laws, the *esprit général* returns us to the generation of laws, to their division into principals and accessories."

76. Montesquieu explains: "A Venetian named Balbi, being in Pegu, was introduced to the king. When the king learned that there is no king in Venice, he began to laugh so loudly, that a cough took him, and it was painful for him to speak with those in his court. Which legislator could propose popular government to such peoples?" (XIX.2.557).
77. Pangle elaborates: "Any attempt to ignore or push aside this spirit, even for the sake of political freedom, leads to 'tyranny'" (*Montesquieu's Philosophy*, 185).
78. Pangle, *Theological Basis*, 25.
79. Spector, "*Esprit général.*" She continues by quoting Montesquieu: "The diverse characters of nations are mixed with virtues and vices, of good and bad qualities. The happy mixes are those from which result great goods, and often one would not suspect it; there are those from which result great evils, and one would not suspect them either" (XIX.10.562).
80. For a discussion of (anti)perfectionism in Montesquieu, see Mosher, "What Montesquieu Taught."
81. Volpilhac-Auger dates the essay 1737–39. See her notes on the essay in "Sur quelques sources prétendues du livre XIV de *L'Esprit des lois*."
82. Montesquieu explains just before this passage:

    We just spoke about the particular education that forms each character; but there is still a general education, that one receives in the society where one is; because there is, in each nation, a general character [*un caractère général*], which those of each particular society attend to more or less. It is the product of two manners: by the physical causes, which depend on the climate ... and by moral causes, which are the combination of laws, religion, *mœurs*, manners, and this species that represents the way of thinking, the air and the silliness of the Court and of the Capital, that spread out far away. (OCII.58)

83. See Krause, "History and the Human Soul," for a discussion of Montesquieu's views on human nature.
84. Hobbes, *Leviathan*, 89.
85. Consider, for example, Gonthier, *Montesquieu and England*.
86. Montesquieu draws a direct connection between the English constitution and character: "I spoke in the eleventh Book of a free people; I gave the principles of its constitution: seeing the effects that must have followed, the character that was able to form, and the manners that resulted from it" (XIX.27.574).
87. For an extended analysis of the role of *inquiétude* in England, see Rahe, *Montesquieu and the Logic of Liberty*, esp. 86–117.
88. Rahe argues, "The partisan conflict inspired by the separation of powers transforms the *inquiétude* characteristic of the English into a vigilance directed against all who might be tempted to encroach on their liberty. This vigilance is the passion that sets the English polity in motion, and it

serves as a substitute for the republican virtue that the English need not and generally do not possess" (*Montesquieu and the Logic of Liberty*, 117).

89. Montesquieu had made a similar remark in *MP*. "They [the English] only esteem two things: riches and personal merit. They have more pride than vanity" (OCI.1334).
90. Consider also Montesquieu's *Notes sur l'Angleterre* (OCI.875–84) for more on his views on England.
91. See Pangle, *Montesquieu's Philosophy*; Pangle, *Theological Basis*; and Rahe, *Montesquieu and the Logic of Liberty*.
92. Consider Montesquieu's *Essai sur le goût* for more on his views on taste and aesthetics.
93. Bandoch, "Forming a European Spirit."
94. Montesquieu famously speaks of a "chain" (*chaîne*) also being present in his *Lettres Persanes*. For more on the "chain" consider Ehrard, *L'Esprit des mots*, 179–92; and Casabianca, *Montesquieu*, 872–85. See also Casabianca's discussion of the design of the work, 885–902.
95. Lowenthal, "Book I," 485; emphasis added.
96. D'Alembert, "Éloge."
97. Voltaire, "L'ABC," *Philosophical Dictionary*, 500, 508.
98. In the introduction to her translation of *EL*, Cohler comments that Montesquieu, both in his work and in his life, "did not seem to require any clear, overt, organizing device. . . . There is no over-arching, organizing image" (Montesquieu, *The Spirit of the Laws*, xxi). Isaiah Berlin labeled the work "a shapeless amalgam of disquisitions on various topics, in no apparent order" ("Montesquieu," 137–38).
99. Samuel writes that proponents include Aron, *Main Currents*, 17–19; Carrese, "Montesquieu's Complex Natural Right," 227–36; and the theses of Lanson, Barkhausen, and Oudin (which theses are summarized by Gressaye (1950, vol. 1, pp. cx–cxxi) ("Design," 305).
100. Samuel, "Design," 305. Samuel continues:

    Book I is typically understood to be the introduction. Books II to VIII are viewed as the political causes of laws, XIV to XVIII as the physical causes, and XIX as the moral causes; XX to XXIII allegedly deal with economic and demographic causes and XIV to XV deal with the religious causes of laws. The rest of the books, however, are said to be unrelated to the previous books: XXVI and XXIX are about the composition and object of the laws, and XXVII, XXVIII, XXX, and XXXI are grouped as the historical books, on the origins of Roman and French law.

101. Ibid., 306. She continues:

    Part 1 frames the determination problem and shows its impact on social and political organization. Part 2 details the path toward social and political liberty. Part 3 puts into relief the threat of material determination, the proposal that humanity is governed strictly by physical causes. The end of Part 3, Book

XIX, is the midpoint of the work, and serves as a transitional book in the sense in which Diana Schaub (1995, 138) argued that there is a movement in Book XIX away from despotism and toward liberty. Pushing Schaub's insight further, I argue that Book XIX provides the key to achieving human freedom over determinism.

Subsequently, Parts 4 to 6 advance the cause of liberty in other spheres of life; in the commercial (or economic), reproductive, and religious spheres; and finally within the particular historical and legal context of the French. These last three parts are in order of praxis.

Clark also argues that the chain that holds not just *EL*, but Montesquieu's work more generally, together is liberty (*Compass of Society*, 82–83).

102. For a thorough investigation of the notion of a secret chain in *EL*, see esp. Volpilhac-Auger, "Une nouvelle 'chaîne secrète.'"
103. Craiutu, *Virtue for Courageous Minds*, 35. Carrese suggests that moderation is "the key to his [Montesquieu's] labyrinthine masterwork" ("Montesquieu's Complex Natural Right," 228). See also 234.
104. Pangle writes, "Montesquieu's investigation focuses first on that factor which he considers most important in the sociopolitical environment: the 'nature' of the government and its 'principle.' The most influential sphere of social life is the political sphere, the sphere in which men deliberately, intentionally, and authoritatively choose and shape a collective way of life" (*Montesquieu's Philosophy*, 44).
105. My claim refers to the general flow of the books. The ordering of the chapters often is more puzzling. Spector suggests an interpretation of the order that is compatible with mine; see *Montesquieu: Liberté, droit, et histoire*, 69–70.
106. Israel, *Enlightenment Contested*, 287.

Chapter Two

1. Rasmussen makes a similar point regarding Montesquieu's flexibility in defining and achieving security, liberty, and prosperity (*Pragmatic Enlightenment*, 90).
2. Rahe, *Montesquieu and the Logic of Liberty*, 98. Rahe contends that Montesquieu thinks a feeling of *inquiétude* actually is necessary for maintaining liberty, at least in England (99–102).
3. Montesquieu explains: "The desire that Hobbes first gives to men of subjugating one another, is not reasonable. The idea of empire and of domination is so composed, and depends so much on other ideas, that it would not be the one that it would have to start with" (I.2.235).

4. About Montesquieu's claim Howse writes: "Montesquieu's bold statement at the outset of Book IX that *no* regime can combine internal health and effective external defense represents an arresting indictment of the entire tradition of political philosophy. The search for the best regime, meaning the best 'city' or the best 'state,' the best 'closed' political community, is utterly futile" ("Montesquieu on Commerce," 4).
5. For more on Montesquieu's assessment of why Rome fell, see especially his *Considérations sur les causes de la grandeur des Romains et de leur décadence.*
6. Mosher, "Montesquieu on Conquest"; Mosher elaborates on his claims in a later, more extensive essay: "Montesquieu on Empire and Enlightenment." Rahe argues that Montesquieu also sees "balance of power" politics as a legitimate reason for conquering (*Montesquieu and the Logic of Liberty*, 205).
7. Rosow notes, "While dismissing cruel treatment of natives as unjust and imprudent, Montesquieu does not outlaw colonialism so long as it follows from the spirit of conservation" ("Commerce, Power and Justice," 363).
8. Howse, "Montesquieu on Commerce," 8.
9. Consider also Spector, *Montesquieu: Liberté, droit, et histoire*, 166.
10. I am grateful to Charles Butterworth for pointing out that the term "juste rigide" evokes that of "le juste milieu" or "the golden mean," where "juste" modifies "milieu." Thus to translate "le juste rigide" as "strict justice" (as Cohler, Miller, and Stone do) or "rigid justice," which captures its modern Hobbesian and Machiavellian connotations or overtones, is not grammatically correct. Admittedly, this term is particularly difficult to translate, and other reasonable alternatives include "balanced severity," "fair strictness," or perhaps "a strict sense of fairness."
11. As Howse observes, "In a remarkable single stroke, Montesquieu endorses the right to conquest as a necessary implication of the right to self-preservation" ("Montesquieu on Commerce," 8).
12. Mosher, "Montesquieu on Conquest," 95.
13. Ibid., 99.
14. Rahe offers an alternative perspective: "Montesquieu did not sanction thereby what we sometimes euphemistically call humanitarian intervention. . . . Instead, he distinguished carefully between the right to go to war, which derived from the right of self-defense and sometimes justified conquest, and the dictates of *droit des gens* with regard to peoples already conquered; and, tellingly, he cited the all-important 'law of natural enlightenment'; solely with regard to the latter (2.10.2–3)" (*Montesquieu and the Logic of Liberty*, 220).
15. Montesquieu's critique of Spanish conquest goes much deeper. For example, as Rosow notes, "Although initially successful the Spanish failed because they pursued political empire at the expense of economic enterprise" ("Commerce, Power and Justice," 350).
16. Mosher, "Montesquieu on Conquest," 103.
17. Mosher, "Montesquieu on Empire and Enlightenment."

18. Mosher, "Montesquieu on Conquest," 108. Mosher explains elsewhere that Montesquieu also admires Alexander's promotion of local government ("Montesquieu on Empire and Enlightenment," 220).
19. See also Larrère, "Montesquieu on Economics and Commerce"; Mosher, "Montesquieu on Empire and Enlightenment"; and Spector, in *Montesquieu: Liberté, droit, et histoire*, for analyses arguing that Montesquieu preferred commercial and maritime empire over territorial and conquering empire.
20. Spector, *Montesquieu: Liberté, droit, et histoire*, 166.
21. Rahe, *Montesquieu and the Logic of Liberty*, 53.
22. For more on this point see Mosher, "Montesquieu on Empire and Enlightenment."
23. Montesquieu continues by noting that if the federal republic contains both monarchies and republics, one state conquering another "shocks less."
24. Spector, *Montesquieu: Liberté, droit, et histoire*, 170.
25. For more on the distinction between "negative" and "positive" liberty, see Berlin, "Two Concepts." Shklar also identifies Montesquieu as a proponent of negative liberty (*Montesquieu*, 86).
26. Rasmussen continues by noting that "*who* governs is ultimately less important than *how* they govern" (*Pragmatic Enlightenment*, 265).
27. See, for example, Rahe, *Montesquieu and the Logic of Liberty*; Pangle, *Montesquieu's Philosophy*; and Pangle, *Theological Basis*.
28. Because Montesquieu identifies this kind of liberty with the person, and focuses on the individual throughout his discussion, I refer to it as personal liberty, rather than "political liberty in relation to the citizen."
29. For an excellent analysis of Montesquieu's views on criminal punishments, and how they diverge from Machiavelli's, see Sullivan, "Against the Despotism."
30. Craiutu explains: "In moderate regimes, the manner of forming judgments is deeply imbued with a spirit of moderation, which requires that scrupulous inquiries be conducted according to that spirit. Neither the prince nor his council exercises judicial power" (*Virtue for Courageous Minds*, 46).
31. Sullivan, "Against the Despotism," 289.
32. Shklar, *Montesquieu*, 89.
33. Craiutu, *Virtue for Courageous Minds*, 45.
34. Spector, *Montesquieu: Liberté, droit, et histoire*, 193.
35. See also XII.7.438.
36. Montesquieu suggests the following standard: Actions "only become crimes when they prepare, accompany, or follow a criminal action" (XII.12.443). Speech alone cannot be criminalized.
37. For a discussion of Montesquieu on China, see esp. Volpilhac-Auger, "Use of the Stick."
38. Shklar suggests that one reason Montesquieu rejects harsh punishments is his experience with them while at the *parlement* of Bordeaux:

> Montesquieu presided over the *Tournelle*, the criminal division, throughout the eleven years of his presidency. There he administered sinister prisons in which the accused were held while they awaited trial, and took part in the infliction of torture, which was a normal part of criminal investigations. He also meted out the usual punishments of execution, deportation to criminal colonies, and service in the galleys. We do not know what he thought about these practices while he was engaged in them, but when he later pleaded for the reform of the criminal law and an end to torture and brutal punishments, he spoke with the voice of someone who had a direct knowledge of these subjects. (*Montesquieu*, 5)

39. Spector, *Montesquieu: Liberté, droit, et histoire*, 200.
40. While Montesquieu speaks of monarchies here, his reasoning applies to republics and other moderate states.
41. For a discussion of Montesquieu's views on taxes, see Spector, *Montesquieu et l'émergence*, 376–86.
42. Craiutu, *Virtue for Courageous Minds*, 46–48.
43. Spector, *Montesquieu: Liberté, droit, et histoire*, 239.
44. For a less absolutist and universalistic reading of Montesquieu's views on slavery, see Rasmussen, *Pragmatic Enlightenment*, 67–69.
45. Richter, *Political Theory*, 59.
46. See also Samuel, "Design," for an analysis on how books XV—XVII continue the discussion of freedom.
47. Consider also Spector's discussions of Montesquieu's critique of slavery in "Il est impossible" and *Montesquieu: Liberté, droit, et histoire*, 214–24.
48. Tomaselli, "Enlightenment Debate on Women," 113.
49. For an excellent analysis of Montesquieu's treatment of women in *LP*, especially with respect to women's unfree status in the harem, see Schaub, *Erotic Liberalism*.
50. Montesquieu's discussion is complicated further when he writes, "In everything here I do not justify customs, but I give reasons for them" (XVI.4.511).
51. In this passage, "they" (*ils*) refers not only to Marseilles, but also to the other places he names here, including Holland and Venice.
52. For more on Montesquieu vis-à-vis Machiavelli, see Sullivan, "Against the Despotism"; Shackleton, "Montesquieu and Machiavelli"; and Carrese, "Machiavellian Spirit."
53. Consider, for example, *Merriam-Webster*'s definition, which is principally economic, but does leave room for a broader understanding. It defines "prosperity" as "the condition of being successful or thriving; *especially*: economic well-being" (accessed June 7, 2017, http://www.merriam-webster.com/dictionary/prosperity).
54. For an examination of East Asian values, see for example, de Bary, *Asian Values*; Bauer and Bell, *East Asian Challenge*.

55. Lowenthal, "Montesquieu," 525.
56. See esp. chap. 10 of Locke's *Second Treatise* (in *Two Treatises*).

Chapter Three

1. Craiutu shows that moderation is "one of the prerequisites" of liberty (*Virtue for Courageous Minds*, 42).
2. Craiutu explains: "liberty can be found in both moderate monarchies and republics and, as Montesquieu put it, it is no farther from the throne than from the senate" (*Virtue for Courageous Minds*, 42).
3. I am grateful to Michael Zuckert for suggesting this way of categorizing the variables and helping me develop the term "subpolitical." I recognize that there is an important difference that my political/subpolitical division does not capture, namely that some of the factors are products of human choice or "voluntary" passions (as Hobbes would call them), as opposed to involuntary (nonchosen) influences like climate. Still, I find the division useful on a number of other grounds, one of which being that Montesquieu clearly does divide the most political variables in parts I and II from the less or "sub" political variables in parts III, IV, and V.
4. Along similar lines, Montesquieu writes, "A good legislator takes a middle way. . . . He does not always inflict corporal punishments" (VI.18.330). Condorcet was critical of Montesquieu identifying the spirit of moderation as the proper spirit of a legislator. Condorcet prefers the spirit of justice to that of moderation: "I do not understand what is contained in this first chapter; but I know the spirit of the legislator should be justice. . . . It is not by the spirit of moderation, but by the spirit of justice, that criminal laws should be mild, that civil laws should tend to equality" (*Observations*, 261). Consider also 262.
5. Montesquieu writes, quoting Ovid:
    When the Sun gave Phaethon his chariot to drive, he said to him: "If you climb too high, you will burn the celestial home; if you descend too low, you will reduce the earth to ashes. Do not go too far to the right, as you will fall into the constellation of the Serpent; do not go too far to the left, as you will go into those of the Altar; keep yourself between the two." (XXX.10.891–92)
6. Craiutu, *Virtue for Courageous Minds*, 33. Consider also Pangle's discussion of moderation, in *Montesquieu's Philosophy*.
7. Rahe, *Montesquieu and the Logic of Liberty*, 75.
8. Mosher notes: "Edmund Burke, a close reader of Montesquieu, took this advice to heart and with it founded modern philosophical conservatism—which is distinct, of course, from any conservatism with a perfectionist project" ("What Montesquieu Taught," 10).
9. Rasmussen explains that Montesquieu "explicitly *opposed* political rationalism, arguing that reform should be carried out gradually and that it

would be foolhardy and dangerous to attempt to impose an abstract or comprehensive scheme on society all at once, no matter how 'rational' it may seem" (*Pragmatic Enlightenment*, 195; see also 205). Consider 206–7 for more on Montesquieu's opposition to revolution. Montesquieu also emphasizes the cautious, methodical approach he recommends later: "Politics is a dull file, which wears out and slowly arrives at its end" (XIV.13.487).

10. Mosher, "What Montesquieu Taught," 10.
11. Sullivan, "Against the Despotism," 287.
12. Craiutu explains: "By distinguishing between moderate and immoderate governments, Montesquieu departed from previous classifications. For him, the fundamental question was no longer *who* exercised power—one, the few, or the many—but *how* power was exercised, that is, moderately or immoderately. Political liberty, he argued, exists only in moderate government and only in those governments in which power is not chronically abused" (*Virtue for Courageous Minds*, 40).
13. Montesquieu continues: "and, as it is always easier to follow its force than stop it, perhaps in the classes of superior people, it is easier to find extremely virtuous people, than extremely wise men" (XXVIII.41.858).
14. We will see in chapter 5 that James Madison in *Federalist* No. 51 draws heavily on Montesquieu's notion that power stops power. In Madison's terms, "ambition must be made to counteract ambition."
15. Craiutu explains that Montesquieu's "key point can be stated as follows: liberty and moderation cannot exist in a state in which power is chronically abused and which lacks proper checks and balances. In order to build moderate government and prevent abuses of power, one must create viable institutional mechanisms that can effectively block attempts at usurping power" (*Virtue for Courageous Minds*, 50).
16. Ibid., 49.
17. Montesquieu continues: "it is a masterpiece of legislation that chance rarely makes, and that one rarely leaves to prudence" (V.14.297).
18. Craiutu, *Virtue for Courageous Minds*, 49.
19. Spector, *Montesquieu: Liberté, droit, et histoire*, 182. Consider more broadly 179–82.
20. See also Charles Eisenmann's works refuting the interpretation that Montesquieu defended a "separation of powers": "*L'Esprit des lois*" and "La pensée constitutionnelle."
21. Craiutu, *Virtue for Courageous Minds*, 53.
22. Ibid., 40.
23. In "Against the Despotism," Sullivan explains:

Montesquieu's recommendations regarding judgments and penalties in the context of his invocation of Machiavelli's name and his challenges to Machiavelli's dictates, serve to emphasize the harshness, the arbitrariness, even the tyrannical character of Machiavelli's republicanism. Given Montesquieu's concerns for the security of individuals, for the happiness of citizens, and for the gentlest possible approach to punishments, what could be further from Montesquieu's spirit than the recommendations that spectacular executions against not only the treasonous but also against the outstanding youth serve to reinvigorate a republic? (289)

24. Commenting on the difference between Montesquieu's typology and that of some of his predecessors, Rahe writes,

   The typology deployed by Montesquieu is peculiar in two regards. On the one hand, it abstracts from questions of moral character. Where Xenophon, Plato, Aristotle, Polybius, and their medieval and Renaissance admirers had distinguished kingship from tyranny, aristocracy from oligarchy, and well-ordered popular government from the regime variously called democracy, anarchy, or mob rule and had done so chiefly with an eye to the character of the ruling individual or group, Montesquieu insists that "the form of the constitution" is alone determinative. (*Montesquieu and the Logic of Liberty*, 66)

25. Samuel, "Design," 308. Samuel interprets the "nature" and "spring" as being deterministic in the sense she uses it throughout her article: "It turns out, then, that the inner workings of the archetypes must endeavor to function like the physical world: all the springs must be in place, and all the laws must support and be derived from the spring and the spring from the nature of the government" (308–9). Consider also Spector: "The State is a machine endowed with a structure ... and moved by a spring—the passion that animates it, that is to say that causes and maintains its movement" (*Montesquieu: Liberté, droit, et histoire*, 121).

26. Carrithers argues: "If there was present in Montesquieu's political philosophy a single most important innovation, it was surely his recognition that the psychology of those persons comprising a given state is as crucial to that state's survival as the very institutions through which governmental power is channeled" ("Not So Virtuous Republics," 255).

27. For more on the place of passions in Montesquieu's thought, see Krause, "Laws, Passion, and Right Action."

28. It is possible, though, for there to be more than one passion in a state, though only one can dominate. Montesquieu explains: "If I said: such a wheel, such a cog is not the spring that makes this watch move, would one conclude from this that they are not in the watch? ... In a word, honor is in the republic, although political virtue is its spring; political virtue is in monarchy, although honor is its spring" (*Avertissement de l'auteur.*228).

29. Montesquieu's usage of the plural *principles (principes)* here is curious.

30. Later Montesquieu makes a similar point: "A state can change in two ways: either because the constitution corrects itself, or because it corrupts itself. If it has conserved its principles, and the constitution changes,

it corrects itself; if it has lost its principles, when the constitution just changed, it corrupts itself" (XI.13.414).

31. Machiavelli, *Discourses*, III, 1.
32. For more on Montesquieu's treatment of fear, see Robin, "Reflections on Fear"; and Robin, *Fear*.
33. Shklar, *Montesquieu*, 69.
34. Spector explains: "The description of despotism is that of a depoliticization of the State: no politics is possible there where men cannot deliberate together about common affairs, or oppose their points of view and negotiate the decisions that concern them" (*Montesquieu: Liberté, droit, et histoire*, 115–16).
35. Ibid., 105.
36. Pangle, *Theological Basis*, 28.
37. Notably, and curiously, Montesquieu does not identify any examples of actions that shock "our small souls."
38. Lowenthal writes, for example: "Of the four forms of government, two republican, Montesquieu clearly regards democracy as best and despotism as worst" ("Montesquieu," 522). See also Hulliung, *Montesquieu and the Old Regime*; Keohane, "Virtuous Republics and Glorious Monarchies"; and Nelson, *Greek Tradition in Republican Thought*.
39. Pangle shows that the virtue Montesquieu describes is different from classical virtue (*Theological Basis*, 53–55).
40. Ibid., 71. More generally, Pangle paints Montesquieu as a critic of ancient republican democracy (71–77). For more on Montesquieu as a critic of this kind of democratic virtue, consider also Pangle, *Montesquieu's Philosophy*, 49–64, 72–90; Rahe, *Montesquieu and the Logic of Liberty*, 69–74; and Krause, "Freedom, Sovereignty, and the General Will."
41. Spector, *Montesquieu: Liberté, droit, et histoire*, 128. Lowenthal also notes the need for "mutual surveillance of all in points of conduct" in democratic republics ("Montesquieu," 518).
42. Pangle, *Montesquieu's Philosophy*, 75. He elaborates:
    Democracy stands or falls by the strict subordination of each to the whole; yet men are selfish enough that they will always be tempted to neglect their political duties in the assembly, in public office, or in war, in order to pursue private pleasure and gain. The community must therefore guide and restrict the private lives of its citizens. The citizens must be enthusiastic about such restriction and control. Enthusiasm about subordinating the private to the public requires education. (72)
43. Montesquieu identifies the force required to establish and maintain political virtue as repressive: "Paternal authority again is very useful for maintaining *mœurs*. We already have said that, in a republic, there is not a force as repressive as in the other governments. It thus is necessary that the laws seek to supplement it there: they do so by paternal authority" (V.7.283).

44. Montesquieu writes: "I was going to say that slaves among the Greeks and the Romans.... But I hear the voice of nature crying out against me" (VI.17.329).
45. For more on the voting process in democracies, see Lowenthal, "Montesquieu," 517.
46. Spector, *Montesquieu: Liberté, droit, et histoire*, 88.
47. Montesquieu writes, for example: "The drawback is not when the State passes from moderate government to moderate government, as from republic to monarchy, or from monarchy to republic; but when it falls and dashes from moderate government to despotism" (VIII.8.356). See also XI, 4 and *MP*, 223, 225, 751, 884.
48. Consider Rahe, *Montesquieu and the Logic of Liberty*; Rahe, "Montesquieu's Critique of Monarchy"; Rahe, "Montesquieu's Natural Rights Constitutionalism"; and Pangle, *Montesquieu's Philosophy* and *Theological Basis*.
49. Scholars translate the term "*stadhouder*" in one of two ways: "stadholder" or "stadtholder." Following Masterson and Levillain, I use "stadholder."
50. Craiutu, *Virtue for Courageous Minds*, 60.
51. Spector presents a thorough discussion of the import of intermediary powers in monarchies (*Montesquieu: Liberté, droit, et histoire*, 93–105).
52. Ibid., 93.
53. For an extended discussion of the *parlements*, see Kingston, *Montesquieu and the Parlement*.
54. *Merriam-Webster Online*, s.v., "honor," accessed June 7, 2017, https://www.merriam-webster.com/dictionary/honor.
55. Lowenthal, "Montesquieu," 520. However, Lowenthal sees this honor as vulgar: "The honor-seeking criticized by Montesquieu cannot simply be identified with the activity attributed by Aristotle to the magnanimous or proud man. Monarchy's system of mores and manners is vulgarized honor, or honor that seeks to be recognized by many, that depends so much more on recognition by others, that succumbs to, rather than resists, the vices (e.g., gallantry) that are popularly taken for signs of boldness" (520–21).
56. Spector, *Montesquieu: Liberté, droit, et histoire*, 147; emphasis added.
57. Ibid., 143.
58. Lowenthal, "Montesquieu," 520.
59. See Krause, "Politics of Distinction" and *Liberalism with Honor*.
60. See also Spector, *Montesquieu: Liberté, droit, et histoire*, 136.
61. See esp. Pangle, *Montesquieu's Philosophy*, 64–69; Radasanu, "Montesquieu on Moderation"; and Rahe, *Montesquieu and the Logic of Liberty*, 67–69, 77–84, 111, 124–6, 154, 186–211, 221.
62. Krause, *Liberalism with Honor*.
63. Lowenthal, "Montesquieu," 520.
64. Craiutu, *Virtue for Courageous Minds*, 61.
65. Krause, *Liberalism with Honor*.

66. De Dijn's earlier work on Montesquieu, *French Political Thought*, is an exception. She presents Montesquieu as an "aristocratic liberal." However, her more recent works, "Montesquieu's Controversial Context" and "Was Montesquieu a Liberal Republican?," seem to contradict her earlier work. She has come to argue that, instead, *De l'Esprit des lois* is a "monarchist tract" and that Montesquieu preferred monarchy to all other forms of government. These diverging theses do not seem to be compatible with one another. Regarding the issue of overlooking aristocracy in Montesquieu, Carrithers points to numerous works where one would expect engagement with aristocracy, but such engagement is not in the texts ("Not So Virtuous Republics," 245).
67. Pangle argues, instead, that Montesquieu sees aristocracy "as an inferior and even defective form of republic" (*Theological Basis*, 52). Rahe also interprets Montesquieu as critical of aristocracies (*Montesquieu and the Logic of Liberty*, 76–77).
68. Carrithers, "Not So Virtuous Republics." Carrithers argues, for example, that in XI, 6 Montesquieu "forthrightly denounced Venice's constitution as producing not liberty but despotism" (268).
69. Carrithers provides a list of twenty classical and modern aristocratic republics of which Montesquieu had knowledge (ibid., 246). While Carrithers labels Holland an aristocratic republic, Montesquieu considered it first and foremost a federal republic.
70. Bandoch, "Aristocracy."
71. Aristotle, *Politics*, 1279a.
72. Montesquieu specifically distinguishes the aristocracy from the nobility in monarchies: "It is not necessary that aristocracy takes the nature and principle of monarchy; that would happen, if the nobles had any personal and particular prerogatives, distinct from those of their body. The privileges should be for the senate, and simple respect for the senators" (V.8.284).
73. See also V, 8 where he speaks of aristocratic families.
74. Lowenthal offers an alternative understanding: "The aristocratic republic is a regime wherein only a part of the people is sovereign, as best exemplified in the early Roman republic and modern Venice. Aristocracy depends upon political and economic inequality between the sovereign nobles and the nonparticipating people" ("Montesquieu," 518).
75. For an alternative interpretation of this passage see Carrithers, "Not So Virtuous Republics," 253–54.
76. Consider Montesquieu's example: "Thus, in Athens when Antipater established that those with less than two thousand drachmas would be excluded from the right of suffrage, he formed the best aristocracy that was possible; because this census was so small that it only would exclude a small number of people, and no one who had any consideration in the city" (II.3.246).

77. On the difference between the two, Samuel explains: "In monarchies, the vital social element also resides with the nobles. However, whereas the nobles of aristocracies must lean toward selflessness, frugality, modesty, simplicity of manners, and moderation, the nobles of monarchies need to cultivate ambition, wealth, self-interest, ornamentation, and honor. This is due to the fact that the political structure of the monarchy is vertically three tiered, not two tiered, as is that of the aristocratic republic" ("Design," 308).
78. Carrithers, "Not So Virtuous Republics," 256.
79. Carrithers notes a tension between what Montesquieu says here about the Venetian inquisitors and his more critical remarks in XI, 6 (ibid., 264–65). For more on checking the nobles, particularly in Venice, consider ibid., 257–58.
80. See esp. ibid., 267.
81. Jefferson, *Portable Thomas Jefferson*, 534.
82. For treatments of the federal model in *EL*, see Larrère, "Montesquieu et l'idée de fédération"; Ward, "Montesquieu on Federalism"; and Wolfe, "Confederate Republic." Other scholars overlook the positive regard in which Montesquieu holds federal republics. De Dijn, for example, does not mention them in her consideration of the form of government Montesquieu preferred ("Was Montesquieu a Liberal Republican?").
83. Montesquieu uses the term "cette forme de gouvernement" (IX.1.369). After referring to "trois espèces de gouvernement" in part I, he begins referring to a "forme de gouvernement" in part II. Consider, for example, XI.2.394. He thus seems to use "form" and "species" interchangeably.
84. Mason seems to think Montesquieu expresses his true opinion about Holland here: "Favored by sea and river, profiting from political intelligence, this regime [Holland] alone may make a bid for immortality" ("Montesquieu and the Dutch," 186).
85. However, Montesquieu says later: "Since all human things have an end . . ." (XI.6.407).
86. For more on the unanimous nature of this consent, see Masterson, "Holland's Fifty Republics," 32–33.
87. Masterson argues that Montesquieu learned from Janiçon that Holland was a union of fifty-six republics and not simply seven provinces. Masterson discusses Montesquieu's footnote from IX, 1, which says: "Elle [Hollande] est formée par environ cinquante républiques, toutes différentes les unes des autres. État des Provinces-Unies, par M. Janisson." Masterson explains:

> it is undeniable that chapter 3 reverts to the seven-Province analysis of the Dutch Republic, in so far as it refers to the weights of the various Provinces in voting and in raising revenue. This is not strictly incompatible with the idea of a fifty-six-town federation, but it seems that Montesquieu was now less conscious of

the idea of the Dutch Republic as an association of towns than he had been in chapter 1. (Ibid., 36)

The difference suggests at a minimum an important revision.

88. Montesquieu explains: "The city of Amsterdam only has its vote, like the others, despite the great inequality of its contribution" (OCI.867).
89. See Bandoch, "Forming a European Spirit," where I utilize Montesquieu's concept of *esprit* to analyze problems facing the European Union. I find the EU's current approach risky since it does not properly account for the different *esprits* of its members. See also Zuckert, "EU's Federalism Deficit."
90. Mansfield elaborates on the importance Montesquieu attaches to an executive (*Taming the Prince*, 213–46).
91. Levillain, in "Glory without Power?," demonstrates how problematic Montesquieu found the lack of a stadholder.
92. Montesquieu later softens his harsh tone. In *MP* he writes first that Holland "is no longer free since they no longer have a stadholder." In the next section, he writes: "Holland has become less free since they do not have a stadholder" (OCI.1432–33).
93. Masterson, "Montesquieu's Stadholder," 81.
94. Ibid., 85.
95. Ibid., 106. Levillain explains that Montesquieu was especially concerned about "the magistrates' misappropriation of public funds in their capacity as tax collectors" ("Glory without Power?," 189).
96. Levillain elaborates: "A stadholder ... brings three things: moderation, unity, and power. Moderation resulted from a 'combination of powers' which allowed one power to balance the other. Unity resulted from the taming of factions.... The stadholder...plays the role of an arbiter between competing factions" (ibid., 189).
97. Masterson explains that the restoration "seemed to present a grave threat to the foreign policy and military situation of France, so Montesquieu decided to be very careful what he published.... In discussing this subject Montesquieu might well have referred to the previous successes, so galling to France, of the last Stadholder, William III of Orange" ("Holland's Fifty Republics," 237).
98. Montesquieu criticizes Louis XIV to make this point:

> The enemies of a great prince who ruled for such a long time have accused him a thousand times, rather, I believe, from their fears than on their reasons, of having formed and pursued the project of universal monarchy. If he had succeeded in it, nothing would have been more fatal to Europe, to its ancient subjects, to him, and to his family. Heaven, who knew the real advantages, served him better by his defeats than it ever would have through his victories. (IX.7.375)
>
> The argument of these "enemies of a great prince" is nearly identical to the one Montesquieu made in his *Réflexions sur la*

monarchie universelle en Europe about the problems related to trying to conquer other states (OCII.17–37).

99. Rahe, *Montesquieu and the Logic of Liberty*; Pangle, *Montesquieu's Philosophy*; and Pangle, *Theological Basis*. See also Israel, *Enlightenment Contested*, 289–90, 293.

100. Pangle, *Theological Basis*, 83; emphasis added. It is true that Pangle goes on to write that

> yet while the English constitution is in some sense 'the model' (11.7), Montesquieu's political science conveys the chastening lesson that the specific English institutions can and ought rarely be applied, and then only with substantial modifications, to other nations (see 11.6, penultimate para.). Even in Europe—where liberty appears to be in some sense indigenous—what should be encouraged and sought out are at most roughly analogous institutional mechanisms and practices, rooted in and thus suited to each nation's peculiar historical spirit. (87–88)

But the entire thrust of Pangle's analysis suggests, instead, that he interprets Montesquieu as viewing England as the best regime. Consider 77–93. Consider also Pangle, *Montesquieu's Philosophy*, 107–60. For example, he writes in this earlier work: "In his presentation of the traditional forms of government, Montesquieu has revealed the inadequacies of their particular principles and the aims which derive from those principles. He has thereby pointed to the desirability of a government having no other purpose than the security and comfort of its citizens. He finds the principles of this desired government in the modern constitution of England" (*Montesquieu's Philosophy*, 107). Pangle also writes: "having presented the correct political principles through his analysis of England in Books XI through XIII, Montesquieu proceeds to show how these principles can be applied to political life elsewhere" (193).

101. See especially Manin's "Montesquieu et la politique moderne," in which he critiques Pangle and seeks to portray Montesquieu as a theoretician of plurality in politics. See also Spector's concerns about the Straussian interpretation of Montesquieu in "Montesquieu et la crise." Spector criticizes Rahe in *Montesquieu: Pouvoirs, richesses, et sociétés*, 385–94, and rejects the notion that England is Montesquieu's model regime in *Montesquieu: Liberté, droit, et histoire*, 192.

102. Rahe, *Montesquieu and the Logic of Liberty*. Consider also Rahe, *Montesquieu's Science of Politics*, 84–90.

103. For more on the judiciary in Montesquieu's thought, see Carrese, *Cloaking of Power*.

104. Montesquieu also writes: "Of the three powers of which we have spoken, that of judging is in some way null" (XI.6.401).

105. Consider Lowenthal, "Montesquieu," 523, for more on how Locke and Montesquieu divided powers differently.

106. Direct democracy can lead to dangerous outcomes, Montesquieu suggests (XI.6.400).
107. Montesquieu does not have high expectations of the people on this matter: "The great advantage of representatives, is that they are capable of discussing business. The people there are not at all appropriate for this; this forms one of the greatest inconveniences of democracy" (XI.6.400).
108. Spector, *Montesquieu: Liberté, droit, et histoire*, 185.

Chapter Four

1. For a discussion of the development of Montesquieu's thought in relation to the climate, see Shackleton, "Evolution" and *Montesquieu*. Shackleton states: "The early works of Montesquieu do not set forth the theory of climatic influence" ("Evolution" 317); and: "It is not until his visit to Italy that he shows serious interest in the effect of climate" (*Montesquieu*, 303). Shackleton also argues that Montesquieu developed his theory of climate in close conjuncture with his concept of *esprit général* ("Evolution," 320). See also ibid., 329: "1734–1741: The formation of the doctrine of *esprit général* with climate as one of its factors." Consider also Casabianca's extensive discussion of the physical causes in *Montesquieu*. Shackleton states about Montesquieu's "theory of the influence of climate on men and societies": "Along with the separation of powers, it is his most influential doctrine" ("Evolution," 317).
2. For a discussion of various theories of climate that existed in the first half of the eighteenth century, see Mercier, "La théorie des climats."
3. Lowenthal ("Montesquieu"), Samuel ("Design"), and Shklar (*Montesquieu*, 93–99) all present Montesquieu as a climate determinist. Discussing the general argument that Montesquieu was a climate determinist, Kriesel writes: "Montesquieu ... has been identified as a determinist or an extreme environmentalist, or, to combine Platt's terms, an environmental determinist. ... In much of the geographical literature concerned with environmental determinists, he has been placed toward the recent end of a chronological continuum which began with Hippocrates, Plato, Aristotle, continued through Ibn Khaldun, Bodin, and Arbuthnot, and gradually came to a close after him with Buckle, Ratzel, Semple, and Huntington" ("Montesquieu," 557–58). Kriesel argues that Montesquieu was not an environmental determinist: for Montesquieu the impact of nature on man was limited; it did not define everything (558). Kriesel states that Montesquieu's "theory of political geography is more properly interpreted as being possibilistic rather than environmentalistic or deterministic" (557). "Montesquieu stated that it was from the physical environment as well as from cultural manifestations that the individual's character arose. That interplay of 'physical' and 'moral' causes was extended . . . to be the factor which established the character of a society

or nation" (560). Kriesel argues that Montesquieu's "blunt statements about the political and governmental manifestations of various types of climate, soil, topography, and land area" "should not be taken out of the context of his *esprit général*, the general spirit of a nation" (565).

Others also reject the notion that Montesquieu was a climate determinist, on the grounds that he viewed man's nature as malleable. Pangle writes:

> In Montesquieu the influence of climate and geography on political life is far greater than it was for Aristotle. This is a consequence of the massive agreement between Montesquieu and those modern thinkers from Machiavelli to Locke who hold that man is much more malleable than the ancients realized. Montesquieu's emphasis on climate and history is an outcome not so much of a return to Aristotle as of a more radical thinking through of the understanding of human nature held by modern political philosophy. (*Montesquieu's Philosophy*, 161–62)

Nyland agrees with Pangle that Montesquieu "was adamant that humans are flexible beings shaped by the ideas and impressions around them" ("Biology and Environment," 394). See also Rahe, *Montesquieu and the Logic of Liberty*, 155; and Carrese, "Montesquieu," 2431.

4. Rasmussen, *Pragmatic Enlightenment*, 257. Rasmussen identifies various works by Montesquieu to corroborate his claim.

5. Pangle notes: "In trying to establish free government on the basis of man's deepest natural needs, the legislator must take into account the natural climatic variation in the capacity to satisfy these needs" (*Montesquieu's Philosophy*, 165).

6. Rahe, *Montesquieu and the Logic of Liberty*, 155. Rahe also writes that Montesquieu's "aim is to achieve an understanding of the special conditions that made possible and perhaps even encouraged the emergence of republics and monarchies in the one place in the world where they happen to have appeared" (159).

7. Shackleton rightly insists that we must view Montesquieu's claims in their historical context:

> The first impression in the mind of the twentieth-century reader, however, may well be that of naïveté of the doctrine; and that impression, if one is to judge by absolute scientific standards, is justified. But if one wishes to understand Montesquieu properly one must judge him in relation to the standards of his own day, and the theories of climate current in the seventeenth and eighteenth centuries often took odd forms. (*Montesquieu*, 313)

8. Pangle suggests that we "see here some of the aberrant enthusiasm generated by Enlightenment scientific research" (*Montesquieu's Philosophy*, 167). He calls this discussion in book XIV "a curious combination of common sense and madness" (167).

9. Lowenthal, "Montesquieu," 526. Pangle identifies temperature as the most influential climatic factor for Montesquieu (*Montesquieu's Philosophy*, 166).
10. For more on the link between climate and servitude in Montesquieu, see Rahe, *Montesquieu and the Logic of Liberty*, 157; and Pangle, *Montesquieu's Philosophy*, 170–72. On despotism see Rahe, *Montesquieu and the Logic of Liberty*, 158.
11. Gourou cites the discussion of hot and cold climates as part of "le déterminisme physique" of Montesquieu ("Le déterminisme physique," 9).
12. Rahe shows that Montesquieu especially had Asia in mind with his analysis of plains and political servitude (*Montesquieu and the Logic of Liberty*, 158–59).
13. For more on Montesquieu's discussion of the English climate, see Pangle, *Montesquieu's Philosophy*, 169–70; and Rahe, *Montesquieu and the Logic of Liberty*, 162–63.
14. See also Rahe, *Montesquieu and the Logic of Liberty*, 156: "Wise legislation may in some measure be able to ameliorate the ill effects of the climate, but it cannot overcome these entirely."
15. Spector, *Montesquieu: Liberté, droit, et histoire*, 212.
16. Craiutu, *Virtue for Courageous Minds*, 55. Pangle also identifies the overcoming of environment-induced laziness as a goal of key import to Montesquieu (*Montesquieu's Philosophy*, 168).
17. Collier, *Bottom Billion*, 53–63.
18. Pangle, *Montesquieu's Philosophy*, 239; emphasis added. Consider also Rosow, "Commerce, Power and Justice," 352; Clark, *Compass of Society*, 87; and Hirschman, *Passions and the Interests*, 81.
19. For an examination of acquisitiveness in Montesquieu, as well as its (anti-)Machiavellian origins, see Hendrickson, "Montesquieu's (Anti-)Machiavellianism."
20. Scholars have differed in their interpretations of Montesquieu's usage of commerce. Mosher, in "Free Trade," and Rosow, in "Commerce, Power and Justice," implicitly suggest that commerce is economic exchange. Rahe puts forth in *Montesquieu and the Logic of Liberty* a broader reading similar to the one I present. Larrère offers yet another perspective: "And sociability can be called *commerce*, since Montesquieu, as was usual among eighteenth-century authors, speaks of commerce in a much broader sense than we currently do, applying it not only to the moneyed exchange of goods, but to all sort of other exchanges, spiritual as well as material, between persons as well as between things" ("Montesquieu on Economics and Commerce," 346). For more on Montesquieu's usage of commerce in *EL*, see Volpilhac-Auger, "L'histoire du commerce." See also also Brühlmeier, "Considérations," for more on Montesquieu's conception of commerce and its relation to markets.
21. Hirschman, discussing Montesquieu and others on the *doux* nature of commerce, explains: "The origin of the epithet *doux* is probably to be

found in the 'noncommercial' meaning of *commerce*: besides trade the word long denoted animated and repeated conversation and other forms of polite social intercourse and dealings among persons (frequently between two persons of the opposite sex). It was in this connection that the term *doux* was often used in conjunction with *commerce*" (*Passions and the Interests*, 61–62).

22. Larrère, "Montesquieu on Economics and Commerce," 356.
23. Rosow, "Commerce, Power and Justice," 355. Rosow does suggest that this dynamic is more present "among merchants and between them and the state."
24. Pangle explains: "commerce impresses upon men and women the fact that they share these needs with the inhabitants of other nations, regardless of their conflicting beliefs and customs. On this solid, because natural, basis, peoples can begin to cooperate with one another. The sympathy that is natural to the human species can emerge and supplant the contempt peoples have come to conceive for one another on account of their different manners and morals" (*Theological Basis*, 100).
25. Spector, *Montesquieu: Liberté, droit, et histoire*, 238–39.
26. Rosow, "Commerce, Power and Justice," 347.
27. Pangle continues: "The establishment of the brotherhood of man comes about through the reduction of all differences to the lowest common denominator—the need for security and the desire for comfort" (*Montesquieu's Philosophy*, 206–7).
28. Pangle argues that the "most important 'destructive prejudices' that commerce can be seen to be curing, the most important kind of 'ferocity' and 'barbarian morals' that commerce can be seen to be softening, are the destructive religious prejudices, and the ferocious, barbarian, or despotic religious morals" (*Theological Basis*, 101). Consider also Pangle's discussion of XX, 1 on commerce's effects on mores (*Montesquieu's Philosophy*, 204–5).
29. Mosher points out that Montesquieu was one of the first people to use communication this way ("Monarchy's Paradox," 186–87).
30. Rahe, *Montesquieu and the Logic of Liberty*, 175.
31. Craiutu, *Virtue for Courageous Minds*, 64–65.
32. Larrère rightly emphasizes that for Montesquieu commerce "is first of all an individual activity, a private profession" ("Montesquieu on Economics and Commerce," 337).
33. Muller discusses how Montesquieu thinks commerce may promote humanity ("Political Economy of Republicanism," 61–75).
34. Spector, *Montesquieu et l'émergence*, 85. She writes: "Because it is necessary for rule to prevail over his spontaneous and selfish inclinations, the good merchant thus can be a good citizen. In this regard, virtue and commerce are no longer opposed. . . . A certain type of commerce can be compatible with a certain type of virtue—not military, but industrious and frugal" (85–86).

35. Rahe continues by noting that in addition to Mandeville, Pierre Nicole and Pierre Bayle were important influences on Montesquieu in this regard (*Montesquieu and the Logic of Liberty*, 176–77). Rahe considers Montesquieu's relation to Mandeville more extensively (176–78). Rahe also contends: "In short, to embrace commerce and the peculiar spirit of cosmopolitanism that it inspires is to embrace moral corruption" (176). Montesquieu cites Mandeville elsewhere regarding how commerce expands (XIX.8.560). Larrère presents an alternative perspective: "In *The Spirit of the Laws*, the private vices/public benefits scheme is valid only in monarchies, where there should be luxury. It is not valid in republics where sumptuary laws are necessary" ("Montesquieu on Economics and Commerce," 347). Consider also Spector, "Vices privés, vertus publiques."
36. For more on the centrality of this passage to Montesquieu's thought, see especially Hirschman, *Passions and the Interests*. Hirschman even selects it as the epitaph to his seminal work on passions and interests.
37. For an extended discussion of luxury in eighteenth- and nineteenth-century French thought, see Jennings, "Debate about Luxury."
38. For more on the distinction between the two forms of commerce, see also Larrère, "Commerce de luxe et commerce d'économie"; Larrère, "Montesquieu on Economics and Commerce," 347; and Clark, *Compass of Society*, 117.
39. Mosher contends that it is "not obvious which kind of political economy Montesquieu prefers, as each tends to create different sets of desirable and undesirable conditions" ("Montesquieu on Empire and Enlightenment," 148). Mosher makes a similar point elsewhere in "Montesquieu on Conquest," suggesting that Montesquieu is ambivalent about the two forms of commerce. Pangle argues that Montesquieu views the commerce of economy as "a superior form of commerce" (*Montesquieu's Philosophy*, 212) while suggesting that Montesquieu sees a place for both forms (211–15). Still, Pangle concludes: "All nations, even those with a commerce of luxury, should try to emulate the universality of English international trade" (239). Rosow concludes that the "benefits of the commerce of economy far outweigh those of the commerce of luxuries" ("Commerce, Power and Justice," 353).
40. Consider Clark, *Compass of Society*, 85, 87.
41. Montesquieu explains: "The riches of a state suppose a lot of industry. It is not possible that in such a large number of branches of commerce, there is not always someone who suffers, and consequently for its workers to not be in temporary necessity" (XXIII.29.713).
42. By contrast, Howse interprets the commerce of luxury as "*taking* something of value from others in order not to have to make it oneself" ("Montesquieu on Commerce," 10–11).
43. Montesquieu highlights the necessity of democratic republics preventing luxury from being established: "As luxury establishes itself in a

republic, the *esprit* turns towards individual interest. To the people for whom there is nothing but necessity, it remains only to desire glory for the country and for themselves. But a soul corrupted by luxury certainly has other desires. Soon it becomes the enemy of the laws that bother it" (VII.2.335).

44. Montesquieu writes: "one has more desires, more needs, more fantasies when one is with others" (VII.1.334).
45. Pangle, *Montesquieu's Philosophy*, 213. Elsewhere Pangle argues that the commerce of luxury is "a stimulus to increased commerce, greater productivity, and the redistribution of wealth from the idle upper to the working and mercantile classes" (*Theological Basis*, 100).
46. Pangle, *Montesquieu's Philosophy*, 212.
47. Clark offers an alternative perspective (*Compass of Society*, 117).
48. According to Montesquieu, it is "the nature of commerce to render superfluous things useful, and the useful things necessary. The State thus will be able to give necessary things to the greatest number of subjects" (XX.23.601).
49. While Montesquieu here is quoting Honorius and Théodose, he seems to share their opinion.
50. Montesquieu writes: "Thus, for the monarchic State to support itself, luxury should be increasing, from laborer to artisan, to merchants, to nobles, to magistrates, to lords, to the principal revenue officers, to the prince; without which everything would be lost" (VII.4.336).
51. Rahe argues that commerce subverts the monarchical principle (*Montesquieu and the Logic of Liberty*, 190).
52. Pangle contends that Montesquieu saw a combination of the two types of commerce as "the greatest hope for progress in much of Europe" (*Montesquieu's Philosophy*, 215).
53. Rosow, "Commerce, Power and Justice," 353.
54. Rosow shows that "prosperity and the good of the state derive from the advantageous participation of the citizens in commerce, not merely from the quantity of gold and silver that the state is able to control. Political conquest must be secondary to economic movement" (ibid., 361). He also contends that "the prosperity of the state, in Montesquieu's view, is determined by the quantity of international trade and by a balance between the amount of money and the total value of commodities in the market" (351).
55. Consider, for example, Rahe, *Montesquieu and the Logic of Liberty*; and Pangle, *Montesquieu's Philosophy* and *Theological Basis*. Pangle writes, "All nations, even those with a commerce of luxury, should try to emulate the universality of English international trade. . . . Wherever possible, all nations should imitate the freedom of movement of persons and goods practiced in England and other commercial republics" (*Montesquieu's Philosophy*, 239–40).

56. Montesquieu continues: "I said: a Dutchman can die at the age of 80 without having ever committed a good deed" (OCI.1338).
57. Montesquieu thinks the Dutch even deceive themselves in a certain respect: "In Holland, taxes on everything that one consumes to live there comprise almost a third of the value of a thing, and it seems that this nation, which calculates its gains and losses so well, consents in this sole case to deceive itself" (OCII.999).
58. *Montesquieu and the Logic of Liberty*, 138. Rahe continues: "for, except in those rare cases in which Montesquieu spells out in his notebooks an idea too controversial to be explicitly addressed and fully explored in his published works, such a procedure could easily result in our giving his passing impressions preference over his considered conclusions, and it invites on the part of his modern students indulgence in a vice to which scholars in all times are prone." Consider, for example, what Levillain writes: "Montesquieu's travel notes offer a picture of a tax-burdened country with a population that had no other choice but to extort money from anyone they could, especially from foreigners" ("Glory without Power?," 186).
59. Montesquieu underwent an important change on Holland, England, and France on this matter. Earlier in *MP* their dominance appears tyrannical. "Europe, which has engaged in commerce in three other parts of the world, has been the tyrant of these three parts. France, England, and Holland, who made the commerce of Europe, have been the tyrants of Europe and of the World; but this will not persist" (OCI.1356). In *EL*, though, he does not make such a claim, suggesting a more mature, positive outlook.
60. Mason, "Montesquieu and the Dutch," 186.
61. For more on the importance Montesquieu attaches to work, see Spector, *Montesquieu et l'émergence*, 85, 347–69.
62. For an excellent discussion of moderation in Montesquieu, see Craiutu, *Virtue for Courageous Minds*. Consider also Manin, "Montesquieu, la république et le commerce," 584.
63. Mosher, in "Montesquieu on Empire and Enlightenment," and Spector, in *Montesquieu et l'émergence*, 399–445, offer careful treatments of empire. Spector also considers the interplay of the *esprit de conquête* and *esprit de commerce* in Montesquieu's works (178–89).
64. Binoche, *Introduction*, 325–26.
65. Spector, *Montesquieu: Liberté, droit, et histoire*, 243, 253–54.
66. Casabianca, *L'Esprit des lois*, 67.
67. Larrère, "Tolérance et liberté religieuse," 153, 158, 162.
68. Kingston, "Montesquieu on Religion," 376.
69. Shackleton, *Montesquieu*, 354.
70. Baum, *Montesquieu and Social Theory*, 89; Conroy, *Montesquieu Revisited*, 101; Dos Santos, "Montesquieu," 173, 177; Gilbert, "Internal

Restlessness," 47; Mason, *Montesquieu's Idea of Justice*, 126–27; Merry, *Montesquieu's System of Natural Government*, 126.
71. Schaub, *Erotic Liberalism*, 144, 149.
72. Samuel, "Design," 317.
73. Pangle, *Montesquieu's Philosophy*, 250.
74. Pangle, *Theological Basis*, 34.
75. Ibid., 128.
76. Bartlett, "Politics of Faith and Reason," 24.
77. Shklar, *Montesquieu*, 44, 84.
78. Lowenthal, "Montesquieu," 533.
79. Cohler, Miller, and Stone say, "Montesquieu never capitalizes *dieu*, 'god'" (Montesquieu, *Spirit of the Laws*, 5, fn. h). This opens Montesquieu up to antireligious and anti-Christian interpretations. But the authoritative Voltaire Foundation manuscript and the Pléiade confirm that Montesquieu capitalized "Dieu." Regarding the substance of Montesquieu's discussion of God in book I, see Bartlett, "Politics of Faith and Reason"; Lowenthal, "Book I"; and Pangle, *Montesquieu's Philosophy* and *Theological Basis*. Waddicor, in *Montesquieu*, considers the relation between religion and natural law in Montesquieu's thought.
80. *Défense de L'Esprit des Lois* (*Défense*) includes a rejoinder against criticisms, especially inside France, of Montesquieu's treatment of religion and charges of being a Spinozist and advocate of natural religion. Spector, in "Naturalisation," examines Montesquieu's relationship to natural religion. His professions of faith may have been a provocative strategy against the censor, or they may have been indicative of a deeper belief in Christian principles. Consider Sonenscher, *Before the Deluge*, to situate Montesquieu's arguments about religious toleration into his French monarchical context.
81. Spector, "Naturalisation," 60.
82. Rahe, *Montesquieu and the Logic of Liberty*, 110.
83. Durkheim, *Montesquieu and Rousseau*, 45.
84. Consider Richter, *Political Theory*, 100; Merry, *Montesquieu's System of Natural Government*, 121–22; and Schaub, "Of Believers and Barbarians," 238.
85. For an extended account of the history of civil religion, from Machiavelli through Heidegger, and one way of fitting Montesquieu into this debate, see Beiner, *Civil Religion*, esp. 189–204.
86. Montesquieu's treatment of Stoicism demonstrates the complicated nature of how he thinks a religion can make "good citizens." He contends that Stoicism "alone knew how to make citizens; it alone made great men; it alone made great emperors" (XXIV.10.721). The Stoics were effective political actors because they "were occupied only in working for men's happiness and in exercising the duties of society." They pursued the common good, not selfish desires; they were "born for society" and "believed that their destiny was to work for it." This is the only

place where he discusses this extinct religion in *EL*. His support is qualified and mostly historical.
87. Zanin, in "Rousseau, Montesquieu, et la 'religion civilie,'" compares Montesquieu and Rousseau on civil religion.
88. For extended analyses of Montesquieu's treatment of Islam, see Bandoch, "Montesquieu's Critique"; and Curtis, *Orientalism and Islam*.
89. Montesquieu calls Islam Mohammedanism, and its followers Mohammedans. Both are incorrect and potentially contentious. He seems to suggest that Muhammad is a leader, not a prophet, and that his followers are worshipping a person, not God. He uses the same terminology in the *Lettres Persanes*, even in the voice of Usbek!
90. Throughout *LP* Montesquieu judges Islam to be harsh on women. Consider XXIV, XXXVIII, LXI–LXIV, and LXVII. See also Schaub, *Erotic Liberalism*, 55.
91. *Esprit*, Montesquieu's core concept, is constituted by the factors he identifies in I, 3 (*esprit des lois*) and XIX, 4 (*esprit général*). The factors vary across time and place. See Bandoch, "Forming a European Spirit"; and Markovits, *Montesquieu*, on *esprit*.
92. Spector, "Naturalisation," 59.
93. Cohler, *Montesquieu's Comparative Politics*, 26, 42.
94. Pangle, *Montesquieu's Philosophy*, 253.
95. Shackleton, *Montesquieu*, 342.
96. Barrera, "Comment certaine," 116–17.
97. Schaub, "Of Believers and Barbarians," 238.
98. Richter, *Political Theory*, 100.
99. For more on Montesquieu vis-à-vis Bayle, see Bartlett, "Politics of Faith and Reason"; Beiner, *Civil Religion*, 176–204; Binoche, *Introduction*, 319–24; Cohler, *Montesquieu's Comparative Politics*, 131; Diop, "Des lectures," 89–90; and Markovits, *Montesquieu*, 206–9.
100. Maire views Montesquieu as a "Catholic author" ("Montesquieu," 214). Shackleton contends that "Montesquieu believes firmly in the existence of God. . . . His belief in God was the foundation of his notions, as they then existed, of morality" (*Montesquieu*, 351). But Shackleton does not find evidence that Montesquieu is definitively Christian. Instead, it is "in deism that is to be found the real religious beliefs of Montesquieu" (352).
101. For an alternative discussion of Montesquieu's treatment of believers and nonbelievers, and how it relates to his stance on toleration, see Schaub, "Of Believers and Barbarians."
102. Shklar, *Montesquieu*, 84.
103. Ibid. Shackleton interprets Montesquieu as less unfavorable to the clergy: "He does not see religion as the invention of dishonest priests; it is not a fraud" (*Montesquieu*, 340). See also Maire, "Montesquieu"; Spector, *Montesquieu: Liberté, droit, et histoire*, 251; and Schaub, *Erotic Liberalism*, 65.
104. Schaub, "Of Believers and Barbarians," 235.

105. Bartlett, "Politics of Faith and Reason," 16.
106. Merry, *Montesquieu's System of Natural Government*, 122.
107. Schaub, "Of Believers and Barbarians," 240.
108. See also Schaub's focus on toleration in connection with other passages in ibid.
109. Kingston, "Montesquieu on Religion," 392.
110. An entry on "troubler" in the *DAF* from 1762 (the edition closest to *EL*'s publication date) supports my reading: "Il signifie encore, Inquiéter quelqu'un dans la possession, dans la jouissance de quelque bien" (It signifies again, Worry someone in the possession, in the enjoyment of some good).
111. Dos Santos, "Montesquieu," 184.
112. Schaub, "Of Believers and Barbarians," 229, 233.
113. Lowenthal, "Montesquieu," 533.
114. Samuel, "Design," 317.
115. Consider also *LP*, XXIX where Rica observes: "I can also assure you that there has never been a realm so prone to civil wars as that of Christ." See also Casabianca, *L'Esprit des lois*, 68.
116. On this point specifically, and in XXV, 9–10 generally, Montesquieu seems to diverge from *LP*. In LXXXV Usbek (though not necessarily Montesquieu) suggests that a state might benefit from having several religions, that members of tolerated religions usually serve a country better than those of the dominant religion, and that the introduction of a new sect can correct abuses in other existing sects.
117. Larrère, "Tolérance et liberté religieuse," 157.
118. An entry in *DAF* supports my reading: "ÉTABLIR signifie aussi Instituer; & il se dit tant des choses qu'on institue pour toujours, que de celles qu'on n'institue que pour un temps" (ESTABLISH also means to Institute; & it means so many things that one institutes forever, than of those that one only institutes for a time).
119. Kingston, "Montesquieu on Religion," 394.
120. An entry in *DAF* supports my reading: "TOLÉRANCE se dit aussi De la condescendance politique qui fait quelquefois que les Souverains souffrent dans leurs États l'exercice d'une autre Religion que celle qui y est établie par les lois de l'État." (TOLERANCE also means From political condescension that sometimes makes the Sovereigns put up with the exercise of another Religion in their States than that which is established by the laws of the State). Consider also Bayle's *Philosophical Commentary*, a prominent Enlightenment defense of toleration. Bayle argues that toleration is not harmful to society, that if the diversity of religions causes evil to the state, it is on account of nontoleration, and that toleration of sects is consistent with public quiet; he contends that "toleration ought to be general," including toward Jews, Muslims, and pagans. Bayle does not equivocate the way Montesquieu does.

121. Consider also *LP*, LXXXV where Usbek suggests: "I admit that history is filled with religious wars, but let us be careful here, for it is not the multiplicity of religions which has produced these wars, but the spirit of intolerance stirring those who believed themselves to be in a dominant position." In *EL* Montesquieu is open to nonviolent intolerance.
122. Durkheim, *Montesquieu and Rousseau*, 41.
123. Ibid.
124. Rahe, *Montesquieu and the Logic of Liberty*, 214.
125. Bartlett, "Politics of Faith and Reason," 18.
126. Pangle, *Montesquieu's Philosophy*, 256–57.
127. Skrzypek, "Montesquieu et les modèles," 143. Consider also *LP*, CXVII.

Chapter Five

1. Lutz, "Relative Influence."
2. The delegates reference Montesquieu on three occasions: Madison, *Notes*, 224, 268, 311. The only other major author cited is Plutarch, and only once.
3. Winthrop, "Modell of Christian Charity." He wrote: "For we must consider that we shall be as a city upon a hill: The eyes of all people are upon us, so that if we shall deal falsely with our God in this work we have undertaken, and so cause him to withdraw his present help from us, we shall be made a story and a by-word through the world." For a brief, crisp formulation of this iteration of Puritan thinking, see Ceaser, *Liberal Democracy*, 14–15. Following Winthrop, President Ronald Reagan later spoke of America as a "shining city." There is extensive literature both on Winthrop and on the notion that America is religiously providential and exceptional. Patrick Deneen labels Winthrop's framework "communal perfectionism": "For Winthrop, America is best understood as a unique example for the rest of the world to follow, and that example is to be fulfilled by means of a particularly difficult attainment of virtue within the context of a political community" ("Cities of Man"). Deneen explains that "Winthrop invokes the image of the 'city on a hill' to highlight his belief that the world at large will be attentive to its success or failure and that God will judge and potentially bless or withhold blessings over the new community, depending on its success or failure. The demands made are over members of the community, and the aim of the self-sacrificial behavior is to provide inspiration to the rest of the world" (35). Consider also Tuveson, *Redeemer Nation*. Brent Gilchrist contends that "the importance of human participation in the unfolding of God's design became increasingly self-evident" to Americans, which then heightened "expectations ... concerning the imminence of the coming millennium and the possibility of America's restoration of itself as a 'city on a hill'" (*Cultus Americanus*, 168). Litke sees Winthrop as the originator of America's

"exemplary" American exceptionalism: "Rather than primarily generating an exception to a pattern, Winthrop calls on the colonists to set a pattern by responding to God's call to live lives of high Christian virtue" (*Twilight of the Republic*, 9). See, more generally, chap. 2, 23–51. Consider also Dreisbach, "Peculiar People." Gamble, in *In Search of a City*, does not find continuity between the biblical phrase of "city on a hill" and more recent political appropriations of this and related notions. He also argues Winthrop's speech is "too narrowly and explicitly Christian" to be interpreted as an "embryonic mission statement for the United States" (45). Kagan dismisses Winthrop's speech as inconsequential in molding early America. In fact, he argues in *Dangerous Nation* that the economic opportunities in the New World pulled colonists away from Puritan morality in favor of worldly pursuits (see esp. chap. 1).

4. Tocqueville highlights Christianity's import throughout *Democracy in America*. Consider, for example, 278–80, 282.
5. For an excellent empirical consideration of America's religiosity vis-à-vis other nations, see esp. Norris and Inglehart, *Sacred and Secular*.
6. Rogers Smith argues that the "aim" and "result" of the Constitution was to create an "overwhelming commercial society in which most citizens had a wide range of formal economic opportunities and more felt impelled by physical necessities, family and social pressures, and personal ambitions to pursue them" ("Our Republican Example," 107).
7. Polls support this. Consider the findings from the Brookings Institution report on "Do Americans Believe Capitalism and Government Are Working?," which is a part of the 2013 Economic Values Survey, http://www.brookings.edu/research/reports/2013/07/18-economic-values-survey-capitalism-government-prri-dionne-galston. Consider also Heimlich, "Little Change."
8. Not everyone views this economic exceptionalism positively. See esp. Beard, *Economic Interpretation*. For more on Beard see the excellent symposium on this work in *American Political Thought* 2, no. 2 (Fall 2013): 259–316.
9. Ceaser identifies studies by notable scholars like Byron Shafer, James Q. Wilson, and Seymour Martin Lipset ("Origins and Character," in *American Political Thought*, 9).
10. *Merriam-Webster Online*, s.v., "exceptional," accessed June 7, 2017, http://www.merriam-webster.com/dictionary/exceptional.
11. Lipset also examines how America is a statistical outlier in *American Exceptionalism*.
12. Cited in Restad, "Old Paradigms," 69.
13. *Merriam-Webster Online*, s.v., "exceptional," accessed June 7, 2017, http://www.merriam-webster.com/dictionary/exceptional.
14. Restad, "Old Paradigms," 55.
15. Davis and Lynn-Jones, "City upon a Hill," 20.
16. Ceaser, "Origins and Character," in *American Exceptionalism*, 16.

17. The Dutch republic shared many of these characteristics but did not have a written constitution, had different institutions, and was not as thoroughly democratic. For more on the Dutch republic see Israel, *Dutch Republic*.
18. Gordon Wood similarly notes this exceptionalism in *Idea of America*, 173–76.
19. Only the United Kingdom, Israel, New Zealand, and Saudi Arabia do not have a written constitution.
20. On America's unique separation of powers, consider also Wood, *Idea of America*, 180.
21. The American founders also relied on thinkers like John Locke, who theorized separating the legislative and executive branches, and Roman thinkers like Cicero, who theorized about Rome's mixed regime.
22. Below we address some important matters of democratic exclusion from the American founding.
23. See esp. *Democracy in America*, vol. 1, pt. 2, chap. 5.
24. As Gordon Wood notes, American principles are deeply embedded in the American people's hearts: "the Revolution made us an ideological people. . . . It is the state, the Constitution, the principles of liberty, equality, and free government that made us think of ourselves as a single people. To be an American is not to be someone, but to believe in something" (*Idea of America*, 320–22).
25. See, for instance, Robert Kagan's argument that, by the early 1800s, Americans firmly believed that "American principles were universally applicable, universally beneficial, and universally desired" (*Dangerous Nation*, 155).
26. Zuckert, *Launching Liberalism*, 215.
27. Zuckert convincingly argues that the Declaration is a quintessentially Lockean document in *Launching Liberalism*, 203–34. See also Zuckert, "Natural Rights and Modern Constitutionalism," 13–40. For more on Locke's influence consider Becker, *Declaration*. Others have identified alternative influences. Garry Willis, in *Inventing America*, emphasizes the potential influence of Francis Hutcheson. Allen Jayne, in *Jefferson's Declaration of Independence*, considers Lord Kames's possible influence. Morton White considers the conceivable influence of J. J. Burlamqui in *Philosophy of the American Revolution*.
28. Declaration of Independence. Zuckert unpacks the meaning of the various phrases like "created equal" and "unalienable" (*Launching Liberalism*, 212–20).
29. Zuckert explains: "Although the Declaration does not use the phrase, these rights clearly are natural rights as opposed to legal or constitutional rights" (ibid., 216).
30. Declaration of Independence.
31. Ibid.

32. Zuckert explains: "the same doctrine of political rights that justifies American independence necessarily also sets criteria for the conduct of legitimate and just government. It was perhaps not inevitable, but it surely was likely that Americans would continue to look to those same justifying principles after their revolution as they did before it" (*Launching Liberalism*, 204).
33. Ibid.
34. Jefferson, Letter to Henry Lee. For an alternative perspective on the letter to Lee, see Detweiler, "Changing Reputation."
35. Jefferson, *Portable Thomas Jefferson*, 585.
36. See Adams, Letter to his wife Abigail, July 3, 1776.
37. Maier, *American Scripture*, xix, 154–55. Justin Litke specifically echoes Maier's claims (*Twilight of the Republic*, 59). Detweiler argues that "the Fathers, although they did not ignore the phrases of the preamble, viewed the Declaration principally as a proclamation of independence" ("Changing Reputation," 557–58). Kendall makes a similar claim ("Equality," 30, 33).
38. Litke, *Twilight of the Republic*, 59–60.
39. Ibid., 63.
40. Zuckert, *Launching Liberalism*, 204.
41. For more on the relationship between the American and French Declarations, consider Janis, "Declaration of Independence."
42. Litke also rejects the universality of the Constitution, suggesting that its scope "is not particularly universal" and noting that the document "has little to say on the question of its own place in history" (*Twilight of the Republic*, 69).
43. Restad, citing Krakau, argues that the Declaration and Constitution "'created' the American nation and its central myths" ("Old Paradigms," 61).
44. Hamilton, Madison, and Jay, *Federalist*, 1; emphasis added.
45. Restad also ties America's Enlightenment principles and universalism together: "By creating a nation based on Enlightenment principles, American nationalism became universalistic. Its nationalism was civic, not ethnic, freed from the 'shackles of history'" ("Old Paradigms," 61).
46. Jefferson, Letter to John Dickinson.
47. In a 1780 letter Adams wrote: "The Americans of this day, have higher notions of themselves than ever. They think, they have gone through the greatest Revolution that ever took Place among Men, that this revolution is as much for the benefit of the generality of Mankind in Europe, as for their own" (Letter to Thomas Digges). Then in 1781 he remarked to his wife: "But the great designs of Providence must be accomplished. Great indeed! The progress of society will be accelerated by centuries by this Revolution. The Emperor of Germany is adopting, as fast as he can, American ideas of toleration and religious liberty, and it will become the fashionable system of all Europe very soon. Light spreads from the dayspring in the west, and may it shine more and more until the perfect day!" (Letter to his wife Abigail).

48. For example, Gamble discusses Ronald Reagan's universalizing interpretation of Winthrop's famous sermon: "America's divine calling summoned the nation to a universal and perpetual task.... Man was born to be free. America had the divine mandate to make that freedom a reality" (*In Search of a City*, 150).
49. For a discussion of Lincoln's key role in developing our understanding of the Declaration and American founding in universalistic terms, see Litke, *Twilight of the Republic*, esp. chap. 4.
50. Lincoln, Letter to Henry L. Pierce and others.
51. Some, of course, strongly disagree with Lincoln's interpretation. See, for instance, Kendall: "What [Lincoln] did, rather, was to falsify the facts of history.... The Declaration of Independence, as signed at Philadelphia, declared the independence of 'the thirteen United States of America'—the independence not of a nation but of a baker's dozen of new sovereignties." To speak of the Declaration as the beginning of America is, he writes, a blatant falsehood, "an act of *political heresy*" ("Equality," 29–30).
52. Lehrman asserts, though without any citations, that Lincoln "based his argument upon the fact that the Declaration was a formal congressional act of American Union and it carried the force of law" (*Lincoln at Peoria*, 109).
53. Calhoun denied that the Declaration had any binding significance on the United States after the Revolution. See especially Calhoun, *Union and Liberty*, 194. Consider also 84, 135, and 566. Consider also Guelzo's analysis on this topic in *Abraham Lincoln*, 193–94.
54. Lincoln, "Second Annual Message."
55. Washington writes, for example: "Against the insidious wiles of foreign influence (I conjure you to believe me, fellow-citizens) the jealousy of a free people ought to be constantly awake, since history and experience prove that foreign influence is one of the most baneful foes of republican government" ("Farewell Address").
56. Deneen, "Cities of Man," 37–38. Deneen sees Washington's speech as the "preeminent expression" of liberal isolationism. For an alternative perspective on Washington's address, see Kagan, who claims the Farewell Address is not an indication of early American isolationist tendencies, but simply the product of a much smaller, more particular foreign policy debate (*Dangerous Nation*, 113–15).
57. Deneen, "Cities of Man," 38–40. See Adams, "Speech on Independence Day."
58. Dunn, "Introduction," 2.
59. Ibid., 2–6.
60. Ibid., 2.
61. Ibid., 3.
62. Ceaser, "Origins and Character," in *American Political Thought*, 16.
63. Ibid., 21.
64. Ibid., 11. Leading up to this point he explains: "In brief, the mission is understood to derive from a religiously inspired errand to promote

liberty or liberal democracy in the world. A line runs from seventeenth-century Puritan thought, to the Revolution, to the mid-nineteenth-century doctrine of manifest destiny, to late nineteenth-century American imperialism, to Wilsonian idealism, to cold war anticommunism, and finally to George W. Bush's unilateralism" (10–11). Ceaser also finds a theological element to these various notions of mission: "These are manifestations of a common theme. Given its theological source—namely, the belief that God provides a warrant for America's mission—many identify it as having a naturally self-righteous dogmatic form. It is not unsurprising, therefore, that, once the power was available, the mission might often express itself in an imperialist or unilateralist form" (10–11).

65. Heclo, "Varieties of American Exceptionalism," 31–32.
66. Ibid., 32. Regarding America's "chosen" status, Peter Onuf writes:
   What makes Americans exceptional is not their institutions or democratic way of life or frontier experience but rather their self-conscious and self-defining embrace of American exceptionalism throughout their history. Americans' belief that their revolution constituted an epochal moment in world history set the terms for subsequent and never-ending arguments about their character and destiny. It also gave their "irritable patriotism" a normative dimension: it was an article of faith for Americans that their form of government was superior to any in history and that they were in some sense—and for some providential purpose—a "chosen people" ("American Exceptionalism," 79).
67. Ibid., 33.
68. Ibid., 34.
69. Ibid.
70. Ibid. Heclo appears to favor this iteration of exceptionalism. He writes: "I think a strong case can be made that America, with all its self-acknowledged shortcomings, has been the greatest human force for good that the world has ever known" (38).
71. Murray, *American Exceptionalism*, 5–6. Murray argues that American exceptionalism is a "fact of America's past" and that it is not something in which you choose to believe, just as one does not choose to believe in "the battle of Gettysburg" (6). (Original is in italics, which I have removed.)
72. Ibid., 6. (Part of quotation is in italics in original, which I have removed.)
73. Wood, *Idea of America*, 2.
74. Fukuyama, *End of History*, xii.
75. Ibid., 42.
76. Ibid., 45.
77. Ibid., 47–50; emphasis in original.
78. Ibid., 200–1.
79. Ibid., 43.
80. Hamilton, Madison, and Jay, *Federalist*, 14.

81. Deneen, "Cities of Man," 41.
82. Regarding the prospects of American commerce, Jay continues:
    The extension of our own commerce in our own vessels, cannot give pleasure to any nations who possess territories on or near this continent, because the cheapness and excellence of our productions, added to the circumstances of vicinity, and the enterprize and address of our merchants and navigators, will give us a greater share in the advantages which those territories afford, than consists with the wishes or policy of their respective sovereigns. (Hamilton, Madison, and Jay, *Federalist*, 14)
83. Jefferson, Letter to George Rogers Clark.
84. Deneen, "Cities of Man," 41.
85. Jefferson, Letter to James Madison.
86. Restad, "Old Paradigms," 67.
87. As Kagan notes, "[Americans] might accept that different cultures ruled themselves differently, but they never really accepted the legitimacy of those differences, and because they did not accept their legitimacy they naturally viewed them as transitory.... Wherever Americans looked in the world, they saw both the possibility and the desirability of change" (*Dangerous Nation*, 103).
88. Ceaser, "Origins and Character," in *American Political Thought*, 14.
89. Ibid., 16.
90. Deneen, "Cities of Man," 45.
91. Litke, *Twilight of the Republic*, 10.
92. There certainly were other justifications for these military interventions. In the case of Afghanistan, it also was a reprisal for 9/11. In the case of Iraq, the belief that Saddam Hussein had weapons of mass destruction was a key factor. Not everyone has accepted exporting democracy as the motive of America's ventures in Iraq and Afghanistan. Some have seen it as an excuse to intervene in the internal politics of these states.
93. Post–World War II Japan and Germany represent exceptions on this matter.
94. Finkelman, *Slavery and the Founders*, 6. While one might argue that the absence of the words "slave" or "slavery" was a victory for northerners, Finkelman contends instead: "Thus, southerners avoided the term [slave] because they did not want unnecessarily to antagonize their colleagues from the North. As long as they were assured of protection for their institution, the southerners at the Convention were willing to do without the word 'slave.'"
95. Ibid., 6–9.
96. Ibid., 9.
97. Ibid., 32.
98. Ibid., 129.
99. Ibid., ix, 152–57.
100. Ibid., ix.

101. Jefferson writes that the king

> has waged cruel war against human nature itself, violating it's most sacred rights of life & liberty in the persons of a distant people who never offended him, captivating & carrying them into slavery in another hemisphere, or to incur miserable death in their transportation thither. this piratical warfare, the opprobrium of infidel powers, is the warfare of the CHRISTIAN king of Great Britain. determined to keep open a market where MEN should be bought & sold, he has prostituted his negative for suppressing every legislative attempt to prohibit or to restrain this execrable commerce.

Some scholars read these passages as proof of Jefferson's antislavery views. Consider Jefferson's "original Rough draught" of the Declaration of Independence, http://www.loc.gov/exhibits/declara/ruffdrft.html. Anastapalo claims: "The slaves in North America were clearly denied the right to liberty: the fierce passage Jefferson had penned for the Declaration and that was stricken by the Congress seems to recognize this denial" (*Abraham Lincoln*, 22). Jaffa proclaims that Jefferson's passage on slavery, if retained, "would have made impossible the perversity of Taney's and Douglas's misrepresentations of the Declaration" (*New Birth of Freedom*, 479). See also Zuckert, *Launching Liberalism*, 278.
102. Finkelman, *Slavery and the Founders*, 130.
103. Ibid., 133.
104. Ibid., 131.
105. Ibid., 160.
106. Levinson, *Our Undemocratic Constitution*.
107. Dahl, *How Democratic*, 122.
108. Ibid., 44.
109. Ibid., 45–46.
110. Ibid., 47.
111. Ibid., 52–53.
112. Ibid., 55.
113. The number of elections was eighteen as of Dahl's writing in 2002. It is now nineteen after Donald Trump's election in 2016.
114. Ibid., 83.
115. Paine, *Common Sense*, 51.
116. Consider Paine's book by that title, *Rights of Man*.
117. For the text of the Virginia Plan see Madison, *Notes*, 30–33.
118. For the text of the New Jersey Plan see ibid., 118–21.
119. See Elbridge Gerry's committee report proposing the compromise in ibid., 237–38.
120. See Hamilton's speech proposing his own plan, which was more extreme than the Virginia Plan, in ibid., 129–39.
121. Tocqueville, *Democracy in America*, 265.
122. Ibid., 265–71.

123. Ibid., 30, 267.
124. Tocqueville is especially interested in how the "constitution of judicial power" checks democracy: "I have shown how the courts serve to correct the aberrations of democracy, and how, without being able to stop the movements of the majority, they will succeed in slowing them down" (274).
125. Ibid., 294.
126. Tocqueville explains his usage of the term *mœurs*: "I understand by this word the sum of the intellectual and moral dispositions that bring men to the state of society" (ibid., 292n8). Consider also 295.
127. Ibid., 276.
128. Ibid., 282.

Conclusion

1. We focus on form of government as one example, while noting that it is necessary to investigate all new developments in order to improve the soundness and comprehensiveness of the politics of place framework.
2. Accounts of communism's immense failures are numerous. Some excellent examples are Malia, *Soviet Tragedy*; Applebaum, *Gulag*; and Yang, *Tombstone*.
3. Bandoch, "Forming a European Spirit."
4. When European citizens have been given the democratic choice as to whether they want to join—or leave—the European Union, or whether they want to give the EU more power, they typically have voted against the European Union. Consider Britain's vote to leave the EU in 2016, Ireland's multiple votes against treaties (and the EU's subsequent browbeating of the Irish to "reconsider"), and the French and Dutch rejections of the EU Constitution in 2005. In most cases integration of countries deeper into the EU has been the doing of political elites.
5. Consider, for example, Simon, *Economic Consequences of Immigration*, for an empirically based argument for the positive benefits of immigration.

Bibliography

Adams, John. Letter to his wife Abigail, July 3, 1776. In *The Adams Papers, Adams Family Correspondence.* Vol. 2, *June 1776–March 1778,* edited by L. H. Butterfield, 29–33. Cambridge, MA: Harvard University Press, 1963. *Founders Online.* National Archives. http://founders.archives.gov/documents/Adams/04-02-02-0016.

———. Letter to his wife Abigail, December 18, 1781. In *Familiar Letters of John Adams and His Wife Abigail Adams during the Revolution with a Memoir of Mrs. Adams,* by John Adams, Abigail Adams, and Charles Francis Adams. New York: Hurd and Houghton, 1875. Project Gutenberg. http://www.gutenberg.org/files/34123/34123-h/34123-h.htm.

———. Letter to Thomas Digges, May 13, 1780. In *The Adams Papers, Papers of John Adams.* Vol. 9, *March 1780–July 1780,* edited by Gregg L. Lint and Richard Alan Ryerson, 307–9. Cambridge, MA: Harvard University Press, 1996. *Founders Online.* National Archives. http://founders.archives.gov/documents/Adams/06-09-02-0189.

Adams, John Quincy. "Speech on Independence Day," July 4, 1821. *TeachingAmericanHistory.org.* http://teachingamericanhistory.org/library/document/speech-on-independence-day/.

Althusser, Louis. *Politics and History: Montesquieu, Rousseau, Marx.* London: Verso Books, 1970.

Amin, Ash. "Regions Unbound: Towards a New Politics of Place." *Geografiska Annaler* 86, no. 1 (2004): 33–44.

Anastapalo, George. *Abraham Lincoln: A Constitutional Biography.* Lanham, MD: Rowman & Littlefield Publishers, 1999.

Applebaum, Anne. *Gulag: A History.* New York: Anchor Books, 2004.

Aristotle. *Politics.* Translated by Carnes Lord. Chicago: University of Chicago Press, 1984.

Aron, Raymond. *Main Currents in Sociological Thought.* Vol. 1. Garden City, NY: Doubleday, 1968.

Baker, Keith M. *Condorcet: From Natural Philosophy to Social Mathematics.* Chicago: University of Chicago Press, 1975.

Bandoch, Joshua. "Aristocracy." In *Encyclopedia of Political Thought,* edited by Michael Gibbons, Diana Coole, Elisabeth Ellis, and Kennan Ferguson, 162–63. Wiley-Blackwell, 2014.

———. "Montesquieu's Critique of Islam." In *The Pilgrimage of Philosophy: A Festschrift for Charles E. Butterworth,* edited by Rene M. Paddags, Gregory A. McBrayer, and Waseem El-Reyes. South Bend, IN: St. Augustine Press, 2018.

———. "Montesquieu's Selective Religious Intolerance in *Of the Spirit of the Laws*." *Political Studies* 62, no. 2 (2016): 351–67.

———. "On the Problem of Forming a European Spirit—Montesquieu's *De l'Esprit des lois* (1748)." In *Ideas of / for Europe: An Interdisciplinary Approach to European Identity*, edited by Teresa Pinheiro, Beata Cieszynska, and Eduardo Franco, 75–87. Frankfurt: Peter Lang, 2012.

Barrera, Guillaume. "Comment certaine religion contredit l'esprit de l'Antiquité et contrarie les temps modernes." In Ehrard, *Montesquieu, l'Etat, et la religion*, 110–24.

Bartlett, Robert C. "On the Politics of Faith and Reason: The Project of Enlightenment in Pierre Bayle and Montesquieu." *Journal of Politics* 63, no. 1 (2001): 1–28.

Bauer, Joanne R., and Daniel A. Bell, eds. *The East Asian Challenge for Human Rights*. New York: Cambridge University Press, 1999.

Baum, Alan. *Montesquieu and Social Theory*. New York: Pergamon Press, 1979.

Bayle, Pierre. *A Philosophical Commentary*. Indianapolis, IN: Liberty Fund, 2005.

Beard, Charles. *An Economic Interpretation of the Constitution of the United States*. New York: Dover, 2004.

Becker, Carl. *The Declaration of Independence*. New York: Knopf, 1942.

Beik, William. *Louis XIV and Absolutism: A Brief Study with Documents*. Boston: Bedford/St. Martin's Press, 2000.

Beiner, Ronald. *Civil Religion: A Dialogue in the History of Political Philosophy*. New York: Cambridge University Press, 2011.

Berlin, Isaiah. "Montesquieu." In *Against the Current: Essays in the History of Ideas*. 1955. Reprint, New York: Penguin Books, 1982.

———. "Two Concepts of Liberty." In *Liberty: Incorporating Four Essays on Liberty*, edited by Henry Hardy, 166–217. Oxford: Oxford University Press, 2002.

Binoche, Bertrand. *Introduction à De l'esprit des lois de Montesquieu*. Paris: Presses Universitaires de France, 1998.

Brühlmeier, Daniel. "Considérations sur l'esprit de commerce et le marché libre chez Montesquieu et Adam Smith." *Revue de théologie et de philosophie* 130 (1998): 301–14.

Burke, Edmund. *Reflections on the Revolution in France*. 1790. Constitution Society Online. http://www.constitution.org/eb/rev_fran.htm.

Calhoun, John C. *Union and Liberty: The Political Philosophy of John C. Calhoun*. Edited by Ross M. Lence. Indianapolis, IN: Liberty Fund, 1992.

Callanan, Keegan. "Liberal Constitutionalism and Political Particularism in Montesquieu's *The Spirit of the Laws*." *Political Research Quarterly* 67, no. 3 (2014): 589–602.

Carrese, Paul. *The Cloaking of Power: Montesquieu, Blackstone, and the Rise of Judicial Activism*. Chicago: University of Chicago Press, 2003.

———. "The Machiavellian Spirit of Montesquieu's Liberal Republic." In *Machiavelli's Liberal Republican Legacy*, edited by Paul A. Rahe. New York: Cambridge University Press, 2006.

———. "Montesquieu, Charles-Louis de Secondat, Baron de (1689–1757)." In *Encyclopedia of Political Thought*, edited by Michael Gibbons, Diana Coole, Elisabeth Ellis, and Kennan Ferguson, 2423–38. Wiley-Blackwell, 2014.

———. "Montesquieu's Complex Natural Right and Modern Liberalism: The Roots of American Moderation." *Polity* 36, no. 2 (2004): 227–50.
Carrithers, David. "Montesquieu's Philosophy of History." *Journal of the History of Ideas* 47, no. 1 (1986): 61–80.
———. "Not So Virtuous Republics: Montesquieu, Venice, and the Theory of Aristocratic Republicanism." *Journal of the History of Ideas* 52, no. 2 (1991): 245–68.
Carrithers, David, Michael Mosher, and Paul Rahe, eds. *Montesquieu's Science of Politics: Essays on* The Spirit of Laws. Lanham, MD: Rowman & Littlefield Publishers, 2001.
Casabianca, Denis de. *L'Esprit des lois, Montesquieu*. Paris: Ellipses, 2003.
———. *Montesquieu: De l'étude des sciences à l'esprit des lois*. Paris: Champion, 2008.
Ceaser, James. *Liberal Democracy and Political Science*. Baltimore: Johns Hopkins University Press, 1990.
———. "The Origins and Character of American Exceptionalism." In Dunn, *American Exceptionalism*, 11–26.
———. "The Origins and Character of American Exceptionalism." *American Political Thought* 1, no. 1 (2012): 3–28.
Chaimowicz, Thomas. *Antiquity as the Source of Modernity: Freedom and Balance in the Thought of Montesquieu and Burke*. New Brunswick, NJ: Transaction Publishers, 2008.
———. *Freiheit und Gleichgewicht im Denken Montesquieus und Burkes: Ein analytischer Beitrag zur Geschichte der Lehre vom Staat im 18. Jahrhundert*. Vienna: Springer-Verlag, 1985.
Clark, Henry. *Compass of Society: Commerce and Absolutism in Old-Regime France*. Lanham, MD: Lexington Books, 2007.
Cohler, Anne M. *Montesquieu's Comparative Politics and the Spirit of American Constitutionalism*. Lawrence: University Press of Kansas, 1988.
Coleman, Patrick, and David Carrithers, eds. *Montesquieu and the Spirit of Modernity*. Oxford: Voltaire Foundation, 2002.
Collier, Paul. *The Bottom Billion: Why the Poorest Countries Are Failing and What Can Be Done about It*. New York: Oxford University Press, 2008.
Condorcet. *Observations on the Twenty-Ninth Book of* The Spirit of the Laws." Published as an appendix to Antoine Louis Claude Destutt de Tracy, *A Commentary and Review of Montesquieu's "Spirit of Laws."* Translated by Thomas Jefferson. Philadelphia: William Duane, 1811.
Conroy, Peter V. *Montesquieu Revisited*. New York: Twayne Publishers, 1992.
Courtney, C. P. *Montesquieu and Burke*. Westport, CT: Greenwood Press, 1963.
Cox, Iris. *Montesquieu and the History of French Laws*. Oxford: Oxford University Press, 1983.
Craiutu, Aurelian. *A Virtue for Courageous Minds: Moderation in French Political Thought, 1748–1830*. Princeton, NJ: Princeton University Press, 2012.
Curtis, Michael. *Orientalism and Islam*. New York: Cambridge University Press, 2009.
Dahl, Robert. *How Democratic Is the American Constitution?* 2nd ed. New Haven, CT: Yale University Press, 2003.
D'Alembert. "Éloge de Monsieur le Président de Montesquieu." In *Encyclopédie, ou Dictionnaire raisonné des sciences, des arts et des métiers*. Vol. 5. Paris. 1755. *Wikisource*.

Accessed June 7, 2017. http://fr.wikisource.org/wiki/De_l'esprit_des_lois_ (éd._Nourse)/Éloge_de_M._le_président_Montesquieu.
Dallmayr, Fred. *In Search of the Good Life: A Pedagogy for Troubled Times.* Lexington: University Press of Kentucky, 2007.
Davis, Tami, and Sean Lynn-Jones. "City upon a Hill." *Foreign Policy* 66 (1987): 20–38.
de Bary, Theodore. *Asian Values and Human Rights: A Confucian Communitarian Perspective.* Cambridge, MA: Harvard University Press, 2000.
Declaration of Independence, 1776. National Archives Online. http://www.archives.gov/exhibits/charters/declaration_transcript.html.
de Dijn, Annelien. *French Political Thought from Montesquieu to Tocqueville: Liberty in a Levelled Society?* New York: Cambridge University Press, 2008.
———. "Montesquieu's Controversial Context: *The Spirit of the Laws* as Monarchist Tract." *History of Political Thought* 34, no. 1 (2013): 66–88.
———. "*On Political Liberty*: Montesquieu's Missing Manuscript." *Political Theory* 39, no. 2 (2011): 181–204.
———. "Was Montesquieu a Liberal Republican?" *Review of Politics* 76, no. 1 (2014): 21–41.
Deneen, Patrick. "Cities of Man on a Hill." *American Political Thought* 1, no. 1 (2012): 29–52.
Desgraves, Louis. *Inventaire des documents manuscrits des fonds Montesquieu de la Biblothèque municipale de Bordeaux.* Geneva: Droz, 1998.
Destutt de Tracy, Antoine-Louis-Claude, Comte. *Commentaire sur L'Esprit des lois de Montesquieu (1819).* Caen, FR: Centre de philosophie politique et juridique de l'Université de Caen, 1992.
Detweiler, Philip F. "The Changing Reputation of the Declaration of Independence: The First Fifty Years." *William and Mary Quarterly* 19, no. 4 (1962): 557–74.
Dictionnaire de l'Académie française. Paris, 1762.
Dionne, E. J., Daniel Cox, Juhem Navarro-Rivera, William A. Galston, and Robert P. Jones. "Do Americans Believe Capitalism and Government Are Working?" Economic Values Survey. The Brookings Institution. 2013. http://www.brookings.edu/research/reports/2013/07/18-economic-values-survey-capitalism-government-prri-dionne-galston.
Diop, David. "Des lectures à l'écriture la question de la laïcisation de l'État dans *L'Esprit des lois* de Montesquieu, selon les apologistes et les encyclopédistes." In Ehrard, *Montesquieu, l'État, et la religion*, 79–109.
Dirlik, Arif. "Place-Based Imagination: Globalism and the Politics of Place." *Review (Fernand Braudel Center)* 22, no. 2 (1999): 151–87.
Dos Santos, Antônio Carlos. "Montesquieu: religion, politique, et intolérance dans le monde ancien." In Ehrard, *Montesquieu, l'État, et la religion*, 172–85.
Doyle, William, ed. *Old Regime France 1648—1788.* New York: Oxford University Press, 2001.
———. *Origins of the French Revolution.* New York: Oxford University Press, 1999.
———. *The Parliament of Bordeaux and the End of the Old Regime 1771–1790.* New York: St. Martin's Press, 1974.
Dreisbach, Daniel. "A Peculiar People in 'God's American Israel': Religion and American National Identity." In Dunn, *American Exceptionalism*, 55–75.

Dunn, Charles W. *American Exceptionalism: The Origins, History, and Future of the Nation's Greatest Strength*. Lanham, MD: Rowman & Littlefield Publishers, 2013.

———. "Introduction: The Magnetism of American Exceptionalism." In *American Exceptionalism*.

Durkheim, Émile. *Montesquieu and Rousseau: Forerunners of Sociology*. Ann Arbor: University of Michigan Press, 1965.

Ehrard, Jean. *L'esprit des mots: Montesquieu en lui-même et parmi les siens*. Geneva: Droz, 1998.

———, ed. *Montesquieu, l'État, et la religion*. Sofia: Éditions Iztok-Zapad, 2007.

Eisenmann, Charles. "*L'Esprit des lois* et la séparation des pouvoirs." *Cahiers de Philosohie politique* 2–3 (1985): 2–34.

———. "La pensée constitutionnelle de Montesquieu." *Cahiers de Philosohie politique* 2–3 (1985): 35–66.

Escobar, Arturo, and Wendy Harcourt. "Women and the Politics of Place." *Development* 45, no. 1 (2002): 7–14.

Finkelman, Paul. *Slavery and the Founders: Race and Liberty in the Age of Jefferson*. 2nd ed. New York: M. E. Sharpe, 2001.

Ford, Franklin. *Robe and Sword: The Regrouping of the French Aristocracy after Louis XIV*. Cambridge, MA: Harvard University Press, 1953.

Fukuyama, Francis. *The End of History and the Last Man*. New York: Free Press, 1992.

Gamble, Richard. *In Search of a City on a Hill: The Making and Unmaking of an American Myth*. New York: Continuum, 2012.

Geenens, Raf, and Helena Rosenblatt, eds. *French Liberalism from Montesquieu to the Present Day*. New York: Cambridge University Press, 2012.

Gilbert, Alan. "'Internal Restlessness': Individuality and Community in Montesquieu." *Political Theory* 22, no. 1 (1994): 45–70.

Gilchrist, Brent. *Cultus Americanus: Varieties of the Liberal Tradition in American Political Culture*. Lanham, MD: Lexington Books, 2006.

Gonthier, Ursula Haskins. *Montesquieu and England: Enlightened Exchanges, 1689–1755*. New York: Routledge, 2016.

Gourou, Pierre. "Le déterminisme physique dans 'L'Esprit des lois.'" *L'Homme* 3, no. 3 (1963): 5–11.

Goyard-Fabre, Simone. *Montesquieu: La Nature, Les Lois, La Liberté*. Paris: Presses Universitaires de France, 1993.

———. *La philosophie du droit de Montesquieu*. Paris: C. Klincksieck, 1973.

Guelzo, Allen C. *Abraham Lincoln: Redeemer President*. Grand Rapids, MI: William B. Eerdmans Publishing Company, 1999.

Hamilton, Alexander, James Madison, and John Jay. *The Federalist*. Edited by J. R. Pole. Indianapolis, IN: Hackett Publishing, 2005.

Hazard, Paul. *La Pensée Européenne au XVIIIème Siècle de Montesquieu a Lessing*. Vol. 1. Paris: Boivin & C, 1946.

Heclo, Hugh. "Varieties of American Exceptionalism." In Dunn, *American Exceptionalism*, 27–40.

Heimlich, Russell. "Little Change in Public's Response to 'Capitalism,' 'Socialism.'" Pew Research Center. 2012. http://www.pewresearch.org/daily-number/little-change-in-publics-response-to-capitalism-socialism/.

Hendrickson, Randal. "Montesquieu's (Anti-)Machiavellianism: Ordinary Acquisitiveness in *The Spirit of Laws.*" *Journal of Politics* 75, no. 2 (2013): 385–96.

Hirschman, Albert. *The Passions and the Interests: Political Arguments for Capitalism before Its Triumph.* Princeton, NJ: Princeton University Press, 2013.

Hobbes, Thomas. *Leviathan.* Cambridge: Cambridge University Press, 1996.

Howse, Robert. "Montesquieu on Commerce, Conquest, War and Peace." *Brooklyn Journal of International Law* 31, no. 3 (2006): 693–708.

Hulliung, Mark. *Montesquieu and the Old Regime.* Berkeley: University of California Press, 1976.

Israel, Jonathan. *The Dutch Republic: Its Rise, Greatness, and Fall 1477–1806.* New York: Oxford University Press, 1995.

———. *Enlightenment Contested: Philosophy, Modernity, and the Emancipation of Man 1670–1752.* New York: Oxford University Press, 2006.

Jaffa, Harry V. *A New Birth of Freedom: Abraham Lincoln and the Coming of the Civil War.* Lanham, MD: Rowman & Littlefield Publishers, 2000.

Janis, Mark W. "The Declaration of Independence, the Declaration of the Rights of Man and Citizens, and the Bill of Rights." *Human Rights Quarterly* 14, no. 4 (1992): 478–84.

Jayne, Allen. *Jefferson's Declaration of Independence.* Lexington: University Press of Kentucky, 1978.

Jefferson, Thomas. Letter to George Rogers Clark, December 25, 1780. In *The Papers of Thomas Jefferson.* Vol. 4, *1 October 1780–24 February 1781*, edited by Julian P. Boyd, 233–38. Princeton, NJ: Princeton University Press, 1951. Founders Online. National Archives. http://founders.archives.gov/documents/Jefferson/01-04-02-0295.

———. Letter to Henry Lee, May 8, 1825. In *Thomas Jefferson: Writings*, edited by Merrill D. Peterson, 1500–1501. New York: Library of America, 1984. TeachingAmericanHistory.org. http://teachingamericanhistory.org/library/document/letter-to-henry-lee/.

———. Letter to James Madison, April 27, 1809. Library of Congress. Exhibitions, Thomas Jefferson. http://www.loc.gov/exhibits/jefferson/149.html.

———. Letter to John Dickinson, March 6, 1801. American History from Revolution to Reconstruction and Beyond. The Presidents of the USA. Thomas Jefferson: The Letters of Thomas Jefferson, 1743–1826. http://www.let.rug.nl/usa/presidents/thomas-jefferson/letters-of-thomas-jefferson/jefl136.php.

———. "'Original Rough Draught' of the Declaration of Independence." Library of Congress. Exhibitions, Declaring Independence: Drafting the Documents. http://www.loc.gov/exhibits/declara/ruffdrft.html.

———. *The Portable Thomas Jefferson.* Edited by Merrill D. Peterson. New York: Penguin Books, 1977.

Jennings, Jeremy. "The Debate about Luxury in Eighteenth- and Nineteenth-Century French Political Thought." *Journal of the History of Ideas* 68, no. 1 (2007): 79–105.

Jones, Colin. *The Great Nation: France from Louis XV to Napoleon 1715–99.* New York: Columbia University Press, 2002.

Juppé, Alain. *Montesquieu: Le moderne.* Paris: Perrin-Grasset, 1999.

Kagan, Robert. *Dangerous Nation: America's Foreign Policy from Its Earliest Days to the Dawn of the Twentieth Century.* New York: Knopf, 2006.
Kant, Immanuel. *Groundwork of the Metaphysics of Morals.* Translated and edited by Mary Gregor. Cambridge: Cambridge University Press, 2008.
Kemmis, Daniel. *Community and the Politics of Place.* Norman: University of Oklahoma Press, 1990.
Kendall, Willmoore. "Equality: Commitment or Ideal?" *Intercollegiate Review* 24, no. 2 (1989): 25–33.
Keohane, Nannerl. *Philosophy and the State in France: The Renaissance to the Enlightenment.* Princeton, NJ: Princeton University Press, 1980.
———. "Virtuous Republics and Glorious Monarchies: Two Models in Montesquieu's Political Thought." *Political Studies* 20, no. 4 (1972): 383–96.
Kingston, Rebecca, ed. *Montesquieu and His Legacy.* New York: State University of New York Press, 2008.
———. *Montesquieu and the Parlement of Bordeaux.* Geneva: Droz, 1996.
———. "Montesquieu on Religion and on the Question of Toleration." In Carrithers, Mosher, and Rahe, *Montesquieu's Science of Politics*, 375–408.
Krause, Sharon R. "Freedom, Sovereignty, and the General Will in Montesquieu." In *The General Will: The Evolution of a Concept*, edited by James Farr and David Lay Williams, 147–74. Cambridge: Cambridge University Press, 2015.
———. "History and the Human Soul in Montesquieu." *History of Political Thought* 24, no. 2 (2003): 235–61.
———. "Laws, Passion, and the Attractions of Right Action in Montesquieu." *Philosophy and Social Criticism* 32, no. 2 (2006): 211–30.
———. *Liberalism with Honor.* Cambridge, MA: Harvard University Press, 2002.
———. "The Politics of Distinction and Disobedience: Honor and the Defense of Liberty." *Polity* 31, no. 3 (1999): 469–99.
———. "The Spirit of Separate Powers in Montesquieu." *Review of Politics* 62, no. 2 (2000): 231–65.
———. "The Uncertain Inevitability of Decline in Montesquieu." *Political Theory* 30, no. 5 (2002): 702–27.
Kriesel, Karl Marcus. "Montesquieu: Possibilistic Political Geographer." *Annals of the Association of American Geographers* 58, no. 3 (1968): 557–74.
Larrère, Catherine. *Actualité de Montesquieu.* Paris: Presses de Sciences Po, 1999.
———. "L'histoire du commerce dans *L'Esprit des lois.*" In *Le Temps de Montesquieu*, edited by Michel Porret and Catherine Volpilhac-Auger, 319–36. Geneva: Droz, 2002.
———. "Montesquieu and Liberalism: The Question of Pluralism." In Kingston, *Montesquieu and His Legacy*, 279–301.
———. "Montesquieu: Commerce de luxe et commerce d'économie." In *Lectures de l'Esprit des Lois*, edited by Céline Spector and Thierry Hoquet, 121–43. Pessac, FR: Presses Universitaires de Bordeaux, 2004.
———. "Montesquieu économiste? Une lecture paradoxale." In Volpilhac-Auger, *Montesquieu en 2005*, 243–66.
———. "Montesquieu et l'idée de fédération." In *L'Europe de Montesquieu*, edited by A. Postigliola and M. G. Bottaro Palumbo, 137–52. *Cahiers Montesquieu.* 2nd ed. Naples: Voltaire Foundation, 1995.

———. "Montesquieu on Economics and Commerce." In Carrithers, Mosher, and Rahe, *Montesquieu's Science of Politics*, 335–73.

———. "Montesquieu: Tolérance et liberté religieuse." In Ehrard, *Montesquieu, l'État, et la religion*, 153–71.

Lehrman, Lewis E. *Lincoln at Peoria: The Turning Point*. Mechanicsburg, PA: Stackpole Books, 2008.

Levillain, Charles-Edouard. "Glory without Power? Montesquieu's Trip to Holland in 1729 and His Vision of the Dutch Fiscal-Military State." *History of European Ideas* 36, no. 2 (2010): 181–91.

Levinson, Sanford. *Our Undemocratic Constitution: Where the Constitution Goes Wrong (and How We the People Can Correct It)*. New York: Oxford University Press, 2008.

Levy, Jacob T. "Beyond Publius: Montesquieu, Liberal Republicanism, and the Small-Republic Thesis." *History of Political Thought* 27, no. 1 (2006): 50–90.

Lincoln, Abraham. Letter to Henry L. Pierce and others, April 6, 1859. In *The Collected Works of Abraham Lincoln*, edited by Roy P. Basler et al. New Brunswick, NJ: Rutgers University Press, 1953–55. Abraham Lincoln Online. http://www.abrahamlincolnonline.org/lincoln/speeches/pierce.htm.

———. "Second Annual Message," December 1, 1862. The American Presidency Project, by Gerhard Peters and John T. Woolley. http://www.presidency.ucsb.edu/ws/?pid=29503.

Lipset, Seymour Martin. *American Exceptionalism: A Double-Edged Sword*. New York: W. W. Norton, 1997.

Litke, Justin. *Twilight of the Republic: Empire and Exceptionalism in the American Political Tradition*. Lexington: University Press of Kentucky, 2013.

Locke, John. *Letter Concerning Toleration*. Edited by J. H. Tully. Indianapolis, IN: Hackett Publishing, 1983.

———. *Two Treatises of Government*. Edited by Peter Laslett. Cambridge: Cambridge University Press, 2003.

Lowenthal, David. "Book I of Montesquieu's *The Spirit of the Laws*." *American Political Science Review* 53, no. 2 (1959): 485–98.

———. "Montesquieu." In *History of Political Philosophy*, edited by Leo Strauss and Joseph Cropsey, 513–58. 3rd ed. Chicago: University of Chicago Press, 1987.

Lutz, Donald S. "The Relative Influence of European Writers on Late Eighteenth-Century American Political Thought." *American Political Science Review* 78, no. 1 (1984): 189–97.

Machiavelli, Niccolò. *Discourses on Livy*. Translated by Harvey Mansfield and Nathan Tarcov. Chicago: University of Chicago Press, 1996.

Madison, James. *Notes of Debates in the Federal Convention of 1787*. New York: W. W. Norton, 1987.

Maier, Pauline. *American Scripture: Making the Declaration of Independence*. New York: Knopf, 1997.

Maire, Catherine. "Montesquieu et la Constitution civile du clergé." In Ehrard, *Montesquieu, l'État, et la religion*, 213–28.

Malia, Martin. *The Soviet Tragedy: A History of Socialism in Russia, 1917–1991*. Free Press: New York, 1994.

Manent, Pierre. *An Intellectual History of Liberalism*. Princeton, NJ: Princeton University Press, 1996.

Manin, Bernard. "Montesquieu et la politique moderne." In *Lectures de l'Esprit des lois*, edited by Céline Spector and Thierry Hoquet, 171–231. Pessac, FR: Presses Universitaires de Bordeaux, 2004.

———. "Montesquieu, la république et le commerce." *Archives européennes de sociologie* 42, no. 3 (2001): 573–602.

Mansfield, Harvey C., Jr. *Taming the Prince: The Ambivalence of Modern Executive Power*. Baltimore: Johns Hopkins University Press, 1993.

Markovits, Francine. *Montesquieu: Le droit et l'histoire*. Paris: Librarie Philosophique, 2008.

———. "Montesquieu: L'esprit d'un peuple, une histoire expérimentale." In *Former un nouveau peuple? Pouvoir, éducation, révolution*, edited by Josiane Boulad-Ayoub, 207–36. Quebec: Presses Universitaires de Laval; Paris: L'Harmattan, 1996.

Mason, S. M. "Montesquieu and the Dutch as a Maritime Nation." *Studies on Voltaire and the Eighteenth Century (SVEC)* 292 (1991): 169–86.

———. *Montesquieu's Idea of Justice*. The Hague: Martinus Nijhoff, 1975.

Masterson, M. P. "Holland's Fifty Republics: François Michel Janiçon and Montesquieu's Federal Theory." *French Studies* 29 (1975): 27–41.

———. "Montesquieu's Stadholder." *SVEC* 116 (1973): 81–107.

Mercier, Roger. "La théorie des climats des 'Réflexions critiques' à 'L'Esprit des Lois.'" *Revue d'Histoire littéraire de la France* 53, no. 1 (1953): 17–37.

Merry, Henry J. *Montesquieu's System of Natural Government*. West Lafayette, IN: Purdue University Studies, 1970.

Montesquieu, Charles Louis Secondat, Baron de La Brède et de. *Œuvres complètes*. Vols. 1 and 2. Paris: Bibliothèque de la Pléiade, 1951.

———. *Œuvres complètes de Montesquieu*. Vol. 3. Edited by M. André Masson. Paris: Éditions Nagel, 1955.

———. *Œuvres et écrits divers*. Vols. 8–9 of *Œuvres complètes de Montesquieu*. Edited by Pierre Rétat. Oxford: Voltaire Foundation, 2003, 2006.

———. *Considerations on the Causes of the Greatness of the Romans and Their Decline*. Translated by David Lowenthal. Indianapolis, IN: Hackett Publishing, 1999.

———. *The Persian Letters*. Translated by George R. Healy. Indianapolis, IN: Hackett Publishing, 1999.

———. *The Spirit of the Laws*. Translated and edited by Anne M. Cohler, Basia C. Miller, and Harold S. Stone. Cambridge: Cambridge University Press, 1989.

Moore, Donald S. "Subaltern Struggles and the Politics of Place: Remapping Resistance in Zimbabwe's Eastern Highlands." *Cultural Anthropology* 13, no. 3 (1998): 344–81.

Mosher, Michael. "Free Trade, Free Speech, and Free Love: Monarchy from the Liberal Prospect in Mid-Eighteenth-Century France." In *Monarchisms in the Age of Enlightenment: Liberty, Patriotism, and the Common Good*, edited by Hans Blom, John Christian Laursen, and Luisa Simonutti, 101–18. Toronto: University of Toronto Press, 2007.

———. "The Judgmental Gaze of European Women: Gender, Sexuality, and the Critique of Republican Rule." *Political Theory* 22, no. 1 (1994): 25–44.

———. "Monarchy's Paradox: Honor in the Face of Sovereign Power." In Carrithers, Mosher, and Rahe, *Montesquieu's Science of Politics*, 159–230.

———. "Montesquieu on Conquest: Three Cartesian Heroes and Five Good Enough Empires." *Revue Montesquieu* 8 (2006): 81–110.

———. "Montesquieu on Empire and Enlightenment." In *Empire and Modern Political Thought*, edited by Sankar Muthu, 112–54. New York: Cambridge University Press, 2012.

———. "The Particulars of a Universal Politics: Hegel's Adaptation of Montesquieu's Typology." *American Political Science Review* 78, no. 1 (1984): 179–88.

———. "What Montesquieu Taught: Perfection Does Not Concern Men or Things Universally." In Kingston, *Montesquieu and His Legacy*, 7–30.

Muller, James. "The Political Economy of Republicanism." In Coleman and Carrithers, *Montesquieu and the Spirit of Modernity*, 61–75.

Murray, Charles. *American Exceptionalism: An Experiment in History*. Washington, DC: AEI Press, 2013.

Nelson, Eric. *The Greek Tradition in Republican Thought*. Cambridge: Cambridge University Press, 2004.

Norris, Pippa, and Robert Inglehart. *Sacred and Secular: Religion and Politics Worldwide*. New York: Cambridge University Press, 2004.

Nyland, Chris. "Biology and Environment: Montesquieu's Relativist Analysis of Gender Behavior." *History of Political Economy* 29, no. 3 (1997): 391–412.

Onuf, Peter. "American Exceptionalism and National Identity." *American Political Thought* 1, no. 1 (2012): 77–100.

Paine, Thomas. *Common Sense*. 1776. Reprint, Mineola, NY: Dover Publications, 1997.

———. *Rights of Man*. 1791–92. Reprint, Mineola, NY: Dover Publications, 1999.

Pangle, Thomas L. *Montesquieu's Philosophy of Liberalism: A Commentary on* The Spirit of the Laws. Chicago: University of Chicago Press, 1973.

———. *The Theological Basis of Liberal Modernity in Montesquieu's* Spirit of the Laws. Chicago: University of Chicago Press, 2010.

Radasanu, Andrea. "Montesquieu on Moderation, Monarchy, and Reform." *History of Political Thought* 31, no. 2 (2010): 283–308.

Rahe, Paul A. "The Book That Never Was: Montesquieu's *Considerations on the Romans* in Historical Context." *History of Political Thought* 26, no. 1 (2005): 43–89.

———. "The Enlightenment Indicted: Rousseau's Response to Montesquieu." *Journal of the Historical Society* 8, no. 2 (2008): 273–302.

———. *Montesquieu and the Logic of Liberty: War, Religion, Commerce, Climate, Terrain, Technology, Uneasiness of Mind, the Spirit of Vigilance, and the Foundations of the Modern Republic*. New Haven, CT: Yale University Press, 2009.

———. "Montesquieu's Critique of Monarchy: A Self-Destructive Anachronism." *Annuaire* 2 (2010): 209–28.

———. "Montesquieu's Natural Rights Constitutionalism." *Social Philosophy and Policy* 29, no. 2 (2012): 51–81.

Rasmussen, Dennis. *The Pragmatic Enlightenment: Recovering the Liberalism of Hume, Smith, Montesquieu, and Voltaire*. New York: Cambridge University Press, 2014.

Restad, Hilde Eliassen. "Old Paradigms in History Die Hard in Political Science: US Foreign Policy and American Exceptionalism." *American Political Thought* 1, no. 1 (2012): 53–76.

Richter, Melvin. *The Political Theory of Montesquieu.* New York: Cambridge University Press, 1977.

Robin, Corey. *Fear: The History of a Political Idea.* New York: Oxford University Press, 2004.

———. "Reflections on Fear: Montesquieu in Revival." *American Political Science Review* 94, no. 2 (2000): 347–60.

Romani, Roberto. "All Montesquieu's Sons: The Place of *Esprit Général, Caractère National,* and *Mœurs* in French Political Philosophy, 1748–1789." *Studies on Voltaire and the Eighteenth Century* 362 (1998): 189–235.

Rosow, Stephen J. "Commerce, Power and Justice: Montesquieu on International Politics." *Review of Politics* 46, no. 3 (1984): 346–66.

Rothschild, Emma. *Economic Sentiments: Adam Smith, Condorcet, and the Enlightenment.* Cambridge, MA: Harvard University Press, 2002.

Rousseau, Jean-Jacques. *Emile or On Education.* Translated and edited by Allan Bloom. New York: Basic Books, 1979.

Samuel, Ana. "The Design of Montesquieu's *The Spirit of the Laws*: The Triumph of Freedom over Determinism." *American Political Science Review* 103, no. 2 (2009): 305–21.

Schaub, Diana J. *Erotic Liberalism: Women and Revolution in Montesquieu's Persian Letters.* Lanham, MD: Rowman & Littlefield, 1995.

———. "Of Believers and Barbarians: Montesquieu's Enlightened Toleration." In *Early Modern Skepticism and the Origins of Toleration,* edited by Alan Levine, 225–47. Lanham, MD: Lexington Books, 1999.

———. "Women, Christianity, and the Modern in Montesquieu's *Considerations on the Romans.*" In *The Pious Sex: Essays on Women and Religion in the History of Political Thought,* edited by Andrea Radasanu, 149–68. Lanham, MD: Lexington Books, 2010.

Shackleton, Robert. "The Evolution of Montesquieu's Theory of Climate." *Revue internationale de philosophie* 33–34 (1955): 317–29.

———. *Montesquieu: A Critical Biography.* Oxford: Oxford University Press, 1961.

———. "Montesquieu and Machiavelli: A Reappraisal." *Comparative Literature Studies* 1 (1964): 1–13.

Shklar, Judith N. *Montesquieu.* Oxford: Oxford University Press, 1987.

———. "Montesquieu and the New Republicanism." In *Political Thought and Political Thinkers,* edited by Stanley Hoffman, 244–61. Chicago: University of Chicago Press, 1998.

Simon, Julian L. *The Economic Consequences of Immigration.* 2nd ed. Ann Arbor: University of Michigan Press, 1999.

Skrzypek, Marian. "Montesquieu et les modèles des rapports entre l'Etat et l'Eglise dans les Lumières françaises." In Ehrard, *Montesquieu, l'État, et la religion,* 142–52.

Smith, Rogers. "'Our Republican Example': The Significance of the American Experiments in Government in the Twenty-First Century." *American Political Thought* 1, no. 1 (2012): 101–28.

Sonenscher, Michael. *Before the Deluge: Public Debt, Inequality, and the Intellectual Origins of the French Revolution.* Princeton, NJ: Princeton University Press, 2007.

Spector, Céline. "*Esprit général.*" In *Dictionnaire Montesquieu*. Online, under the direction of Catherine Volpilhac-Auger. ENS de Lyon, 2013. http://dictionnaire-montesquieu.ens-lyon.fr/fr/article/1376474276/fr/.

———. "'Il est impossible que nous supposions que ces gens-là soient des hommes': La théorie de l'esclavage au livre XV de *L'Esprit des lois*." *Lumières* 3 (2004): 15–51.

———. "Montesquieu était-il libéral?" In *La Pensée libérale*, edited by G. Kevorkian, 55–69. Paris: Ellipses, 2010.

———. "Montesquieu et la crise du droit natural modern: L'exégese straussienne." *Revue de Métaphysique et de Morale* 1 (2013): 65–78.

———. *Montesquieu et l'émergence de l'économie politique.* Paris: Champion, 2006.

———. *Montesquieu: Liberté, droit, et histoire.* Paris: Michalon Éditions, 2010.

———. *Montesquieu: Pouvoirs, richesses, et sociétés.* Paris: Hermann Éditeurs, 2011.

———. "Naturalisation des croyances, religion naturelle et histoire naturelle de la religion: Le statut du fait religieux dans *L'Esprit des lois*." In Ehrard, *Montesquieu, l'État, et la religion*, 40–78.

———. "Quelle justice? Quelle rationalité? La mesure du droit dans *L'Esprit des lois*." In Volpilhac-Auger, *Montesquieu en 2005*, 219–42.

———. "Vices privés, vertus publiques: De la *Fable des abeilles* à *L'Esprit des lois*." In Coleman and Carrithers, *Montesquieu and the Spirit of Modernity*, 127–57.

Sullivan, Vickie B. "Against the Despotism of a Republic: Montesquieu's Correction of Machiavelli in the Name of the Security of the Individual." *History of Political Thought* 27, no. 2 (2006): 263–88.

Tocqueville, Alexis de. *Democracy in America.* Translated and edited by Harvey C. Mansfield and Delba Winthrop. Chicago: University of Chicago Press, 2000.

———. *Correspondance D'Alexis de Tocqueville et de Louis Kergorlay.* Paris: Gallimard, 1977.

Tomaselli, Sylvana. "The Enlightenment Debate on Women." *History Workshop* 20 (1985): 101–24.

Tuveson, Ernest Lee. *Redeemer Nation: The Idea of America's Millennial Role.* Chicago: University of Chicago Press, 1968.

Van Doren, Carl. *The Great Rehearsal: The Story of the Making and Ratifying of the Constitution of the United States.* New York: The Viking Press, 1948.

Velema, W. R. E. "Republican Readings of Montesquieu: *The Spirit of the Laws* in the Dutch Republic." *History of Political Thought* 18, no. 1 (1997): 43–63.

Volpilhac-Auger, Catherine, ed. *Montesquieu en 2005.* Oxford: Voltaire Foundation, 2005.

———. "On the Proper Use of the Stick: *The Spirit of Laws* and the Chinese Empire." In Kingston, *Montesquieu and His Legacy*, 81–96.

———. "Sur quelques sources prétendues du livre XIV de *L'Esprit des lois*. De l'Essai sur les causes à *L'Esprit des lois*: La théorie des climats existe-t-elle?" 2017. http://montesquieu.ens-lyon.fr/spip.php?article872.

———. "Une nouvelle 'chaîne secrète' de L'Esprit des lois: L'histoire du texte." In *Montesquieu en 2005*, 85–216.

Voltaire. *Philosophical Dictionary.* New York: Harcourt, Brace and World, 1962.

Waddicor, Mark. *Montesquieu and the Philosophy of Natural Law.* The Hague: Martinus Nijhoff, 1970.

Ward, Lee. "Montesquieu on Federalism and Anglo-Gothic Constitutionalism." *Publius* 37, no. 4 (2007): 551–77.
Washington, George. "Farewell Address," 1796. The Avalon Project: Documents in Law, History, and Diplomacy. Lillian Goldman Law Library. Yale Law School. http://avalon.law.yale.edu/18th_century/washing.asp.
White, Morton. *The Philosophy of the American Revolution*. New York: Oxford University Press, 1978.
Williams, David. *Condorcet and Modernity*. Cambridge: Cambridge University Press, 2007.
Willis, Garry. *Inventing America: Jefferson's Declaration of Independence*. New York: Vintage Books, 1979.
Winthrop, John. "A Modell of Christian Charity," 1630. Hanover Historical Texts Collection. Hanover College. History Department. https://history.hanover.edu/texts/winthmod.html.
Wolfe, Christopher. "The Confederate Republic in Montesquieu." *Polity* 9, no. 4 (1977): 427–45.
Wood, Gordon. *The Creation of the American Republic, 1776–1787*. New York: W. W. Norton, 1969.
———. *The Idea of America: Reflections on the Birth of the United States*. New York: Penguin Press, 2011.
Wright, Johnson. "Montesquieuian Moments: *The Spirit of the Laws* and Republicanism." *Proceedings of the Western Society for French History* 35 (2007): 149–69.
Yang, Jisheng. *Tombstone: The Great Chinese Famine, 1958–1962*. New York: Farrar, Straus, and Giroux, 2012.
Yung, Laurie, Wayne A. Freimund, and Jill M. Belsky. "The Politics of Place: Understanding Meaning, Common Ground, and Political Difference on the Rocky Mountain Front." *Forest Science* 49, no. 6 (2003): 855–66.
Zanin, Sergey. "Rousseau, Montesquieu, et la 'religion civile.'" In Ehrard, *Montesquieu, l'État, et la religion*, 186–212.
Zuckert, Michael P. "The EU's Federalism Deficit: A Madisonian Perspective." In *The New Frontiers of Europe: The Enlargement of the European Union; Implications and Consequences*, edited by Daniel S. Hamilton, 41–75. Washington, DC: Center for Transatlantic Relations, 2005.
———. *Launching Liberalism: On Lockean Political Philosophy*. Lawrence: University Press of Kansas, 2002.
———. "Natural Law, Natural Rights, and Classical Liberalism: On Montesquieu's Critique of Hobbes." In *Natural Law and Modern Moral Philosophy*, edited by Ellen Frankel Paul, Fred D. Miller, and Jeffrey Paul, 227–51. New York: Cambridge University Press, 2001.
———. "Natural Rights and Modern Constitutionalism." *Northwestern Journal of International Human Rights* 2 (2004): 1–25.

Index

Adams, John, 163, 166, 227n47
Adams, John Quincy, 167
Alexander the Great, 51, 71
Anti-Federalists, 179
Appleby, Joyce, 159
aristocracy, 47, 56, 85, 99–104, 210n72, 210n76, 211n77. *See also* nobility
Aristotle, 4, 66, 79, 87, 99, 193n19, 194n204
Aron, Raymond, 3

Bartlett, Robert C., 142, 154
Bayle, Pierre, 146, 218n35, 223n120
Bentham, Jeremy, 1, 2, 189n1
Berlin, Isaiah, 3
Bill of Rights, 160
Binoche, Bertrand, 3, 141
books, 37–38
branches, of government, 112–17, 177–78
Burke, Edmund, 5, 191n25, 194n25, 205n8
Bush, George W., 171
Butterworth, Charles, 202n10

Calhoun, John C., 166, 228n53
Callanan, Keegan, 191n20
capitalism, 75–76, 158. *See also* commerce
Carrese, Paul, 29, 193n7, 193n9, 201n103, 211n79
Carrithers, David, 99, 103–4, 207n25, 211n79
Ceaser, James, 167–68, 170, 190n13, 225n9

change: caution with, 80–81; commerce and, 125–40; conquest and, 52; *esprit* and, 28–29; moderation and, 83–84; politics of place and, 42–43; power and, 82–83; religion and, 152–54; in states, 4–5; universalism and, 17
checks, on power, 117–19
China, 60, 133, 139
Clark, George Rogers, 170
clergy, 90, 92, 118. *See also* religion
climate, 27, 41, 66, 120–25, 121, 180, 199n82, 205n3, 214n1, 214n3. *See also* physical environment
Cohler, Anne, 29, 145, 198n67, 200n98
Collier, Paul, 125
commerce, 75–76, 120; as agent of change, 125–40; competition and, 133–34; conquest and, 52; as destructive, 126; of economy, 130–31; *esprit* and, 34, 154, 197n61; in Holland, 136–40; laws and, 135–36; liberty and, 134; of luxury, 125, 130–32, 218n39, 218n42, 219n45, 219n55; morals and, 23, 129, 217n28; nobility and, 132–33; peace and, 49, 127–28; prosperity and, 68–70; religion and, 154; virtue and, 129–30, 217n34
Common Sense (Paine), 176
competition, 75, 133–34, 140
Condorcet, Nicolas de, 16–17, 195n32, 205n4
confederation, 109–10
conquest, 49–54, 70–71, 96

247

constitution: in Aristotle, 4; change and, 207n30; commerce and, 130, 135; immigration and, 188; laws and, 56, 84, 91; moderation and, 101; political liberty and, 21, 55, 192n3; religion and, 153; republicanism and, 105; rights and, 22
Constitution: English, 40, 74, 111–12, 115, 117–18, 199n86, 213n100; German, 106; US, 1, 157–60, 162, 165, 167, 170, 172–73, 174–81, 178, 189n4, 225n6, 227n42
Correggio, Antonio da, 13
corruption, 40, 85–86, 96, 100, 102, 110, 129, 136–37
Craiutu, Aurelian, 15, 21, 39, 80, 82, 83, 124, 191n24, 194n25, 203n30, 205nn1–2, 206n12, 206n15
Crimea, 46
criminal code, 57–62

Dahl, Robert, 174–75
d'Alembert, Jean le Rond, 38
Declaration of Independence, 1, 162–65, 226n27, 228n51, 228n53
De Dijn, Annelien, 210n66, 211n82
defense, 40, 47–50. *See also* security
De la politique (Montesquieu), 26
De l'Esprit des lois (Of the Spirit of the Laws) (Montesquieu), 2, 4–5, 6; introduction of, 10–13; political science in, 10; prejudices in, 12–13; principles in, 11–12; as prohibited book, 11
democracy, 52, 71, 81, 87–88, 100–101, 114, 171–72, 208n38, 230n92
Democracy in America (de Tocqueville), 179–80
Deneen, Patrick, 170, 224n3, 228n56
despotism, 208n38; confederation and, 110; *esprit* and, 34; monarchies and, 97; offensive force and, 53; rejection of, 86–87;

religion and, 145; security and, 40, 48–49
Detweiler, Philip F., 227n37
Dickinson, John, 165–66
Dictionnaire de l'Académie française, 25, 196n51
Discourses on Livy (Machiavelli), 86
Dos Santos, Antônio Carlos, 150
Dunn, Charles, 167
Durkheim, Émile, 3, 153
Dutch. *See* Holland

economic conquest, 51–52. *See also* commerce
economic liberty, 41, 62, 64, 66, 70, 77–78
economic security, 62–63
education, 32–33, 40, 42–43, 74, 103, 124, 199n82
elections, 100–101, 114
electoral system, American, 175–76
"*Éloge de Monsieur le Président de Montesquieu,*" 38
End of History (Fukuyama), 189n4
England, 114–16, 199n86; commerce and, 70–71, 133, 134; *esprit* in, 35–36; liberty in, 73–74, 74–75; as mixed regime, 111–12
English Bill of Rights, 160
Enlightenment: American, 173–74, 227n45; "pragmatic," 7, 15; reason in, 165; universalism and, 1, 2, 16
environment, physical, 41, 120–21, 121–25, 214n1
esprit, 10; conquest and, 54; defining, 24–33; in *Dictionnaire de l'Académie française*, 25; in England, 35–36, 199n86; examples of, 33–37; French, 33–34, 95; in Holland, 34–35; laws and, 22–24, 27, 37–42, 142–43; liberty and, 30–31; as normative concept, 31; of republics, 105; society and, 28–29

Essai sur les causes qui peuvent affecter les esprits et les caractères (Montesquieu), 32
Ethiopia, 145
European Union, 36–37, 107, 232n4
exceptionalism: American, 8–9, 158, 159–82, 224n3; historical, 159–61; particularistic, 158, 176–82; unfortunate, 158, 172–76; universal, 158, 162–72
executive branch, 112, 116

Fable of the Bees (Mandeville), 35, 129
fear: aristocracy and, 102; criminality and, 58–59, 60–61; despotism and, 48, 87, 97, 144; government and, 40; liberty and, 56–57; religion and, 147; republics and, 86; security and, 45; taxes and, 64
Federalist Papers, 2, 83, 118, 158, 160, 161, 165, 176
federal republics, 104–11, 161. *See also* republics
feminism, 66–67
Feyerabend, 195n36
Finkelman, Paul, 173–74, 230n94
France, 33–34, 48, 72–73, 95
freedom. *See* liberty
French Revolution, 81
Fukuyama, Francis, 168–69, 189n4

Gamble, Richard, 228n48
geography, 121–25, 214n3. *See also* environment, physical
Germany, 105, 107
Gilchrist, Brent, 224n3
Gourou, Pierre, 216n11
governance: branches of government in, 112–17; corruption and, 85–86; law and, 13–14, 39–40; liberty and, 77–78; moderation and, 83; nature and, 84–86; principle and, 84–86; prosperity and, 70. *See also* democracy; laws; mixed regime; monarchies; republics

Greece, 68–69
Guasco, Ottaviano, 109

Hamilton, Alexander, 158, 165
Heclo, Hugh, 167, 168, 229n66
Hegel, G. W. F., 1, 2, 5, 168–69
Hirschman, Albert, 216n21
Hobbes, Thomas, 6–7, 13, 20, 33, 46, 194n20, 194n25, 201n3
Holland, 211n87, 212n92, 220n57, 59; commerce and, 27, 75–76, 126, 130, 136–40, 220n59; *esprit* in, 34–35; physical environment of, 124; representation in, 114–15; as republic, 89, 105–10, 161, 210n69, 212n92; taxes in, 220n57
honor: ambition and, 93; criminality and, 61; despotism and, 97; education and, 95; false, 96; in French *esprit*, 34, 74; monarchy and, 83, 89, 92–93, 98, 207n28, 209n55; morality and, 94; nobility and, 56, 91, 94–95; in republics, 85; war and, 96
Howse, Robert, 202n4, 202n11, 218n42
human nature, 17, 33, 76–77, 215n3
Hume, David, 7

Index Librorum Prohibitorum, 11
inequality, 71, 88, 101–2
Inquisition, 92
intolerance, religious, 141–56
Iraq War, 171–72, 230n92
Ireland, 123
Islam, 46, 73, 135, 144, 145–46, 148, 151, 155, 172, 187, 222n89

Japan, 133, 139–40, 152
Jay, John, 169–70, 230n82
Jefferson, Thomas, 19, 163, 165–66, 170, 173–74, 231n101
judiciary, 112, 113–14. *See also* lawmaking; laws

Kagan, Robert, 226n25, 228n56, 230n87
Kant, Immanuel, 189n3
Kendall, Willmoore, 228n51
King, Martin Luther, Jr., 98
Kingston, Rebecca, 141
Kojève, Alexandre, 168–69
Krause, Sharon, 94, 98
Kriesel, Karl Marcus, 214n3
Kuhn, Thomas, 195n36

Larrère, Catherine, 3, 126, 141, 151, 217n32
lawmaking, 11–24. *See also* judiciary
laws: aims of, 14–15; commerce and, 135–36; criminal, 57–62; defined, 13; *esprit* and, 22–24, 27, 37–42, 142–43, 197n55; governance and, 13–14, 39–40; liberty and, 12, 54–55; in monarchies, 89–90, 98; prosperity and, 69; religion and, 143–44, 148; rights vs., 20–21; terrain and, 124. *See also* governance; judiciary; legislative branch
Lectures on the Philosophy of World History (Hegel), 1
Lee, Henry, 163
legislative branch, 112, 114, 115
Lehrman, Lewis E., 228n52
Leviathan (Hobbes), 33
Levillain, Charles-Edouard, 212nn95–96, 212n96, 220n58
liberty, 54–68; branches of government and, 112; commerce and, 134; criminal law and, 57–62; defined, 54; determination and, 38–39; economic, 41, 62, 64, 66, 70, 77–78; *esprit* and, 30–31; honor and, 74; laws and, 12, 54–55; negative, 54–55; personal, 56–59; political, 40–41, 45, 55–56, 81–82; politics and, 2, 11, 192n3; politics of place and, 15–16, 73–74; prosperity and, 77–78;

punishment and, 60–62; religion and, 75; rights vs., 21; security and, 77–78; security as, 45; security vs., 59–60; servitude and, 67–68; slavery and, 64–68; society and, 4; taxation and, 62–64; in US Constitution, 1
Lincoln, Abraham, 166–67, 228n52
Lipset, Seymour Martin, 167
Litke, Justin, 163–64, 224n3, 227n37
Locke, John, 1, 2, 6–7, 189n1; human nature in, 33; judiciary in, 113; rights in, 18–19; United States and, 226n21
Louis XIV, 33–34, 48, 89, 97, 212n98. *See also* monarchies
Lowenthal, David, 20, 37, 142, 197n56, 208n38, 208n41, 209n55, 210n74, 214n3
luxury: aristocracy and, 103; commerce and, 133; commerce of, 125, 130–32, 218n39, 218n42, 219n45, 219n55; democracy and, 88, 218n43; government and, 40; inequality and, 131–32; monarchy and, 53, 218n35, 219n50; slavery and, 65. *See also* prosperity
Lycia, 106
Lynn-Jones, Sean, 159

Machiavelli, Niccolò, 83, 86, 194n25
Madison, James, 2, 83, 118, 157, 160, 161, 170, 173, 176, 206n14
Magna Carta, 160
Mandeville, Bernard, 35, 93–94, 129, 218n35
manifest destiny, 170–71, 229n67
Manin, Bernard, 3, 195n26, 213n101
Margolis, Joseph, 195n36
maritime empires, 52
Markovits, Francine, 23, 197n58, 198n75
marriage, 66–67
Martin, Luther, 179
Marx, Karl, 194n25

Mason, S. M., 211n84
Masterson, M. P., 211n87, 212n97
Mazarin, Cardinal, 92
Mes Pensées (Montesquieu), 26–27, 136, 137, 212n92
Metamorphosis (Ovid), 13
Mexico, 51, 54, 180
mixed regime, 111–18
moderation, 5, 27, 29–30, 39, 42, 45, 56, 63, 77, 79–84, 181
monarchies, 85, 89–98, 110, 211n77; conquest by, 52–53; security in, 47–48. See also Louis XIV
Montesquieu: as particularist, 2–4, 44; political science of, 10–43; principles of, 11–12, 42–43
Mosher, Michael, 29, 51, 191n22, 202n6, 203n18, 205n8, 216n20, 217n29, 218n39
Muller, James, 217n33
Murray, Charles, 167, 168, 229n71

natural rights, 18–22, 76–77, 178
negative liberty, 54–55
Netherlands. See Holland
Nicole, Pierre, 218n35
nobility, 56, 90–91, 94–97, 132–33, 210n72, 211n77. See also aristocracy
Notes on Debates in the Federal Convention of 1787 (Madison), 157
Nyland, Chris, 215n3

offensive force, 49–54
Onuf, Peter, 229n66
Ovid, 13, 80, 205n5

Paine, Thomas, 176–77
Pangle, Thomas, 14, 29, 39, 87, 142, 145, 154, 194n20, 195n38, 198n65, 199n77, 201n104, 208nn39–40, 208n42, 210n67, 213nn100–101, 213n100, 215n3, 215n5, 215n8, 216n9, 217n24, 217nn27–28, 218n39, 219n45, 219n52

Paris school, 3
parlements, 34, 56, 90–92, 109, 203n38
particularism, 2–4, 15, 18, 22, 43, 44, 54–55, 73–76, 79–80, 111–13, 118–19, 125–40, 176–82, 190n14, 191n20
personal liberty, 56–59. See also liberty
Peter the Great, 55
physical environment, 41, 120–21, 121–25, 214n1, 214n3
Plato, 79, 99, 143, 194n25, 195n36
Politics (Aristotle), 99
politics of place, 2, 4–6; American founding and, 177; change and, 42–43; climate and, 122; defined, 15; lawmaking and, 11–24; liberty and, 15–16, 73–74; universalism and, 17; use of term, 190n12
polygamy, 66–67. See also marriage
Portugal, 92, 140
prejudices, 12–13, 65–66
"problems of politics," 14–15
prosperity, 4, 15, 22, 44–47, 62, 68–78, 87–89, 126, 130–31, 134–35, 154–55, 204n53, 219n54
Protagoras, 195n36
punishment, 59–62. See also criminal code

racial prejudice, 65–66
Rahe, Paul A., 19, 29, 35, 45, 196n39, 199n88, 201n2, 202n14, 207n24, 213n101, 215n6, 216n12, 216n14, 216n20, 218n35, 219n51
Rasmussen, Dennis, 7, 15–16, 21, 121, 189nn1–2, 195n28, 195n35, 205n9
reading, 37–38
Reagan, Ronald, 224n3, 228n48
Reflections on the Revolution in France (Burke), 5
Réflexions sur la monarchie universelle en Europe (Montesquieu), 34
relativism, 4, 17–18, 43, 195nn35–36, 195n36

252 INDEX

religion, 11, 25, 58, 75, 141–56, 158, 192n4. *See also* clergy
republics, 47, 85, 89, 104–11, 161, 208n43
Restad, Hilde Eliassen, 170, 227n43, 227n45
revolution, 1, 28–29, 81, 152–53, 166, 206n9
Richelieu, Cardinal, 89
Richter, Melvin, 64
rights, 18–22, 76–77, 178
rights claims, 196n48
Rome, 47, 65, 107
Rosow, Stephen J., 202n17, 202n15, 216n20, 217n23, 219n54
Rothschild, Emma, 195n32
Rousseau, Jean-Jacques, 13, 19–20, 30, 33, 194n25
Russia, 46, 55, 61
Russian Revolution, 81

Samuel, Ana, 38–39, 85, 141, 198n64, 200nn99–101, 207n25, 211n77, 214n3
Schaub, Diana, 29, 141, 146
Secondat, Charles Louis de. *See* Montesquieu
Second Discourse (Rousseau), 33
Second Treatise (Locke), 1, 18–19, 33
security, 40, 45–54, 59–60, 73, 77–78
self-knowledge, 12–13
servitude, 67–68
Shackleton, Robert, 141, 215n7
Shklar, Judith N., 29, 56–57, 87, 142, 147, 195n35, 198n67, 203n25, 203n38, 214n3
Skrzypek, Marian, 155
slavery, 64–68, 173–74
Smith, Adam, 7
Smith, Rogers, 225n6
social contract, 6. 20, 22
society, 4, 14–15, 17, 28–29, 46, 194n20
Spain, 51, 54, 65, 92, 202n15

Spector, Céline, 3, 15, 26, 29–30, 31, 82–83, 88, 93, 143, 193n19, 196n47, 197nn59–60, 199n79, 201n105, 208n34, 213n101, 217n34
Stoics, 143, 221n86
Sullivan, Vickie B., 195n35, 206n23
Switzerland, 105, 107, 123

taxation, 62–64, 136–37
terrain, 122–24. *See also* environment, physical
Tocqueville, Alexis de, 3, 5, 159, 179–81, 232n124, 232n126
tolerance, religious, 141–56
totalities, 29, 198n63

Ukraine, 46
uniformity, 16–18, 85, 176–77
United States, 1–2, 76, 118, 157–82
universalism, 1–2, 14–17, 22, 43, 76–77, 163–65, 169–72, 176–77, 189n1, 189n3, 191n20, 196n48, 227n45
US Constitution, 1–2, 157, 159–60, 178, 189n4

virtue: aristocracy and, 56, 103–4; bourgeois, 129–32; climate and, 122; commerce and, 128–29, 217n34; democratic, 87–88, 194n22; ethics, 79; moderation and, 101; political, 11, 207n28, 208n43; republican, 142–43; slavery and, 65; vice and, 15
Voltaire, 7, 38, 221n79
voting, 100–101, 114, 175–76
Voyage de Gratz à la Haye (Montesquieu), 99
Voyage en Hollande (Montesquieu), 34–35, 136

Washington, George, 167, 173, 228n55

wealth. *See* prosperity
Weightman, Roger, 163
William I of Orange, 108
William III of Orange, 212n97
Williams, David, 195n32
Willis, Gary, 226n27

Winthrop, John, 158, 167, 224n3
women, 66–67, 144, 204n49
Wood, Gordon, 226n24

Zuckert, Michael, 19, 21, 163, 164, 205n3, 226n27, 226n29, 227n32

www.ingramcontent.com/pod-product-compliance
Lightning Source LLC
Chambersburg PA
CBHW051608230426
43668CB00013B/2022